Windows® XP Professional

Security

Windows® XP Professional
Security

Chris Weber
Gary Bahadur

McGraw-Hill/Osborne

New York Chicago San Francisco
Lisbon London Madrid Mexico City Milan
New Delhi San Juan Seoul Singapore Sydney Toronto

The McGraw·Hill Companies

McGraw-Hill/Osborne
2600 Tenth Street
Berkeley, California 94710
U.S.A.

To arrange bulk purchase discounts for sales promotions, premiums, or fund-raisers, please contact **McGraw-Hill/**Osborne at the above address. For information on translations or book distributors outside the U.S.A., please see the International Contact Information page immediately following the index of this book.

Windows® XP Professional Security

1234567890 FGR FGR 0198765432

ISBN 0-07-222602-1

Publisher
  Brandon A. Nordin
Vice President & Associate Publisher
  Scott Rogers
Senior Acquisitions Editor
  Jane K. Brownlow
Project Editor
  Leslie Tilley
Acquisitions Coordinator
  Martin Przybyla
Technical Editor
  Timothy Mullen
Copy Editor
  Cleo Dorápan

Proofreader
  Paul Tyler
Indexer
  Valerie Robbins
Computer Designers
  Tabi M. Cagan, Tara A. Davis,
  Kelly Stanton-Scott
Illustrators
  Michael Muller, Melinda Lytle,
  Lyssa Wald
Series Design
  Peter F. Hancik, Lyssa Wald
Cover Series Design
  Jeff Weeks

This book was composed with Corel VENTURA™ Publisher.

To Mom and Dad, "tamam."

Chris Weber

This is dedicated to a talented team at Foundstone.
It is a pleasure to work with them on a daily basis.

Gary Bahadur

ABOUT THE AUTHORS

Chris Weber

Chris Weber works for Foundstone as a security consultant and trainer. He specializes in product analyses, attack and penetration tests, web application reviews, and security architecture reviews. Chris also provides Foundstone training through the Ultimate Hacking set of courses. Prior to Foundstone, Chris worked as a network administrator for VisionAir performing enterprise network assessments and mission-critical systems implementations for police and sheriff's departments across the United States.

Chris's public work includes developing courseware and teaching for SANS. Chris was a security tutorial honoraria speaker at the USENIX 10th Annual Security Symposium in 2001, served as a co-instructor at CSI's 2001 Network Security conference, and has taught classes at several of the Black Hat Briefings.

His published works include *Securing Windows 2000 Professional Using the Gold Standard Security Template* (SANS Press, 2002), and *Privacy Defended: Protecting Yourself Online* (Que, 2002). Chris has also authored several articles with SecurityFocus.com and Global Knowledge.

Chris holds a double B.S. in Information Systems and Marketing from the University of North Carolina at Wilmington. His industry certifications include Microsoft Certified Systems Engineer and the GSEC from the SANS Institute. Chris can be reached at chris@securingxp.com.

Gary Bahadur

Gary Bahadur is CIO and a co-founder of Foundstone. He has been involved with numerous penetration studies and network reviews covering various firewalls, UNIX, Windows NT, Novell networks, web servers, Internet connectivity, SAP security, and many others.

Prior to joining Foundstone, Gary held positions of manager in the Security Profiling Services group of Ernst & Young, and senior consultant in Price Waterhouse's Enterprise Security Solutions practice. Gary developed methodologies for network security at both companies.

Gary is a featured speaker and teaches security seminars at various industry conferences. He is widely published in industry magazines and co-authored *Privacy Defended* with Chris Weber and Will Chan.

Gary holds a B.S. in Information Systems/Finance from New York University and is a Certified Information Systems Security Professional (CISSP). Gary can be reached at gary@securingxp.com.

About the Contributing Authors

Tom Lee is the IT manager at Foundstone. Tom has more than 10 years' experience in systems administration and security. He has served as technical editor on several security publications, including *Hacking Exposed*, 3rd edition (Osborne, 2001).

Yen-Ming Chen is a principal consultant at Foundstone, specializing in wireless network security, web application testing, intrusion detection, and penetration tests. Yen-Ming is a contributing author of *Hacking Exposed* and *Hacking Exposed Web Applications,* and his articles have been published in *SysAdmin, UnixReview, DevX, PCWeek,* and other technology-related magazines. He has been a speaker at MISTI and Global Knowledge and an instructor for the Ultimate Hacking classes. Yen-Ming also contributed to the open source project Snort. Yen-Ming holds a B.S. in Mathematics from the National Central University in Taiwan, and an M.S. in Information Networking from Carnegie Mellon University. He also holds several professional certificates, including CISSP and MCSE.

Dane Skagen is Foundstone's director of training. Dane is responsible for instructors, class logistics and equipment, development and publication of class material, and training management. He has more than 15 years of training and training-management experience in both civilian and military environments. Dane holds a Bachelor of Commerce degree from the University of Calgary, Canada, and an M.S. in Systems Management from the University of Southern California. Dane is a Microsoft Certified Systems Engineer (MCSE), a Microsoft Certified Trainer (MCT), an A+ Certified Technician, and a Certified Technical Trainer (CTT).

Nishchal Bhalla is a security consultant at Foundstone, specializing in web application testing and product testing. Nish draws his experience from being a network security consultant for clients ranging from members of the Fortune 500 to startups, where he gained knowledge of several types of security technologies. Nish has a bachelor's degree in Commerce from Bangalore University, a master's in Parallel Processing from Sheffield University, and is a post-graduate in Finance from Strathclyde University. He is also GSEC (SANS) and AIX certified.

Clinton Mugge is a director of consulting for Foundstone. He has been a regular contributing author to the internationally best-selling Hacking Exposed series of books, as well as technical reviewer for the ground-breaking book *Incident Response: Investigating Computer Crime* (Osborne, 2001). Clinton's technical and managerial experience has been developed working with Fortune 100 clients in the financial, software, services, and manufacturing markets as well as the government sectors and law enforcement. Clinton holds a B.S. degree from Southern Illinois University and an M.S. from University of Maryland. He is a Certified Information Systems Security Professional (CISSP).

Matt Pepe is a senior investigator at Foundstone. He has performed digital evidence discovery and computer forensics in more than 100 federal investigations for the Air Force Office of Special Investigations, FBI, and other government agencies.

In addition to criminal and counterintelligence cases, he has contributed to the successful resolution of several multimillion-dollar civil litigation suits. His prior experience includes host and network security assessments, intrusion detection, and incident response program development. Matt is a contributing author of *Incident Response*.

About the Technical Editor

Timothy Mullen is CIO and chief software architect for AnchorIS.com, a developer of secure enterprise-based accounting solutions. Mullen is also a columnist for Security Focus's Microsoft Focus section and a regular contributor of InFocus technical articles. Timothy, also known as "Thor," is the founder of the Hammer of God security co-op group.

AT A GLANCE

CONTENTS

Part I   **Securing the Operating System**

Part II   Network Security

Part III	Active Directory, .NET Framework, and Internet Services

FOREWORD

f you are reading this, the presence of Windows XP in your personal or business computing environment is probably a foregone conclusion. Like millions of people around the world, you have chosen to build a digital framework around Microsoft's operating system because of its ease of use, robust feature set, integration of current technology standards, operational stability, and widespread acceptance as the dominant standard in desktop computing.

With all of these things in its favor, why do you need a book on XP security?

Maybe the recent hyper-sensationalized headline on the latest Microsoft security flaw has you scared. Or maybe you're tired of being made fun of by your friend who runs Linux and you want to let the air out of his blustering hyperbole. Or perhaps you realize that all the things that make Microsoft technologies dominant in their respective markets conversely also make them a ripe target for opportunistic vandals currently roaming computer networks, both public and private.

Yes, on the security front, Microsoft has become a victim of its own success, and its customers bear a heavier burden for it. In general, for all of the new features included in each successive generation of Windows, security has decreased. Likewise, as ease of use has improved, security has often been weakened. As deployment of Windows has grown so has the complexity of the OS and, concomitantly, its potential insecurity. This doesn't mean that Windows is architecturally flawed—it simply means that users of Windows need to remain diligent about how to configure and operate it securely. This is the unfortunate reality for any commercially viable computer operating system today, and especially the most popular one.

Picking up this book is thus a good first step—you recognize that you face a challenge. The only remaining question is, "Does this book provide the best solutions?" As someone who has worked closely with the authors over the past few years helping enterprises deploy and secure Windows technologies, I can answer with a resounding "Yes!"

This book will give you the insider's tips on how to deploy Windows XP securely and manage it for ongoing security. It also gives you practical policies for dealing with the inevitable changes that are sure to surface down the road for the Windows product line. *Windows XP Professional Security* offers expert overviews of technology from an experienced, professional security perspective. It delivers dozens of recommendations for technical configurations to amplify out-of-the-box security, tailored to specific scenarios and environments. In addition to the bit- and byte-level advice, you get high-level policy recommendations from experienced enterprise practitioners and consultants who have "been there, done that" and have seen where uninformed security decisions can lead. Checklists follow each chapter to ensure comprehension and provide a convenient mechanism for gauging compliance in your environment.

As for specific topics that impressed me as I reviewed drafts of the manuscript, *Windows XP Professional Security* explores how XP is more secure by default than Windows 2000 in many ways, including file system and registry ACLs and improved security settings. It discusses at length managing Windows XP in a Windows 2000–based domain, with emphasis and examples on how and why Group Policy can be a life-saver if used properly or a career-ender if used inappropriately. It covers the gamut of security-related technologies new in XP and improved from Windows 2000, including SAFER, EFS (with specific solutions for known security problems), ICF, anonymous access controls, IPSec, and more. Finally, the last section of the book treats XP penetration testing and security incident response with clarity and precision.

In short, *Windows XP Professional Security* is the operator's manual for Windows XP security—don't boot up without it. So what are you waiting for? Start turning the pages and learn how to strengthen the defenses on your XP deployment today.

Joel Scambray
Senior Director of Security, Microsoft MSN,
and co-author of *Hacking Exposed*, 3rd edition;
Hacking Exposed Windows 2000;
and *Hacking Exposed Web Applications*
August 2002

ACKNOWLEDGMENTS

This book would not have been possible without the dedication of such a talented group of people; they poured countless hours of thought and experience into every bit of content. We sincerely hope to honor them all here and apologize to anyone we have overlooked.

First and most properly, enormous thanks to our families for continuing to support us through the many months of excessive research and writing. Without their understanding none of this would have been possible.

Next we would like to thank all of our colleagues for their contributions. Experience and talent run deep in this industry, and the fine folks at Foundstone are a true demonstration of this. The efforts of our contributing authors—Clinton, Tom, Dane, Nish, Matt, and Yen-Ming—truly help in making this book a valuable read.

Many thanks to Timothy Mullen, our technical editor, whose precise knowledge and attention to detail shook out more bugs in this book than we care to admit.

And a huge Aussie thanks to Ben Bower of Cerberus IT, a true security expert from the land Down Under, for his speedy and accurate aid during the technical-editing process.

More big thanks, for the thoughtful foreword, go to Joel Scambray—a fine person whose unshakeable commitment has finally awoken some sleeping giants. See you at the Kitchen, brother!

Our respect and admiration to all the individuals who bring life to computer security through their teachings, code, and tools, including Stephen Northcutt, David Litchfield, Arne Vidstrom, Mark Mortimore, Rain Forest Puppy, and all the other extraordinary people who perform this important work every day.

The exceptionally focused team at McGraw-Hill/Osborne deserve their own round of thanks, for spending days, evenings, and weekends sifting through our materials and keeping everything on track. Thanks to our acquisitions editor, Jane Brownlow, for always keeping an open ear and providing valuable insight; our project manager Leslie Tilley, who always remained calm, no matter how big the storm; and the rest of the team, who kept it all moving.

And most important of all, thanks to our readers for deciding to invest in this book. We hope it serves you all well!

INTRODUCTION

The past several years have seen the snowballing of computer security as a top priority. Even before Bill Gates's January 2002 public committal to a security-minded Microsoft over the next decade, organizations the world over were struggling to discover the delicate balance between a secure system and a usable one. Although many people today are still in the dark about the fundamentals of information security, ever larger numbers are recognizing the need for firewalls, tightened operating systems, and patch management, among other security concerns.

Unfortunately, rapidly changing technologies continue to place inhuman demands on IT professionals, who must continually struggle to balance the requirements of managers and appetites of end users with what it takes to keep an enterprise running smoothly. On top of that, Microsoft products have suffered from a recent rash of public vulnerabilities, which can sometimes be exploited even despite a well-hardened operating system. For instance, in the summer of 2002, months after the much-publicized UPnP vulnerability, a severe remote SMB vulnerability appeared in the spotlight along with a flaw in the processing of digital certificates (used largely during SSL transactions), both of which affected all versions of Windows. Without security in the enterprise, chaos ensues.

The question of where security starts and ends is easy to answer—in both cases the answer is "with people," and technology is the fulcrum in the middle. In the information age we live in, the chain of technology plays a leading role in organizations every day. If people don't understand the technology, then security can break down anywhere in the chain, compromising the integrity of the entire enterprise.

To any administrator, consultant, or manager responsible for designing and implementing this chain of security, the challenge immediately becomes complex and at times seemingly insurmountable. The client OS presents one of the biggest challenges—not surprisingly, considering it is often the most widely distributed technology in the enterprise.

The Challenge of the Distributed Client

In this book we show you how to meet this challenge. By the time you've finished reading the book, you should have a solid understanding of the many security options available in Windows XP Professional and Windows .NET Server. You will learn what makes Windows XP more secure by default than Windows 2000 (contrary to popular belief) and the many options you have for taking security to the extreme. Not only is each technical setting explained, but solutions are presented in a real-world context garnered from our experience in the trenches.

Where do we, the authors, get this experience? From years of being hired by the world's largest companies to break into their networks and advise them on security configurations—that's our job.

Our approach to divulging this experience and knowledge is to focus delivery on a few key points. First, we discuss all the options and configurations that are available;, then we give examples of where and how they can best be applied. Along the way, we highlight where significant changes and improvements have been made in Windows XP over Windows 2000, and point out important details that should not be overlooked. Second, we focus the discussion on the most likely scenario in the coming years—an enterprise with mixed Windows operating systems. For example, we will explain the best plan of action for implementing Windows XP group policy objects in a Windows 2000 domain that contains both Windows XP and Windows 2000 clients.

HOW THIS BOOK IS ORGANIZED

Any book is the sum of its parts, and this one is no exception. Each of the four parts collects a number of related topics.

Part I: Securing the Operating System This part describes how to use Windows XP's built-in security features and mechanisms to tighten and protect the OS. Microsoft has beefed up security by enhancing default settings and providing more options for fine-tuning the OS. However, you shouldn't rush to implement any configurations without first understanding their behavior completely. Chapter 1 offers a full rundown and describes how Windows XP security settings have changed from Windows 2000.

Chapter 2 discusses what software restriction policies are and how you can best use them. Registry security is the topic of Chapter 3, while Chapter 4 covers file system security, including the improvements that have been made to the Encrypting File System (EFS). Chapter 5 covers other security enhancements, including logging options and system services. Finally, Chapter 6 discusses user and group constructs.

Part II: Network Security   This part describes how to supplement your OS security settings with solid network defenses that protect against hostile attacks. In Chapter 7 you will explore what makes IPSec tick in Windows, and in Chapter 8 you will learn how ICF can be used for host protection as well as the ICF caveats you need to be aware of.

Chapter 9 teaches the fine points of designing a secure wireless network infrastructure by presenting you with two proven alternatives. Finally, Chapter 10 explains new options for remote administration and enterprise-wide patch management solutions you can choose from.

Part III: Active Directory, .Net Framework, and Internet Services   Active Directory provides the foundation for a security infrastructure. When it is combined with Group Policy, as described in Chapter 11, enterprise-wide security is literally just a few clicks away. As the mixed-OS network continues to evolve, you will need to understand how this AD–Group Policy infrastructure can work best, without backward-compatibility problems.

Chapter 12 looks to the future, when .NET Framework will come into play and managed code will gradually take over as the security solution of the application layer.

Internet services, the topic of Chapter 13, include the IIS web server in Windows XP (IIS 5.1) and Windows .NET (IIS 6.0), as well as Internet Explorer. Considering that these are some of the most active and exposed applications, they deserve separate attention.

Part IV: Preparing for the Worst   This part contains two chapters designed to provide methodologies that will round out and heighten security in your organization. Performing penetration testing on your own network (Chapter 14) is important both to understanding it and to staying one step ahead of the hostile attackers or worms that wish to own it. Having a working incident response plan in place (Chapter 15) will keep anarchy at bay on the day your systems are broken into.

Appendix   For convenient reference, the appendix contains a concise listing of default security and service settings in Windows XP along with recommended settings.

Blueprints   Like its siblings in the Osborne Networking series, this book includes several pages of blueprints illustrating key configurations and designs. In our blueprints, you will find a network map that is referenced throughout the book. We have included Active Directory concept designs, such as cross-forest trusts, trees, and organizational units. You will also find wireless network diagrams to illustrate options for secure designs.

Modularity and Unique Elements   This book has been designed as a reference that can be read either one chapter at a time or from start to finish as a progression of security topics. Each chapter is a self-contained subject, and to help tie everything together we made references to other chapters whenever we could.

Several elements common to the Osborne Networking series are used throughout the book. Be sure to check out these elements for pointers and other useful information.

- **Security Alert**   Although this entire book is about security, Security Alerts call your attention to specific circumstances where a security issue might arise.

- **Note**   Notes supplement running text by highlighting a bit of relevant information.

- **Caution**   This element provides a warning about something that could cause problems, but would not jeopardize security. Cautions will point out pitfalls to avoid, workarounds to employ, or "gotchas" to be aware of.

- **Challenge**   Most chapters include a boxed Challenge describing a real-life scenario that either has or could occur.

- **Checklist**   Each chapter ends with a checklist summarizing the proper security actions you should take.

ONLINE RESOURCES

Computer security is always changing, so we are providing our readers with an online source for the latest material available: http://www.securingxp.com.

In addition to updated information, this site gives you a way to reach the authors directly via e-mail:

- chris@securingxp.com

- gary@securingxp.com

We encourage you to visit the site frequently for updated information that supplements this book.

A FINAL WORD

A good computer security book is one that provides practical real-world options and solutions. We know you're an experienced computer professional who provides solutions to your organization daily. You know that client computer security starts with preparations like end-user awareness and antivirus software, but you want more answers about the advanced options available to you. Lots of research and many weekends went into this book, so we hope that it will serve you well as a time-saver in designing and rolling out your security infrastructure. Attaining client operating system security can be an elusive responsibility, but rest assured that the knowledge in this book will keep it firmly in your grasp.

PART I

Securing the Operating System

CHAPTER 1

Security Settings

Group Policy is the single most comprehensive and useful feature for managing security in Windows 2000/XP networks. However, it is the security settings specifically, or *Local Security Policy,* that is the crux of some of the most important security configuration options available.

In pre–Windows 2000 days, an administrator had to navigate through a hodgepodge of user interfaces and registry settings in order to properly secure a system. Windows NT 4.0 tools such as Security Configuration Editor and System Policy were the best things available for managing security in a Windows NT network. Then came Windows 2000 and the introduction of Group Policy and the Security Settings user interface (UI). With the evolution to Windows XP/.NET, Group Policy has taken on even more functionality with over 200 new administrative template settings, including new categories such as Software Restriction Policies and Wireless Network Policies.

KNOW YOUR INTERFACES

There are quite a few interfaces available, several of which ultimately do the same thing. A few things should be familiar, such as the MMC (Microsoft Management Console), snap-ins, containers, and objects. These terms and concepts were introduced late in the lifetime of Windows NT 4.0, and were completely integrated into the release of Windows 2000. They continue to play an important role in the administration of Windows XP/.NET systems as well.

The MMC is Microsoft's all-in-one tool for managing the Windows environment. Click Start → Run and type **MMC** to launch it. The MMC basically provides a framework for *snap-ins* to run. The snap-ins provide interfaces to manage most everything on a Windows system or network. For example, in this chapter, we will be using the Local Security Settings snap-in, previously named Local Security Policy. (We will use these terms interchangeably.) To launch the MMC for Local Security Settings, type **secpol.msc** at the command prompt.

Containers and objects can be equated to folders and files, respectively. For example, after launching Secpol.msc, you will see several containers on the left-hand side, as shown in Figure 1-1.

In the MMC and Active Directory alike, containers are everywhere. For example, a domain is a container, and so is an organizational unit. You will see default containers for users in which each user is considered an object. (We cover Active Directory in detail in Chapter 11.)

Since there is often some confusion regarding the tools used to implement security policy, let's take a quick look at what separates them:

- **Local Security Policy (Secpol.msc)**   Renamed Local Security Settings in Windows XP/.NET, this is the interface for configuring some of the most important "security settings" related to the operating system. These settings are included as a subset of Group Policy, and contain the relevant configurations for Password Policy, Audit Policy, Security Options, Software Restriction

Policies, and IP Security Policies. Configurations set through Local Security Policy are only applied to the local machine.

- **Group Policy (GPedit.msc)**   This is the MMC snap-in that is used to edit and apply group policy objects (GPOs). It is accessible either by running GPedit.msc from the command line or by right-clicking a domain or organizational unit in Active Directory and selecting Properties → Group Policy. *Group Policy* is basically a concept term that refers to the use of settings that control computer and user configurations. It is a pretty straightforward concept: you apply the same computer and user configurations to a group of computers or users. On a local machine, Group Policy can also be used to apply local configurations.

- **Group Policy Object**   GPOs are a logical collection of specific settings that control operating system and application behavior on a computer or user basis. You can apply one or more GPOs to a relevant Active Directory container such as a domain or organizational unit.

- **Security Configuration and Analysis**   This powerful toolbox provides a means of configuring all the security settings related to Local Security Policy as well as many more related to the file system, registry, restricted groups, and services. Access the Security Configuration and Analysis snap-in by opening the MMC and selecting File → Add/Remove Snap-in. This tool, which reappears throughout this book, can be used to perform the following tasks:

  - Analyze system security based on a security template
  - Apply system security based on a security template
  - Export a security template file that can be imported into an Active Directory container GPO

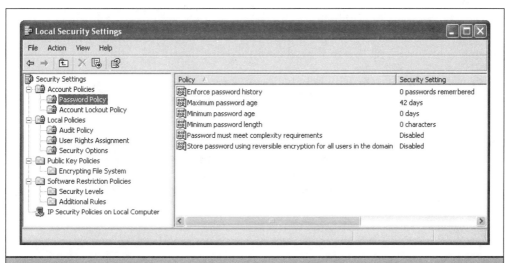

Figure 1-1.   Local Security Settings—containers on the left, objects on the right

SECURITY SETTINGS

The core of this chapter is a discussion of security settings. These are configurable locally via Local Security Policy (Secpol.msc) and across a network via Active Directory and the Group Policy Security Settings container. One thing that should come across in the end is the granularity of Windows security. Files are just one of the 14 or so objects capable of being protected by Access Control Lists (ACLs). Others include such obscure objects as named pipes, mutexes, semaphores, events, and devices.

As you go through these security settings, consider how you would use them throughout your network. Remember that with a well-thought-out plan they can most effectively be applied to groups of users and computers through Active Directory. The appendix to this book provides a concise table listing the recommended values for each of these settings.

Account Policies

This container provides settings for password and account lockout security. It is worth repeating that these settings are most effectively enforced at a domain or organizational unit level within Active Directory. These provide one of the most basic means of networkwide security.

Password Policy

Planning and implementing a password policy is crucial. If you do not configure password policies for your domains, then you allow your users to create weak passwords that are never required to be changed. In such a scenario, an attacker will have a much higher degree of success trying basic password-guessing attacks. The following password policy options are available.

Enforce password history   Windows will prevent your users from reusing passwords by remembering their old ones. Set the number of passwords you want Windows to remember; otherwise set this to zero (default).

Maximum password age   Specify how long in days a password is valid (42 days is the default). At that time it expires and the user is forced to change it. Setting this to zero will prevent a password from ever expiring.

Minimum password age   To prevent users from working around the "Enforce password history" setting, set the minimum time in days that a password must be used before it can be changed. For example, if you had a password history of 5 defined, a user could simply change their password 5 times within the same day to get to their old favorite again.

Password must meet complexity requirements   Enable this setting to make people use strong passwords. By enabling this setting, Windows will enforce the following minimum password requirements:

- Cannot contain even part of a person's username
- Must be six characters long
- Must contain characters from at least three of the four categories: A–Z, a–z, 0–9, and alphanumeric, such as $, !, #, %

Store passwords using reversible encryption   This setting should never be enabled, as it essentially stores passwords in plain text instead of as a hashed value.

Account Lockout Policy

These settings determine when an account should be locked out and for how long. They should always be configured in a domain to provide maximum security. Without lockout policies defined, you give attackers free rein to guess passwords all day long.

Account lockout duration   Specify the time in minutes that an account should be locked out for after a specified number of failed logon attempts have been made (see "Account lockout threshold"). It is often standard practice to set a lockout duration such as 30 minutes, after which time the account is automatically unlocked for use again. It is up to you to decide whether you want this automatic unlock feature enabled, or whether you want your administrators to know about and react to every account lockout (not always a bad idea).

Account lockout threshold   This has to be set before any of the other options in this section can be configured. A standard recommended threshold is five failed login attempts, but it's really up to your organizational policy.

Reset account lockout counter   This must be set to less than or equal to your account lockout duration (e.g., 30 minutes). This is the time in which failed logon attempts are being tallied up. If you set it to 30 minutes, then failed logins will be tallied until either the threshold is reached and the account is locked out or the lockout counter is reset.

NOTE   What happens when somebody starts guessing passwords in the middle of the night? If you have lockout duration set for 30 minutes, and allow five invalid logon attempts before locking out an account, then an attacker can guess about ten passwords in an hour.

Local Policies

This most popular container has very important settings for auditing, user rights, and other security options.

Audit Policy

All auditing is disabled by default. It is important to know just what you want to audit and how to enable it. Some of the overlap in terminology can get a bit confusing (such as "account logon events" versus plain old "logon events") if you are not certain of exactly what you want to log.

CAUTION   All auditing is disabled by default in Windows. Make sure you enable auditing in a practical manner.

Audit account logon events   This setting is more suited to a domain controller, because you are not auditing where an account logon/logoff occurs but rather where the account lives and is validated. This setting will record every remote logon attempt (success or failure) and logoff, for which this computer confirms the account. For example, if you use a domain account to log on to a workstation named Cottons, this "account logon" will show up in the security event logs of the domain controller that validated the account credentials.

Audit account management   This setting logs any successful or failed changes to user or group accounts. These changes include adds, deletes, and modifications such as changing group membership, renaming, or setting a new password.

Audit directory service access   This setting logs successful and/or failed Active Directory object access attempts. It is not applicable to a workstation, only to a domain controller.

Audit logon events   Once you enable this setting to log success and failure, all logon and logoff events to the local machine will be logged. This setting is suitable to any machine, including workstations and domain controllers. Logon events to the local computer include console logon/logoff, network logon, and RDP/terminal services logons. For example, whether you use a domain or a local account to log on to a workstation named Cottons, the event will be logged in the local security event logs of Cottons.

Audit object access   When this setting is enabled, objects such as NTFS files, folders, registry keys, and printers will be ready for auditing. However, you still have to manually configure SACLs, or auditing settings, on the devices and actions you want to log. Additionally, enabling auditing here prepares the system to log actions on global system objects, such as mutexes, semaphores, and events.

Audit policy change   Policy changes include modifications to user rights assignments, audit policies, and trusts.

Audit privilege use   You can log each occurrence of an account exercising a user right by enabling this audit setting. Not all user rights, however, will actually be audited. Rights such as debugging programs, creating a token object, backing up files and directories, and restoring files and directories will not be audited unless you enable the "Audit: Audit the use of Backup and Restore privilege" setting in Security Options.

Audit process tracking   You can have a log entry created every time a process is successfully or unsuccessfully executed and exited. Process tracking is not normally something you would want to audit successes on, because of the large performance overhead it carries. Many organizations do like to audit failures here so that they can see which processes users are attempting to launch without correct permissions.

Audit system events   It's pretty important to audit such events as system restarts or shutdowns, so this setting should definitely be enabled for both successes and failures.

User Rights Assignment

This section lists a description of each user right as offered in the Local Security Policy GUI. Chapter 6, on user and group management, will go into more detail on some of these specific settings. Through the GUI you can control which users and groups have each right.

Access this computer from the network   The groups and users given this right will be allowed to connect remotely to the local computer via SMB sessions (i.e., basic Windows shares). As a general rule, you should define only the specific groups that need remote access via SMB. Remove the Everyone group (added by default) and replace it with Authenticated Users (at a minimum), and remove Guest. This setting has no effect on other services such as FTP and Terminal Server.

Act as part of the operating system   There is a good reason that no users have this right by default. A user who possesses this low-level privilege can essentially bypass all other security permissions, rights, and privileges on the system. For example, an anonymous token could be created that includes any or all access permissions, thus evading security and auditing.

Add workstations to domain   This right lets the specified users or groups add new workstations to the domain. Many large organizations like to give this right to all Authenticated Users, which is a questionable practice. Obviously, unauthorized or improperly secured machines could be added to the trusted domain. Once on the domain, a computer will be updated with any domain services and service accounts, for which passwords are stored in clear text in the registry.

Adjust memory quotas for a process   Adjusting the amount of memory available to a process may be necessary for fine-tuning a system, but it could be used either intentionally or unintentionally to create a denial of service type of attack.

Allow logon through Terminal Services   Users can be explicitly allowed the ability to log on through terminal server/RDP sessions.

Back up files and directories   Do not give this right away lightly. It defaults to Administrators and Backup Operators, and users allowed the "Back up files and directories" right can essentially bypass all file and folder DACLs (Discretionary Access Control Lists) in order to back up a file. The main thing to keep in mind here is that you don't want the same user having both backup and restore rights simultaneously.

Bypass traverse checking   Users with this right are allowed to traverse directories that some ACL denies them access to. The users cannot list directory contents, but only pass through the directory to get to another one. For example, say you have three chained directories, C:\temp\middle\target. Your user account is allowed access to \temp and \target, but denied access to \middle. With the "Bypass traverse checking" right, you are allowed to pass through the \middle directory in order to access the \target subdirectory.

Change the system time   Because accurate system time is critical to auditing, application, and authentication functions such as Kerberos, this right is limited to Administrators and Power Users by default. Depending on how much power they really need, best practice indicates that Power Users should be removed so that only Administrators hold this right. Keep in mind that changing the system time can corrupt audit logs and disable Kerberos—and don't give this right away lightly.

Create a pagefile   Administrators are the only ones who by default can create the pagefile on a Windows system. The pagefile is necessary to normal computer operation, and it is security sensitive because it acts as virtual memory, storing process variables and functions. Unless you have a unique situation, Administrators should be the only group with this right.

Create a token object   No accounts should ever possess this right, unless you want to completely jeopardize all other security defenses. This right provides the ability to call system APIs that create an access token which defines an account's permissions at logon. If access tokens can be arbitrarily created then there is no security. Access tokens are described further in Chapter 6.

Create permanent shared objects   Certain kernel mode components already possess this right, which they use for extending an object namespace. This right should never be given to a user or group account.

Debug programs   Administrators only have this right by default, and they should be removed from it. This right allows a user to attach a debugger to a process, which may be necessary for developers and Visual Studio installations. Having this right also allows tools such as LsaDump2.exe to be used; it dumps clear text service account passwords from the registry.

Deny access to this computer from the network   Use this right to force accounts to log on at the console, instead of via SMB across the network. They will receive a "permission denied" error message when attempting SMB connections remotely. A Deny rule takes precedence over an Allow rule, so, for example, if an account is given both the Allow and Deny access right, the remote logon will be denied.

Deny logon as a batch job   Batch job logons may be used instead of interactive logons. A batch logon can be executed, for example, by the Schedule service. A Deny rule takes precedence over an Allow rule, so, for example, if an account is given both the Allow and Deny logon right, the logon will be denied.

Deny logon as a service   Service accounts are used to register a process as a service. Use this setting to specifically deny an account this ability. A Deny rule takes precedence over an Allow rule, so, for example, if an account is given both the Allow and Deny logon right, the logon will be denied.

Deny logon locally   Accounts specified here will not be allowed to log on at the console. They can still log in via Terminal Services, Telnet, SMB, and other services. As usual, a Deny rule takes precedence over an Allow rule.

Deny logon through Terminal Services   Accounts specified here will be explicitly denied logon via Terminal Services. They can still log in locally via the console, Telnet, SMB, and other services. Again, a Deny rule takes precedence over an Allow rule.

Enable computer and user accounts to be trusted for delegation   Typically, on a client workstation such as Windows XP, no one will have this right, as is the case by default. Delegation is a Windows function used most often in multitiered applications where servers need to pass user contexts from one to another. Users with this right have the ability to set the "Trusted for delegation" setting on a user or computer object in Active Directory. This option is accessible on a user object in Active Directory, for example, under the Account tab and Account options. On a Windows 2000/.NET domain controller, Administrators possess this right by default.

Force shutdown from a remote system   Users with this right can call APIs to shut down the computer from a remote system. There is not much reason to let anyone but the Administrators group have this right.

Generate security audits   A process will be allowed to use accounts specified here to add events to the Security Event log.

Increase scheduling priority   Users with this right can increase the priority of a process. For example, a process's priority can be increased through the Task Manager by right-clicking the process and selecting Set Priority. The highest definable level is named Realtime, and it essentially commits the operating system to give all available CPU resources to the process. Setting high priorities can quickly consume all computer resources and result in a denial of service attack.

Load and unload device drivers Device drivers run in privileged kernel mode and should therefore be scrutinized and controlled. Best practice dictates that only Administrators have this right, as is the case by default.

Lock pages in memory Locking pages in physical memory (RAM) means preventing them from being written to the system pagefile. If someone were to abuse this right, they could create a denial of service condition by consuming all available RAM while preventing the use of the pagefile. For good reason, nobody has this right by default.

Log on as a batch job Batch job logons may be used instead of interactive logons. A batch logon can be executed, for example, by the Schedule service.

Log on as a service Service accounts are used to register a process as a service. Use this setting to specifically allow an account this ability. Accounts will be automatically given this right once you specify that a service can "Log on as" a certain account through the Service GUI of the MMC (Services.msc). Be aware that a service accounts password will be stored in clear text in the registry, so refrain from using domain administration level service accounts.

Log on locally Accounts must have this right if they are to have console access. This setting has no effect on an account's logon permissions for Terminal Services, Telnet, SMB, and other services, including IIS (see the following Caution). Best practice dictates that the defaults here are too permissive, and should be tightened up to only allow the exact groups who need it. This typically means removing all groups except the Administrators and Users groups.

CAUTION When running IIS, the IUSR account must be given the "Log on locally" right. That may not be of as much concern, however, as that any user who needs to access a Basic Authentication–protected virtual directory also needs the "Log on locally" right! That's correct—if you have a site set up to require Basic Authentication, then any remote user needing access will require this right.

Manage auditing and security log Users with this right have two very important capabilities. First, they can enable auditing on individual objects such as files, folders, and registry keys. Second, they can view and clear the Security Event log. For this reason, it is recommended that only Administrators carry this right.

Modify firmware environment values This right allows an account to modify the systemwide environment variables, as opposed to the individual user environment variables. Because system environment variables can be used to point at malicious programs, it is recommended that only Administrators possess this right, as is the default.

Perform volume maintenance tasks   These tasks include using such built-in APIs as disk cleanup and disk defragmenting, both actions that should only be carried out by Administrators.

Profile single process   This setting defines who can monitor the performance of non-system-related process counters.

Profile system performance   This setting defines who can monitor the performance of system-related process counters.

Remove computer from docking station   Users with this right can undock a workstation without logging on. Without this right, a user must log on and use the Start → Eject PC menu option to undock the computer. Obviously, without physical controls, a computer could be forcefully undocked regardless of this right.

Replace a process level token   An account with this right can use a parent process to replace the access token for a subprocess. This is a highly privileged right, usually reserved for kernel mode components.

Restore files and directories   As with the complementary "Back up files and directories" right, users allowed this right can essentially bypass all file and folder permissions (DACLs) in order to restore a file. It defaults to Administrators and Backup Operators, which means that your secret design plans can be restored, or overwritten, by any member of these groups, despite your specified DACL. Again, the thing to keep in mind is that the backup and restore rights should be separated between different user accounts.

Shut down the system   Users with this right can shut down the system, typically something that needs to be done for a workstation, especially a laptop that travels.

Synchronize directory service data   This right is relevant only to domain controllers and gives an account the ability to synchronize directory service data (i.e., the Active Directory database).

Take ownership of files or other objects   A user that can take ownership of objects (including files, folders, and registry keys) can bypass all security permissions on that object. *Read that one more time.* This functionality is designed to give administrators the ability to access files and folders regardless of their DACL. For example, if an employee hastily leaves your organization, you may still want access to their protected files.

Security Options

One of the first things seasoned administrators will notice is that the settings in this container have been newly categorized. In Windows 2000 they were simply presented in alphabetical order. In Windows XP/.NET they are presented in this format:

Category: title or short description

The *Category* piece is fairly straightforward, meaning that "Accounts" will be settings applied to user accounts, while "Network Security" will be settings meant to affect network security. The short description is not always as straightforward, which is why we are presenting a longer description in this chapter. The appendix will include a table of the recommended settings.

Accounts: Administrator account status   This setting is not applicable (by default) unless you have created another user account that is a member of the local Administrators group. There is nothing fancy here; by setting this to Disabled, you are disabling the built-in Administrator account just as you could through another UI such as the Local Users and Groups MMC snap-in.

Accounts: Guest account status   This is another place from which you can enable or disable the local Guest account, which is disabled by default. Be aware that if you have the "Network access: Sharing and security model for local accounts" setting set to "Guest only," then the local Guest account must be enabled or else network logons (such as SMB-based logons) will fail.

Accounts: Limit local account use of blank passwords to console logon only   This setting is enabled by default. Remote interactive logons, such as those by Terminal Services and Telnet, will not be allowed if the local user account being used has a blank password. Additionally, remote connections to SMB services (such as network shares) will not be allowed for users with blank passwords.

Accounts: Rename administrator account   This is another example of how security settings that can be made in other user interfaces are being brought together under one roof. There are several reasons for this, including making the administrator aware of what can be done and providing the ability to propagate such settings through Group Policy. Rename the Administrator account to something less obvious if you want to, but be aware that its RID (Relative Identifier) will always be 500 (see Chapter 6). A more paranoid technique is to actually rename and disable the built-in Administrator account.

Accounts: Rename guest account   Renaming the Guest account to something less obvious is another arguably weak attempt at obfuscation.

Audit: Audit the access of global system objects   Disabled by default, when enabled, this setting will set Windows to create system objects such as mutexes, events, and semaphores with auditing enabled. This is usually unnecessary in most environments, but it illustrates the level of security configuration granularity that Windows provides. Enabling this setting is a prerequisite for auditing system objects. You will then actually have to set an audit policy for "Audit object access" for events to show up in your logs.

Audit: Audit the use of Backup and Restore privilege   Disabled by default, this setting requires that you have an audit policy set up for "Audit privilege use" before events will actually be written to your logs. Once you enable it, however, all user privileges will be audited, including the use of the backup and restore privileges.

Audit: Shut down system immediately if unable to log security audits   This setting is disabled by default for good reason. You would only want to enable this in high-security settings where the system should not operate unless it can log security events. Once enabled, the system will actually crash with a Stop error BSOD (blue screen of death) when the security event log is full and cannot be written to.

Devices: Allow undock without having to log on   This setting only works for laptops that cannot be mechanically undocked, since software cannot protect against that. When it is disabled (not the default), a user will actually have to log on to undock the computer and be granted the Remove Computer from Docking Station privilege. This works in conjunction with the "Remove computer from docking station" user right.

Devices: Allowed to format and eject removable media   This control is granted to Administrators by default, but you can relax it if necessary by allowing Administrators and Power Users, or Administrators and Interactive Users, the right to format and eject removable media.

Devices: Prevent users from installing printer drivers   This setting affects only network printers, not locally connected printers. If you enable this setting (it is disabled by default), then only Administrators and Power Users can install network printer drivers, unless a trusted path has been set up for the network printer drivers.

Devices: Restrict CD-ROM access to locally logged-on user only   This setting is disabled by default. If you want to protect against network access to your CD-ROMs, then enable this setting. Keep in mind that it only applies when you are logged in interactively. Once you log out, the CD-ROM is still accessible from the network.

Devices: Restrict floppy access to locally logged-on user only   If you want to protect against network access to your floppy drives, then enable this setting; it is disabled by default. Keep in mind that it only applies when you are logged in interactively. Once you log out, the floppy disk is still accessible from the network.

Devices: Unsigned driver installation behavior   Installed drivers are loaded into kernel space and therefore have serious security implications. This setting controls how drivers are installed through the Setup API. By default, Windows will "Warn but allow installation." If you want to be ultrasecure then set this to "Do not allow installation," which will not stop a driver from being installed by other means, such as manually. Keep in mind that Administrators by default are the only ones with the "Load and unload device drivers" user right.

Domain controller: Allow server operators to schedule tasks   Because the Schedule service can be used to launch programs in the context of the all-powerful SYSTEM account, it is recommended that this setting be disabled. Otherwise, a member of the server operators group could abuse this ability to elevate their own privileges.

Domain controller: LDAP server signing requirements   Applicable to domain controllers only, this setting determines whether the LDAP server requires the LDAP client to sign the traffic. Setting to "not defined" (the default) or None does not require the LDAP client to sign. Setting this to "Require Signature" will require the LDAP client to negotiate signing methods, unless SSL/TLS is being used.

Domain controller: Refuse machine account password changes   This domain controller–specific setting is not typically something you would want to enable. The reason is simply that it prevents a computer password from being changed on a domain controller. Since these passwords are randomly generated and strong, you should not let your users change them unless they know what they are doing.

Domain member: Digitally encrypt or sign secure channel data (always)   This setting is disabled by default to allow for interoperability with clients and servers that cannot set up signed or encrypted channels. In large mixed environments, you will probably want to leave this disabled. However, in specific segments, organizational units, or networks with all Windows NT 4.0 SP4 and later OSs, you should consider enabling this.

When it is enabled, the Windows XP client will always attempt to encrypt or sign the secure channel used for communication with a supportive domain controller (Windows NT 4.0 SP4 and later). If an encrypted or signed channel cannot be set up, then communication will fail altogether. When disabled, a secure channel can still be set up, but the signing and encryption parameters are negotiated, and not required. Secure channel communication with a domain controller usually involves NTLM passthrough authentication, SID/Name lookups, and other types of domain authentication traffic.

NOTE   Interoperability is a recurring theme throughout this book, and is something you will always want to keep in mind. Microsoft is providing such granular settings as "always" and "when possible" to give you the flexibility to either require security or allow it to be negotiated more transparently.

Domain member: Digitally encrypt secure channel data (when possible)   This setting should always be enabled (as it is by default) so that encrypted communication with a domain controller is preferred to unencrypted. An encrypted, secure channel will be negotiated, but is not required, so that interoperability with incapable systems still works.

Domain member: Digitally sign secure channel data (when possible)   This setting should always be enabled (as it is by default) so that signed communication with a domain controller is preferred to nonsigned.

Domain member: Disable machine account password changes   This setting is disabled by default for good reason. Leave it that way unless you have some pressing need to change machine account passwords. These passwords are managed transparently by Windows and the domain controllers and should not require human intervention. If you need to reset machine account passwords, you can do so through the Active Directory Users and Computers snap-in by right-clicking a machine name and selecting "Reset Account." By default these passwords are automatically changed every 30 days, as specified in the next setting, "Maximum machine account password age."

Domain member: Maximum machine account password age   Defaulting to 30 days, this setting specifies how often a machine account password is to be automatically reset by Windows.

Domain member: Require strong (Windows 2000 or later) session key   If your domain controllers are all Windows 2000 or later, and you require that certain computers communicate with them only over secure channels with strong, 128-bit encryption, then put those computers in an organizational unit and enable this setting. Communication with a DC usually involves NTLM passthrough authentication, SID/Name lookups, and other types of domain authentication traffic. This setting is not related to SMB traffic (Windows networking with Server Message Block), which is covered in upcoming text. It is disabled by default, which means Windows XP hosts will tolerate weaker encryption keys to set up secure channels.

Interactive logon: Do not display last user name   While this setting is still disabled by default, you should enable it to prevent the last logged-on user's name from appearing at the login screen. This typically enforced setting usually gets enabled through a GPO for all computers in the domain.

Interactive logon: Do not require CTRL+ALT+DEL   The familiar CTRL-ALT-DEL sequence that precedes a Windows 2000 login is not the default in stand-alone Windows XP Professional computers. Instead, Fast User Switching is enabled, which doesn't invoke the secure logon channel that pressing CTRL-ALT-DEL does. Once a Windows XP Professional machine joins a domain, however, this setting is automatically disabled, and the secure CTRL-ALT-DEL sequence is required.

Interactive logon: Message text for users attempting to log on   This is another setting typically enforced through a GPO at the domain level, because an organizational login message is normally required by policy. If you are not already using this feature, you should enable it for all your network computers. In some legal cases, message text at the logon prompt can be required to show that users were warned not to attempt unauthorized access to a system.

Interactive logon: Message title for users attempting to log on   This is the text for the title bar that accompanies the message text at logon.

Interactive logon: Number of previous logons to cache (in case domain controller is not available)
The past ten unique logon credentials will be cached by default. This is considered insecure, because these credentials are stored in a protected part of the system registry where they could possibly be retrieved by someone with Administrator privileges. The problem may not seem obvious at first, but suppose that some of your users have Administrator rights on their personal machines, and one day your domain administrator has to log into one of those machines to do some work. Are you comfortable knowing that the domain administrator's credentials have just been cached in the registry of that computer?

The most paranoid mind will set this to zero, so that no domain logon credentials are cached. However, this would mean that domain accounts will not be able to log into the machine if a domain controller is not available. For laptops and traveling employees, you should probably set this to at least 1, so that the last logon is cached. This will ensure that they can still log on to their computer when disconnected from the network (provided they were the last ones to log on). Configure this setting wisely.

Interactive logon: Prompt user to change password before expiration   By default, users are prompted 14 days prior to a required password change. Set this to the number of days' advance notice you want users to have that a password change will be required.

Interactive logon: Require Domain Controller authentication to unlock workstation   Once enabled, a workstation cannot be unlocked with a domain account unless a domain controller is present. If you have a group of traveling employees with laptops, you do not want to enable this for them, and you might consider placing them in a separate organizational unit with their own GPO.

Interactive logon: Require smart card (Windows.NET AD only)   In Windows .NET Active Directory, smart card authentication can be required for user interactive logons. This setting is disabled by default, but it can be enabled and applied to a GPO if desired to require an organizational unit or domain to use smart cards for logon. Smart cards provide some of the strongest authentication methods possible today.

Interactive logon: Smart card removal behavior   When a smart card is removed for a logged-on user, one of three things can be configured to happen. Either no action is taken, the workstation is locked, or the user is forcefully logged off. In most cases, setting this to "Lock Workstation" will provide a good security measure.

Microsoft network client: Digitally sign communications (always)   When both a client and a server sign their packets, message integrity can be achieved and man-in-the-middle attacks can be prevented. This is called *mutual authentication* and provides the most security. The type of communications that this setting is concerned with is a client using Server Message Block (SMB) to connect to a server. This setting is disabled by default, because in most mixed OS environments, some legacy systems will not be capable of signing SMB communications. If your network is purely Windows 2000 and higher, then you should definitely enable this setting for maximum security. The server requirements defined in "Microsoft network server: Digitally sign communications (always)" must be enabled to provide the "mutual authentication" mentioned.

NOTE   Digitally signing packets does incur a CPU performance penalty on the client and server.

Microsoft network client: Digitally sign communications (if server agrees)   This setting is enabled by default and should remain so. It attempts to negotiate secure, signed communications, but will not fail the communication if the other computer is not capable of signing.

Microsoft network client: Send unencrypted password to third-party SMB servers   This setting is disabled by default and should stay that way. It prevents the client from sending plaintext passwords to SMB servers that do not support encryption during the authentication process. If you have some specific need to enable this setting, you should create an organizational unit for only the computers that need it, and warn everyone of the consequences. If someone can put a sniffer on the network or trick a machine into sending its plaintext credentials, then those credentials can be reused on the network.

Microsoft network server: Amount of idle time required before suspending session   You can set a timeout for SMB communications. This setting is undefined for Windows XP workstations by default, and set to 15 minutes for servers. For example, if an established SMB connection with a server has been idle for 15 minutes, the server will disconnect it.

Microsoft network server: Digitally sign communications (always)   In a perfectly networked world, digital communications would always be signed, so that the identity of each party could be validated. However, in the real world of backward compatibility, hybrid environments, and incapable clients (and even servers), you can only enable this setting when you have absolute certainty that every computer is capable of signing. This is not to say that once this setting is enabled (it's disabled by default) you will be more secure, but your Windows 2000/XP/.NET computers will at least require that all SMB communications with their Server service be signed by the remote client computer.

Microsoft network server: Digitally sign communications (if client agrees)   This setting is disabled on workstations and enabled on servers, but it won't hurt to enable this on your Windows 2000 and XP workstations. In fact, it's a good idea. Once you do, the SMB server of the workstation will attempt to set up signed communications with whatever remote computer is attempting connection. If the remote computer does not agree to sign its communications, they will still be allowed.

Microsoft network server: Disconnect clients when logon hours expire   When this setting is enabled, remote sessions with the workstation's local SMB server will be forcibly disconnected once the logon hours of the account have expired. While it is undefined by default, you should enable it if you want logon hours to be enforced on your network.

Network access: Allow anonymous SID/Name translation   New to Windows XP/.NET, this setting is disabled on workstations and enabled on servers. Certain aspects of authentication with a domain controller require that anonymous SID-to-name translation be allowed, but it is certainly not necessary for all servers. You should leave this setting disabled on workstations to prevent remote, anonymous users from being able to illicit SIDs by username, or usernames by SID. SID/Name translation is a common technique used by hackers to enumerate administrator (and other users) account names and SIDs on remote machines.

Network access: Do not allow anonymous enumeration of SAM accounts   RestrictAnonymous has been much improved in Windows XP to include more granular control of anonymous access without the past Windows 2000 problems of breaking domain functionality. The old RestrictAnonymous setting of Windows 2000 is now split into several separate settings. This option corresponds to a new registry value named RestrictAnonymousSam and, as it is enabled by default, will prevent user account information from being enumerated by an anonymous user.

NOTE   RestrictAnonymous has been newly designed for Windows XP. In Windows 2000, setting RestrictAnonymous=2 prevents null users from even connecting to the IPC$ share, which ends up killing down-level client access and trusted domain enumeration. This isn't the case in Windows XP/.NET, however, which gives you more control over restricting anonymous access by providing the following finely tuned options:

- Network access: Do not allow anonymous enumeration of SAM accounts
- Network access: Do not allow anonymous enumeration of SAM accounts and shares
- Network access: Allow anonymous SID/Name translation
- Network access: Let Everyone permissions apply to anonymous users

In its own way, each setting contributes to the permissions that an anonymous user has on a system. Remember, too, that these are in addition to other settings that control anonymous access to named pipes and registry keys.

Network access: Do not allow anonymous enumeration of SAM accounts and shares   Enabling this setting is somewhat similar to setting RestrictAnonymous to 1 in Windows 2000, although you should remember that the functionality has changed in Windows XP/.NET. In Windows XP/.NET, this setting still allows an anonymous connection to IPC$ as null, but it won't allow user account and share enumeration.

It is disabled by default, which means that while user account information can be enumerated, share information cannot. You should enable this setting on any Windows XP/.NET computer that does not need to allow anonymous users to remotely enumerate both user accounts and shares. Note that enabling this may break some applications, so test first.

CHALLENGE

You have a development department that needs a higher level of network security that can only be configured in a purely Windows 2000 SP2 and later network. Luckily, you just finished a complete desktop upgrade to Windows XP for this department, and you know that all their domain controllers are at least Windows 2000 SP2. The file and print servers in this department have also recently been upgraded from Windows NT 4.0 to Windows 2000 SP2.

So what are the strongest security settings you can enable that will be supported by both Windows 2000 and Windows XP?

You can actually enable a lot of security in a network where only Windows XP and Windows 2000 computers exist. By configuring the following settings for Windows XP and the corresponding settings for Windows 2000, you will increase security for network operations such as domain authentication, SMB file shares, and anonymous user access:

- **Domain member: Digitally encrypt or sign secure channel data (always)** Enabled

- **Domain member: Require strong (Windows 2000 or later) session key** Enabled

- **Microsoft network client: Digitally sign communications (always)** Enabled

- **Microsoft network server: Digitally sign communications (always)** Enabled

- **Network access: Allow anonymous SID/Name translation** Disabled

- **Network access: Do not allow anonymous enumeration of SAM accounts and shares** Enabled

- **Network security: Do not store LAN Manager hash value on next password change** Enabled

- **Network security: LAN Manager authentication level** Send NTLMv2 response only\refuse LM. (Ideally, if you can set this value to "Send NTLMv2 response only\refuse LM & NTLM" then you should do so. Be sure to test this, however, as we have seen this break functionality in different environments.)

- **Network security: Minimum session security for NTLM SSP based (including secure RPC) clients** Require each message integrity, message confidentiality, NTLMv2 session security, and 128-bit encryption

---

CHALLENGE *(continued)*

- **Network security: Minimum session security for NTLM SSP based (including secure RPC) servers**   Require each message integrity, message confidentiality, NTLMv2 session security, and 128-bit encryption
- **System cryptography: Use FIPS compliant algorithms for encryption, hashing, and signing**   Enabled
- **System objects: Default owner for objects created by members of the Administrators group**   Administrators Group

Note that a few questions arise here. First, how do we intend to apply Windows XP–specific security settings through a Windows 2000 domain controller, when these settings don't even show up in the Group Policy MMC snap-in on the DC?

Chapter 11 will answer this question, when it describes how you can use your Windows XP Professional computer (or Windows .NET member server) to manage the Active Directory and GPOs.

Another question is, how in the world do these Windows XP–specific settings map over to the Windows 2000 computers, and vice versa? Or more importantly, how can a single GPO be created that applies these settings to both Windows 2000 and Windows XP?

The answers are that they do map over (but not in the way that you would expect), and that you cannot create a single GPO for both operating systems (unless you want to wreak havoc on your network). The section on managing Windows XP GPOs in Chapter 11 will answer these questions as well.

Network access: Do not allow storage of credentials or .NET Passports for network authentication
This setting is disabled by default. Credentials and .NET passports used for network connections will be stored in the new Credential Manager. They will be used transparently when an integrated authentication package (Kerberos, NTLM, etc.) requires them. The Credential Manager acts like a key ring. It can be managed through the User Accounts control panel applet by clicking the "Manage my network passwords" link.

Network access: Let Everyone permissions apply to anonymous users   A brand new and powerful setting in Windows XP/.NET lets you control whether or not Everyone permissions apply to the Anonymous user token. When this setting is disabled, the Anonymous account (security principal) will not be considered a member of the Everyone group, and its token therefore will not carry the SID for the Everyone group.

NOTE   A security token is a collection of SIDs that define the access permissions for an account, as discussed further in Chapter 6.

Without being a member of the Everyone group, the Anonymous user is even more limited than it was Windows 2000 and Windows NT. Because this may break some applications, you can easily enable this setting for troubleshooting.

Network access: Named Pipes that can be accessed anonymously   Named pipes are communications channels between computers on a network. Services and applications will set up and use these channels. The list here can also be found in the registry key `HKEY_LOCAL_MACHINE\SYSTEM\CurrentControlSet\Services\ lanmanserver\parameters` under the `NullSessionPipes` value, where the configuration ultimately resides.

This list represents the anonymously accessible named pipes, but there can exist many other named pipes that are not accessible with null credentials, and hence do not appear on this list. You probably do not need all the default pipes here, but deleting them is something you should only do in a test lab, one by one, to figure out which ones are needed for the applications you run. For example, a print server will require that the SPOOLSS exist. Most other systems will require the EPMAPPER, LLSRPC, and LOCATOR for most networking functions.

Network access: Remotely accessible registry paths   As described further in Chapter 3, on registry security, the remotely accessible registry paths correspond to the `HKLM\SYSTEM\CCS\Control\SecurePipeServers\winreg\AllowedPaths` key values. The paths specified here can, more precisely, be accessed remotely by Anonymous users. The best method for removing them is one by one in a test lab, figuring out which ones do and don't break your applications and network management needs. For instance, if the host is not serving as a print server or a terminal server, then there is most likely no need for the System\CurrentControlSet\Control\Print\Printers and the System\CurrentControlSet\Control\Terminal Server paths.

Network access: Restrict anonymous access to Named Pipes and Shares (.NET AD only)
Enabled by default on a Windows .NET domain controller, this setting effectively overrides both the "Network access: Named Pipes that can be accessed anonymously" and the "Network access: Shares that can be accessed anonymously" settings. Enabling this setting restricts anonymous access for named pipes and shares specified in the two mentioned settings.

Network access: Shares that can be accessed anonymously   Most shares in Windows require some form of authentication, unless you specifically add the Anonymous SID. In this case the shares listed here have that SID, and while they are not created by default on a Windows XP host, they will allow anonymous access once a share with that name is created. However, the Anonymous user will not have any permissions unless specifically defined. For maximum security, you should remove the shares listed here (COMCFG, DFS$) unless your applications (typically COM+ and DFS) require them.

Network access: Sharing and security model for local accounts   Touted as one of Windows XP's new features, this setting controls whether or not remote network connections to the XP computer will be forced to authenticate as a guest account or another account. This is irrelevant in domain environments, where this setting is forced to "Classic—local users authenticate as themselves," which essentially means any local account can be used for authentication from a remote machine. This setting was mainly added to help protect the networked user, by allowing (the default) remote connections to authenticate with only minimal Guest privileges.

Network security: Do not store LAN Manager hash value on next password change   As described further in Chapter 3, this setting was first introduced in Windows 2000 SP2 as a registry hack. Now in Windows XP it is a Security Policy setting. You should definitely enable it (it is disabled by default), as it will prevent older LAN Manager–style password hashes, which are more easily crackable, from being stored on the computer. Be careful if you are using applications that require the LAN Manager (LM) hash, and test this setting in a lab. Also remember that once you flip it to enabled, you must make a password change before the old LM hash disappears.

NOTE   You can achieve this same setting in both Windows 2000 and Windows XP by creating a password 15 characters or longer, for which a LM hash will not be generated.

Network security: Force logoff when logon hours expire   Logon hours are defined by user either locally or in Active Directory, by domain or organizational unit. This setting is disabled by default, but if you are serious about your network's logon hours, then you should enable it. It applies only to client SMB connections, meaning it will only affect users logged in across the network. To see current SMB connections type **net session** from the command line.

Network security: LAN Manager authentication level   This is another setting that allows you to balance between backward compatibility and network security. Figure 1-2 illustrates the options you can choose from. Although Kerberos authentication is at the center of a Windows 2000/XP/.NET domain, LAN Manager and NTLM will still be used with down-level clients (or servers) and when Kerberos authentication fails.

Windows 2000/XP/.NET all default to "Send LM & NTLM responses," which happens to be the weakest but most compatible stance. If someone can capture, or *sniff*, traffic on your network and get LM hashes, the hashes can be easily cracked with tools such as L0phtCrack to gain the username and password. NTLM is stronger but has its own set of problems, although it is not as readily criticizable. At a *minimum*, you should override the default setting in your default domain policy and pick the second one: "Send LM & NTLM—use NTLMv2 session security if negotiated." This will ensure backward compatibility while providing an option for stronger NTLMv2. If your

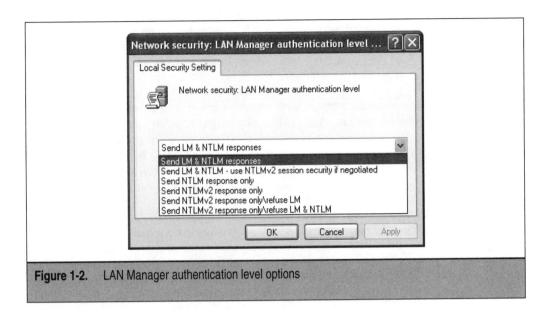

Figure 1-2. LAN Manager authentication level options

network is all Windows NT 4.0 and later, then you could choose "Send NTLM response only." If it is all Windows 2000 and later, then you could choose "Send NTLMv2 response only\refuse LM & NTLM," as we did in this chapter's Challenge.

NOTE Windows NT 4.0 SP4 brought support for NTLMv2, although it needs to be turned on through the registry. Also, Windows 95/98 clients can support NTLMv2 if you install the Directory Services Client from the Windows 2000 installation CD and enable the LMCompatibility registry key setting. See Microsoft Knowledge Base article Q239869 for more details.

Network security: LDAP client signing requirements "Negotiate signing" is the middle of the road and the default choice. In this way, network security will be achieved by the LDAP client requesting signed communications with the server. If the server agrees, then signed communications will commence; otherwise, communications will go by unsigned. The exception to this is if TLS/SSL is being used, in which case signing will not even be requested.

Network security: Minimum session security for NTLM SSP based (including secure RPC) clients
This setting affects the behavior of the computer when it acts as a network client, and was also available in Windows 2000 and Windows 9x clients using the dsclient software. By default, there are no minimum security requirements set on application-to-application SSP (Security Service Provider)–based communications. As administrator, you can require none or any combination of the following: message integrity, message confidentiality, NTLMv2 session security, 128-bit encryption.

Network security: Minimum session security for NTLM SSP based (including secure RPC) servers
This setting affects the behavior of the computer when it acts as a network server. As administrator, you can require none or any combination of the following: message integrity, message confidentiality, NTLMv2 session security, 128-bit encryption.

Recovery console: Allow automatic administrative logon   This setting should always be disabled unless you have some aggravating needs that require you to completely jeopardize security. By allowing automatic administrative logon to the recovery console, no logon information (such as username and password) is required for administrative access to the system. Anyone with physical access to the server can shut it down and boot straight to the recovery console with full admin rights.

Recovery console: Allow floppy copy and access to all drives and all folders   By default, the recovery console allows access only to the system partition and a limited set of commands. Enabling this setting will provide access to all local drives, including the floppy, as well as open up some additional commands. Typically, default access to the system partition is enough to perform most troubleshooting or maintenance tasks that the recovery console is designed to do.

NOTE   The recovery console is not installed by default, even though these settings exist. To install it, insert the setup CD and run **\i386\winnt32.exe /cmdcons**.

Shutdown: Allow system to be shut down without having to log on   By default, Windows workstations can be shut down from the initial logon screen, while servers cannot. By disabling this setting, the logon screen option to shut down will be grayed out and a user will have to log on before it is enabled.

Shutdown: Clear virtual memory pagefile   Since the paging file contains data swapped from physical memory, it can contain sensitive information such as passwords and encryption keys. While the operating system does a good job of protecting the pagefile while the system is running, there is nothing to stop someone with physical access from powering off a machine and rebooting to an alternate OS to access the data stored in the pagefile. After all, it is just a file on disk that simulates RAM. If this setting is enabled, be prepared for a slight performance hit; it will take longer to shut down and reboot.

System cryptography: Use FIPS compliant algorithms for encryption, hashing, and signing
This is a new crypto setting for Windows XP/.NET that allows you to force stronger encryption algorithms when it is enabled. For TLS/SSL, encryption algorithms are forced to use Triple DES, rather than their default DESX. Also, the RSA public key algorithm is forced for the key exchange and authentication, and only the SHA-1 hashing algorithm will be used for hashing negotiations. This setting also applies to EFS encryption algorithms and will force Triple DES rather than DESX.

System objects: Default owner for objects created by members of the Administrators group   On Windows XP Professional, this setting defaults to "Object Creator," meaning that if a member of the Administrators group creates an object (such as a new file or folder), their user SID will be designated the owner of that object. This is as opposed to the SID for the Administrators group being designated the owner of the object. On Windows .NET servers this setting defaults to "Administrators Group," which is the more secure choice. This setting requires a reboot in order to take effect.

SECURITY ALERT   A serious threat to system integrity can be caused by setting this to "Object Creator." Imagine a scenario where Lisa is a member of the Administrators group, and she creates some new top secret folders and files for use by Administrators on one of the administrative workstations. If a few months later she takes a new position and is removed from the Administrators group, she will still have ownership rights to those files and folders, which means she can give herself full control and remove other user's permissions.

System objects: Require case insensitivity for non-Windows subsystems (Windows .NET only)
The Win32 subsystem is case-insensitive by default, a feature that cannot be changed. Win32 will however support case sensitivity in subsystems such as POSIX. By default this setting is enabled, and case insensitivity is enforced for all subsystems except Win32.

System objects: Strengthen default permissions of internal system objects (e.g. Symbolic Links)
Enabled by default, this setting tightens security by setting stronger DACLs on shared system objects such as mutexes, semaphores, and DOS device names. Instead of carelessly giving out full control to everyone, these objects will be created so that nonadministrative users can read but cannot modify them. There is no good reason to disable this setting.

TOOLS OF THE TRADE

Several tools are used to implement security policy. Security settings can be managed locally by system or domainwide through Group Policy. In addition, the security settings can be exported to an .inf template file with the Security Configuration and Analysis tool, and imported either locally or as a part of a group policy object.

Local Security Policy (Secpol.msc)   Renamed Local Security Settings in Windows XP/.NET, this is the interface for configuring some of the most important "security settings" related to the operating system. These settings are included as a subset of Group Policy, and contain the relevant configurations for Password Policy, Audit Policy, Security Options, Software Restriction Policies, and IP Security Policies. Configurations set through Local Security Policy are only applied to the local machine, regardless of the logged-on user.

Group Policy (GPedit.msc)   This is the MMC snap-in that is used to edit and apply Group Policy Objects. It is accessible either by entering **gpedit.msc** from the command line or by right-clicking a Domain or Organizational Unit in Active Directory and selecting Properties → Group Policy. You use it to apply the same computer and user configurations to a group of computers or users in Active Directory. On a local machine, Group Policy can also be used to apply local configurations.

Security Configuration and Analysis   This powerful toolbox provides a means to configure all the security settings related to Local Security Policy, as well as many more related to the file system, registry, restricted groups, and services. Access the Security Configuration and Analysis snap-in by opening the MMC and selecting File → Add/Remove Snap-in.

CHECKLIST: SECURITY SETTINGS

The security settings, which provide some of the most important security configurations, have changed significantly from Windows 2000 to Windows XP. Configuring these wisely can drastically improve OS security on your network. To successfully implement them, you need to understand the effects of each setting and the effects of combining multiple settings. Do not plan your Windows XP rollouts without designing a solid baseline of security settings.

The following checklist highlights some of the key points made throughout this chapter:

- ☐ Local Policy is applied for a single machine, to all users on the machine.
- ☐ Group Policy is more powerful, allowing you to apply policy to sites, domains, and organizational units in Active Directory on a per user/computer or per group basis.
- ☐ Several interfaces exist to accomplish similar goals. Get familiar with the MMC, Local Security Policy (Secpol.msc), Group Policy (GPedit.msc), and the Security Configuration and Analysis MMC snap-in.
- ☐ Plan a security policy baseline that can be applied across your organization.
- ☐ When planning your baseline, consider the need for interoperability with older Windows clients.
- ☐ Configure your account policies so they can be applied at the domain or organizational unit level, through a group policy object.
- ☐ Enable Auditing, which is disabled by default.
- ☐ Tighten up user rights assignments to match your own needs; do not give everyone rights that they do not need.
- ☐ Understand each of the security options available. Remember that some options that talk of signing or encrypting traffic are repeated for different types of traffic, such as SMB, LDAP, and session security.

CHAPTER 2

SAFER Software Restriction Policies

One of the most important new security features of Windows XP/.NET is Software Restriction Policies (SAFER). It gives Windows administrators more control than ever over executable code.

If you have used Appsec.exe before (it was included in the Windows 2000 Server Resource Kit) then you will be familiar with some of the limitations of earlier software restriction techniques. Appsec.exe allowed administrators to specify whether an executable would be allowed to run based on a configured path such as C:\program files\application. If strict NTFS access controls were not used in conjunction with the paths, then users could find ways to circumvent this security by renaming executables or moving them to different directories. Other methods that prevented software from running in Windows 2000 included removing shortcuts from the Start menu or hiding the Run command.

SAFER is one of the most notable additions to Windows XP/.NET. SAFER provides a much more advanced system for controlling executable code. In fact, some may argue that its granularity can lead to complexities that leave end users and administrators with difficult problems to troubleshoot. For this reason, it is important to carefully plan your software restriction policies and think through the goals and deployment scenarios you want to achieve.

Software restriction policies can provide to an organization the following types of benefits:

- **Protection from malicious code such as viruses, Trojans, and worms**
  Consider a policy that prevents unsigned VBScript files from executing,
  or Trojan code such as SubSeven or BackOrifice from launching.

- **Safety from nonmalicious code that might unintentionally cause problems**
  Think of an unsupported application that tries changing computer
  configurations, or some software that conflicts with critical applications.

- **Control over what users can and cannot do with their computers**
  Think of preventing users from running registry-modification tools,
  running downloaded executables, and allowing only signed scripts to run.

IMPORTANT CONSIDERATIONS

To get familiar with software restriction policies, consider the following questions you will eventually have to ask yourself, each of which can realistically be answered with SAFER:

- Do I want a default policy of allowing all executable code or denying all?

- Do I want my additional rules to apply to all users, including administrators?

- Do I want my additional rules to apply to all software, including DLLs?

- What should be considered executable code? File extensions might include
  .cmd, .chm, .exe, .hlp, .lnk, .mdb, .msi, .reg, and .scr.

- Should I control executable code based on cryptographic hashes, certificates, paths, or security zones?

You will also need to consider how you want to apply the policy:

- Do I want a local computer policy or a Group Policy Object (GPO) applied through Active Directory?

If you are going to use a GPO for the policy, you should create one that is separate from your other GPOs. This will make it a lot simpler for you to change and troubleshoot. If you need to quickly remove the GPO, you will not have to affect your other policies. When going the GPO route, ask yourself:

- Do I want to apply these settings to machines or users?
- Do I want to apply this GPO to an entire domain or a specific OU?
- Are there certain users or groups I will want to remove the "Apply Policy" permission for?

Now let's see how these questions can realistically be answered.

Software restriction policies are built using a few *umbrella* settings that "set the stage," so to speak. Once the stage is set, you can begin configuring the *additional rules*, which actually provide the core of the policy. These additional rules are where you define the specific software that can and cannot run, while the umbrella settings define the conditions under which these rules function.

CONFIGURE SOFTWARE RESTRICTION POLICIES

Software restriction policies can be configured through a few different interfaces. To configure a local security policy on a single machine, just go Start → Run → Secpol.msc to launch the console and select Software Restriction Policies from the list on the left.

Another way to configure software restriction policies on a local machine is to launch Gpedit.msc and configure the policies under Computer Configuration. To configure a GPO for an Active Directory site, domain, or OU, simply launch Dsa.msc, right-click the domain or organizational unit you want, and navigate to Properties → Group Policy → Edit. In addition, you can edit the GPO directly by running the Windows XP MMC and adding the Group Policy snap-in, at which point you can browse and select a domain GPO to manage or create a new one (provided the Windows XP computer is a domain member).

NOTE The Dsa.msc console is installed on a Windows 2000/.NET domain controller by default, and on a Windows XP workstation when you install the Administration Tools Package (AdminPak.msi) from Microsoft.

WINDOWS 2000 INTEGRATION

Software restriction policies can be used in a Windows 2000 Active Directory by simply managing the group policy objects from a Windows XP computer. The process for doing this is almost as simple as it sounds—just run the MMC and add the Group Policy snap-in from a Windows XP computer in the domain, and then select the GPO you want to manage. You must of course be logged in with administrative permissions.

From Windows XP, you will see the container for Software Restriction Policies under Computer Configuration → Windows Settings → Security Settings. Once you finish configuring your policies, they are saved as any normal GPO would be. Surprisingly, however, they will not appear when you view the GPO from a Windows 2000 computer or domain controller, but rest assured that they are there.

Chapter 11 goes into detail about creating Windows XP GPOs in a Windows 2000 domain, but for now remember that the Windows 2000 domain controllers do not need to be upgraded. Any software restriction policies configured will be enforced by Windows XP/.NET machines, and ignored by Windows 2000 computers.

NOTE   It is good practice to create separate GPOs for your software restriction policies.

UMBRELLA SETTINGS

The umbrella-type settings are the ones that define the default policy rules, under which all additional rules operate. These settings are listed in the Local Security Settings console, as shown in Figure 2-1, and are named as follows:

- Security Levels
- Additional Rules
- Enforcement
- Designated File Types
- Trusted Publishers

You should fully understand each of your options before planning any settings. Rest assured, by the time you finish reading this chapter, you will be able to come back to this point and know exactly what you want to do with each setting.

Security Levels

First of all, when creating a new software restriction policy, you create a default rule similar to one you would on a firewall. You set up a default rule to either allow all or deny all code execution. Microsoft's terminology is a bit different, however, as you can see in Figure 2-2.

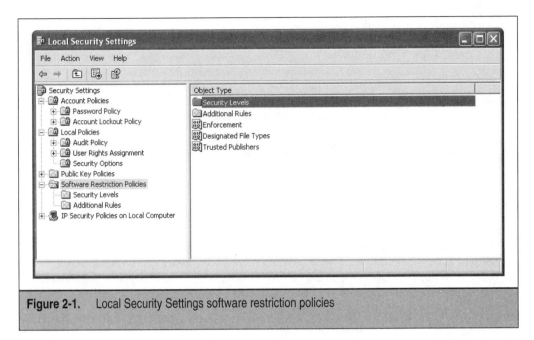

Figure 2-1.   Local Security Settings software restriction policies

The Security Levels subcontainer of Software Restriction Policies is where the default rule is defined. Just double-click or right-click Disallowed or Unrestricted, and select "Set as Default." As noted in Table 2-1, Disallowed corresponds to a familiar "deny all" type of policy, and Unrestricted to "allow all."

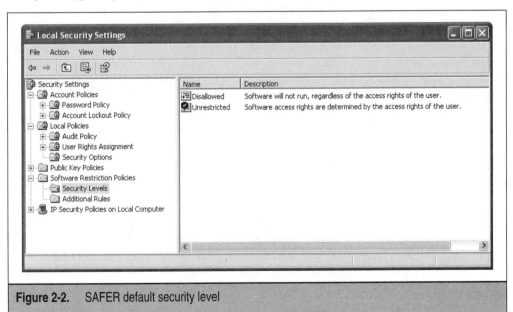

Figure 2-2.   SAFER default security level

Security Level	Description
Disallowed	When set as the default, all software considered executable code will be prevented from running. You will have to set up additional rules to specifically allow the software that you want to run.
Unrestricted	When set as the default, all software considered executable code will be allowed to run. You will have to set up specific additional rules that disallow software you do not want to run.

Table 2-1.   Security Levels

CAUTION   Without proper planning, setting a default Disallowed security level will cause serious problems. To demonstrate this, try setting up a test box with a Disallowed default rule that applies to all users. At the next reboot, your administrator will not even be able to log in, because executable code that the operating system depends on will not be allowed to run (everything in the %systemroot% and %programfiles% directories). If you set this default, you would normally want to create an additional path rule that would allow executable code in these directories to run.

Enforcement

This ever-important configuration is where you answer the two questions from above: "Do I want my additional rules to apply to all users including administrators?" and "Do I want my additional rules to apply to all software including DLLs?" As shown in Figure 2-3, these questions are answered using the radio buttons in the UI.

Applying General Software Restriction Policies

By default, software restriction policies are applied to "All software files except libraries (such as DLLs)," which is the recommended general purpose setting. The only time you might want policies applied to "All software files" is in a highly sensitive security environment. This setting turns on DLL checking, which can be a nightmarish fate.

It is recommended that you leave the default setting active for a number of reasons. As an example, consider Internet Explorer, which consists of an executable file, IExplore.exe, and many supporting DLLs.

- With a default "Unrestricted" security level, only the executable file would need to be specified to prevent the program from running, so being required to disallow each associated DLL would be an unnecessary and burdensome task.

- With a default "Disallowed" security level, not only would the executable, IExplore.exe, need to be specified as allowed to run, but each of the DLL files it depends on would need to be specified as well. With the several files that Internet Explorer depends on, this task can easily get out of hand.

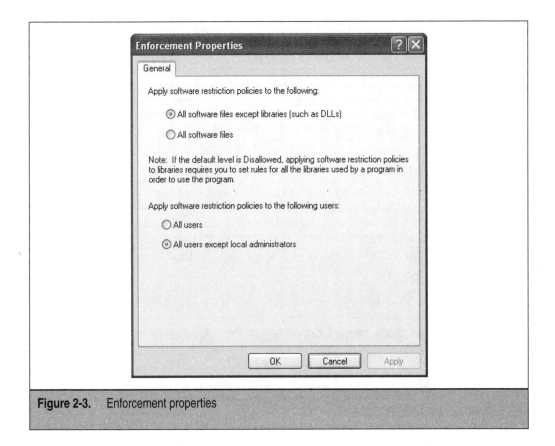

Figure 2-3.   Enforcement properties

- A severe performance penalty can be experienced if policy is applied to "All software files," since policy needs to be checked not only for each program but for each file that loads with the program as well.

NOTE   To view an executable file's dependencies on DLLs and other files, you can use a tool like Dependency Walker (Depends.exe) from the Windows 2000 Resource Kit.

Applying Software Restriction Policies to Users

In most scenarios, it is recommended that you apply your policy to "All users except local administrators." This way your administrators will not risk configuring a policy that comes back to haunt them. As noted in the preceding Caution, if you want to see how fast an administrator can get locked out of their own machine, configure a policy with a default security level of Disallowed and an enforcement setting of "All users." Following the next reboot, the administrator will not even be able to log in.

In a high-security scenario, you may want to apply the policy to "All users," instead of exempting administrators. However, this configuration requires that you either have the security level set to Unrestricted, or else you must explicitly define all software necessary for administrators to perform their necessary functions.

NOTE   If you are applying software restriction policies through a GPO applied to an organizational unit, and you plan to skip administrators, it's a good idea to use a different approach. To cut down on network traffic and CPU cycles, create a group in Active Directory for the administrators, and set the GPO to deny the "Apply Group Policy" permission for the group.

Designated File Types

The rules you set up for a software restriction policy will only apply to the file types defined here. The Designated File Types dialog box is where you can easily delete these existing file types and add new ones. As shown in Figure 2-4, a default list includes many file types already, including BAT, CHM, EXE, SCR, and more. It does not include scripting files, such as Visual Basic and JavaScript files. You can customize this list of file types for any policy you create.

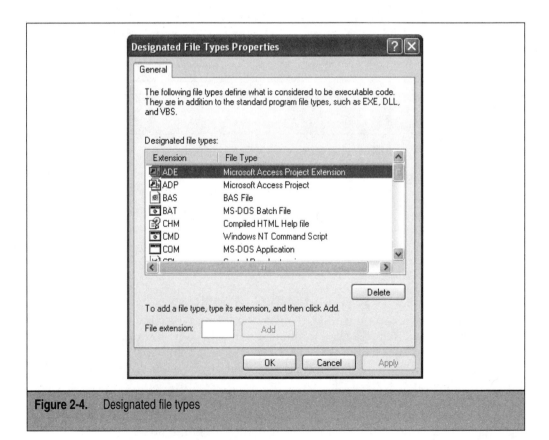

Figure 2-4.   Designated file types

Trusted Publishers

This final umbrella setting lets you define the behavior for signed content such as ActiveX controls. As shown in Figure 2-5, you can control two things:

- Which users can select trusted publishers
- Certificate revocation behavior

Active content often comes via web browsers, for example, when a message box asks if you want to allow installation of certain software. There is usually an option to add the publisher of the software to a list of "trusted publishers" so you will not be prompted to make the same decision in the future. In that case, software by a trusted publisher will be installed and launched transparently.

You have the option to allow any user the ability to designate trusted publishers for signed active content. To be more restrictive, you could allow only "Local computer administrators" or only domain administrators ("Enterprise administrators").

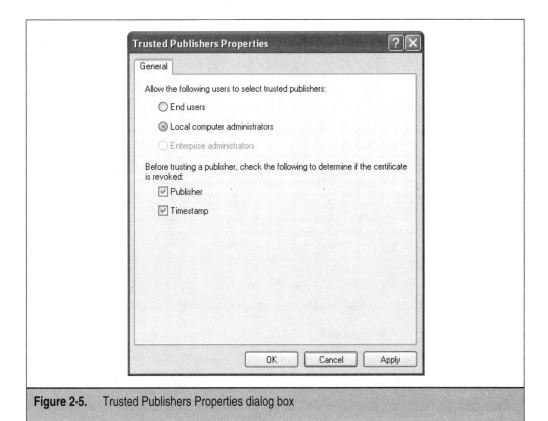

Figure 2-5.   Trusted Publishers Properties dialog box

You can also control how Windows will check if a certificate has been revoked, by selecting one, none, or both of the following settings:

- Publisher: The certificate of the software publisher will be verified.
- Timestamp: The certificate of the organization that time-stamped the active content will be verified.

THE ADDITIONAL RULES

There are four types of additional rules that you can set up to control which software can and cannot execute. These rules override the default security level and provide the meat of your policy, much as a firewall ruleset would. Your options are to define a rule based on a hash, certificate, Internet zone, or path rule.

Hash Rule

A hash rule provides the most specific way to identify executable code. A file hash is created that cryptographically fingerprints a file with either an MD5 or SHA-1 value, so that it can be identified no matter where it is moved or what it is renamed to. For example, to create a hash rule to Disallow tftp.exe, follow these steps:

1. Right-click Additional Rules and select New Hash Rule.
2. Browse to the file you want to create a fingerprint for.
3. Set the security level for this rule to Disallowed.
4. Type a description that helps identify your rule.

Certificate Rule

You can allow or disallow software to run, based on a software publisher's "code signing" certificate. For example, if you wanted to be sure that all your organization's Visual Basic scripts were allowed to run, you could create an Unrestricted certificate rule, and sign your scripts with that certificate.

Internet Zone Rule

Windows Installer (*.msi) packages can be identified according to the Internet zone they are downloaded from and controlled with either an Unrestricted or Disallowed rule.

Path Rule

Three types of path rules are available to identify software:

- File or folder path
- UNC path
- Registry path

Path rules are less specific and less secure than hash and certificate rules; however, they provide a level of flexibility that is often needed when creating a software restriction policy. Consider the following challenge, which is designed to prevent malicious VBScript files from running.

CHALLENGE

You want to restrict all Visual Basic script files from running in your organization, unless they are signed with your IT department's certificate. How do you go about this? You have heard of several techniques in the past, such as placing strict ACLs on Wscript.exe and Cscript.exe that deny Users execute rights. Other ideas you have heard of involved unmapping the VBS file type, and deleting Wscript.exe and Cscript.exe altogether. While these techniques could work OK, they are difficult to implement and manage. Worse than that, they make it nearly impossible for your organization to execute its own VBScript files.

You want a new approach that simplifies implementation and management. You first decide to create a GPO that will be applied at the domain level. The GPO is separate from your default domain policy, so that you can easily apply or remove it without affecting other domain policy settings. You name the GPO "SAFER VBS restrictions" and apply the following settings in the software restriction policy:

Default security level	Unrestricted
Enforcement	All users
Certificate rule:	
IT department's certificate	Unrestricted
Path rules:	
*.VBS	Disallowed
*.VBE	Disallowed
*.WSC	Disallowed
*.WSF	Disallowed
*.WSH	Disallowed

Since certificate rules take precedence over path rules, *.vbs files will be allowed to run if they are signed with your IT department's certificate, and disallowed otherwise. Implementation of this GPO is simple; just apply it to the domain container in Active Directory. If you decide later that you want to disallow JavaScript files from executing as well, you can just update the policy by adding path rules for *.js and *.jse.

Wildcards and Environment Variables

Wildcards, such as * and ?, and environment variables can be used in file or folder and UNC path rules, but not in registry path rules. For example, the following path rules are acceptable:

- **\\server??** will match any share from \\server01 and \\server02.
- ***\Program Files** will match C:\Program Files and D:\Program Files.
- **C:\win*** will match C:\winnt and C:\windows.
- **%USERPROFILE%** will match the user's home directory, for example, C:\Documents and Settings\username.

Registry Path Guidelines

When specifying a registry path, you should keep the following rules in mind:

- The registry path must be in the form of *hive**key**value*.
- A registry path must not end with a backslash.
- Percent signs must surround the registry path.
- The hive name must be spelled out completely, not abbreviated.
- Wildcards cannot be used.
- The registry value named must be a string (either REG_SZ or REG_EXPAND_SZ).

Therefore, this path would be acceptable

```
%HKEY_LOCAL_MACHINE\Software\Microsoft\Windows\CurrentVersion\Run\app%
```

while this one would not

```
HKLM\Software\Microsoft\Windows\CurrentVersion\Run*
```

A registry path rule must point directly to a specific value name, not just a registry key. You can also use a registry path rule in combination with a folder name. For example, the following rule will match any subfolder named My* in the path indicated by the registry value, "%USERPROFILE%My Documents":

```
%HKEY_CURRENT_USER\Software\Microsoft\Windows\CurrentVersion\Explorer\
User Shell Folders\Personal%My*
```

The environment variable %USERPROFILE% will be expanded at run time. So, as an example, with a Disallowed rule, no executable code located in "C:\Documents and Settings\username\My Documents\My Downloads" would be allowed to run.

SECURITY ALERT Without registry, folder, and file ACLs in place, most path rules can easily be defeated by changing the location or name of the application.

RULE PRECEDENCE

Some rules carry more weight than others. That is, when many rules are in place, one has to take precedence. Rules will be applied in the following order, from most specific to least specific:

1. Hash
2. Certificate
3. Path
4. Zone
5. Default

In general, the more specific rule wins. Use a hash rule to make exceptions to a certificate rule. Use a certificate rule to make exceptions to a path rule. A path rule specifying C:\windows\system32*.exe will be less specific than C:\windows\system32\tftp.exe.

BOUNDARIES FOR SOFTWARE RESTRICTION POLICIES

There are exceptions to even software restriction policies. In general, the following code is exempt from any policy:

- Drivers and kernel mode code
- Programs run by the SYSTEM account
- Macros run from Microsoft Office
- Code designed for the Microsoft .NET Common Language Runtime
- 16-bit programs, which could be disabled in a roundabout way by disallowing Ntvdm.exe (Microsoft has a fix available for this, as noted in Knowledge Base article Q319458.)

In addition, SAFER is not enabled when Windows boots into Safe Mode. This is a recovery feature designed to help troubleshoot problematic policies.

BEST PRACTICES

It is assumed that most people will use SAFER to apply policies in an Active Directory environment. In this case, you will create group policy objects for either users or machines, and apply the GPOs to sites, domains, and organizational units. To save yourself some headaches, consider some of the following best practices.

For easier management and troubleshooting:

- Keep software restriction policy GPOs separate from other GPOs.
- Do not modify your default domain policy.
- Test thoroughly before deploying.

For better performance:

- When using the "except local administrators" enforcement option in a GPO for a domain or OU, you can save on network bandwidth by setting the GPO to deny the "Apply Group Policy" permission for the Administrators group. This saves bandwidth by preventing the policy from being downloaded by Administrators.
- Do not link to another domain's software restriction policy.

LOGGING

SAFER events are logged to the System Event Log with Event IDs, as shown in Table 2-2. Auditing does not need to be enabled for these events to be recorded.

There is also an advanced logging mechanism, designed to give you more details than the event logs do. Setting up advanced logging will create a text file that keeps a running log of every process created and what the effective policy applied to it was. To enable advanced logging for SRP, set the following registry key value as REG_SZ:

```
HKLM\SOFTWARE\Policies\Microsoft\Windows\Safer\CodeIdentifiers\
LogFileName
```

The value of *LogFileName* should be a path and filename for the log file. For example, C:\srplog.txt will create a log file named srplog.txt on the C:\ partition.

Event ID	Type of Rule
865	Default security rules
866	Path rules
867	Certificate rules
868	Zone or hash rules

Table 2-2.   Event IDs for SAFER events

KIOSK SCENARIO

Many organizations use kiosks in lobbies and other public places. Cities will often place kiosks in public libraries for people to search card catalogs and the Internet. We have even seen a case where a single government building housed the police station, city hall, and the public library, and every computer in the building was connected on the same network. The kiosk in the library could actually see the computers used for 911 dispatching and the databases used for maintaining criminal records. That was a scary situation.

How could you lock down something like that? Well, the first thought is to remove the kiosk from the network, and yes, that probably is best. But you may not have that option all the time. Let's design a software restriction policy that can make the situation better. The following matrix shows a possible SAFER configuration:

Default security level	Disallowed
Enforcement	All Users except Administrators
Designated file types (in addition to default)	VBS, VBE, JS, JSE, PL
Path rules:	
%WINDIR%	Unrestricted
%PROGRAMFILES%	Unrestricted
Hash rules:	
%WINDIR%\regedit.exe	Disallowed
%WINDIR%\system32\cmd.exe	Disallowed
%WINDIR%\system32\tftp.exe	Disallowed
%WINDIR%\system32\ftp.exe	Disallowed
%WINDIR%\system32\taskmgr.exe	Disallowed

The default security level disallows all software from running and applies only to Users, not Administrators. We have also expanded the default list of file types to include scripts such as VBScript, JavaScript, and Perl. Then some exception rules are set up that allow the computer to continue to function normally, such as allowing programs in %WINDIR% and %PROGRAMFILES% to run, since many of them are needed for basic Windows XP functionality.

You may be thinking that this will not be very effective, because many of the programs installed in these folders do not need to be run on a kiosk and can in fact be used to hack Windows. Well, you may be right in part, but remember that this kiosk is protected with NTFS and User Rights. The Users group does not have rights to add or delete programs from either %WINDIR% or %PROGRAMFILES%. Whatever applications they download with Outlook or Internet Explorer will be stored in their %USERPROFILE% directory, in which software is disallowed by the default policy.

The hash rules provide some additional exceptions by specifying software that should not run, even though it exists in the unrestricted paths. These rules could be path rules instead, in which case they would have precedence over the other path rules because they are more specific.

This set of rules will help protect Users against many things, including the execution of malicious code that was downloaded unknowingly. Registry editing tools and the command prompt are disabled, as well as FTP and TFTP tools. You can see that this sort of configuration can get much more granular. The list of exceptions could be expanded more, for example, by adding a path rule that allows scripts to be run from a scripts share on your domain controllers.

TOOLS OF THE TRADE

At present, only the MMC snap-ins are available for configuring and managing software restriction policies. Other general tools can aid in troubleshooting, such as Gpresult.exe, which is useful for listing software restriction policy rules. Look for more tools to manage SAFER policies in future Resource Kits and online from Microsoft.

Gpresult.exe   Gpresult.exe is the command line equivalent of the Resultant Set of Policy MMC snap-in discussed further in Chapter 10. Since we have a preference for command line tools, let's see what it does.

Gpresult.exe queries and displays all group policy settings for a computer or user, to display the end result of all policies that may be applied. The following syntax and output shows its usage. We redirect the output to a file named C:\safer.txt. The /SCOPE parameter will accept either COMPUTER or USER, in which case a username must also be specified with the /USER switch. The /V option is used to produce verbose output, but /Z can be used for even more verbose output. Just type **gpresult.exe /?** from the command prompt to see all options and syntax. Gpresult even works on remote machines with the /S switch.

When you open the safer.txt log, go through the initial information about the computer configuration until you get to the "Administrative Templates" section. Details about each rule are not displayed, but the rule GUID is, as shown in the following output from a local group policy GPO.

```
C:\Gpresult /SCOPE COMPUTER /V > C:\safer.txt
        File System Settings
        -------------------
            N/A


        Public Key Policies
        -------------------
            N/A
```

```
       Administrative Templates
       -----------------------
            GPO: Local Group Policy
Setting: Software\Policies\Microsoft\Windows\Safer\CodeIdentifiers\0\
Hashes\{0835c618-237a-400e-a3f9-ceeba33d9595}
            State:   Enabled

            GPO: Local Group Policy
Setting: Software\Policies\Microsoft\Windows\Safer\CodeIdentifiers\0\Hashes\
{55529b18-9f7d-4b19-b52d-d6dbbb2f3086}
            State:   Enabled

            GPO: Local Group Policy
Setting: Software\Policies\Microsoft\Windows\Safer\CodeIdentifiers\262144\
Paths\{90cf039f-bcee-4569-9e34-4bc84e828d59}
            State:   Enabled

            GPO: Local Group Policy
Setting: Software\Policies\Microsoft\Windows\Safer\CodeIdentifiers\262144\
UrlZones\{c7720a63-2ada-444b-986e-3e3802314342}
            State:   Enabled

            GPO: Local Group Policy
Setting: Software\Policies\Microsoft\Windows\Safer\CodeIdentifiers
            State:   Enabled
```

You can use the GUID to track down the exact rule in either the Local Security Policy or the GPO that was applied, and even in the registry, where the applied policies are stored. In fact, the registry path is included in the output, and it basically gives away the type of rule that is applied.

CHECKLIST: SAFER SOFTWARE RESTRICTION

Software restriction policies will probably gain attention in the coming years. They provide a completely new, integrated solution for managing security in a Windows XP environment. At first glance, their power seems well designed for controlling executable code with flexibility, while their ability to work as expected is unparalleled by previous applications, such as Appsec.exe, that attempted to do the same thing. By investing the time to fully understand and utilize these policies, you can control which code is allowed to run and which is not, to build more secure desktops for end users and harden public systems such as terminals and kiosks.

- ☐ Plan your software restriction policies thoroughly before testing them.

- ☐ Decide whether you will configure local security policies, or group policies to be pushed through Active Directory.

- ☐ When using Active Directory–based GPOs, create a new, separate GPO for your software restriction policy so that it can be easily updated or removed without affecting your other security policies.

- ☐ Remember, you can create separate GPOs to apply to separate domains or organizational units, in keeping with the security needs of each.

- ☐ Decide on and configure the default security level—will all software be set to Unrestricted or to Disallowed?

- ☐ Configure the other important umbrella settings such as Enforcement, Designated File Types, and Trusted Publishers.

- ☐ When configuring the specific additional rules, keep in mind the policy boundaries and path syntax guidelines.

- ☐ Rules are applied in order of precedence, with more specific rules taking higher precedence (a hash rule will always be more specific than a path rule).

- ☐ For troubleshooting, look in the System Event Log, and turn on advanced logging through the registry key hack.

- ☐ For advanced troubleshooting, use the Resultant Set of Policy MMC snap-in or its command line equivalent, Gpresult.exe.

- ☐ Use Gpresult.exe to show the effective result of all policies applied to a user or computer, including the software restriction policies.

CHAPTER 3

Registry Security

T he Windows registry is more important than it has ever been. Windows XP has turned up the juice by enhancing the registry's performance and security and tools you use to access it.

You are probably pretty familiar with the Windows registry. After all, every version of the Windows operating system depends on it. The registry is a centralized database that stores most of the operating system and application configuration settings. This includes the local user profiles, hardware configurations, installed applications, network settings, and more. The registry is the brain of the Windows operating system: The kernel needs it to load drivers, start subsystems, and just get up and running. The Local Security Authority (LSA) needs it to pass authentication information to the Winlogon process, so you can get logged onto the desktop. And nearly all of the other services and applications need the registry to run, too!

Most people know the registry through the Regedit.exe or Regedt32.exe applications. You also know it by the files that make it up, which are stored in the %SYSTEMROOT%\system32\config directory.

The Windows XP registry hasn't changed too much from previous versions; however, the product team has made some significant strides forward in the following areas:

- Faster queries
- No more size limits
- Loaded into cached memory instead of paged pool
- New Regedit.exe

The Windows XP registry has been optimized to yield faster access times than the Windows NT and Windows 2000 registries. In past versions, the problem of locality between related keys could cause performance degradation. Because related information was sometimes stored in separate hives, file-access times for system and security files would be slowed down due to I/O requests and page faults. The new XP registry has an improved algorithm for keeping related information closer together, thus speeding up access times.

The size limits that accompanied Windows NT and Windows 2000 are removed in Windows XP. Earlier versions loaded the registry into the paged pool region of memory, which is limited to approximately 160MB maximum in 32-bit kernels. Windows XP does not use the paged pool area of memory to store the registry; it instead uses the cache manager to provide mapped views of the registry files.

TIP The registry size in Windows NT/2000 can actually be changed by modifying the registry key `HKLM\SYSTEM\CurrentControlSet\Control\RegistrySizeLimit`, as described in the Microsoft Knowledge Base article Q94993.

Most people will be pleased with the new Regedit.exe application. This is the tool used to access and modify the registry. It is also used to import and export registry hives and keys. Regedit.exe is still very similar to previous versions: you can still connect to remote computer registries, and you can easily locate the familiar Find feature used to search the registry. The new Regedit.exe also incorporates many important new features. For example, it eliminates the need for the separate Regedt32.exe program by absorbing its functionality for managing the security, auditing, and permissions of various keys. In fact, the two programs are now one and the same: Regedit.exe.

So we will first look at what makes up the registry files and the registry's "beehive" structure. Then we will discuss securing the registry through permissions, auditing, and specific keys that require strict ACLs. Following that is a look at the registry hacks that are considered important for establishing higher security. Finally we will take a look at some tools available for local and remote registry management.

Keep in mind that most things discussed in this chapter apply to Windows NT, Windows 2000, and Windows XP. Differences between the various OSs will be noted throughout the chapter. The goal of understanding registry security is to come up with a realistic operating system build that will work well in your enterprise. If you can fine-tune your builds before deploying them, you have a greater chance of maintaining security. Otherwise, you will find yourself looking for creative ways to manage an enterprise of haphazard registries.

NOTE   This chapter discusses modifications to the registry. Before making any of these modifications in a production environment, you should have a current full working backup of your system and its registry available. Also, you should try out any new settings in a test environment before implementing them in production.

REGISTRY FUNDAMENTALS

The registry consists of static and dynamic information. When Windows boots up, the registry is called upon by various processes and is loaded into memory. Most of what is loaded is determined by the files, or *hives*, that make up the registry. And there is also dynamic data being written to and deleted from the registry during the course of operation.

Hives, Keys, and Values

A registry hive is one of several files stored on disk that contain registry information. A hive contains a top-level key that provides the starting point for the hierarchically stored subkeys and values. As you will notice, hives do not automatically match up with the root keys you are used to seeing (like HKEY_LOCAL_MACHINE), but may instead represent a subkey thereof (such as HKEY_LOCAL_MACHINE\SECURITY). The determining factor is that a hive consists of nonvolatile data that is stored in a file on the disk. An example of a dynamically generated key is HKEY_LOCAL_MACHINE\HARDWARE.

Some of the registry keys are really just links pointing to another key. For instance, the HKEY_CURRENT_USER root key is a reference to the HKEY_USERS*SID*, where *SID* is the security ID of the currently logged-on user. Also, HKEY_CLASSES_ROOT derives its values from the HKEY_LOCAL_MACHINE\SOFTWARE\Classes key. Table 3-1 lists the root keys that make up the registry.

Each root key contains subkeys and values. If a subkey is like a folder on your hard drive, then a value is like a file. The file is stored in the folder, has a name, and contains some data. Values are similar in that they have a name and they contain some data. In fact, the three parts of a value, as we consider them here, include Name, Type, and Data.

For example, for the key HKLM\SOFTWARE\Microsoft\Command Processor\ the values are

- Value Name: CompletionChar
- Value Type: REG_DWORD
- Value Data: 0x00000040 (decimal)

This example uses the REG_DWORD value type. However, several data types exist in the registry, including REG_BINARY (binary data), REG_SZ (text string), REG_MULTI_SZ (multi string), and others.

CAUTION   Changing a value's type or adding a value of the wrong type can have unpredictable and sometimes disastrous consequences.

Root Key	Description
HKEY_CLASSES_ROOT	In this root key is stored information on all the existing COM objects and file associations on the system.
HKEY_CURRENT_USER	This root key contains the currently active user's profile information. Everything necessary to load up a customized working environment is stored here.
HKEY_LOCAL_MACHINE (HKLM)	HKLM is one of the most used and most interesting root keys. The tons of configuration information stored here is used by applications, device drivers, and the operating system. This is also home to the SAM and SECURITY subkeys.
HKEY_USERS	This root key contains the default user profile and all active user profiles.
HKEY_CURRENT_CONFIG	This root key is actually a reference to the HKLM\System\CurrentControlSet\Hardware Profiles\Current registry key. Information for the currently loaded hardware profile is stored here.

Table 3-1.   The Registry Root Keys and Their Descriptions

As mentioned, the registry hives are related to files on the disk. Table 3-2 lists the standard registry hives with their related files.

All the hive files mentioned in Table 3-2 can be found in the %SYSTEMROOT%\ system32\config folder, except for the NTUSER.DAT and ntuser.dat.log files, which are stored in each user's %HOMEPATH%, typically C:\Documents and Settings\ *Username*. You will also notice that the System.alt file has been eliminated from Windows XP. This is due to the registry enhancements that render it unnecessary.

Regedit.exe

There are several tools available for accessing and modifying the registry. The GUI tool Regedit.exe is probably the most popular. Regedit.exe can be found in the %SYSTEMROOT% directory, or typically C:\Windows\. There is also a backup copy stored in %SYSTEMROOT%\system32\dllcache. Since no shortcuts are installed, you have to launch it either at the command prompt or through Start → Run → regedit.

The Windows XP version of Regedit.exe lets you add new keys and values. It provides an extended set of value types as well, letting you add not only string data, binary data, and DWORD data (as in Windows NT/2000) but also add multi string and expandable string data. This all-in-one tool also helps in managing security settings associated with the registry, such as security permissions, auditing, and even viewing the effective permissions for a user.

CAUTION   There is no longer a read-only mode for Regedit.exe. Any changes you make will be committed, so be careful!

Viewing the effective permissions of a registry key is easier than ever with Windows XP (and Windows .NET). Open up Regedit.exe and navigate to any root key or subkey. For example, if you right-click the HKEY_LOCAL_MACHINE\SOFTWARE subkey, select Permissions, and then click the Advanced button and the Effective Permissions tab, you will see a screen similar to that in Figure 3-1.

Registry Hive	Related Files
HKEY_CURRENT_USER	NTUSER.DAT, ntuser.dat.log
HKEY_LOCAL_MACHINE\SAM	SAM, SAM.log
HKEY_LOCAL_MACHINE\SECURITY	SECURITY, SECURITY.log
HKEY_LOCAL_MACHINE\SOFTWARE	software, software.log, software.sav
HKEY_LOCAL_MACHINE\SYSTEM	system, system.log, system.sav
HKEY_USERS\.DEFAULT	default, default.log, default.sav
HKEY_CURRENT_CONFIG	system, system.log, system.sav

Table 3-2.   Registry Hives and Files

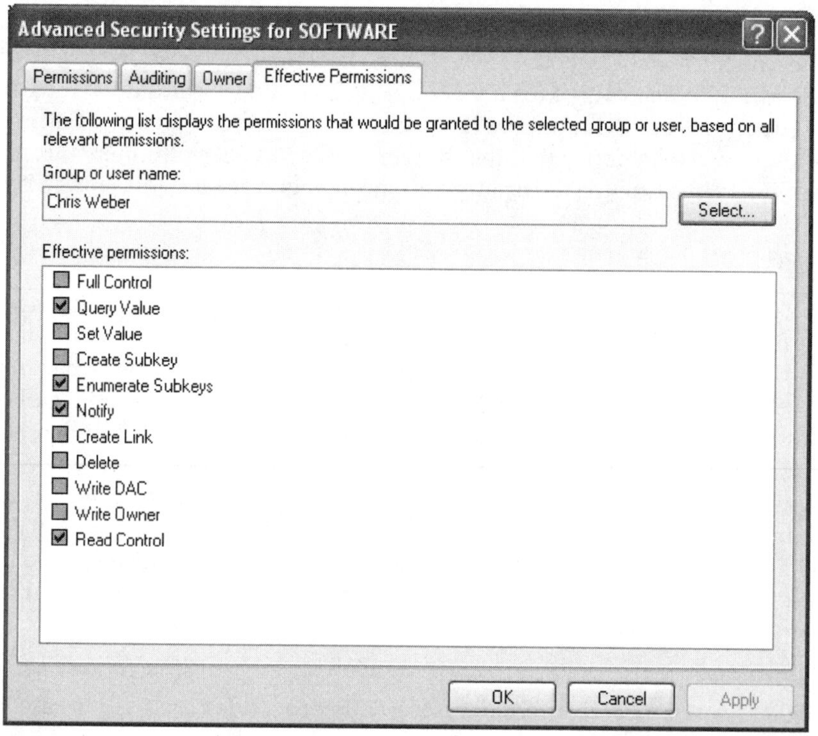

Figure 3-1.   The Effective Permissions tab of Regedit.exe

This example shows the effective permissions for Chris Weber, a normal user on the system.

By clicking the Select button, you can choose any group or user account that you want to calculate effective permissions for. The effective permissions are equal to all the permissions a user, group, or computer object has on this key, based on group memberships as well as explicit and inherited permissions.

As you can see in Figure 3-1, Chris Weber, a normal user account, has limited permissions on the SOFTWARE subkey. Because the SOFTWARE subkey will serve as the parent for any subkeys beneath it, its permissions will be inherited by each child subkey. Remember, however, that the child subkeys can (and do) each have explicit permissions defined that change or remove these inherited permissions.

SECURING THE REGISTRY

On the subject of permissions, the level of registry security has improved with each new version of Windows. Windows XP provides a better set of Access Control Entries than previous versions, and Longhorn (the next version of Windows) is sure to provide even better.

In the following sections, we describe some relevant keys, their recommended settings, and a description of what they achieve. Our standard format for presenting this is as follows:

Key: The path to the registry key

Value Name: The name of the key's value

Value Type: The acceptable type of value, such as string, binary, DWORD, multi string, or expandable string

Recommended Setting: The recommended setting for increased security

Default Setting: The default data value, if Windows XP has one

Description: A long description of what this registry key's settings can achieve and what the valid data settings can be

We also use some shorthand when listing a key's location. You will probably already know the following translations for the root hives:

- HKCR = HKEY_CLASSES_ROOT
- HKCU = HKEY_CURRENT_USER
- HKLM = HKEY_LOCAL_MACHINE
- HKU = HKEY_USERS
- HKCC = HKEY_CURRENT_CONFIG
- CCS = CurrentControlSet

When securing the registry, first start at the physical level and protect the files that make up the registry. Second, consider the default registry key permissions that Microsoft sets and how to enable auditing on keys that might be important to your applications. Third, you should take a look at some of the specific registry keys that can be configured to provide heightened security for your Windows XP clients.

Registry Files That Need Protection

We looked at the files that make up the registry earlier, in Table 3-2. Security of these files starts with the following two important actions:

1. Providing physical security of the computer
2. Installing the Windows operating system on an NTFS partition

Before going any further you should understand the importance of the SAM and Security files/hives. Two registry hives—SAM and Security—hold all of the operating system's security configurations, including user accounts and passwords. The SAM file is essentially a database that holds all Windows usernames and passwords. Although these passwords are stored encrypted, there are tools available to decrypt and crack the SAM file, such as @stake's L0phtCrack 4 (http://www.atstake.com), one of the more popular password crackers. This is why access to the SAM is so important.

The other important hive is the Security hive, which contains the LSA Secrets cache. If you have any service accounts configured on your computers, such as agent services for backup software, the password for that account is stored in the cache known as the LSA Secrets, a part of the Security hive. This can be immensely dangerous when administrators configure backup services to run with domain admin user accounts and passwords! (Just where did you think those passwords were being stored?) If possible, you want to prevent access to SAM and Security, whether the computer is online or offline. Since Windows manages online security of these files rather well, you are most concerned with offline access.

Service account passwords stored in the LSA Secrets are easily retrieved using tools like BindView's LSADUMP2.exe (http://www.bindview.com). If you configure service accounts with domain administrator privileges to run on your Windows XP clients, then you are jeopardizing your entire domain!

First and foremost, the registry files in %SYSTEMROOT%\system32\config need the security of an NTFS partition. On a default install of Windows XP, the ACLs on this directory look like those shown in Table 3-3. These permissions are similar to those in Windows 2000 Professional, and they provide good out-of-the-box security. In fact, there is not much left for you to tweak here, since Microsoft has done a good job of it.

Even though these files can be read, they cannot be copied or moved by anyone, not even Administrators. The files are locked in use by the system to provide you this level of protection. Keep in mind that members of the Administrators group can still use tools like Regdmp.exe (discussed in the "Regdmp.exe" section, later in the chapter) to extract the contents of the registry to a readable text file.

User or Group	Permissions
Users	List Folder Contents
Power Users	List Folder Contents
Administrators	Full Control
Creator Owner	Full Control (Creator Owner is actually "special permissions" because the Full Control permissions only apply to subfolders and files, not the /config folder itself)
System	Full Control

Table 3-3.   Default Windows XP Permissions on %SYSTEMROOT%\system32\config

Backups Will Haunt You

Your biggest concern at this point is really the backup copies of the registry. Whenever you back up the System State data, backup copies of the registry files are written to the %SYSTEMROOT\Repair (Windows XP) or %SYSTEMROOT\Repair\Regback (Windows 2000) folder.

Users can only list files in this directory, unless you upgraded from Windows NT, in which case permissions are inherited! For the most part, the default permissions on the \Repair folder are similar to those on the \config folder, with one rather important difference: Power Users have rights to read and modify the \Repair folder and subfolder. The registry files have their own permissions, however (which are not inherited), and only the Administrators group has access to the individual files in \Repair.

The real threat with backups lies in the way you store them. You should be asking who has access to your backup tapes. If you use a backup server that stores all backups to disk before writing them to tape, then you should also ask who has access to that server and how secure it is. The point to remember is that if somebody has access to your backups, then they have access to the SAM and Security files.

Offline Access Will Destroy You

Physical access always has the upper hand. If somebody has access to shut down the computer, then the game is over. They would just shut down, boot to an alternate file system, and copy the SAM offline. Unless you used some form of disk encryption, such as EFS, the files can be easily accessed in a number of ways. An attacker could boot to Linux and mount the NTFS partition, or they could boot to DOS and use Sysinternals' almighty NTFSDOS tool (http://www.sysinternals.com) to mount the NTFS partition. At that point, they simply copy the registry files they need and run the SAM file through L0phtCrack to get your computer's passwords.

In this case, your best protection would be controlling who can shut down the computer, as well as installing disk encryption that protects the disk when the computer is shut down. Rights to shut down the computer are controlled through the "Shut down the system" local security setting, accessed through Local Policies → User Rights Assignment → "Shut down the system" user right, as shown in Figure 3-2. By default, the following groups have this right in Windows XP:

- Administrators
- Backup Operators
- Power Users
- Users

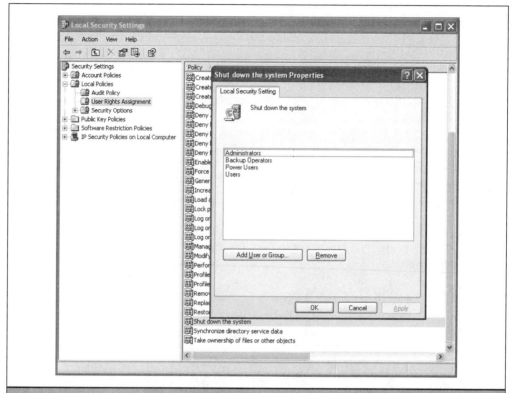

Figure 3-2.   Rights to shut down a computer can be configured through Local Policies.

If you're willing to risk a lot more support calls each day, you may want to configure things so that only Administrators have this right. Most likely this is not a realistic solution for an enterprise, so at a minimum, you should keep in mind that the SAM and Security files are no longer in your control when the system is shut down. This means that any passwords you store on the local SAM can possibly be cracked, and those you store in LSA Secrets can be discovered. In this case, your best defense is to use strong, complex passwords for local user accounts and refrain from using service accounts whose passwords you wouldn't want advertised in the break room.

TIP   Use complex passwords for local administrator accounts, and use low privileged accounts for service accounts. Having access to the SAM hive means having access to any usernames and passwords you have on the system. Depending on how complex the passwords are, they can be cracked with publicly available tools like L0phtCrack.

Security Permissions and Auditing

Registry permissions are very similar to NTFS file and folder permissions; however, different permissions apply. These rights can be configured at a granular level, allowing you to specify the following individual permissions, which have not changed since Windows NT 4.0:

- Full Control
- Query Value
- Set Value
- Create Subkey
- Enumerate Subkeys
- Notify
- Create Link
- Delete
- Write DAC
- Write Owner
- Read Control

General Default Access Rights to the Registry

Windows XP installs with default access rights that use the following built-in security groups. Keep in mind that if you join the Windows XP computer to a domain, its permissions will be determined by the settings of that domain.

Administrators   Much as in Windows NT/2000, Administrators have full control of the computer. Most of the registry subkeys grant the Administrators group full control, including any currently logged-on user's HKEY_CURRENT_USER subkeys and most of the HKEY_LOCAL_MACHINE subkeys. Administrators, by default, have very limited access (Write DAC and Read Control) to several subkeys, including

- HKEY_LOCAL_MACHINE\SAM
- HKEY_LOCAL_MACHINE\SECURITY

Subkeys to which Administrators do not have access at all include

- HKEY_LOCAL_MACHINE\SOFTWARE\Microsoft\Windows NT\ CurrentVersion\Winlogon\Credentials
- HKEY_LOCAL_MACHINE\SYSTEM\CurrentControlSet\Control\Class\ {4D36E965-E325-11CE-BFC1-08002BE10318}\Properties (CD/DVD)

- HKEY_LOCAL_MACHINE\SYSTEM\CurrentControlSet\Control\Class\
{4D36E97B-E325-11CE-BFC1-08002BE10318}\Properties (SCSI)

- HKEY_LOCAL_MACHINE\SYSTEM\CurrentControlSet\Services\
MRxDAV\EncryptedDirectories

As expected, members of the Administrators group are still owners of these and other registry keys, meaning they can grant themselves any privileges they want. If you don't want Administrators having this type of access, then you would deny them the "Take ownership of files and other objects permissions" user right (otherwise known as SE_TAKE_OWNERSHIP_NAME). However, this is *not* a recommended practice, as the stability of the Windows operating system depends on this functionality!

Backup Operators   Members of this group have limited access to just one registry key: HKEY_LOCAL_MACHINE\SOFTWARE\Microsoft\Windows NT\CurrentVersion\ Asr\Commands. Backup Operators also have the Backup Files and Directories user right, meaning they have access to files and folders regardless of their permissions. If you read that again, it means that any user with this right can bypass NTFS file and folder permissions, in order to back up a file, including the hive files!

Network Configuration Operators   Members of this group have access to query and set values on several of the network-related subkeys in the HKEY_LOCAL_MACHINE hive. After all, this group was designed with specific rights to configure networking features for different interfaces, such as IP addresses.

Power Users   As the name implies, the Power Users group tends to have powerful rights, somewhere between those of the Administrators level and the Users group. In the following sections we will point out specific keys where Power Users have potentially dangerous permissions. In general, the Power Users group has access to create subkeys and set values in many subkeys under the HKEY_LOCAL_MACHINE\ SOFTWARE subkey. Power Users have the ability to install applications that can be used by all members of the Users group. Membership in the Power Users group should not be granted haphazardly.

Users   The Users group has minimal access privileges to the operating system registry and files in a new default install of Windows XP. Keep in mind, however, that upgrading to Windows XP from previous versions of Windows will leave the pre–Windows XP permissions intact. In general, the Users group has Read access to most parts of the HKEY_LOCAL_MACHINE registry hive, and Users have Read/Write access only to their own profiles. A good practice for maintaining system integrity is to include all end users in the Users group.

Auditing

Windows NT/2000/XP/.NET all allow for auditing of individual registry keys. Auditing is easily enabled in Windows XP through Regedit.exe, by right-clicking a key and selecting Permissions →Advanced → Auditing.

You enable auditing by specifying the user or group accounts and access successes or failures you want to audit. You should enable auditing for any critical registry keys, including the `winreg` key described in the next section. If, for example, you run an application that stores encryption keys in a registry subkey, you will probably want to enable auditing of that key. Any audited events will be written to the Security Event Log.

You must have Audit Object Access enabled through the Local Security Settings before any registry events will be written to the Event Log. To audit Object Access on a local system, open Secpol.msc (or open Local Security Settings from Administrative Tools) and navigate to Local Policies → Audit Policies → Audit Success and Failure for Object Access. Be aware, however, that this may fill up your Event Logs rather quickly, depending on what other objects you have enabled auditing on, such as NTFS files and folders.

Registry Keys That Need Protection in Windows NT/2000/XP

Some registry keys require special protection because they either contain or give access to sensitive information. The keys in this section will be found on every installation of Windows XP and can be considered some of the more valuable keys. It goes without saying that if you have a certain application that stores sensitive information in the registry, such as passwords or encryption keys, it will require its own protection. In such a case, you should modify the Access Control Entries for that key to allow only necessary users the specific permissions they need. In addition, you will probably want to enable auditing of certain events surrounding that key.

To modify the permissions for a registry key, take the following steps:

1. Open Regedit.exe.
2. Navigate to the key.
3. Right-click the key and select Permissions.

The Security tab will appear, as shown in Figure 3-3.

From this GUI you can modify a registry key's access permissions. At the Security tab, you can add or remove users and groups as necessary. Click the Advanced button to configure more granular permissions, configure auditing, change the key owner, and view effective permissions.

Many of the following keys served the same purpose in Windows NT and 2000 as they do in Windows XP. Before changing any registry permissions on your production systems, you should definitely test them in a lab setting.

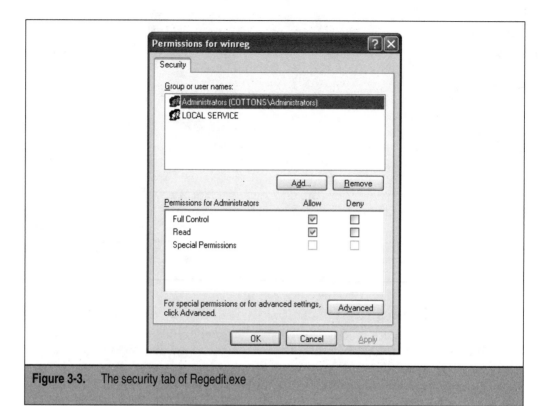

Figure 3-3. The security tab of Regedit.exe

Winreg: Doorway to a Remote Registry Connection

Key: HKLM\SYSTEM\CCS\Control\SecurePipeServers\winreg

Remote access to the registry is required by some applications and Windows services. For example, on a system running directory replication, the Replicator account needs access to certain remote registry keys. The ACL permissions on the winreg key determine which users have remote access to the computer's registry. The last thing you want to see here is that the Everyone group or the Anonymous user has access. By default, Administrators have Full Control, Backup Operators have read-only access, and the Local Service account has read-only access.

NOTE If one of your applications needs anonymous, or null, access to the registry, you should consider its importance and find a possible alternative. If you must give a wide range of users remote access to the registry, then give the Authenticated Users group read-only access.

If the winreg key does not exist (it is only in Windows NT Workstation by default) then any remote user will have access to the registry. For maximum registry security, create this key and set its ACLs to allow a minimum of Administrators Full Control, the Local Service account Read access, and any other account permissions you require. Windows NT Server, Windows 2000 Professional and Server, and Windows XP Professional all have this key by default.

Don't forget the allowed paths! It is true that exceptions always occur, and the `winreg` key is no different. Under the `winreg` key, there exists by default a subkey named `AllowedPaths`. The paths listed in this key will be available to anonymous users despite the permissions you set on `winreg`. Since some Windows services require remote access to the registry—such as the Spooler service when it is connecting to a network printer, and the Directory Replicator service—you may need to allow access to the corresponding keys.

Delete the `AllowedPaths` subkey if it does not break any of your applications (such as print servers and directory replication). Otherwise, modify the following two values so that they contain only the registry keys you want to allow anonymous remote access to. The `Machines` value exists by default, the `Users` value does not. The `AllowedPaths` data for the `Machines` value can also be edited through the Local Security Settings GUI (or through Group Policy), in the Local Policies → Security Options → "Network Access: Remotely accessible registry paths" setting. The value for `Users` is not accessible because it does not exist by default.

Key: HKLM\SYSTEM\CCS\Control\SecurePipeServers\winreg\
AllowedPaths

Value Name: Machines

Value Type: REG_MULTI_SZ (multi string)

Recommended Setting: Remove all values that do not break your applications.

Default Values:

```
SYSTEM\CurrentControlSet\Control\ProductOptions
SYSTEM\CurrentControlSet\Control\Print\Printers
SYSTEM\CurrentControlSet\Control\Server Applications
SYSTEM\CurrentControlSet\Services\Eventlog
SOFTWARE\Microsoft\OLAP Server
SOFTWARE\Microsoft\Windows NT\CurrentVersion
SYSTEM\CurrentControlSet\Control\ContentIndex
SYSTEM\CurrentControlSet\Control\Terminal Server
SYSTEM\CurrentControlSet\Control\Terminal Server\UserConfig
SYSTEM\CurrentControlSet\Control\Terminal Server\
DefaultUserConfiguration
```

Description: The registry paths listed can be accessed by remote machines, provided the explicit permissions on these keys do not say otherwise.

Key: HKLM\SYSTEM\CCS\Control\SecurePipeServers\winreg\
AllowedPaths

Value Name: Users

Value Type: REG_MULTI_SZ (multi string)

Recommended Setting: Remove all values that do not break your applications.

Default Value: Does not exist.

Description: The registry paths listed can be accessed by remote users, provided the explicit permissions on these keys do not say otherwise.

Remember that just because a user has read-only access to the `winreg` key, that doesn't mean they have read-only access to the entire registry. Once remote registry access is allowed, access to the registry's other keys is determined by their individual Access Control Entries.

CurrentVersion Keys and Subkeys

Key: `HKLM\SOFTWARE\Microsoft\Windows NT\CurrentVersion`

Key: `HKLM\SOFTWARE\Microsoft\Windows\CurrentVersion`

In the past, Microsoft has officially made recommendations to change the security permissions of registry subkeys under these two `CurrentVersion` keys. In Windows XP, the default permissions on these two keys give the following permissions:

- Full Control to Administrators and System
- Special Permissions to Power Users (includes the Delete and Set Value permissions)
- Read-only access to Users
- Full Control on all SubKeys to Creator Owner

The one that should raise a flag here is the Power Users' right to delete and set values. Granted, many of the subkeys specify their own explicit permissions that give Power Users read-only access at best, such as the `AeDebug`, `Asr\Commands`, `SeCEdit`, `SvcHost`, `Windows`, and `Winlogon` subkeys. The Power Users are a powerful group in Windows XP, which should be a reminder to think twice before granting a user these excessive rights. If you don't like the default type of access, then consider modifying these subkey ACLs to suit your environment.

System Performance Data

Key: `HKLM\SOFTWARE\Microsoft\Windows NT\CurrentVersion\Perflib`

The conditions set by this key are the same in Windows NT/2000/XP, but the ACL on this key is not. Performance data can be queried by remote users who have permissions to access this key. Just like the `winreg` key, you secure `Perflib` by modifying the ACLs it has set. You would want to secure this key because some performance information, such as running processes, can be considered sensitive. In Windows NT 4.0, the Everyone group has Read access to this key, and it is recommended that you remove this ACL. In Windows XP, the default ACL on this key is generally considered good enough, allowing Administrators Full Control and Interactive as well as Network Service groups read-only access.

Run Keys

Key: HKLM\SOFTWARE\Microsoft\Windows\CurrentVersion\Run

Key: HKLM\SOFTWARE\Microsoft\Windows\CurrentVersion\RunOnce

Key: HKLM\SOFTWARE\Microsoft\Windows\CurrentVersion\RunOnceEx

The infamous Run keys have gained widespread attention since the appearance of viruses and backdoor programs like BackOrifice. The Run keys appear the same in nearly every version of Windows, and each of the three keys has similarities and differences. Essentially, if the path to a program (e.g., C:\program files\virus software\ myvirusscanner.exe) is included in one of these keys, that program will be run the next time Windows starts up.

 SECURITY ALERT   The Run key is persistent, meaning whatever values are set there will remain after they are executed and between reboots. Values in RunOnce and RunOnceEx are automatically deleted after execution. Additionally, RunOnceEx will display a status box when items are run.

Do you see the trouble here? It doesn't matter which user logs in, because the Run keys are in the HKEY_LOCAL_MACHINE hive of the registry. So if an Administrator logs in, that program will run with Administrator privileges. This is why viruses love to put executable code in the Run keys: the next time an Administrator logs in, the virus can have its way with the computer, setting up services, mangling user accounts, or whatever.

Unfortunately for these types of malicious code, the three Run keys in Windows XP only allow Administrators and System Full Control. The Users group has only Read access to the three keys. The Power Users group also has Read access to the three keys, but it has special permissions for the first Run key, including the ability to change current values and create new ones.

It is generally recommended that you change the permissions of the Run keys so that only Administrators and System have Full Control, while Authenticated Users have only Read access.

REGISTRY HACKS

This section presents some of the security-related registry key values that can be modified in Windows XP. In several cases, direct registry editing will work. But it is not required, as several of these settings can be configured through a provided GUI (such as the Local Security Settings snap-in). Also, many of the registry changes will not work until the system is rebooted. Several of these keys are not new to the Windows XP registry but in fact existed in Windows 2000 and in some cases in Windows NT.

General Security Settings

Some general settings that should help fine-tune the security of your Windows XP clients are described in the following sections.

Changing a Terminal Server or Remote Desktop's Listening Port

Key: HKLM\SYSTEM\CCS\Control\Terminal Server\Winstations\RDP-Tcp

Value Name: PortNumber

Value Type: REG_DWORD (decimal)

Recommended Setting: Any port number you wish to use, such as 5001

Default Setting: 0xd3d (3389)

Description: Terminal Server services, or what is also known as Remote Desktop in Windows XP, listen for incoming connections on TCP port 3389 by default. Administrators can change this to their port of choice by editing this registry value. When you use the Windows XP Remote Desktop Connection client software to connect, you can specify this port with the computer name followed by a colon (:) and the port number, as shown here. The computer is named "COTTONS" and the port number is 777.

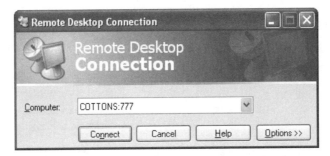

Configure Forceguest Feature for Display of NTFS Security Settings

Key: HKLM\SYSTEM\CCS\Control\Lsa\

Value Name: forceguest

Value Type: REG_DWORD (Boolean)

Recommended Setting: None

Default Setting: 1

Description: Only available in Windows XP/.NET, the Forceguest security setting works with a value of either 0 or 1. There is also a corresponding Local Security setting named "Network access: Sharing and security model for local accounts," which can be set to Guest Only (1) or Classic (0). This setting ties into the Simple File Sharing model, which installs by default on Windows XP and hides the Security tab from NTFS files and folders. When you set the forceguest value to 0, you are enabling the Classic Security UI, which displays the NTFS Security tab when you right-click a folder or file and select Properties. Forceguest defaults to 1 for stand-alone Windows XP computers that are part of a workgroup, and remains that way when joined to a Windows 2000 domain.

Prevent Storing LANMAN Hashes in the Local SAM or Active Directory

Key: HKLM\SYSTEM\CCS\Control\Lsa\

Value Name: NoLmHash

Value Type: REG_DWORD (Boolean)

Recommended Setting: 1 (true)

Default Setting: 0

Description: This key actually became available in Windows 2000 SP2, but you have to manually create it. In Windows XP and .NET the key is included by default, but it is set to 0, or disabled. It is also included in the Local Security Settings GUI of Windows XP/.NET, as "Network Security: Do not store LAN Manager hash value on next password change."

Setting this key to 1 will prevent the LANMAN password hash from being stored in the SAM or Active Directory database. Instead, only the user's NTLM password hash will be stored. Remember, however, that the LANMAN hash will not be removed until the next time the user changes his or her password.

This feature increases security of the user passwords because the LANMAN hash has been proven to be cryptographically weak and easily crackable. The LANMAN hash is still included with Windows operating systems to allow for backward compatibility with older applications and Windows OSs. If you do not require the LANMAN hash on your network, definitely set this value to 1.

NOTE Setting a password greater than 14 characters long will disable the LANMAN hash on Windows 2000 SP2 and Windows XP on an account-by-account basis.

Disable 8.3 Filename Creation

Key: HKLM\SYSTEM\CCS\Control\Filesystem

Value Name: NTFSDisable8dot3NameCreation

Value Type: REG_DWORD (Boolean)

Recommended Setting: 1 (true)

Default Setting: 0

Description: This value accepts either a 0 (false) or 1 (true), and was available with Windows NT/2000 as well as Windows XP. With NTFS (32-bit) partitions, you can disable the creation of 8.3 filenames, which are used as compliant short-name equivalents of NTFS long filenames. Several past attacks have utilized vulnerabilities in 8.3 filenames, including web server and file system attacks.

CAUTION Some older, 16-bit applications require the use of 8.3 filenames (an eight- character-maximum filename with a single three-character extension), so disabling their creation will break these apps.

Prevent Users from Saving RAS Passwords

Key: HKLM\SYSTEM\CCS\Services\RasMan\Parameters

Value Name: DisableSavePassword

Value Type: REG_DWORD (Boolean)

Recommended Setting: 1

Default Setting: None

Description: This functionality has been offered since Windows NT 4 (see the Microsoft Knowledge Base article Q172430 for details). By default, users are allowed the Save Password option for RAS-related network connections such as dial-up and VPN. When a user checks the Save Password box, the password is cached in the registry so it will be automatically reused the next time the RAS connection is used. The problem with this is that the password is stored in a portion of the registry known as the LSA Secrets cache. As mentioned earlier, these passwords can be easily retrieved with administrative access using publicly available tools like LSADUMP2.EXE. When you set this registry value, the Save Password option will be grayed out, so users will have to type in the password each time they want to connect.

 SECURITY ALERT Any previously saved passwords are still cached in the LSA Secrets cache even after this setting is enabled. To remove these previously saved passwords from the cache, you need to delete the RAS entry and recreate it.

Remove Default Administrative Shares

Key: HKLM\SYSTEM\CCS\Services\LanManServer\Parameters\

Value Name: AutoShareWks

Value Type: REG_DWORD (Boolean)

Recommended Setting: 0 (false)

Default Setting: None

Description: This value produces the same result in Windows XP as it did in Windows NT and 2000. The default administrative shares on a Windows XP system include the hidden partition shares, such as C$ and D$, which share the entire drive partition, as well as the hidden ADMIN$ share, which maps to your %systemroot%, usually C:\Windows. To view the shares on your system just type the command **net share** at the command prompt. Windows XP does not allow the permissions on these shares to be modified, although only the Administrators group has access. By setting the AutoShareWks value to 0, you are preventing these shares from being created upon the next and successive reboots. On any server version of the Windows operating system, you should use the `AutoShareServer` value name instead. This is a fairly standard security control aimed at preventing brute-force attacks on your critical, open shares.

NOTE Some enterprise management systems and network-based backup programs rely on the default administrative shares. Make sure that disabling these shares will not have any negative effects in your network.

Disable CDROM AutoRun

Key: HKLM\SYSTEM\CCS\Services\CDROM\

Value Name: AutoRun

Value Type: REG_DWORD (Boolean)

Recommended Setting: 0 (false)

Default Setting: None

Description: By default, when a CD is loaded into the CD-ROM drive, Windows XP will automatically run any code the CD is enabled with. This can present a security risk, since malicious code can be compiled onto the CD and launched without the user's intention. With the `AutoRun` value set to 0, Windows XP will not automatically execute code from a loaded CD, ensuring that the user must intentionally do so. This setting is the same in Windows NT and 2000.

CHALLENGE

If an attacker learns the administrator name and password, could she just remotely recreate and access these shares? Although these default administrative shares can be easily removed by an administrator, they can be just as easily added back by anyone with Administrator privileges. With this in mind you might ask, What is the real value in disabling these default shares?

Well, consider the case of a future worm that propagates not only via HTTP port 80 but via open NetBIOS shares (sounds similar to Nimda, right?). This new worm attacks an IIS server to gain the administrator username and password, and then enumerates trust relationships that the credentials have access to. Shares are an easy way to spread files, so the worm scans for C$ and D$ shares that it can access. These well-known share names are quickly found, and the worm uses them to spread its payload from computer to computer. Before you know it, an entire domain is infected with the worm as it spreads its files from share to share. In this case, not only IIS servers running the web service are victimized, but any Windows computer with default administrative shares is infected too.

Force a Memory Dump on a Hung Computer

Key: HKLM\SYSTEM\CCS\Services\i8042prt\Parameters\

Value Name: CrashOnCtrlScroll

Value Type: REG_DWORD (Boolean)

Recommended Setting: 1

Default Setting: None

Description: Enabling this registry key will allow you to generate a Memory.dmp file by holding down the right CTRL key and pressing SCROLL LOCK twice. *Yes, doing this will crash your computer!* But that may be what you want in the case of a hung computer. The type of dump depends on how you have the Startup and Recovery settings configured for the computer. (To do so, in Control Panel, choose System. Then select Advanced, Startup and Recovery, Settings, and Write Debugging Information.) This setting will not work with nonlegacy computers that use, for example, a USB keyboard.

CAUTION   By utilizing this functionality, you are forcing your computer to halt—also known as a crash, complete with Blue Screen of Death!

Display Hidden Files and Extensions

Key: HKCU\SOFTWARE\Microsoft\Windows\CurrentVersion\Explorer\Advanced

Value Names:

    Hidden
    HideFileExt
    ShowSuperHidden

Value Type: REG_DWORD

Recommended Settings:

    Hidden = 1
    HideFileExt = 0
    ShowSuperHidden = 1

Default Settings:

    Hidden = 2
    HideFileExt = 1
    ShowSuperHidden = None

Description: Displaying hidden files is not something you want to do for the majority of users on your network. That's why we saved this for the last of the General settings. Instead, you should reserve these settings for administrative Windows XP workstations and Windows 2000/.NET servers. To let Explorer show hidden files and folders, set the Hidden value to 1. Set HideFileExt to 1 so that file extensions are also shown.

To show the protected operating system files, set ShowSuperHidden to a value of 1. Note that the hive in this key is HKCU, not HKLM.

In addition, you will notice that when you first view certain folders in Windows Explorer, such as Program Files and Windows, their contents will be hidden until you agree to have them shown. This feature is also controlled by the registry settings in the following subkey:

```
HKCU\SOFTWARE\Microsoft\Windows\CurrentVersion\Explorer\
WebView\BarricadedFolders\
```

In this subkey several values exist, including shell:Windows and shell:ProgramFiles. Changing these values from 1 to 0 will ensure that the contents of these folders are displayed when you first visit them.

We show this registry key merely as a convenience in case you want to, for example, spread these settings via a script. As with many of the settings we mention in this chapter and others, there is a GUI available for doing the same thing. In this case, you can modify these same registry keys through Windows Explorer, by selecting Tools → Folder Options and clicking the View tab. The related options are listed in the advanced settings: Show Hidden Files and Folders, Hide Extensions for Known File Types, and Hide Protected Operating System Files.

TCP/IP-Related Denial of Service Protection

Several settings are designed to help protect against different types of TCP-based denial of service (DoS) attacks, which are not often targeted toward client workstations. The most likely candidates for protection against DoS attacks are your servers, especially Internet-facing systems like your web servers; however, these settings work in all Windows 2000, XP, and .NET systems. (Although this book is about Windows XP, we realize that you could still load IIS 5.1 and run a web server if you choose to do so. That's why this section is here.)

These recommended settings reflect generally accepted practices as derived from sources such as Microsoft and several professional computer security organizations. Many of these keys do not exist in the registry, and will have to be created. Once that's done, a reboot is required for them to take effect. Keep in mind that many of these settings are designed to protect against various DoS attacks and may have undesirable consequences on your network. Try out these settings in a test environment before using them in production.

Windows stores all the TCP/IP configuration information in the registry, where it can be used by the protocol driver, tcpip.sys. The HKLM\SYSTEM\CCS\services\ tcpip\parameters\ key's settings apply to each adapter installed on the system; however, specific configurations can be set or overridden by adapter. Under the Interfaces subkey exist specific keys that correspond to each of the hardware (e.g., NIC) and software (e.g., remote access) adapters created on the computer.

Allow ICMP Redirects

Key: HKLM\SYSTEM\CCS\Services\Tcpip\Parameters\

Value Name: EnableICMPRedirect

Value Type: REG_DWORD (Boolean)

Recommended Setting: 0 (false)

Default Setting: 1 (true)

Description: When a router sends an ICMP redirect packet to a target computer, it instructs the target to change its route table to reflect a change in routing on the network. Setting this value to 0 turns off this functionality, so a Windows computer will not happily change its routing table based on any old ICMP redirect packet it receives.

Protect Against Path MTU Vulnerabilities

Key: HKLM\SYSTEM\CCS\Services\Tcpip\Parameters\

Value Name: EnablePMTUDiscovery

Value Type: REG_DWORD (Boolean)

Recommended Setting: 0 (false)

Default Setting: None

Description: This key accepts a value of either 1 (true) or 0 (false). The Maximum Transmission Unit is the largest packet that can be sent across a network. It is different for various networks (e.g., X.25, Token Ring); Ethernet networks have an MTU of 1500 bytes. When packets are transmitted across networks, Windows uses its own algorithms to determine the Path MTU (PMTU), which represents the smallest packet size that will be allowed across all the networks involved. For example, when a 10KB packet needs to cross an Ethernet network using an MTU of 1500 bytes, both computers will exchange MTU information. With this information, the computers will fragment the packet into smaller packets that can traverse the network.

CAUTION   By setting this value you are disabling an important part of Window's dynamic networking functionality, which could prevent packets from getting to their destinations.

There is a vulnerability affecting mainly Windows computers that perform routing between two or more networks. Essentially, an attacking computer can force the target computer to lower its MTU for a given destination to 68 bytes, the lowest allowable MTU. The attacking computer can then flood the target with multiple streams of data that must be fragmented and forwarded, and eventually they will consume the resources of the target. By default, PMTU discovery is enabled in Windows. However, if you set this value to 0, you are forcing Windows to always use a value of 576 bytes for the MTU. You should be very familiar with your network and understand the effects of disabling PMTU discovery before you enable this setting.

Protect Against SYN Attacks

Key: HKLM\SYSTEM\CCS\Services\Tcpip\Parameters\

Value Name: SynAttackProtect

Value Type: REG_DWORD

Recommended Setting: 1

Default Setting: None

Description: Windows allocates memory and processing resources whenever a TCP three-way handshake is in course. A SYN attack occurs when an attacking computer sends out a bunch of SYN packets to a target computer in order to force the initiation of the three-way handshake on the target. The target computer starts allocating resources to each SYN request it receives, and eventually runs out of resources while it is waiting for all of these incomplete handshakes to finish.

The SynAttackProtect registry value will accept a denial value of 0, 1, or 2. This setting defines the number of retries and the retry interval that Windows will use to complete a handshake. Setting this value to 2 is strongest, and in effect it has Windows free up resources at a much faster rate than its default. Setting this value to 2 can cause connectivity problems on high-latency networks. To provide at least some protection for Internet-facing computers, set this value to 1. As always, test this in your own test labs before going live. This setting requires that the TcpMaxConnectResponseRetransmissions value be set to at least 2.

If you want to have a look at how many TCP connections are currently open on your computer, type the following at the command prompt:

```
Netstat -n -p tcp
```

Prevent Users from Manipulating Type of Service Bits in Outgoing IP Packets

Key: HKLM\SYSTEM\CCS\Services\Tcpip\Parameters\

Value Name: DisableUserTOSSetting

Value Type: REG_DWORD (Boolean)

Recommended Setting: 1 (true)

Default Setting: None

Description: The DisableUserTOSSetting can be set to either 0 (false) or 1 (true). By setting the value to 1, you can prevent applications from manipulating the Type of Service (ToS) bits found in the header of outgoing IP packets. In Windows XP, this registry value does not exist by default, which is essentially the same as if it were set to 0, or false. In Windows 2000, this value defaults to 1, or true. Most of your network clients will not need to have this value enabled (set to 1). If they do, you should know that they will have the ability to defeat system policy controls such as Quality of Service (QoS) bandwidth settings.

Generic DoS Prevention Settings in TCP

Table 3-4 lists the other TCP settings you can modify in the registry, along with references for more information. These settings do not exist by default, but may be created by some application you install. Otherwise, you would want to enable these settings on systems (mainly Internet-facing servers), which are at risk of DoS attacks.

References for these keys and values include the Microsoft Knowledge Base article "Internet Server Unavailable Because of Malicious SYN Attacks" (Q142641) and the REGENTRY.CHM help file from the Windows 2000 Resource Kit.

IPSec-Related Settings

The following settings apply specifically to the IPSec implementation in Windows XP and 2000. For more details of IPSec default exemptions and functionality in Windows XP, see Chapter 7.

Registry Subkey and Values	Recommended Setting
HKLM\system\CCS\services\tcpip\parameters	
TcpTimedWaitDelay	96
KeepAliveTime	300,000
TcpMaxHalfOpen	100
TcpMaxPortsExhausted	1
TcpMaxHalfOpenRetried	80
TcpMaxDataRetransmissions	3
TcpMaxConnectResponseRetransmissions	2
EnableDeadGWDetect	0
EnablePMTUBHDetect	0
HKLM\system\currentcontrolset\services\afd	
DynamicBacklogGrowthDelta	10
EnableDynamicBacklog	1
MaximumDynamicBacklog	20
MinimumDynamicBacklog	20
Interfaces\{InterfaceID}	
PerformRouterDiscovery	0

Table 3-4. DoS Registry Key Value Settings

Disable Default Exemptions

Key: HKLM\SYSTEM\CCS\Services\IPSec\

Value Name: NoDefaultExempt

Value Type: REG_DWORD

Recommended Setting: 1

Default Setting: None

Description: By default, certain types of traffic are excluded from protection of the IPSec filters that you set up (see Chapter 7 and Microsoft Knowledge Base article Q253169 for more information). This traffic includes Kerberos, broadcast, IKE, RSVP QoS, and multicast. Setting this value to 1 disables the exemption for RSVP and Kerberos traffic, meaning they will be protected by your IPSec filters.

Enable the Oakley Log and Advanced Logging of IKE Events

Key: HKLM\SYSTEM\CCS\Services\PolicyAgent\Oakley

Value Name: EnableLogging

Value Type: REG_DWORD (decimal)

Recommended Setting: 1

Default Setting: None

Description: Logging Oakley-related events can provide some valuable information to aid in troubleshooting or traffic analysis. When this key is created and set to a value of 1, all ISAKMP negotiations for Main mode and Quick mode are written to a log file. The log file is created each time the Policy Agent is started, and it is stored in %SystemRoot%\debug as Oakley.log. Previous versions are saved as Oakley.log.sav.

Checking the Certificate Revocation List (CRL)

Key: HKLM\SYSTEM\CCS\Services\PolicyAgent\Oakley

Value Name: StrongCRLCheck

Value Type: REG_DWORD

Recommended Settings:

1 = Reject the certificate validation only if the server returns an affirmative answer that the certificate has been revoked.

2 = Reject the certificate if any error occurs during the CRL check. This essentially means that the CRL distribution point must positively respond that the certificate has not been revoked. Any other errors that occur, such as the network or server being unreachable or the server saying that it never issued such as certificate, will cause the certificate to be rejected.

Default Setting: None

Description: When using certificates for IPSec in Windows 2000 or XP, you probably want to ensure that they have not been revoked. By setting this registry to a value of either 1 or 2, you will force the IPSec Policy Agent to check the certificate server's Certificate Revocation List (CRL) to determine the status of the certificate. Keep in mind that the CRL checks may be different for various certificate servers, so this setting may not always work the way you expect. Before enabling this check, ensure that your IPSec authentications are working with certificates, and enable the Oakley log to get a closer look at the details of the certificate authentication. Then test this setting in your test environments to see that it works as you expect.

NOTE   This setting must be tested prior to being used in production! Coordinate testing with your IPSec and Certificate Server administrators.

You have to restart the Policy Agent for this setting to take effect, unless your system is acting as a VPN with L2TP support, in which case you need to reboot. To disable the StrongCRLCheck, simply restart the Policy Agent or the VPN server, as appropriate.

NetBT-Related Settings

NetBIOS is still alive and well in the latest versions of Windows. What you don't want to hear is that its vulnerabilities have more or less followed it throughout the evolution of Windows. *NetBIOS over TCP* (NetBT) is a networking protocol that Windows computers use for NetBIOS communications over a TCP/IP network, hence the name. The essential functions performed, or delivered, via NetBT include file sharing, netlogon, NetBIOS name–to–IP mappings, browsing, and messenger service.

NetBIOS communications have almost no security, such as encryption and authentication, associated with them. Because of this, you should either disable NetBIOS communications between critical systems or protect them with IPSec or some application-layer security. Since there is no authentication, Windows computers will respect almost any NetBIOS type of traffic that is sent to them. As you will see in the coming sections, this makes it easy for an attacker to cause a denial of service condition for computers on your network, by corrupting the methods they use to perform name resolution.

Aside from the registry keys that follow, a good prevention against NetBIOS DoS attacks is to use DNS name resolution on your network. DNS has priority over WINS and NetBIOS name broadcasts, so your enterprise will first use DNS when trying to resolve computer names.

All of the configuration parameters for NetBT are stored in the registry subkey HKLM\SYSTEM\CCS\Services\NetBT\Parameters. The following two registry keys are of concern regarding NetBT security.

Protect from Name Release Datagram Denial of Service Attacks

Key: HKLM\SYSTEM\CCS\Services\NetBT\Parameters

Value Name: NoNameReleaseOnDemand

Value Type: REG_DWORD

Recommended Setting: 1 (true)

Default Setting: None

Description: This value accepts data of either 0 (false) or 1 (true), and requires Windows 2000 Service Pack 2 or later. A couple of vulnerabilities inherently exist in NetBIOS networking. A Windows computer will release its NetBIOS name when it receives a name-conflict datagram indicating that there is a name conflict on the network. Most Windows administrators have seen it before: when two computers come online with the same NetBIOS name, there is a conflict, and neither of the names will work on the network. Not only are the names put into a state of "conflict," but NetBIOS functionality is essentially destroyed, and such things as file sharing and netlogon will not work until the conflict is resolved, usually by changing the computer name.

CAUTION   NetBIOS communications are essential on most Windows networks. By setting this value, you are altering the basic functionality of NetBIOS, which is to release a NetBIOS name when receiving a name-conflict datagram. Be aware that by setting this value, the computer will ignore name-conflict datagrams and keeps its NetBIOS name even when another computer online is using it.

Because NetBIOS communications are essential on most Windows NT/2000/XP networks, when a computer receives a name service datagram indicating a name conflict, it can prevent the following types of NetBIOS name services from working:

- Computer Browser service can prevent browsing the network with tools such as net view, Network Neighborhood, and My Network Places.
- Netlogon service can prevent domain logons.
- Server and Workstation services can prevent shared network resources from being accessible.

See Microsoft Knowledge Base article Q269239 for more details and step-by-step remediation for all versions of Windows.

The problem is that an attacker on your network could send a NetBIOS name–conflict datagram to any target Windows computer utilizing NetBIOS and NetBT, and that target will happily release its name and stop participating in NetBIOS communications.

Microsoft's fix for this came out with Security Bulletin MS-0047, which can be found at http://www.microsoft.com/technet/security/bulletin/MS00-047.asp. By setting the NoNameReleaseOnDemand registry key to a value of 1, you protect the computer from releasing its name after receiving a name-conflict datagram.

You can view the state of NetBIOS names in the local cache by typing **nbtstat –n** at the command line. You will see output similar to the following:

```
Node IpAddress: [10.0.2.67] Scope Id: []
                NetBIOS Local Name Table

        Name                Type         Status
   ---------------------------------------------

        COTTONS       <00>  UNIQUE      Registered
        COTTONS       <20>  UNIQUE      Registered
        WORKGROUP     <00>  GROUP       Registered
        WORKGROUP     <1E>  GROUP       Registered
```

The Status will show up either as Registered, Registering, or Conflict. In the case of a Conflict, the computer's NetBIOS communications will be severely debilitated.

Spoofed Packets Can Corrupt the Cache, Causing a Denial of Service Condition

Key: HKLM\SYSTEM\CCS\Services\NetBT\Parameters

Value Name: CacheTimeout

Value Type: REG_DWORD

Recommended Setting: 60000 (decimal for 1 minute)

Default Setting: 600000 (decimal for 10 minutes)

Description: This value accepts a decimal value from 60000 to 4294967295. This value defines the time in milliseconds for which NetBIOS names are stored in the local cache. The NetBIOS name cache is updated when computers on the network send out name service datagrams. As usual, NetBIOS will happily process anything it receives in one of these datagrams, so an attacker can maliciously spoof datagrams that contain false information and corrupt NetBIOS name caches on your network. The only protections against this are to either firewall NetBIOS traffic or lower the CacheTimeout value to periodically empty the cache.

NOTE   Lowering the CacheTimeout value will result in more NetBIOS name resolution traffic throughout your network, if the network is heavily dependent on WINS instead of DNS.

TOOLS OF THE TRADE

Several tools are available to directly manage the registry through either a GUI or command line interface. As an administrator, you have the option to connect to individual registries for modification or to use a script or group policy to modify an entire network of registries. Many of these tools have been available through the Windows NT or Windows 2000 Resource Kits, and Microsoft has even included some of them by default with Windows XP/.NET.

Regedit.exe We covered the ever-useful Regedit.exe tool early in the chapter (see "Regedit.exe"). This is Microsoft's tool for accessing and modifying most all aspects of the registry.

Regmon.exe Another awesome tool, from Sysinternals' Mark Russinovich and Bryce Cogswell (http://www.sysinternals.com), Regmon.exe will let you see registry activity in real time. This tool provides a look into the heart of the Windows operating system, showing registry values that are being queried and set, by the processes that are requesting the action. You can even filter the activity and save it out to a log file for analysis. Figure 3-4 shows Regmon.exe in action.

Regini.exe Regini.exe is the command line tool for modifying registry key permissions. If you need to automate this process or script it up for a large network, then this is the tool for you. Take a look a Microsoft's Knowledge Base article Q237607 for the details of how to use Regini.exe. Installed in the %SYSTEMROOT%\system32\ directory on Windows XP, this tool can also be found in the Windows 2000 Resource Kit.

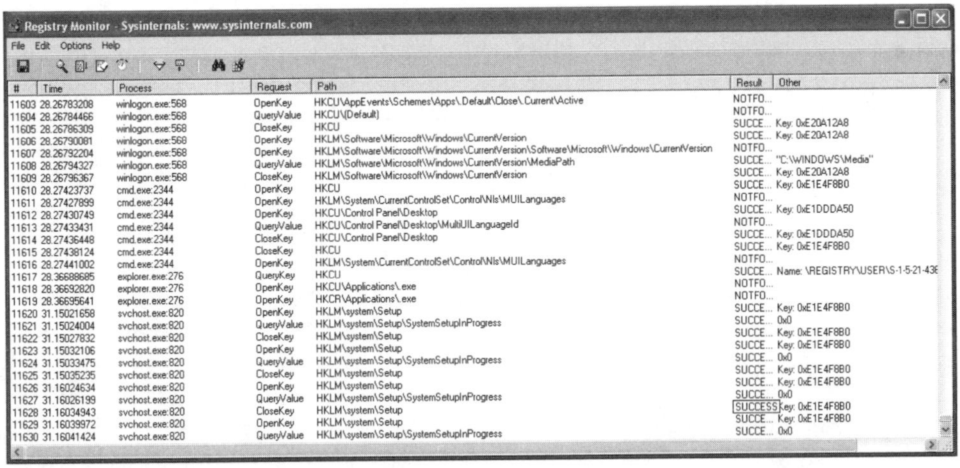

Figure 3-4. Regmon.exe in action, showing real-time registry activity

Reg.exe This command line tool is installed in the %SYSTEMROOT%\system32\ directory on Windows XP, and can also be found in the Windows 2000 Resource Kit. Reg.exe version 3.0 is included with Windows XP, offering new switches such as /compare, /export, and /import. Reg.exe is an all-purpose registry tool, giving you the ability to perform most common registry tasks, except for modifying key permissions. Note that keys can be abbreviated similar to what we have done in this chapter, HKLM, HKCU, HKCR, and HKCC.

Regdmp.exe Although it's from the Windows 2000 Resource Kit, this tool still works on Windows XP. It will literally dump the contents of any registry hive or subkey that you specify. This can be very useful for auditing a system. For example, the following command will dump the contents of the \Services subkey, providing output as shown in Figure 3-5.

```
regdmp HKEY_LOCAL_MACHINE\system\CurrentControlSet\Services
```

Of course, this output can easily be redirected to a file instead of the screen by simply using a redirect symbol. The next command shows an example of redirecting output to a simple text file:

```
regdmp HKEY_LOCAL_MACHINE\system\CurrentControlSet\Services > file.txt
```

Regfind.exe Regfind.exe is another command line Resource Kit utility. It allows you to do string-search or search-and-replace operations in local or remote registries.

Regback.exe and Regrest.exe Both of these are command line tools from the Windows 2000 Resource Kit. Regback.exe lets you back up any hive while it is open and in use by the system. The hive will be backed up to a folder and filename that you define. Later, you can use Regrest.exe to restore the hive, or portion of the registry, that you backed up with Regback. Together, these tools can make for scriptable registry backup solutions.

Windows Script Host RegRead, RegWrite, and RegDelete Built into the Windows XP operating system is Microsoft's Windows Script Host (WSH). It may seem clear that these three methods of the WSH provide the ability to read, write, or delete a value from the registry, just by their names. Unfortunately, these methods are limited and only allow for operations on one value at a time. So you cannot, for example, use the RegRead method to easily list all of the values in the Run keys. You cannot enumerate subkeys either. You can, however, run these methods on local or remote machines, and therefore easily script them up.

Figure 3-5. Regdmp.exe dumping the contents of the \Services subkey to the console

An example script that reads a registry value follows. To run this on your system, just create a file named regread.vbs and add these lines. Then run the script from the command prompt by entering **regread.vbs**.

```
Dim WSHShell
Dim sKey
Dim sValue
```

```
Set WSHShell = Wscript.CreateObject ("Wscript.Shell")
sKey = "HKLM\System\CurrentControlSet\Control\Lsa\forceguest"
sValue = WSHShell.RegRead (sKey)
Wscript.echo "The forceguest value is set to " & sValue
```

NOTE   This script should be run with the Cscript.exe scripting host. This can be done by running **cscript regread.vbs** from the command line, or by registering Cscript as the default scripting host by running **cscript //H:cscript** from the command line.

You can change the sKey string in Regread.vbs to any registry key value of your choice, as long as your credentials are allowed.

WMI StdRegProv   Windows Management Instrumentation (WMI) also provides some more advanced methods for accessing the system registry. With the WMI Standard Registry Provider (StdRegProv), you can retrieve and modify data in the registry as well as receive notifications when values change. (Further discussion is beyond the scope of this book, but a wealth of additional information is available at http://msdn.microsoft.com/scripting.)

CHECKLIST: REGISTRY SECURITY

The registry is in many cases the brains of the Windows operating system. If you understand it and take care of it, it will take care of you. Registry security starts with understanding some of the registry's structure, and depends on individual key settings and key ACLs.

- [ ] Make your system partition NTFS, so the registry files can be properly secured.
- [ ] Consider the security of your backups that contain the registry hives.
- [ ] Protect offline access to the SAM and Security registry hives and files, as they contain passwords for the local system's users and service accounts.
- [ ] Don't run services such as backup agent software with Domain Administrator service accounts. Remember, these passwords are stored in the LSA Secrets cache.
- [ ] You must enable Audit Object Access through the Local Security Settings before you can enable auditing on any registry keys.

☐ Manage user accounts wisely, and put end users in the Users group. Use the Power Users group only in specific circumstances, when you are willing to sacrifice certain levels of security and system integrity.

☐ Set strict ACLs on the `winreg` key to specify who has remote access to the registry.

☐ Delete the `AllowedPaths` subkey of `winreg` for maximum security, but be careful that this doesn't break your applications (such as printer servers and Directory Replication).

☐ Determine the necessity for enabling the TCP denial of service defensive keys for machines on your network. Most likely DoS defenses are more appropriate for Internet-facing servers such as web servers, but some keys may be appropriate for your Windows XP clients, such as the NetBT `NoNameReleaseOnDemand` setting.

CHAPTER 4

File System Security

Windows XP supports three file systems: FAT, FAT32, and NTFS. (OK, technically it also supports FAT12, UDF, and CDFS, but we won't concern ourselves with those here.) Of course, in any security-related context, files systems in Windows XP can mean only NTFS.

Like Windows 2000, Windows XP supports both basic and dynamic disks. Microsoft really wants you to use dynamic disks—you won't be able to use software RAID without upgrading to dynamic. Dynamic disks also use the Master File Table (MFT), which is more resilient since a copy is kept on both disks, unlike the basic disk's partition table.

NTFS

Aside from getting a new version number—3.1—NTFS in Windows XP is largely unchanged from the one we all know and love from Windows 2000. Out of all the supported file systems, only NTFS implements files and directories as securable objects— thus letting you set file and directory permissions and stop John in Marketing from seeing all the, uh, unfinished poetry in your My Documents folder. In addition, NTFS provides EFS—the Encrypted File System.

Security concerns aside, there are many other reasons to use NTFS, including

- Data recoverability (transactional file system)
- Storage fault tolerance (RAID)
- Dynamic bad-cluster remapping (flag bad sectors and remap data to good ones)
- File and folder compression
- Directories as volume mount points

Some of the main differences in Windows XP are the new UI changes, such as the Effective Permissions tab. As far as EFS is concerned, Microsoft has also improved its design, using lessons learned in Windows 2000. To understand the best practices for NTFS and EFS, read on.

How Permissions Do Their Job

Many things are taking place behind the scenes to protect your spreadsheets and databases from would-be crackers. When you log on to a Windows XP system, the system produces an access token. The token is actually made up of many pieces of information, including your user account SID, your group SIDs, a logon SID, an owner SID, the SID for the primary group (who let this many SIDs into the party anyway?), the source of the token, and more. When this user attempts to access a file, the system looks to see if this token has access to the security descriptor of the file. (You can find more details on the access token in Chapter 6.)

In Windows 2000, if you create a new file in the root of your C: drive, what permissions are on that file? Yes, you guessed it—Everyone has Full Control, as shown in Figure 4-1.

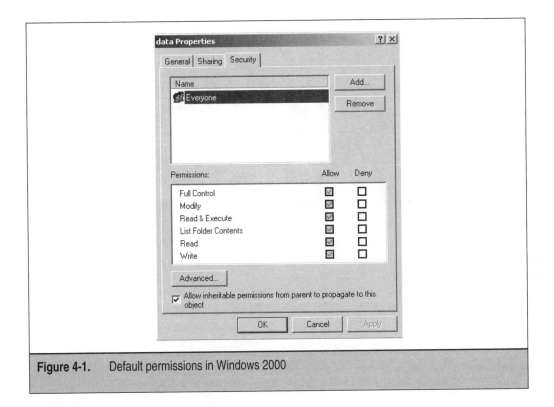

Figure 4-1.   Default permissions in Windows 2000

Now, create a subfolder without changing the permissions on it, and create a file in that subfolder. What permissions are on that file? Sure, the same—Everyone has Full Control. This is because the *inherited permissions* are propagating through your folders, starting with Everyone Full Control at the root. This isn't exactly a great way to start off a "secure" file structure.

In Windows XP, however, if you create a new file in the root of C:, it will not be wide open to the world. If you check the permissions, you will see that the Creator Owner of the file has Full Control, along with the System (inherited) and the local Administrators group (inherited), and the Users group has Read & Execute (inherited), as shown in Figure 4-2.

Now that is much better—foreshadowing, perhaps, the more "secure by default" environment that Microsoft seems to be embracing, to borrow a phrase from OpenBSD.

Auditing All Access

More good news about NTFS is that each access attempt can be audited by the system—and these audit logs can only be seen by the administrator or other users with appropriate permissions. Many system administrators make use of file and folder auditing, but there is a wealth of information to be had—when users access files, create files, delete

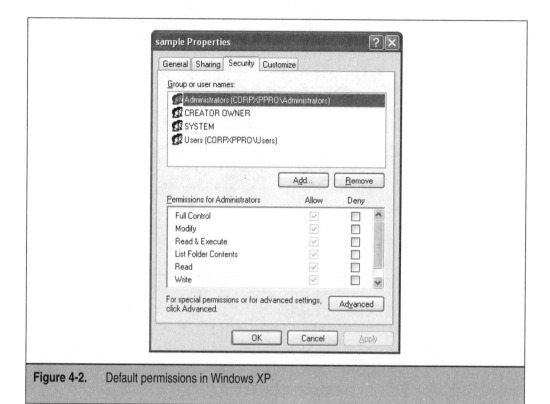

Figure 4-2. Default permissions in Windows XP

files, and so forth. Auditing serves as your electronic watchdog, which is very useful for when the boss wants to know just who accidentally deleted the latest sales report. You access auditing options by right-clicking the folder in Explorer, selecting Properties, and then selecting the Security tab. Then click the Auditing tab of the Advanced Security Settings dialog box, choose Add, and select the users or groups you would like to track, as shown in Figure 4-3.

NOTE Make sure that object auditing is enabled in the local security policy or GPO for the computer. As discussed in Chapter 1, object auditing is enabled in the Security Settings → Local Policies → Audit Policy → Audit object access setting.

Who Has Permission?

When you want to change permissions on a file or folder in Windows XP, right-click it to choose Properties, and click the Security tab.

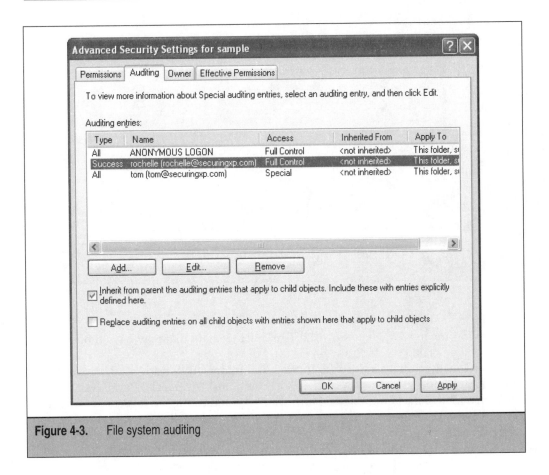

Figure 4-3.   File system auditing

NOTE: If you have Simple File Sharing enabled the Security tab will be hidden.

When you click the Add button, the dialog box shown in Figure 4-4 comes up, letting you choose a user or group to add. This dialog box has changed—you can now search for users or groups much more easily than in Windows 2000.

You can filter the object type by a user, group, or by a "built-in security principal," which means the default groups that are included in Windows XP: Administrators, Power Users, System Operators, and so on. You can click the Locations button to pick from a list of machines or domains you are currently authenticated to. Then you can enter the object name to select—you are even shown examples. To go one step further, there is an Advanced button that lets you search, which is a welcome addition when

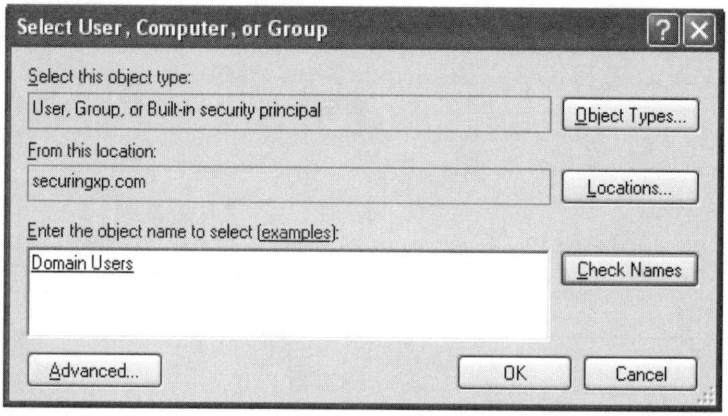

Figure 4-4. Select User, Computer, or Group dialog box

you are working in a large Windows 2000 or .NET domain that may have thousands of objects. The dialog box is shown in Figure 4-5.

When looking at the Security tab for files and folders in Windows XP, versus the same tab in Windows 2000, some differences stand out. The Special Permissions item has been added to the bottom of the Permissions list, indicating the presence of extended permissions on the object. To see the extended permissions, click the Advanced button on the main Security tab screen, and then highlight one of the permissions entries, and click the Edit button. The same extended permissions existed in Windows 2000, with the exception of the Full Control permission, which is now listed at the top.

Something missing on the Security tab is the "Allow inheritable permissions from parent to propagate to this object" check box. This was somewhat redundant in Windows 2000, as the same check box appeared when you clicked the Advanced button. Windows XP replaces it with some more verbose text: "Inherit from parent the permission entries that apply to child objects. Include these with entries explicitly defined here." This is a nice change—it describes the full effect of combining the inherited permissions with the explicitly defined ones.

The second check box for resetting permissions on child objects and enabling propagation of inheritable permissions has a more circuitous and less effective explanation: "Replace permission entries on all child objects with entries shown here that apply to child objects."

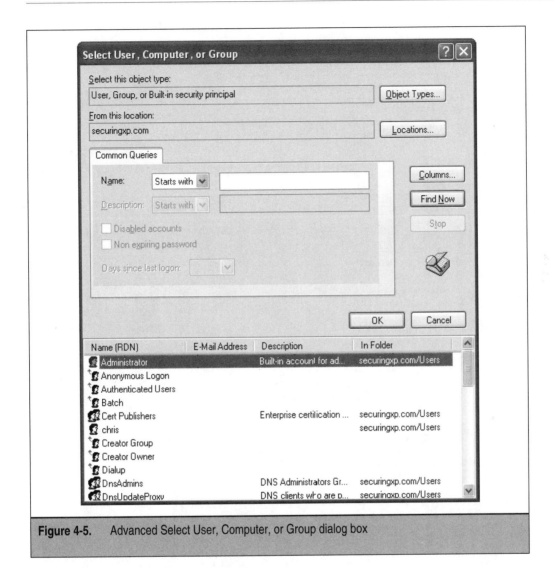

Figure 4-5.   Advanced Select User, Computer, or Group dialog box

What Are the Effective Permissions?

A welcome addition to the Advanced Security Settings screen in Windows XP is
the Effective Permissions tab. This new feature in Windows XP lets administrators
check their work by selecting a user or group and seeing the sum of that user's or
group's permissions for the object in question. This can be very helpful when you have
both inherited permissions and explicit permissions being applied to many groups.
Figure 4-6 shows what the effective permissions will be.

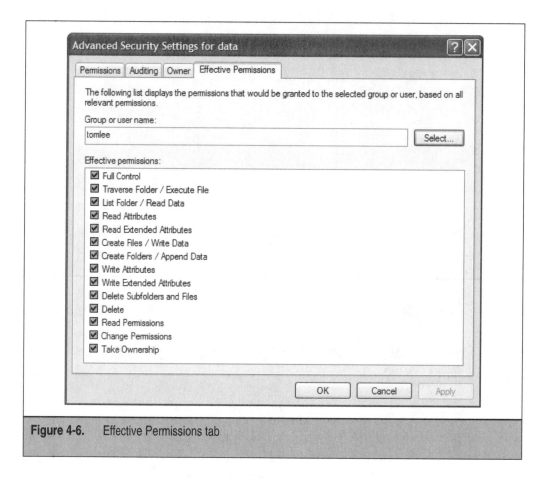

Figure 4-6. Effective Permissions tab

THE ENCRYPTING SYSTEM KEY (SYSKEY)

The system startup keys protect several sensitive areas of the system. For maximum protection, the Syskey wizard can be invoked to protect sensitive information including

- Master keys used to protect private keys
- Protection keys for user account passwords stored in Active Directory
- Protection keys for passwords stored in the registry in the local SAM registry key
- Protection keys for LSA data
- Protection key for the administrator account password used for system recovery startup in Safe mode

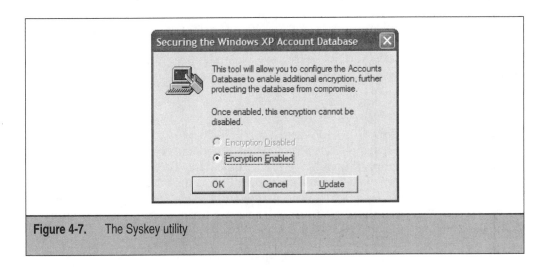

Figure 4-7. The Syskey utility

Running the Syskey command at the command prompt will let you configure the system to use a computer-generated random key as the startup key. You can store it in one of two ways: either randomly distributed throughout the registry (enabling restarts without the need to enter the startup key), or on a floppy disk (which must be inserted into the system for it to boot). A strong password should be assigned when using Syskey, (shown in Figure 4-7), with either the stored locally or floppy disk method.

The Syskey-on-floppy method may be the ultimate in security, but is also the most dangerous if the floppy is lost or damaged or the password forgotten. In that case, the only way to recover the system is to use a repair disk to restore the system registry to a time before Syskey protection was enabled.

CAUTION   Once enabled, the Syskey startup protection can't be disabled, only configured to operate at different security levels.

Once the startup key has been enabled, system startup occurs when the startup key is retrieved from either the locally stored key, a manually entered password, or the insertion of the startup disk. The startup key is then used to decrypt the master protection key, which is used to derive the per-user account password encryption key, which decrypts the password information in Active Directory or the local SAM registry key.

ENCRYPTING FILE SYSTEM

A well-thought-out file permissions strategy is important to any Windows XP security plan. However, if an attacker can get physical access to a machine, then all bets are off.

If someone can dismount your physical media and bring it up on their own machine, your carefully crafted permissions scheme will be bypassed, effectively giving up full access to your files. This would not be the case, however, if you have encrypted your sensitive files with the *Encrypting File System* (EFS).

How EFS Works

First available in Windows 2000, EFS uses a public-private key pair and a per-file encryption key to encrypt and decrypt your files. When a user encrypts a file, EFS generates a File Encryption Key (FEK) to encrypt the data. The FEK is encrypted by using the user's public key, and the encrypted FEK is then stored with the file. Windows 2000 and Windows XP Professional encrypt using DESX encryption by default, and 3DES is an option. .NET server uses 256-bit AES encryption by default, and can optionally use 3DES as well.

NOTE   As described in Chapter 1, the new Security Options setting "System cryptography: Use FIPS compliant algorithms for encryption, hashing, and signing" is used to force EFS encryption to use Triple DES algorithms.

Files and folders can be encrypted by right-clicking the file or folder, selecting Properties, then selecting the Advanced button on the General property tab. Next you click the Encrypt Contents to Secure Data check box. Optionally, you can also use the Cipher.exe utility. Files cannot be both compressed and encrypted, and system files or files in the %SYSTEMROOT% folder cannot be encrypted.

NOTE   NTFS files cannot be both compressed and encrypted.

Figure 4-8 shows an example of the EFS dialog box.

If you need command line functionality for scripting or other reasons, you can use the `cipher` command to perform the same functions. Entering **cipher /?** at the command line will give you the switches you can use. The example below shows how to quickly encrypt a directory.

```
C:\temp>cipher /e
Encrypting directories in C:\temp\
encrypteddirectory  [OK]
1 directorie(s) within 1 directorie(s) were encrypted.
```

EFS Best Practices

EFS encryption is transparent to the end user. Files stored in encrypted folders are automatically decrypted when opened and re-encrypted when closed. The EFS File System Run Time Library (FSRTL) is the module within the EFS driver that handles

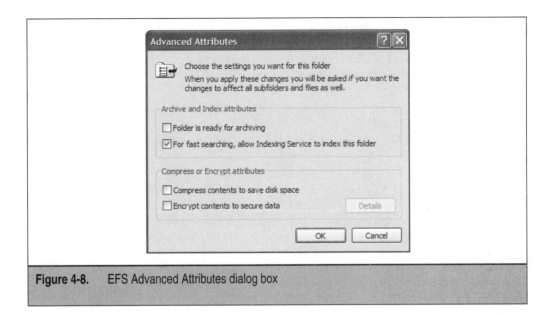

Figure 4-8.   EFS Advanced Attributes dialog box

the various file system operations performed on encrypted files, such as reads, writes, and opens.

EFS has been in use long enough for people to have been bitten and learned a few things. We've rounded up several best-practice recommendations in the following sections.

Use Smart Cards for Authentication

Your best bet when managing EFS security in a network of users is to distribute smart cards. Smart cards can require a biometric mechanism or a PIN to log in to a computer. By requiring smart card authentication for your users, you can significantly protect the private keys stored locally on the hard disk. To access the files, a user needs both the smart card and private key, or else access is denied.

The certificate store keeps the private keys encrypted with 3DES until you log on to the system. At that point, the store and keys are unlocked, or unencrypted, for general use, as long as you are logged in.

A smart card solution for domain authentication is very strong and easy to manage. It usually comes down to the old question of ROI (return on investment): is it more cost effective to purchase and distribute smart cards to gain the added security or to just tolerate the risk of storing private keys locally, saving the cash?

SECURITY ALERT!   By implementing the standard method of domain logon through a username and password, you leave your user's computers open to a simple possibility of attack. If an attacker can steal the computer, and obtain the user's credentials, they can simply log in as that user and access all of their encrypted files. This is another area where smart cards can offer a strong defense.

With smart cards in place, attackers would need more than just the user's credentials; they would need the physical smart card and the PIN. If the smart card uses biometrics, then attackers have even more problems. Without the smart card to log in with, the certificate and private key store remain encrypted on the disk with the 3DES protection provided by Windows.

Use Encrypted Folders

It is preferred to encrypt folders, and to then place files to be encrypted in those folders, rather than encrypting individual files. The reason for this is that when EFS encrypts an individual file, it first writes all data streams of the file to a plaintext file in the system's temporary folder before it generates the necessary keys and actually encrypts the data. As you probably know, when files are deleted, even in NTFS, they are not really gone for good, and can often be recovered with the correct tools. When a unencrypted file is placed into an encrypted folder, no plaintext temporary file is written.

TIP   Create encrypted folders rather than individually encrypted files.

Secure Temporary Files

Something else to keep in mind is that many programs, such as Microsoft Word, create temporary files while you create and edit your potentially sensitive data. You may think that you're safe if you move your file into an encrypted folder after you're finished editing it, figuring you're eliminating the possibility of creating the plaintext temporary file. However, almost as soon as you started editing the document, Word created a temporary file. So for maximum effectiveness, it's a good idea to encrypt your My Documents folder or whatever the default file location for temporary files is in your application.

If you do choose to encrypt the Temp directory, you should keep that decision in the front of your mind, because many applications put temporary setup files in the Temp directory during installation. If the setup routine impersonates a different user during the installation, such as System, the installation can fail.

Overwrite Slack Space

If you have encrypted individual files and want to overwrite the system slack space to avoid any possible recovery of sensitive data, make use of the Cipher.exe utility by executing **cipher.exe /w**, which will remove data from available unused disk space on the entire volume. Cipher.exe has many other switches that allow you to encrypt and decrypt files and folders from the command line, among other things. Just running Cipher.exe in a directory will bring back a listing of all files and folders and will show which ones are encrypted. Use **cipher /?** to check all the options available.

Encrypting Offline Files

With Windows XP, users can keep offline copies of files shared from network servers on their computers. The implementation of offline files in .NET server is not compatible with Remote Desktop. To enable offline files on .NET server, first make sure Remote Desktop is disabled: right-click My Computer, choose Properties, and go to the Remote tab. In the Remote Desktop section, clear the "Allow users to connect remotely to this computer" check box, and then click OK.

For both Windows XP and .NET server, to turn on offline files, start Windows Explorer, go to the Tools menu, select Folder Options, and go to the Offline Files tab, as shown in Figure 4-9. Choose both Enable Offline Files and Encrypt Offline Files to Secure Data, and click OK. Offline files will now be encrypted locally, even if file encryption was not enabled on the server. This is a key option to enable for traveling users, so that even if their laptop is lost or stolen, the data is still protected by encryption.

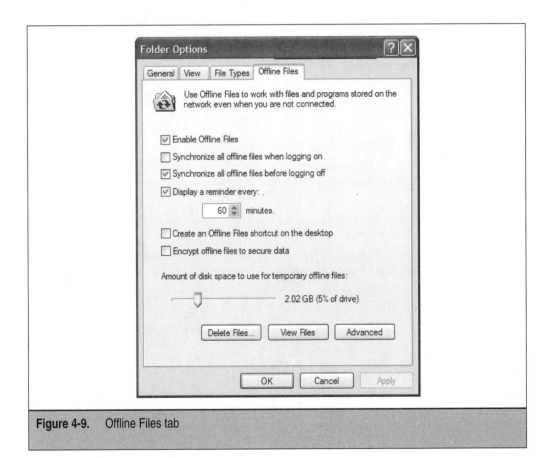

Figure 4-9.   Offline Files tab

The registry key that sets Windows XP to encrypt offline content is `HKEY_LOCAL_ MACHINE\SOFTWARE\Microsoft\Windows\CurrentVersion\NetCache`. It is a `REG_DWORD` named EncryptCache that should be set to 1. Although configuring Administrative Template (.adm) files is outside the scope of this book, from an administrative security standpoint it would be a good idea to push this out to all of your users via a group policy by creating an .adm file and setting the option to encrypt.

File Operations on Encrypted Files

File copy, rename, and move operations have different effects on encrypted files, depending on whether the files are moved or copied between volumes or within a volume, and on whether the commands are entered on the command line or performed through the GUI. It's important to understand these effects in case, for example, scripts are used to move or copy files between encrypted and unencrypted volumes. An easy way to visually determine if a file is encrypted is to select the option to "Show encrypted or compressed NTFS files in color": select Tools | Folder Options, click the View tab, and click in the check box to enable this option.

Local EFS File Operations

Here we list certain things to watch out for when performing file operations with encrypted files from the command line. Make sure that you understand the effects of what you do with encrypted files so that you don't inadvertently decrypt sensitive information.

- When an unencrypted file is moved or copied via Windows Explorer or copied via the command line to an encrypted folder on the same volume, the file is encrypted.

- When an unencrypted file is moved via the command line to an encrypted folder on the same volume, the file is *not* encrypted.

- When an unencrypted file is moved via the command line to an encrypted folder on a different local volume, the file is encrypted.

- When an unencrypted file in an encrypted folder is renamed via Windows Explorer, the file is encrypted.

- When an unencrypted file in an encrypted folder is renamed via the command line, the file is *not* encrypted.

Remote EFS File Operations

As with local operations, it is critical to understand the effects of certain remote operations on encrypted files. These are operations performed between systems over the network.

- When an encrypted file is moved or copied to or from a network file share on a remote computer, the files are decrypted locally, transmitted unencrypted, and re-encrypted on the target volume if the remote computer is trusted for delegation and is using NTFS. If the remote system is not trusted for delegation, the transfer fails. If the remote system is trusted for delegation but is not using NTFS, the transfer will succeed but the file will no longer be encrypted.

 SECURITY ALERT: Note that encrypted files are sent in clear text over the wire. Make sure to use other methods (web folders or HTTPS, for example) to transfer encrypted files.

- Encrypted files transmitted to or from web folders remain encrypted during transmission. Enabling Web Folders with WebDAV will decrease your administrative burdens by transparently keeping files encrypted across the network and preventing the need for alternative options.

If you don't like the idea of files sent in clear text between SMB shares, and you do not want to implement Web Folders, you can always implement a secure IPSec design that encrypts all traffic to and from an SMB share.

EFS and Certificates

A user must have a certificate to encrypt files with EFS. For Windows XP users not connected to a domain or for stand-alone servers, this will mean a self-signed certificate. If you encrypt a file in these environments, Windows XP will automatically create a self-signed certificate for you. You can verify the type of certificate you have by going into the Certificates—Current User MMC snap-in. In an MMC console, go to the File menu, choose Add/Remove Snap In, and add the Certificates snap-in. Choose My User Account when prompted. Navigate to the Personal folder, and click the Certificates subfolder, as shown in Figure 4-10. If the certificate inside is issued by the same person it is assigned to, then it is a self-signed certificate.

These self-signed certificates are set to expire 100 years after they are issued. It is recommended from a security, manageability, and data recovery standpoint that certificates be managed from a Certificate Authority (CA) in any domain environment. Keep in mind that there are some problems with integrating third-party PKI solutions, as listed in Microsoft Knowledge Base articles Q281245 and Q291010.

In a domain environment, when a server is designated a CA by installing Certificate Services, it can be used to store and manage user certificates for the domain. In this case, a user can request a certificate by going into the Certificates snap-in as just described, right-clicking the Certificates subfolder, and going to All Tasks → Request New Certificate. If the permission to request a certificate has not been revoked via a policy, then the user can receive a valid certificate.

Renewing Certificates

EFS will automatically attempt to renew certificates. Since self-signed certificates do not expire for 100 years, renewal is not an issue unless the user is immortal. However, for certificates assigned by a CA renewal is necessary, since the certificates are generally only viable for a year or two. If EFS cannot automatically renew a certificate, then files can no longer be encrypted using that certificate. However, files that were previously encrypted by that certificate can still be decrypted, since EFS stores existing private keys.

To move to an environment that uses certificates issued from a Certificate Authority from one that used self-signed certificates, a user can issue the `cipher /k` command. This will archive the existing self-signed certificate and request a new certificate from an enterprise CA. The user can still decrypt files with the previous self-signed certificate, and then they can be encrypted with the new public key when they are resaved. If the user cannot obtain a certificate from a CA, then a new self-signed certificate is installed.

NOTE   If you use the `/k` option, you can then use the `/u` option to go through and update all the user's keys once they've changed.

Authorizing Access to Encrypted Files

Any user who has access to an encrypted file can add other users' certificates to the list of users that can decrypt that file. For this reason, it is very important to authorize only trusted users. The exception is if the user does not have Write permission to the file. The user then cannot modify the file, nor can they let other users decrypt the file. To perform this operation, simply right-click a file, select Properties, click the Advanced button on the General tab, and click the Details button. The Encryption Details dialog box appears, as shown in Figure 4-11.

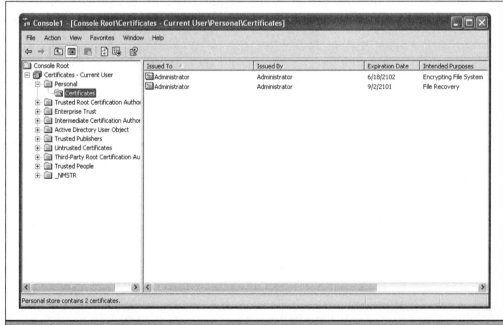

Figure 4-10.   Local certificate store

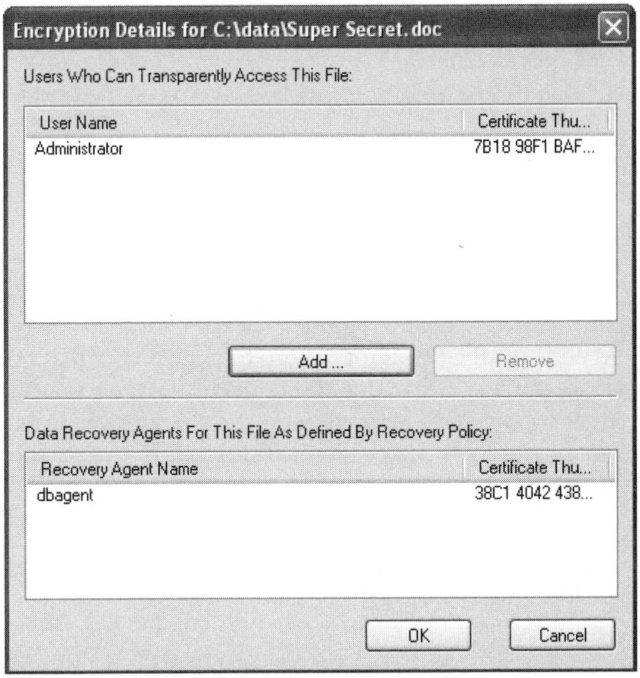

Figure 4-11.   Encryption Details dialog box

This dialog box will show all users who can decrypt the file, including any data-recovery agents (DRAs) specified by the domain EFS policy. By clicking the Add button, you can add other users to this authorization list. The default list of certificates that Add brings up includes all the certificates in the Other People and Trusted People certificate stores. Clicking the Find Now button will allow the user to search Active Directory for other certificates to add.

NOTE   When manually importing certificates, always choose the Trusted People certificate store. Self-signed certificates can only be used when placed in this store.

Adding other users will enable them to decrypt individual files but not folders.

Recovering Encrypted Files

When you encrypt files, some occasions require file recovery—when a user leaves the organization, for example. The user's profile may become damaged or deleted, meaning that the private key used to encrypt the files is gone. Deleting profiles is somewhat common; the problem is that it also destroys your keys. If you go to System → Advanced → User Profiles and delete a profile, you don't even receive a warning that you will lose the keys! In these cases, there are four recovery methods.

Data Recovery Agents

When an EFS recovery policy is in effect, DRAs can decrypt any encrypted file within the scope of the policy, because every encrypted file includes the DRA's public key. Also, all DRA certificates are cached in the computer's certificate store. By default in a domain environment, the Domain Administrator account on the first domain controller installed is automatically designated as the DRA for the domain. This is set in the EFS recovery policy, and additional DRA accounts can be specified in that policy. To specify the policy in Windows .NET server, open the Policy Editor, and under Computer Configuration navigate to Windows Settings → Security Settings → Public Key Policies → Encrypting File System. Here you may specify additional DRAs for the domain, as shown in Figure 4-12.

CAUTION   By default, no DRAs are specified for stand-alone computers. It is highly recommended to have at least one DRA, in case recovering files is necessary.

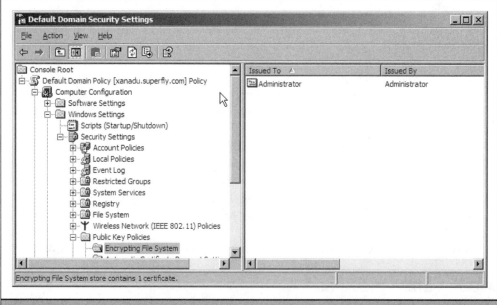

Figure 4-12.   Specifying additional DRA certificates

Unlike in a Windows 2000 environment, with .NET server it is possible to enable EFS without having a designated DRA. However, this must be manually configured, since the Domain Administrator account is automatically set to be a DRA. Note that it is *not* recommended to encrypt files with the DRA account if there is only one DRA—the effectiveness of a DRA would be lost, because the account is both the creator and the DRA.

Export and Import EFS and DRA Certificates and Private Keys

For extra protection against laptop theft or having certificates and private keys otherwise stolen, lost, or corrupted, certificates can be exported to a .cer file, and certificates and private keys can be stored in a password-protected .pfx file.

TIP   For maximum security, when exporting the private keys use strong passwords to protect the .pfx file, securely wipe the exported private keys from the system after export, and make sure to store the exported keys in a physically secure location.

After the private keys are exported, they can be removed from the system for extreme security. In this case, however, it is of paramount importance that the exported keys be physically secure with a strong password and that they are put on reliable media and not misplaced. This is especially true for the DRA accounts, as anyone who obtained the DRA private key could import it and use it to decrypt files.

NOTE: For simplified management and increased security, smart cards can be used as the certificate store, providing a secure and reliable storage media. But you should still test your backups and plan for the worst, remembering that smart cards can be easily lost, stolen, or damaged.

To export certificates, go to the Certificates snap-in, expand the Personal folder, and right-click the certificate to export. Then choose All Tasks → Export. The Certificate Export wizard will appear and guide you through the process of exporting the certificate. The most secure solution is to export the private key and then choose to delete it from the system if successful. This should be the option chosen for the DRA accounts, for maximum security. Do not delete the private key from the user's Windows XP certificate, as then they would have to provide the backup private key every time they wanted to decrypt a file.

The same basic process is followed to import a certificate into the certificate store, choosing All Tasks → Import. The .pfx or .cer file will then have to be provided, along with the password if one was used when the certificate was exported.

Backing Up and Restoring Encrypted Files

Encrypted files remain encrypted when they are backed up and restored. Backup files remain encrypted when transferred across the network or when copied or moved onto any storage medium, including non-NTFS media. If backup files are restored onto a new computer that does not contain the user's profile and the private key needed to decrypt the files, an EFS certificate and private key can be imported.

The integrated Windows XP backup program is accessed through the Start →
Accessories → System Tools menu.

Recovering and Archiving Keys

.NET server offers Certificate Services for key archival and recovery purposes in the
event of lost or damaged keys, or in order for an administrator to assume the role of
a user to access or recover data.

To enable key archiving, on the server the administrator needs to open the Certificate
Templates MMC snap-in. Then go to the properties of the template where you want to
enable archiving. On the Request Handling tab, select the Archive Subject's Encryption
Private Key check box. Then go to the Certificate Authority file, right-click the name of
the Certification Authority and choose Properties. Then click the Recovery Agents tab,
and choose Archive the Key. The keys can then be recovered by using the `Certutil`
`-recoverkey` command line utility.

EFS Recovery Changes in Windows XP

Windows XP fixes a flawed implementation of EFS on Windows 2000. EFS users
on Windows 2000 machines are at risk because their password is not used to encrypt
the EFS certificate's private key. Consider this scenario: A user's machine is stolen. The
thief uses the Ntpasswd utility to change the user's password and then logs on to the
system. This attacker can now access the user's encrypted files. This may seem handy
from a usability standpoint—when a user forgets their password, the administrator
can change it for them, and the user automatically has access to their encrypted files.
However, the security loophole this creates is not worth the convenience.

NOTE This Windows 2000 flaw is not as pronounced in a domain environment, because there the
user's password hash is not stored locally in the SAM but on the domain controllers.

Microsoft recognized this, and uses a new technology in Windows XP called the
Credential Manager, in which the EFS certificate's private key is encrypted with the user's
password. If an administrator changes the user's password, then they will no longer
have access to their encrypted files. The user can regain access to their files by either
using a password-recovery disk, restoring their EFS certificate from a backup, or having
a DRA recover their files for them. The user must remember to recreate their password
recovery disk after each password change. If they don't, the second time they use the
disk they will still be able to log in to the system, but they won't be able to decrypt
their files.

EFS Security Risks

When EFS is enabled, users will rely on it to secure their data. However, a few security
risks still remain. The following sections describe solutions to these risks.

Export EFS Certificates and Private Keys

Mobile users are at the highest risk for losing access to their encrypted master keys, because without a connection to the domain, master keys cannot be automatically backed up. If a disconnected user were to lose access to their master keys, they would be unable to decrypt their data. In the event of a corrupted profile, for example, if an EFS data recovery agent was not configured for the system, the only way to recover the encrypted files would be to use a floppy disk that the user had previously exported their EFS certificates and private keys to.

Export and Remove Private Keys

As described previously, export the private keys for the recovery accounts and recovery certificates, store the media in a safe location, and remove the private keys from the system. That way, in the case of a system being stolen, the attacker would not be able to use the recovery account to decrypt files.

Unencrypted Data Stored in Paging or Hibernation File

When encrypted files are decrypted by the operating system for use by users, the unencrypted contents of the files may be written to the system paging file. The pagefile.sys cannot be encrypted, so measures must be taken to ensure that the unencrypted data cannot be recovered by unauthorized users. Access to the paging file data is possible on any Windows system by booting the system with another operating system, thus bypassing the local system security. The same situation occurs if hibernation is enabled on the system—which is more likely on a portable PC—and unencrypted data is stored in the hibernation storage file.

To eliminate these vulnerabilities, the following two actions should be taken:

- Hibernation mode should be disabled. In Control Panel, choose Power Options, click the Hibernate tab, and clear the Enable Hibernation check box.

- System Policy should be configured to clear the virtual memory pagefile upon system shutdown, a setting available through the Security Settings UI, as discussed in Chapter 1.

Encrypt the My Documents Folder

It is a good idea for EFS users to encrypt the My Documents folder, so that newly created files and temporary files are encrypted by default.

Encrypt Folders, Not Files

Encrypting folders rather than individual files ensures that no confidential data is ever stored on the file system unencrypted. This also catches temporary files, so that they are encrypted when file access occurs.

CHALLENGE

Jim, the security administrator at Big Movie Corporation, was very strict and thorough with security. He had pushed down strict security settings to all of his users through group policies, implemented EFS through his Windows XP network, and taught users to encrypt sensitive files for enhanced security. Jim's users did not complain about using encryption, as it was built into the operating system and did not require much extra effort to use.

Harry, an executive at BMC, frequently traveled the globe to meet with writers, directors, and actors that worked with his company. Harry used EFS to encrypt his sensitive files, especially the new movie scripts at BMC, which were the most guarded of the company's secrets.

One day, Harry was at the airport, on his way home from a particularly long business trip. He placed his laptop on the airport's X-ray machine and was about to proceed through the metal detector when the person in front of him set off the detector several times. It seemed like no matter how many objects the man pulled from his pockets, the metal detector still kept squealing. "What more can happen on this trip?" Harry thought. Finally, airport security took the man aside and manually swept his person with a wand. However, when Harry got to the other side of the detector, his bag was nowhere to be found. He had been too tired to remember to make sure there was no one in front of him when he placed the bag with his laptop on the conveyor belt.

Jim was upset to hear of the laptop loss, but confident in his security scheme. With all the encryption and safeguards he used, the thief might be able to sell the laptop for parts but would not be able to get any company secrets off of it.

Several months went by without incident, until one day Harry angrily strode into Jim's office. "What do you think of this?" Harry asked, slamming down the entertainment section of the newspaper. On the front page, Jim read about the new movie that was being released by their chief competitor, Star Light Movies. It was a new action adventure flick, which didn't seem out of the ordinary until Harry said, "It's the same movie that we're supposed to come out with this summer." Star Light had used BMC's script. How did they get a hold of it?

Although Jim was having all of his users use EFS encryption, he had neglected to enable an important Security Option in the domain security policy setting described in Chapter 1: "Shutdown: Clear virtual memory pagefile." The thief had used forensic tools to recover the script in the pagefile of the computer and had sold it to Star Light.

Only Use the Recovery Account for Recovery

Encrypting files with the recovery account can be disastrous because if the private keys are lost there would be no way to recover the data.

Alternatives to EFS

With all its features, EFS can be complicated to implement effectively. Some non-Microsoft programs exist to encrypt data, but they generally lack enterprise-level management features and Group Policy integration. These programs include PGP from Network Associates, although it is no longer being actively developed. Some other solutions include SecurStar's DriveCrypt (http://www.drivecrypt.com) and Jetico's BestCrypt (http://www.jetico.com). Because of their lack of integration within Windows XP, these programs generally take more effort to use on a daily basis—and, of course, will require added cost over and above your operating system purchase.

FILE SHARING

File shares are the means by which Windows users access files on remote systems. They are easy to set up but can be dangerous if not secured. File-sharing capabilities are provided by the SMB/CIFS (Server Message Block/Common Internet File System) protocols. If you are concerned about files being transferred across your network in clear text via SMB, you should use IPSec to protect them.

Windows XP introduces Simple File Sharing, which is important to understand. Also, system administrators should know how to audit the file shares that are available on their network and how to turn off unnecessary file sharing.

Simple File Sharing

By default in stand-alone mode (not joined to a domain), Windows XP Professional uses the same method of sharing files as XP Home—Simple File Sharing. This method of sharing files is not secure and should be avoided. To disable Simple File Sharing, in Windows Explorer choose Tools → Folder Options →View. In the Advanced Settings, scroll down to the bottom, where you will find the "Use simple file sharing" check box, and clear it, as shown in Figure 4-13. If you're using simple file sharing, you're sharing files without passwords or permissions. After you clear the check box, then sharing will be back to the way you remember it in Windows 2000.

NOTE When your Windows XP computers are joined to a domain Simple File Sharing is automatically disabled, along with Fast User Switching.

Looking for Shares

File shares give Windows XP systems the ability to let users connect to machines and access files. File sharing in Windows XP works like it did in Windows 2000. To share a folder, right-click it and choose Sharing and Security, and then pick Share This Folder. You will then be able to give a name to the folder share. To access this folder from the network, users can use the UNC format *machinename**sharename* to either map a drive letter to the share or access it directly.

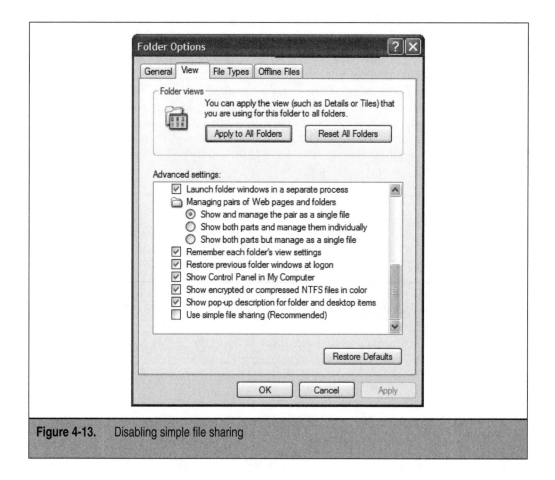

Figure 4-13. Disabling simple file sharing

Permissions can also be set on shares, but they will intersect with NTFS permissions to define the effective permissions a user has to a file, even when accessing it through a share. The share permissions do not have any meaning when a user is accessing files locally on the machine (not through the share). Share permissions are either Full Control, Change, or Read. A user's effective permissions consist of their most restrictive share permission plus their least restrictive NTFS permissions. So if you have full permissions on the share, and the user belongs to one group with NTFS read permissions and another group with NTFS read-write permissions, the effective permissions for that user are read-write. Rights can never exceed the user rights placed on the share, so if you had a share with read-only permissions and NTFS permissions of Full Control, the user would have read-only access to the files within the share. The only caveat here is that explicit Deny rights trump all other rights. So, a Full Control share with a user who had explicit Deny rights to the files and directories in that share would have no access.

Have you ever audited your network, looking for file shares? That's what an attacker would do once they gained access through your network's outer defenses. Don't think

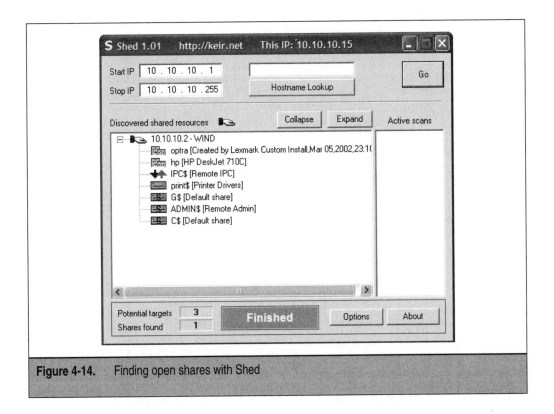

Figure 4-14. Finding open shares with Shed

that putting a $ after your share name will hide them from attackers, either. There are several free tools that can be used to query your network for open shares. One such program is the very fast Shed tool, by Robin Keir (http://www.keir.net), shown in Figure 4-14.

The simple Net.exe program is still around in Windows XP, and by issuing a Net View command, for example, you will be able to see nonhidden shares on your network.

Shadow Copy Restore

A new feature slated to arrive with .NET server is Shadow Copy Restore. This feature is not enabled on shares by default, but it can be activated to give users the ability to immediately restore previous versions of files or folders, at the expense of disk space. Shadow Copy is convenient in that users will no longer have to wait while the administrator retrieves a backup copy of a lost file from tape. This is because enabling Shadow Copy turns on a checkpoint backup feature, which stores a certain number of the older file versions in the background. As modifications are made, users can revert to an old (previous checkpoint) version of a file through Windows Explorer. To turn on Shadow Copy, right-click the folder, choose Properties, and go to the Shadow Copies tab, shown in Figure 4-15.

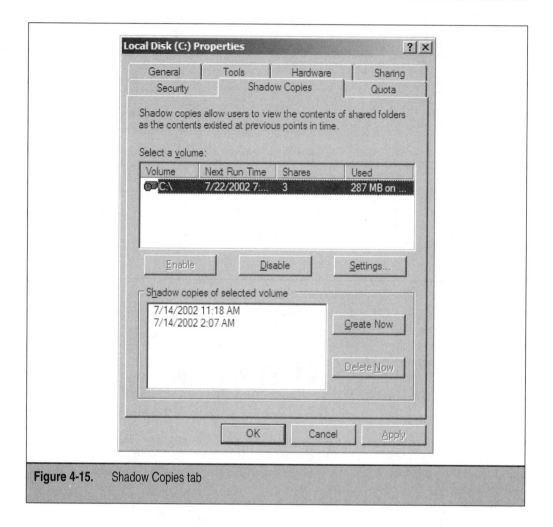

Figure 4-15.   Shadow Copies tab

By default, the system will take shadow copies of the data twice a day, but that can be changed. Shadow Copy is convenient because users will be able to see what previous versions of files exist for them to restore, and they can complete the restoration procedure themselves through Windows Explorer without contacting an administrator.

TOOLS OF THE TRADE

We have discussed a number of built-in tools that you can use to secure your file systems. Windows XP and Windows .Net have provided enhancements in the areas of encryption and access controls, and you should take advantage of these features.

Cipher.exe   This utility lets you display or alter the encryption status of directories or files on NTFS partitions. It's handy to use from scripts. The `cipher /u` option lets you re-encrypt all files on a local drive when changing to a new certificate.

Syskey.exe   You can modify Syskey protection to further increase the security of your system. Choose to store the startup key either on the system or on a floppy disk that must be provided at system startup. Make sure to use a strong password. Type **syskey** from the command prompt to use it.

Net.exe   Net.exe has been built in since Windows NT. The `net share` option shows, adds, or deletes local shares, and `net view` lists remote shares. Net.exe is another handy command line utility that can be scripted. There are many additional options as noted throughout this book. Type **net** by itself at the command line to see available options.

Cacls.exe and Xcacls.exe   Cacls.exe, which was introduced in Windows NT, will let you change ACL permissions on files from the command line. To see the various options just run these commands in a command window.

This utility is handy when you need to script file permissions changes in a batch file or logon script. The Xcacls.exe command line tool from the Windows XP Support Tools does the same thing, but has the `/y` option, to automatically answer the "Are you sure?" confirmation.

Without any switches, Cacls.exe will show the current ACLs on a file:

```
C:\>cacls test2.txt
C:\test2.txt BUILTIN\Administrators:F
             NT AUTHORITY\SYSTEM:F
             STARSHIP\Tomlee:F
             BUILTIN\Users:R
```

NOTE   Make sure to use the `/e` switch if you want to add to the current ACL instead of replacing it.

The next listing uses the `/e` parameter to keep the current ACLs and then the `/g` parameter to add or change permissions to the CORPXPPRO\tomlee account:

```
C:\>cacls test2.txt /e /g CORPXPPRO\tomlee:C
processed file: C:\test2.txt

C:\>cacls test2.txt
C:\test2.txt BUILTIN\Administrators:F
             NT AUTHORITY\SYSTEM:F
             STARSHIP\Tomlee:F
             BUILTIN\Users:R
             CORPXPPRO\tomlee:C
```

CHECKLIST: FILE SYSTEM SECURITY

File system security is a large factor in the overall security posture of any computer. In Windows this includes NTFS file and folder permissions, share permissions, and encryption of sensitive files. Planning your Encrypting File System is crucial, as this chapter has shown; you need to consider such things as the recovery agent, temporary files, and offline storage of the private keys.

The following checklist highlights some of the key points made throughout this chapter:

- ☐ Always use NTFS.
- ☐ Understand and check permissions on created files to delegate only the permissions needed, and nothing more.
- ☐ Use file and folder auditing where it makes sense.
- ☐ Secure critical programs.
- ☐ Implement EFS for maximum file protection.
- ☐ Use smart cards for authentication and certificate/private key stores, or else export private keys and remove them from systems.
- ☐ Utilize data recovery agents in EFS.
- ☐ Don't create files with the recovery agent account.
- ☐ Clear the system pagefile with the security option mentioned in Chapter 1.
- ☐ Enable Syskey startup protection, using the appropriate method (integrated, password, or startup disk) for your environment.
- ☐ Encrypt the My Documents folder.
- ☐ Disable Simple File Sharing.
- ☐ Audit your network for shares and remove unnecessary ones.

CHAPTER 5

Operating System Enhancements

There are numerous enhancements in Windows XP Professional edition that have made security easier to implement on a granular level. Some of these enhancements take the place of third-party security tools that may have been necessary with older versions of the Windows operating system.

In Chapter 1, we covered security policies, and in Chapter 4 we covered the file system, so we will only briefly reiterate some of those topics. We will cover in detail the following:

- New functionality provided by Windows XP Professional
- New services that enable security or need to be restricted
- Utilization of event logs for auditing
- Accessing system information

NEW SECURITY FEATURES

Windows XP has numerous new security features. Many of these features are discussed throughout this book, including new restrictions for anonymous users, new restrictions for network and console logons, new ACL defaults, and much more. It shouldn't be difficult for you to quickly comprehend the new changes mentioned in this section. One key aspect of security to keep in mind is that some features change when you are connected to a domain, as opposed to working in a stand-alone or workgroup setting. The polices discussed in Chapter 1 will significantly affect your system both locally and when you are part of a domain. Also, using group policy objects (GPOs) gives you the greatest control of enterprise-wide security.

Fast User Switching

A very handy feature of Windows XP and .NET is the ability to switch user accounts without having to log off the current user. If the computer is part of a workgroup, then this feature can be enabled; however, Fast User Switching is not (yet) supported in a domain. To turn Fast User Switching on or off, in Control Panel → User Accounts, select "Change the way users log on or off." From here, you can clear the Use Fast User Switching check box.

NOTE   Fast User Switching will not work with offline folders. Fast User Switching also cannot be enabled if the computer is part of a domain.

As the administrator, you can log off other users on the system by running Task Manager (Taskmgr.exe) and selecting the Users tab. Remember that as the administrator, you have to set the Fast User Switching service to Automatic.

CAUTION   If you have Fast User Switching turned on and you audit logon events, you will get numerous failures in your Security Log. Windows XP will try to log on for all users on the Welcome screen when switching users, and generate a failure event.

Internet Connection Firewall (ICF)

The Windows XP Professional product provides basic built-in firewall features. Whether you are using a broadband connection, VPN, or dial-up connectivity, you can protect the connection using ICF. ICF functionality is discussed in detail in Chapter 8.

Shared Documents Folder

The Shared Documents folder is considered by most to be more of a security hazard than a feature. If there are multiple users on the same computer in a workgroup, the Shared Documents folder will enable them to share documents with one another. While users can each have their own My Documents folder, which can be restricted with a password, the Shared Documents folder gives all users on the system a central place to share files.

Microsoft does not provide a way to remove the Shared Documents folder through the GUI, but most administrators will want to remove it altogether for Windows XP computers in the enterprise. This can be easily done by deleting a subkey. In this registry key

```
HKLM\SOFTWARE\Microsoft\Windows\CurrentVersion\Explorer\
My Computer\NameSpace\DelegateFolders
```

delete the subkey:

```
{59031a47-3f72-44a7-89c5-5595fe6b30ee}
```

SECURITY ENHANCEMENTS IN WINDOWS XP PROFESSIONAL

Many of the "new" security features in Windows XP are really enhancements to those in the Windows 2000. Windows XP Professional's security enhancements give more granular control to both you, the administrator, and to the end user, as discussed in the sections that follow.

Certificate Services

Certificate Services can allow one of your internal Windows 2000/.NET servers to act as a Certification Authority (CA). Windows XP Professional supports offline and online Certificate Authorities. The public key certificates are stored in a personal certificate store, usually by user profile in Documents and Settings*username*\\ApplicationData\\ Microsoft\\SystemCertificates\\My\\Certificates.

Roaming profiles can be set up to access server resources for mobile users. Certificates can be stored on the server so that when a user logs in from a different computer, they will have access to their stored certificate information. If you want to restrict users from using roaming profiles, you can do so by changing the option with Gpedit.msc under Local Computer Policy → Computer Configuration → Administrative Templates → System/User Profiles → Only Allow Local User Profiles.

Each user's private keys for cryptographic service providers (CSPs) are stored in their user profile, in C:\\Documents and Settings*username*\\Application Data\\Microsoft\\ Crypto\\RSA. Application Data is hidden by default. When a user switches computers in a domain, the private key can be stored in the RSA folder on the domain controller. The keys stored in this directory will allow the user access to the key as they move between computers and log into the domain. Wherever the user logs on, the key will be downloaded and used until the user logs off.

Private keys in the RSA folder are encrypted. The user's master key (which is automatically generated and 64 bytes in length) is generated by a random number generator, which is then used to encrypt the private keys.

User Certificate Autoenrollment

User certificate autoenrollment was introduced in Windows 2000, but it has been improved in Windows XP to provide applications with a more convenient means of using Certificate Services. The autoenrollment function can be enabled through Group Policy and Active Directory to provide for smart card enrollment. Using autoenrollment, a user can manually or automatically request a certificate from a Windows .NET Server CA or a Windows 2000 CA. Once approved by an administrator, the autoenrollment function will install the certificate automatically.

Internet Connection Sharing (ICS)

ICS is used to share one Internet connection among multiple computers. It makes routing traffic through one gateway and setting up a small network very simple. The host computer running ICS broadcasts its information using UPnP and uses DHCP to give out IP addresses for other systems on the network. ICS will be discussed in detail in Chapter 8.

Smart Card Support

Smart card support has been embedded in Windows 2000 and Windows XP/.NET. Smart cards can be used to store such information as certificates and private keys and to perform functions such as authentication, digital signing, and key exchange. Smart cards must meet ISO 7816-1, 7816-2, and 7816-3 standards to work with Windows 2000/ XP/.NET. A number of drivers are already included with Windows 2000/XP/.NET.

The two services associated with smart card functionality are Smart Card and Smart Card Helper.

Smart cards authenticate to a domain by interactive logon using the Active Directory service. Remote logon uses a public key certificate with the Extensible Authentication Protocol (EAP) and Transport Layer Security (TLS). And client authentication is accomplished by mapping a public key certificate to an Active Directory account. By using smart cards to authenticate to the domain, you will have access to your domain resources.

Smart card login to a network uses Active Directory and Kerberos v5 protocol authentication. It will not work with local account login. Users can have certificates assigned by administrators using autoenrollment and stored on a smart card, which can then be used to verify the user's identity at log-in time.

Smart card support has been greatly enhanced with Windows XP/NET. For example, Windows .NET Terminal server logins, Runas.exe, and Net.exe all now support smart cards. The net command looks like this:

```
net use [devicename | *] [\\computername\sharename[\volume] [password | *]] /smartcard
```

Administrators should make a practice of logging into their workstations as a normal user and executing the runas.exe command to launch specific processes like Cmd.exe and Compmgmt.msc with administrative privileges. Logging in as a normal user enables you to execute most programs with limited privileges (like Outlook and Internet Explorer), thereby limiting the amount of damage they can do should they be infected with malicious code.

Using smart cards for Windows .NET Terminal Server authentication can greatly increase security for your critical and Internet-facing systems. By implementing smart card logins, you keep attackers from using brute-force logins or guessing passwords.

A useful tool for validating a smart card is Dsstore.exe, available in the Windows 2000 Resource Kit. Just type **dsstore.exe /checksc** to validate the certificate on your smart card.

SECURITY CONFIGURATION AND ANALYSIS SNAP-IN

This MMC snap-in has been carried over from Windows 2000. The Security Configuration and Analysis (SCA) tool is designed to do any of the following three things:

- Configure the gamut of security options for the computer (security policies, registry keys, and file/folder ACLs, to name a few)

- Compare a computer's security configuration against a security template (.INF file)

- Apply a security template (.INF file)

The SCA snap-in provides an incredible amount of control over the security configuration of the computer. You can use any of the security templates included with Windows to either compare or configure the security settings of your computer. Security templates are designed as plain ASCII text files that can be edited with notepad. The preinstalled templates are located in C:\WINDOWS\Security\templates, and are denoted with a .INF file extension. By opening one of these files, you can easily see how configuration options are categorized to include the following:

- Account Policies
- Local Policies
- Event Log
- Restricted Groups
- System Services
- Registry access permissions
- File System access permissions
- Registry key values (although these don't show up in the SCA GUI)

All of these categories show up in the GUI as well, except for the registry key values, which are only contained in the template file. But rest assured, when you apply a template, these registry values get set as well!

One of the most fundamental uses of the SCA is to analyze the configuration of a computer to see how the computer settings match up to the security template settings. You first access SCA through Start → Run → MMC → Console → Add/Remove Snap-in, and then add the Security Configuration and Analysis snap-in. The first thing you need to do is create a database by right-clicking the Security Configuration and Analysis container and selecting Open Database. You can type in any name you want, and you will then be prompted to select a template file to use as the security baseline. You can browse to the templates included with Windows in the C:\Windows\Security\templates directory. The last thing you need to do is select the path for the error log, which actually stores detailed information about the analysis the SCA tool performs.

The database has two functions. First, it stores the baseline configuration settings in the security template; then, it stores the actual corresponding configurations of your computer. Once your database is set up, one of the first things you do is right-click the SCA container and select Analyze Computer Now. Your computer's settings will then be compared against the security template.

Let's put this tool to work by using an imaginary security template from NIST, NSA, SANS, and CIS called the Windows XP Gold Standard (although the template will probably be a reality one day). Figure 5-1 shows the results after comparing a default build of Windows XP against this template.

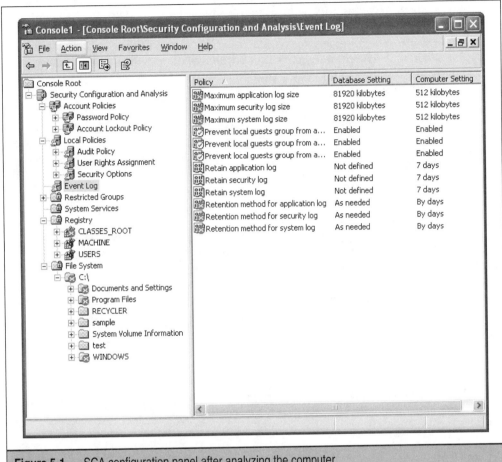

Figure 5-1.   SCA configuration panel after analyzing the computer

In particular the computer's Event Log settings differ heavily from those defined in the security template. Quite simply, a red circle with a white X denotes where a computer setting differs from that of the security template. A white circle with a green checkmark indicates that the computer setting matches up directly that of the template. Where there is no icon, it means that the setting was "Not defined" in the template, and hence could not be used for a comparison. You can see this by looking at the two columns titled Database Setting and Computer Setting. The Database Setting column holds the configuration defined in the template and will state "Not defined" when a setting simply was not configured in the template.

At this point, you can modify settings in the database if you want. When you do, it affects neither your computer setting nor the security template; it only changes the setting in the database. For example, you can modify each individual setting manually by double-clicking it. The changes are automatically written to the database. Of course, once you decide to select Configure Computer Now, all of the settings stored in the database will be applied.

Let's continue by applying the configuration stored in the database (remember this was originally obtained from the security template file). To do so, right-click Security Configuration and Analysis and select Configure Computer Now. Once your hard disk has finished churning, you can then use the Analyze Computer Now option to check the database settings with the actual computer settings again. As shown in Figure 5-2, you will now see that each of the Event Log settings has a circle with a green check mark, meaning that each Computer Setting item matches up perfectly with the corresponding Database Setting item.

If you have multiple computers to set up, you can create your own security template .INF file and apply this template to each computer. You can configure security options of your choice in SCA, export the template, and import it onto other computers by right-clicking Security Configuration and Analysis. Even better, you can create a GPO (group policy object) and import the .INF file by right-clicking Security Settings and selecting Import Policy. The GPO can then be easily applied to an entire organizational unit or domain in Active Directory.

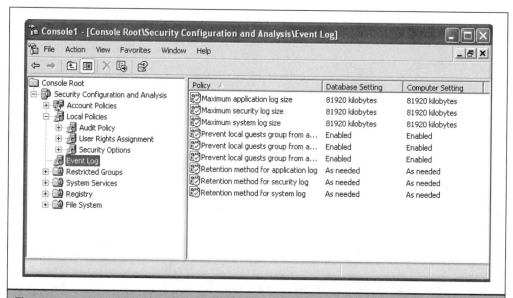

Figure 5-2.   Event Log settings after applying the security template stored in the database

CHALLENGE

The installation of a new Windows XP Professional system for your corporate users has been mandated by your CIO. What you haven't been told is exactly how you must secure these systems or what parameters to follow. The first questions you must address include

- How in-depth should your security stance be?
- What services should you have running on the end users' desktops?
- How do you restrict users from modifying their systems?

As you should know by now, it's better to have strong security up front than to have to retrofit a large environment with security. Corporate desktops contain a wealth of information that is not stored on servers, and end users' desktops need to be protected as much as servers.

Open services are the death of any server, and the same holds true for desktops. Lock down the desktop services and you won't have to worry as much about the end user being hacked up by some virus or some internal attacker.

By limiting the functionality of the end user on the system and removing their access to powerful system utilities, you will better control the damage they can do to their own system and minimize your maintenance headaches.

SERVICES

The Services options have been expanded in Windows XP. You get better descriptions of what services are and their dependencies. Unfortunately, there are even more services for you to worry about. About 78 services are installed by default on a typical installation of Windows XP Professional—sometimes more, in certain OEM installations. Although not all are running, the list of those services that are running can seem excessive. As usual, it is generally better to keep services disabled and enable them only when necessary. See the appendix to this book for recommended settings for each of these services.

 SECURITY ALERT   In the appendix you will notice that we recommend that many services be disabled. The general rule is that you should turn off anything you are not using. For example, disable SSDP if you really don't need it. It listens on port 5000 and looks for UPnP devices. SSDP allows clients to discover network services by providing for multicast discovery support. There have already been known problems associated with UPnP involving a remotely exploitable buffer overflow attack, a denial of service attack, and a distributed denial of service attack. Although Microsoft has addressed these issues with a patch, we still recommend disabling any unneeded service.

You can access the services listing through Start → Control Panel → Administrative Tools → Services, or by running Services.msc. A great command line tool is Sclist.exe from the Windows 2000 Resource Kit. Sclist.exe works locally and remotely to show you a readable list of all services on a computer and their current state—Running, Stopped, Paused, or otherwise.

We recommend that you follow most of the settings in the appendix to secure the basic services that are running, and then begin to enable services on an as-needed basis. For example, you will want to enable Remote Desktop Help Session so you can use Remote Assistance. Likewise, enabling Windows Image Acquisition would help users extract images from cameras with native Windows software. And, as you will learn in Chapter 9, wireless can be made secure, and enabling the Wireless Zero Configuration service is useful for automatically configuring wireless security.

Command Line Service Control

If you're a command line fanatic, you can see which services are running in each process using the command `tasklist /svc` as shown in the following output:

```
C:\>tasklist /svc
Image Name                   PID Services
========================================================================
System Idle Process            0 N/A
System                         4 N/A
SMSS.EXE                     376 N/A
CSRSS.EXE                    476 N/A
WINLOGON.EXE                 560 N/A
SERVICES.EXE                 604 Eventlog, PlugPlay
LSASS.EXE                    616 NtLmSsp, PolicyAgent, SamSs
SVCHOST.EXE                  788 RpcSs
SVCHOST.EXE                  916 AudioSrv, Browser, CryptSvc, Dhcp,
                                 dmserver, EventSystem, helpsvc,
                                 lanmanserver, lanmanworkstation,
                                 Netman, Nla, RasMan, Schedule,
                                 SENS, SharedAccess, ShellHWDetection,
                                 srservice, TapiSrv, Themes,
                                 uploadmgr, W32Time, winmgmt,
                                 WmdmPmSp, wuauserv, WZCSVC
SVCHOST.EXE                 1096 Dnscache
SVCHOST.EXE                 1152 LmHosts, SSDPSRV, WebClient
SPOOLSV.EXE                 1252 Spooler
MSDTC.EXE                   1496 MSDTC
```

To see which services are listening on open TCP and UDP ports, execute the command **netstat -ano** at the command line. The output looks like this:

```
C:\>netstat -ano
Active Connections
```

Proto	Local Address	Foreign Address	State	PID
TCP	0.0.0.0:21	0.0.0.0:0	LISTENING	1772
TCP	0.0.0.0:135	0.0.0.0:0	LISTENING	788
TCP	0.0.0.0:445	0.0.0.0:0	LISTENING	4
TCP	0.0.0.0:1025	0.0.0.0:0	LISTENING	916
TCP	0.0.0.0:1026	0.0.0.0:0	LISTENING	1496
TCP	0.0.0.0:1032	0.0.0.0:0	LISTENING	1772
TCP	0.0.0.0:1033	0.0.0.0:0	LISTENING	4
TCP	0.0.0.0:1801	0.0.0.0:0	LISTENING	292
TCP	0.0.0.0:2103	0.0.0.0:0	LISTENING	292
TCP	0.0.0.0:2105	0.0.0.0:0	LISTENING	292
TCP	0.0.0.0:2107	0.0.0.0:0	LISTENING	292
TCP	0.0.0.0:3449	0.0.0.0:0	LISTENING	3716
TCP	0.0.0.0:3452	0.0.0.0:0	LISTENING	3716
TCP	0.0.0.0:5000	0.0.0.0:0	LISTENING	1152

As you can see, the new Windows XP version of Netstat.exe now maps the listening port to a PID. This is extremely useful information that could previously be found only in tools like Foundstone's Fport.exe (http://www.foundstone.com). Netstat still leaves you wanting more, however, wishing that the PID would just be resolved to the actual process name. Otherwise you just have to look up the PID yourself with another tool like Tasklist.exe!

One way you can check services that should be started automatically is to change the settings of all services to Manual. Once you reboot, the services that need to be started will be started regardless and those that are not absolutely needed will not be started. You can then check which services were started and which were not, and change those not started to Disabled. Be careful not to disable a service that the system depends on.

You can use the command line program Sc.exe to interact with services locally or on remote machines. This program was previously included in the Windows 2000 Resource Kit, and now comes installed with Windows XP. You can perform functions such as starting or stopping a service, modifying or creating a service, and querying a service for information. In the output below, we are querying the Messenger service, and we see that it is stopped.

```
C:\>sc query messenger
SERVICE_NAME: messenger
        TYPE               : 20  WIN32_SHARE_PROCESS
        STATE              : 1   STOPPED(NOT_STOPPABLE,
                                 NOT_PAUSABLE,IGNORES_SHUTDOWN)
        WIN32_EXIT_CODE    : 1077          (0x435)
        SERVICE_EXIT_CODE  : 0   (0x0)
        CHECKPOINT         : 0x0
        WAIT_HINT          : 0x0
```

Typing just **sc query** at the command line will give you this output for every installed service on the computer.

Setting Permissions on Services

As an administrator, you may have wondered how you can give a certain user or group rights to control a service. Other than for domain-based Group Policy, there is no direct interface available in Windows NT/2000/XP/.NET for actually setting permissions on a service. Say, for example, that you want your normal Users group to be able to stop and start the Print Spooler service in case they have a hung print job. Well, by default Windows XP does not provide the Users group with permissions to stop and start the Spooler service. Or maybe you want to deny Everyone including Administrators the right to start the Server service. There is a way to assign these types of permissions. Although it seems roundabout, it can be done through the Security Configuration and Analysis snap-in.

NOTE   A command line tool called Gsd.exe is available from Arne Vidstrom at http://www.ntsecurity.nu. This tool will get the security permissions for any service and display them by user or group.

The MMC Security Configuration and Analysis snap-in discussed earlier can be used to apply security settings to services. You first create a database with the MMC and use a template of security setting to base your settings. A security template can be used to change permissions for users. To set up security of services based on users, perform the following steps:

1. Select Start → Run and type **MMC**.

2. From the Console menu, select Add/Remove Snap-in → Add.

3. Select the Security Configuration and Analysis snap-in, click Add → Close → OK.

4. In the MMC, right-click the Security Configuration and Analysis item, click Open Database, and name the database to create a new database.

5. Select a security template to import; you can modify it later.

6. In the MMC, right-click the Security Configuration and Analysis item, click the Analyze Computer Now option, and save the file somewhere.

7. Once the file is saved, double-click System Services, right-click a service, select Properties → "Define this policy in the database" → Automatic, and then click Security.

8. Click Edit Security, and then add user accounts and modify permissions.

9. Apply the settings by right-clicking Security Configuration and Analysis item and selecting Configure Computer Now. This will update the system with the permissions you have set.

SSDP and UPnP Discovery Host were disabled in the service listing, but a regular user can configure the startup options, recovery options, and even the logon context of these services, and then re-enable them. Figure 5-3 shows an example of this type of service modification.

> **NOTE** An even easier way to apply permissions to services is through an Active Directory–based group policy object. In a domain or OU GPO, there is a container for Services, which lets you simply double-click a service to edit the permissions for groups to start, stop, or have full control of it.

After you have selected the user and added permissions to the user, the service permissions for that user would look like Figure 5-4.

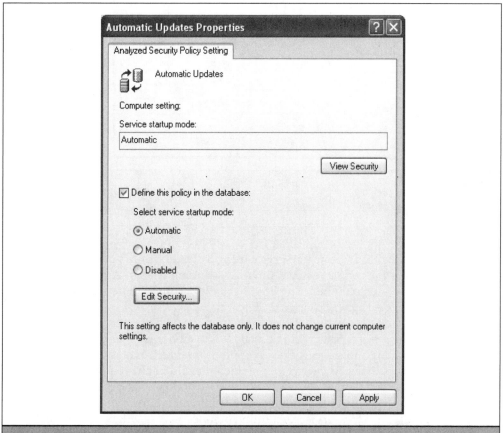

Figure 5-3.   Accessing the properties of the Automatic Updates service

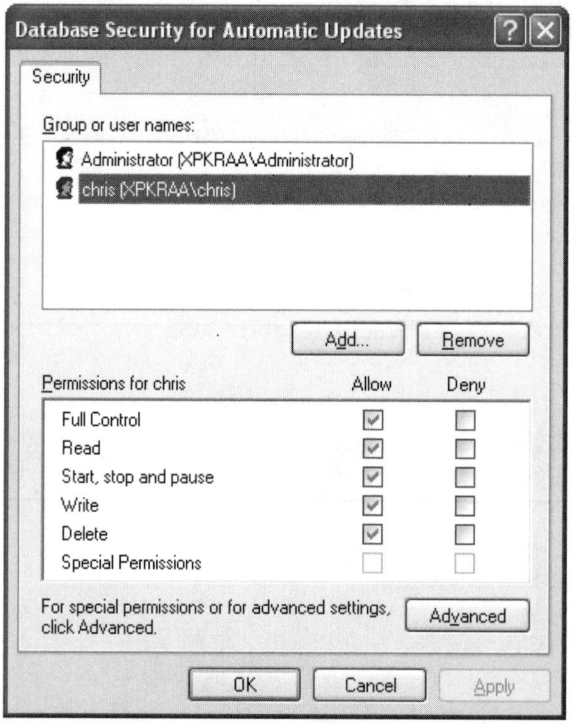

Figure 5-4. Modifying the service to restrict to two users

You can see in Figure 5-5 how the service list will appear before you use Configure Computer Now. As you can see, several services, including Alerter, Automatic Updates, and Clipbook, have been modified. The Investigate flag is on for these services. Once you apply the changes, this flag will change to "OK."

In addition to adding a group with specific permissions to a service, you can audit the use of the service. Select Edit Security when modifying a service; then select Advanced → Auditing, and select the audit options you need, as shown in Figure 5-6.

If a user attempts to modify a service to which they do not have permission, then they will get an "access denied" message. When you modify a service to give users access rights, by default Administrators, Power Users, and Authenticated Users will have rights to start and stop services. Auditing of failed events will be turned on by default as well.

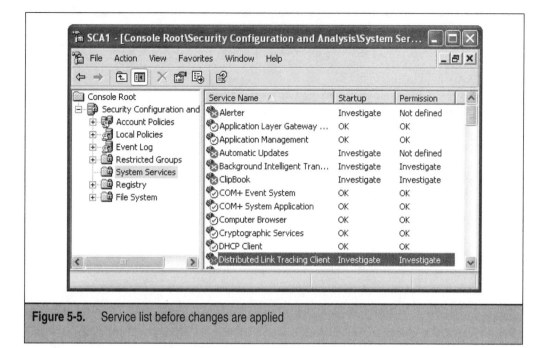

Figure 5-5.   Service list before changes are applied

EVENT LOGS

Logging has been improved in Windows XP. The Event Viewer is used to view system information and notify you of any problems and security violations that the system has the ability to monitor. The three standard event logs are Application, Security, and System. Usually these will be stored in %SystemRoot%\System32\Config as the AppEvent.evt, SecEvent.evt, and SysEvent.evt files. Each log is responsible for the following:

- **Application Log**   Contains information logged by programs. Each program has its own error events. These will be recorded in the log if logging is turned on for applications.

- **Security Log**   Security-related events will be recorded here. If you have auditing turned on, the audit events will be written to this log. This log records information such as failed login attempts. If you have enabled object access auditing for specific NTFS files or even registry keys, the access events will be recorded in the Security event log.

- **System Log**   Events of system components, such as services and drivers, are sent to this log.

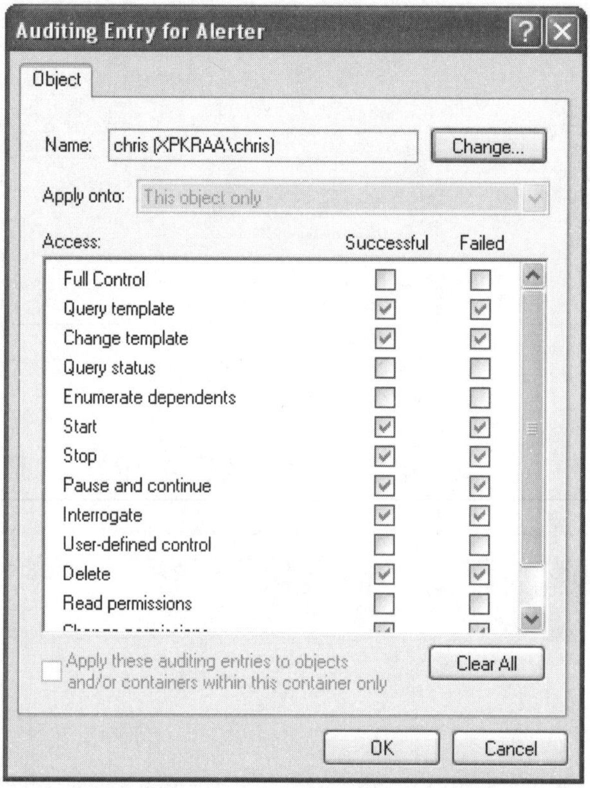

Figure 5-6. Audit options for an individual service

The Event Log service must be running for logging to take place. You probably want to set its startup mode to Automatic, which is the default. You can access the Event Viewer through Start → Control Panel → Administrative Tools → Event Viewer, or by running Eventvwr.msc, as shown in Figure 5-7.

You can view each event detail by clicking on the event, as shown in Figure 5-8. You can copy the event by clicking the Copy button in the Properties window. Each event has the following information: Date, Time, Type, User, Computer, Source, Category, Event ID, and Description. Events are categorized by type: Information, Warning, or Error (see Figure 5-7). You can search through the events using the Find or Filter menu option.

You can manage the size of the log files. By default they are set to 512KB. This is too small for most logs, as newer events will overwrite older events. To change the size and overwrite options, right-click Event Log, select Properties, and set the size.

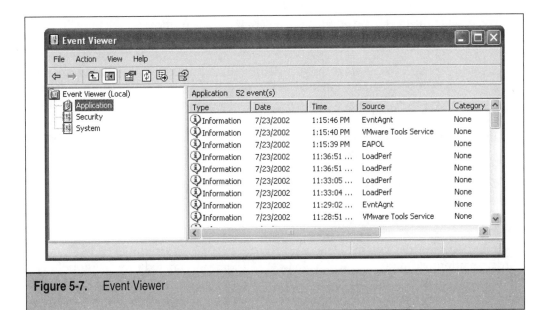

Figure 5-7. Event Viewer

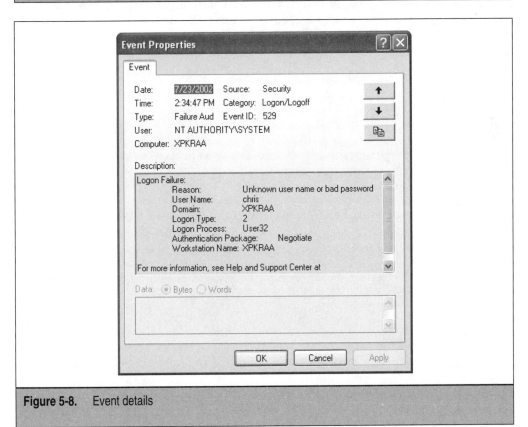

Figure 5-8. Event details

You can change the overwrite options to Never Overwrite or increase the time limit to overwrite. You can also save the log to a file using the Save Log File As option and start a new log.

You will probably never want the security log of critical systems to overwrite itself. You should save it periodically and start a new security log. In the Security Log, you should always check on event IDs 529 "Unknown user or bad password," 680 "Account logon," and 517 "Security Log Cleared."

For most systems, your setting on log files should be the following, at a minimum:

- **Application Log**   Max Log Size (80MB), "Overwrite Events as needed"
- **Security Log**   Max Log Size (80MB), "Do Not Overwrite Events (save manually before they are full and clear)"
- **System Log**   Max Log Size (80MB), "Overwrite Events as needed"

Setting the Security Log to "Do Not Overwrite Events" will definitely add to the burden of administration. You will have to set up some automated process (hopefully not manual!) for saving and clearing the log before it is full. Using tools like Elogdmp.exe (from the Windows 2000 Resource Kit) and Elsave.exe, you can dump the contents of a local or remote event log to a file and clear the log. For example, Elogdmp.exe will dump the contents of any event log to the screen in comma-delimited format. By redirecting the output, you can easily save it to a file using the greater than symbol (>), as in the following example:

```
Elogdmp.exe computername system >  syslog.txt
```

Elsave.exe can then be used to clear the local or remote log. You can easily script these tools together to set up an automated process that will dump and clear the security event logs of your critical systems.

You can also change the path where the event logs are stored. Go to Start → Run → **regedit** and modify the following registry keys:

- **System Log** HKLM\System\CurrentControlSet\Services\ EventLog\System. Select the file and change to your desired path.
- **Application Log** HKLM\System\CurrentControlSet\Services\ EventLog\Application. Select the file and change to your desired path.
- **Security Log** HKLM\System\CurrentControlSet\Services\ EventLog\Security. Select the file and change to your desired path.

EVENT TRIGGERS

You can create Event Triggers to launch a program when an event occurs in the logs. Using the new Windows XP command line program Eventtriggers.exe, you can run commands based on activity in the log files. You can create, delete, or query triggers.

The output of a trigger that executes the Task Manager every time an error occurs in the System Log is shown here:

```
C:\>eventtriggers /create /tr "Taskmanager Execution" /L System
/t ERROR /tk c:\windows\system32\taskmgr.exeSUCCESS: The Event Trigger
"Taskmanager Execution" has been created.
```

Another way to gather Event Log information from the command line is by using the new Windows XP EventQuery.vbs VBscript. This will list the events and event properties from one or more event logs in a command window. The output is shown here:

```
C:\> CSCRIPT c:\windows\system32\EventQuery.VBS
Microsoft (R) Windows Script Host Version 5.6
Copyright (C) Microsoft Corporation 1996-2001. All rights reserved.
Listing the events in 'application' log of host 'KRAA'
```

Type	Event	Date Time	Source	ComputerName
information	2023	5/29/2002 1:22:48 PM	SysmonLog	KRAA
information	2023	5/29/2002 1:22:46 PM	SysmonLog	KRAA

```
Listing the events in 'security' log of host 'KRAA'
```

Type	Event	Date Time	Source	ComputerName
audit failure	680	5/29/2002 1:27:02 PM	Security	KRAA
audit failure	680	5/29/2002 1:26:55 PM	Security	KRAA

```
Listing the events in 'system' log of host 'KRAA'
```

Type	Event	Date Time	Source	ComputerName
information	7036	5/29/2002 1:27:10 PM	Service Control	KRAA
error	7034	5/29/2002 1:27:02 PM	Service Control	KRAA

EventQuery.vbs works on local and remote machines alike and gives you filters to more granularly run the query and display the output. It will even dump output as a CSV (comma-separated value) file.

SYSTEM INFORMATION

Windows XP has enhanced the amount of system information that you can retrieve. There are some new tools as well as enhanced tools that give you more control over your system.

Winmsd.exe

Using Winmsd.exe, you can retrieve a lot of system information, and this information can even be saved as an .nfo file or exported to a plain text file.

From Winmsd.exe you can access other tools, including:

- **Network Diagnostics**   Gathers system hardware, software, and network information
- **System Restore**   Undoes damage done via some installation of software or system crash
- **File Signature Verification**   Checks for digitally signed or unsigned files
- **DirectX Diagnostic Tool**   Reports information on DirextX components and drivers
- **Dr. Watson**   Sets up parameters for Dr. Watson, such as file location and save options

SFC.exe

SFC.exe is a utility for checking protected files and replacing incorrect versions with the correct Microsoft version. You can invoke the program from the command line. You will see the program checking files in a pop-up window when you run `sfc /scannow`. SFC gets its configuration from the following registry key and values:

```
HKEY_LOCAL_MACHINE\SOFTWARE\Microsoft\WindowsNT\CurrentVersion\Winlogon\
SFCDisable (REG_DWORD)
```

0 = enabled (default)

1 = disabled, prompt at boot to re-enable (debugger required)

2 = disabled at next boot only, no prompt to re-enable (debugger required)

```
SFCScan (REG_DWORD)
```

0 = do not scan protected files at boot (default)

1 = scan protected files at every boot

2 = scan protected files once

`SFCQuota (REG_DWORD)`

n = size (in megabytes) of dllcache quota

FFFFFFFF = cache-protected system files on the local hard drive

`SFCShowProgress (REG_DWORD)`

0 = System File Checker progress meter is not displayed.

1 = System File Checker progress meter is displayed (default).

`SFCDllCacheDir (REG_EXPAND_SZ)`

Path = local location of dllcache directory (default is %Systemroot%\system32\dllcache).

The options to SFC are

- `/scannow` Scans all protected system files immediately
- `/scanonce` Scans all protected system files at the next boot
- `/scanboot` Scans all protected system files at every boot
- `/revert` Windows XP: Return to default settings (in case you used `/scanonce` or `/scanboot`)
- `/purgecache` Purges the file cache
- `/cachesize=x` Sets the file cache size

NOTE   SFC creates a log every time it is scheduled to run. Open the log through Start → Run → Winmsd → Tools → File Signature Verification Utility.

MSConfig.exe

Windows XP has the System Configuration Utility (SCU), which provides both information and the ability to modify various system functions. You can access the SCU by launching MSConfig.exe from Start → Run. Various startup file and registry key functions can be accessed and modified through the SCU, including System.ini, Win.ini, Boot.ini, Services, and Startup options. Through the SCU, you can also change the startup mode (Normal, Diagnostic, or Selective), as well as launch the System Restore functionality. Figure 5-9 shows the SCU in action.

Programs can be run from the registry and these will be found in the `HKLM\SOFTWARE\Microsoft\Windows\CurrentVersion\Run` key. Deleting the values under these registry keys will prevent the programs from running at startup. (See Chapter 3 for more information about the Run keys.) In SCU, if you have disabled startup programs, you can remove them from the SCU Startup box by removing the registry keys from `HKLM\SOFTWARE\Microsoft\Shared Tools\MSConfig\startupfolder`.

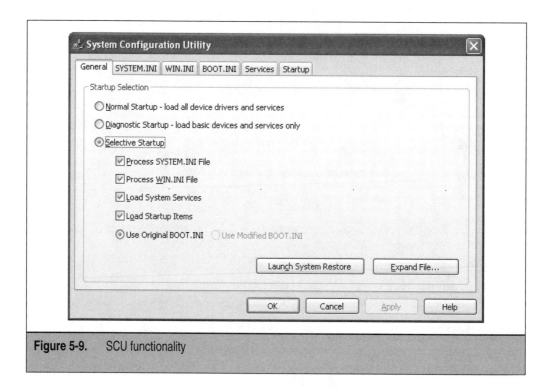

Figure 5-9.   SCU functionality

SPCheck.exe

The SPCheck.exe utility can be used to find the level of the service pack of components. It is installed with the Support Tools MSI package found in the Support folder of your Windows XP CD. You first download the spcheck.ini file from Microsoft and run the SPCheck program to generate a report. It must be run by an administrator account. SPCheck uses the Path environment variable to find files, which makes it less accurate than HFNetChk.exe (see Chapter 10).

Verifier.exe

Driver Verifier (Verifier.exe) is used to test kernel-mode drivers that can cause damage to the operating system. You can launch it through Start → Run → verifier.exe. It finds problems during testing by looking for improper IRQL handling. This program was included with Windows 2000 and is in Windows XP. Verifier can be run at the command line or through the GUI. Figure 5-10 shows the Driver Verifier Manager.

You can specify drivers and levels of verification as well as monitor statistics. You can enable Verifier through the registry using the key HKLM\SYSTEM\ CurrentControlSet\Control\Session Manager\Memory Management\ VerifyDrivers. Set the REG_SZ key to the case-insensitive names of the drivers for testing.

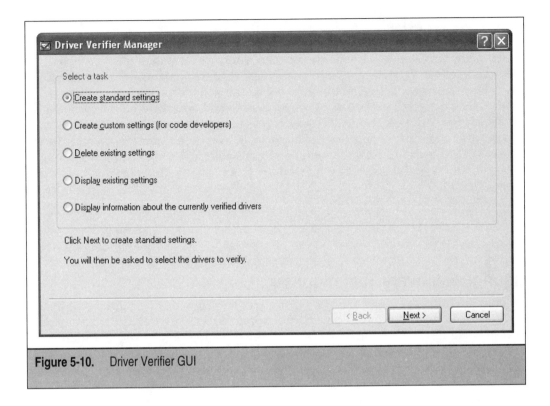

Figure 5-10.   Driver Verifier GUI

You can set the verification level using the key HKLM\SYSTEM\
CurrentControlSet\Control\Session Manager\Memory Management\
VerifyDriverLevel.

Driver Verifier monitors the following forbidden actions:

- Restore IRQL by calling KeLowerIrql
- Raise IRQL by calling KeRaiseIrql
- Requesting a size-zero memory allocation
- Allocating or freeing paged pool at an IRQL above APC_LEVEL
- Allocating or freeing nonpaged pool at an IRQL above DISPATCH_LEVEL
- Trying to free an address that was not returned from an allocate call
- Trying to free an address that was already freed
- Acquiring or releasing a fast mutex at an IRQL above APC_LEVEL
- Acquiring or releasing a spin lock at an IRQL other than DISPATCH_LEVEL
- Double release of a spin lock
- Specifying an illegitimate or random (uninitialized) parameter to any one of several APIs

SYSTEM RESTORE

System Restore is used to generate snapshots of your critical system files and store these snapshots as a *restore point*. If some problem occurs that damages your system, you can restore from the last good restore point. This is done via the System Restore service when a *trigger event* occurs. A trigger event could be when a new application is installed, a new driver is installed, or a Windows update is run. As the administrator, you can also create a manual restore point through Start → Programs → Accessories → System Tools → System Restore. System Restore controls can also be configured through Group Policy under Computer Configuration → Administrative Templates → System → System Restore.

NOTE   System Restore can noticeably affect system performance when it is running. Before trying to using System Restore, remember that you may have disabled it, as we discussed earlier in the chapter.

Configuring Recovery Techniques

You can modify the settings that allow you to recover from a failure through the Startup and Recovery options. To access these options, select Start → Control Panel→ System → Startup and Recovery Settings, and select Settings under System Failure.
You have the following options:

- Write an event to the System log
- Send an administrative alert (Microsoft Knowledge Base article Q310490 has more information on setting up alerts.)
- Automatically restart
- Write debugging information:
  - Small Memory Dump shows some information on the problem; it requires a paging file of at least 2MB. You can find this memory dump in %SystemRoot%\Minidump.
  - Kernel Memory Dump shows kernel memory and requires 50MB to 800MB for the paging file. You can find this memory dump in %SystemRoot%\Memory.dmp.
  - Complete Memory Dump records all contents of system memory. A lot of memory will be needed on your boot volume, at least the size of your RAM plus 1MB to hold header information. You can find this memory dump in %SystemRoot%\Memory.dmp.

NOTE   For multidrive machines, the page file must be on the System drive for the memory dump files to work.

Boot Logging

Boot logging allows you to identify problems with drivers at startup. You can identify where problems occur using the boot log file.

To enable boot logging, restart your computer and press F8. You can then select Enable Boot Logging from the Windows Advanced Options menu. The log file will be created in the %systemroot% directory. It will be named Ntbtlog.txt and can be viewed using Notepad. The log lists drivers as either "Loaded driver" or "Did not load driver."

TOOLS OF THE TRADE

Windows XP has enhanced programs from previous versions of Windows as well as added new ones. Resource kit tools and built-in tools provide a lot of functionality to secure and manage your system. But don't forget those Support Tools either (installed from the Support folder of your Windows XP installation CD).

Taskmgr.exe   This is always a good program for seeing what's going on in your system. The enhanced version in Windows XP provides a great deal of information about your system, including performance statistics and connected users.

Netstat.exe   Netstat has been around forever, but using the new -o switch in Windows XP provides more functionality by mapping the listening ports to a PID (process ID).

SC.exe   Using SC.exe gives a lot of command line flexibility for interacting with Services.

SCList.exe   While SCList is not built into Windows XP, using it from the Windows 2000 Resource Kit will let you quickly list all services and their states (e.g., Running, Stopped) on local and remote computers.

EventQuery.vbs   Use the VBscript program EventQuery to gather log information. This is a good tool if you like scripting and automating administrative tasks.

Eventtrigger.exe   You can use the command line program Eventtrigger to set up alerts and run programs when some specific type of event occurs in your log files.

SPCheck.exe   SPCheck is a tool for checking the status of your service packs. There are better ways, such as using Hfnetchk from Microsoft and using the Windows Update feature, but it's good if you want to do some scripting.

SFC.exe   SFC is used to check the versions of your system files and compare them with correct Microsoft versions.

Secedit.exe   Secedit is the trimmed-down command line version of the Security Configuration and Analysis MMC snap-in. It can be used to automatically create and apply security templates, and to analyze system security from scripts or on the fly via the command line. (We know many of you are command line junkies.) The Secedit commands include

- `secedit /analyze`
- `secedit /configure`
- `secedit /export`

CHECKLIST: OS ENHANCEMENTS

Most of the tools we have discussed in this chapter are all built-in and provide new functionality to the Windows XP environment. Enhancements to tools you are accustomed to using such as Netstat and event logs will greatly enhance your ability to control security of your Windows XP system.

☐ Enable ICF on your stand-alone computer or use some other firewall.

☐ Remove the Shared Documents folder if you don't use it.

☐ Turn off all unnecessary services.

☐ Be aware of what services are running and investigate any service you don't know about or that seems suspicious. Use `netstat -ano` to look for strange listening ports and Sclist.exe to list all services.

☐ Turn on auditing and store security log files off the server. Check your logs frequently, especially for failed logon attempts. Increase the size of your event logs to 80MB for the security logs, and set them to "Do not overwrite" for critical systems. When a security incident does happen, you will not want to be without these logs.

☐ Use Eventriggers to notify you when key events occur.

☐ Use restore points for up-to-date snapshots of your system settings, in case something gets royally bollixed up.

☐ Turn on boot logging to track down those pesky driver problems.

☐ Use SFC to check that system files are the correct Microsoft version.

☐ Use Winmsd to run diagnostics on your system and create a report of the system's hardware and software configurations.

☐ Use MSConfig to modify startup programs and see what is running on the system at startup.

CHAPTER 6

User and Group Management and Authorization

In this chapter we will discuss users and groups in Windows XP. Many things will be familiar from Windows 2000, but some things have changed. We will discuss some basic concepts, note the changes and new features, and look at security issues to consider. If you are responsible for a large domain, you will probably be using unattended installation technologies and will certainly be controlling local administrator accounts. In this case, you will be most interested in this chapter's details on Windows XP's new user accounts, groups, and password management.

Security principals are the basis of all things related to users and groups. The definition of a security principal and how it functions is central to our discussion. We will deal with SIDs, RIDs, access tokens, and security context, all of which define security principals. With this information we can better understand what users and groups are and how they are managed.

Microsoft has developed some interesting user tools to improve users' efficiency and help administrators do their jobs more easily, including storing usernames and passwords and preventing forgotten passwords. While both of these are excellent ideas that work as advertised, if not carefully managed they pose very real security risks.

SECURITY PRINCIPALS

In this section we discuss security principals, or *special identities*, and how you can use them to enhance security. Without security principals, virtually nothing could happen on our Windows computers.

Quite simply, security principals are the users, groups, computers, and services that are used to establish an identity in the operating system. Rights and privileges are granted based on this identity, some of which are configurable through User Rights Management, as discussed later in this chapter and in Chapter 1. As far as the operating system is concerned though, a security principal is identified using a SID.

SID Structure

SIDs are used to uniquely identify specific security principals. They are variable in length but organized in a consistent manner. The basic organization is *S-R-X-Y-Y-Y-Y-RID*. The *S* will actually be the literal character "S" and indicates that the SID is a *string value*. The *R* is the *revision level* of the SID and is currently 1 for all SIDs. The *X* is an *Identifier Authority* value from 0 to 5. The multiple *Y* values are *domain identifiers* and vary in length. The *RID* value is the *Relative Identifier,* which is incrementally and sequentially created to uniquely identify a Security Principal.

Using the Whoami Resource Kit utility, we can discover the SID of the currently logged-on user. This value is unique to the computer or domain where the account is created. The following output shows that the entire value `S-1-5-21-839522115-1078145449-195779448-1003` is the SID on the CORPXPPRO computer for the user called User1. User1 is not User1 to Windows. The name User1 is just a human-readable label for what Windows knows as

S-1-5-21-839522115-1078145449-195779448-1003. Whatever User1 does on the computer or the network is now tracked, logged, monitored, and restricted based on this value.

```
C:\>whoami /user /sid
[User]    = "CORPXPPRO\user1"   S-1-5-21-839522115-1078145449-195779448-1003
```

The last section of the SID, the Relative Identifier or RID value (1003 in this case) is used to create and track specific accounts. The four sections preceding the RID, 21-839522115-1078145449-195779448, are the domain identifier. These are unique for each computer or domain where SIDs are created and managed. As an example, the domain securingxp.com will use the same domain identifier value for every domain account that exists in the Active Directory. By contrast, every Windows XP machine in the domain will each have its own unique domain identifier for any local, nondomain accounts.

As stated, Windows uses the RID to create and track specific accounts. It does so sequentially and incrementally for local accounts: RID 1000 is created first and is always the HelpAssistant account on a stand-alone Windows XP system. RID 1001 is created next and is always the HelpServicesGroup. RID 1002 is created next and is always Support_388945a0 and so on. Since Windows creates accounts sequentially and incrementally, the RID value of the next account created will be 1003, followed by 1004, then 1005, and so on. For domain accounts, a similar sequential and incremental numbering of RIDs happens. Now we can decode the rest of the SID. The S-1-5-21 slots of the SID, labeled *S-R-X-Y*, are decoded as in Table 6-1.

Table 6-2 contains the Identifier Authority values for SIDs. This value represents the authority level that issued the SID. As a rule, the higher the Identifier Authority value the greater the initial power or permissions of that account. For example, the Everyone group has an Identifier Authority of 1, while the Administrators group has 5.

The next section after Identifier Authority can be specific subauthorities, part of the domain identifier (as in our example above), or other group or user characteristics.

SID Value	Placeholder	Description
S	*S*	Identifies the SID as a string value; this never changes.
1	*R*	The revision version of the SID (it is still 1, indicating that there are no Service Packs or hotfixes for the SID); this also does not change.
5	*X*	This slot is the Identifier Authority and indicates the level of authority that can issue SIDs for this Security Principal. It can have values of 0 to 5. In this case it is 5, which is NT Authority (see Table 6-2).
21	*Y*	This slot begins the domain identifier, but it also can relate directly to specific groups, users, and their characteristics. In this case it is 21, which is part of the domain identifier. There can be as many as five sections (see Table 6-3).

Table 6-1.   SID Prefix Values

Identifier Authority	Value	Important Characteristics
Null SID	S-1-**0**-0	A group with no members. Often used when a SID value is not known.
World	S-1-**1**-0	A group that includes all users.
Local	S-1-**2**-0	Users who log on to terminals locally (physically) connected to the system.
Creator Owner ID	S-1-**3**-0	A security identifier placeholder to be replaced by the security identifier of the user or group who created a new object. This SID is used in inheritable ACLs.
Nonunique	S-1-**4**-0	A nonunique SID authority.
NT Authority	S-1-**5**-0	Accounts created by the OS or users, generally Administrators. These may include well-known users, groups, and computers.

Table 6-2.   Identifier Authority Values

Table 6-3 shows examples of these values. Note the number 32 in the first Y section of the Administrators group. The number 32 indicates that this is a built-in group that can be directly affected by Administrators. Also note that these SIDs are quite short and well known. These will exist on every Window XP installation.

The operating system creates many built-in users and groups on every installation. This implies many well-known users and groups with corresponding well-known SIDs that will always be the same in every installation. The groups in Table 6-3 are all well-known groups with SIDs consistent across installations.

 SECURITY ALERT   SIDs of well-known accounts are predictable. The true Administrators account will always have a SID ending in a RID of 500, even if the account is renamed. Hacker tools can ferret out this attempt at "security through obscurity." Two tools, Sid2user and User2sid, can remotely query and display the SID of any account on a machine with NetBIOS enabled and no anonymous user restrictions set. Luckily, as noted in Chapter 1, Windows XP can prevent this when security option "Network access: Allow anonymous SID/Name translation" is set to Disabled.

SID Prefix	Name	Important Characteristics
S-1-5-2	Network group	Members of this group are logged on using a network connection.
S-1-5-3	Batch group	Members are logged on using a batch queue such as the Task Scheduler.
S-1-5-4	Interactive group	Members are logged on interactively.
S-1-5-11	Authenticated Users	Members are users whose identity has been authenticated.
S-1-5-32-544	Administrators group	Members are Administrators on the local machine.
S-1-5-32-545	Users group	Members are Users on the local machine.

Table 6-3.   Subauthorities and Well-Known SIDs

Access Token

When programs are executed they must be executed as security principals that are assigned a SID. When you log on and surf the Internet, you are doing so as a security principal. When Windows runs the winlogon process, for example, it does so as a security principal. Major aspects of security principals are these:

- They can initiate actions such as installing or starting an application.
- They have SIDs and are specifically identified in the SAM and/or Active Directory.
- They can log on provided they have the appropriate user right (recall our discussion from Chapter 1), including computer security principals, or computer accounts.
- They can access resources.
- They can be added, disabled, reset, and deleted. (Yes, even computer security principals can be disabled; groups, however, cannot.)

When a security principal such as a user logs on, an *access token* is created. (Groups are unique in this situation, as a group cannot log on, so groups do not have access tokens.) In its simplest form, the access token is composed of three things:

- The user SID
- SIDs of all security groups the user belongs to
- User rights and privileges

Using Whoami, we can see the access token, including user rights and privileges, by typing **whoami /user /all**. The following output shows SIDs of the seven groups User1 is a member of, as well as User1's rights. This is part of the access token that is created when the user logs on.

```
C:\>whoami /user /all
[User]     = "CORPXPPRO\user1"  S-1-5-21-839522115-1078145449-195779448-1003
[Group  1] = "CORPXPPRO\None"   S-1-5-21-839522115-1078145449-195779448-513
[Group  2] = "Everyone"  S-1-1-0
[Group  3] = "BUILTIN\Administrators"  S-1-5-32-544
[Group  4] = "BUILTIN\Users"  S-1-5-32-545
[Group  5] = "LOCAL"  S-1-2-0
[Group  6] = "NT AUTHORITY\INTERACTIVE"  S-1-5-4
[Group  7] = "NT AUTHORITY\Authenticated Users"  S-1-5-11
(X) SeChangeNotifyPrivilege           = Bypass traverse checking
(O) SeSecurityPrivilege               = Manage auditing and security log
(O) SeBackupPrivilege                 = Back up files and directories
(O) SeRestorePrivilege                = Restore files and directories
(O) SeSystemtimePrivilege             = Change the system time
(O) SeShutdownPrivilege               = Shut down the system
(O) SeRemoteShutdownPrivilege         = Force shutdown from a remote system
(O) SeTakeOwnershipPrivilege          = Take ownership of files or other objects
```

```
(O) SeSystemEnvironmentPrivilege         = Modify firmware environment values
(O) SeSystemProfilePrivilege             = Profile system performance
(O) SeProfileSingleProcessPrivilege      = Profile single process
(O) SeIncreaseBasePriorityPrivilege      = Increase scheduling priority
(X) SeLoadDriverPrivilege                = Load and unload device drivers
(O) SeCreatePagefilePrivilege            = Create a pagefile
(O) SeIncreaseQuotaPrivilege             = Adjust memory quotas for a process
(X) SeUndockPrivilege                    = Remove computer from docking station
(O) SeManageVolumePrivilege              = Perform volume maintenance tasks
```

A quick look shows us the SID for User1. We also see Group1, CORPXPPRO\None, has a SID ending in 513, which is the SID for the Domain Users group. In our case it is a placeholder, since this computer is not a domain member. There is no local group called CORPXPPRO\None. When joined to a domain, ComputerName\None is removed. Group 2 is the Everyone group. Group 5 is the Local group, showing the user is locally logged on to this machine. The bottom section shows user rights granted to User1 based on group membership and user rights specifically granted to the individual user.

This is a snapshot of the access token for the security principal User1 on the CORPXPPRO machine, created when User1 logs on. It is presented when resource access is requested, when applications are run, or when User1 attempts to do anything on the computer. If group membership or user rights change while User1 is logged on, the user must log off and then log back on to rebuild the access token in order for those changes to take effect.

NOTE   An access token is built only when a user logs on. If group membership or user rights change, the user must log off and log back on to get a new access token and have those changes take effect.

Access Tokens and Security Context

Every user action initiated is executed using this access token. When a resource is requested, for example, the access token is presented as the credential that will allow access. When the access token is presented, compared, and accepted, the *security context* is created and in effect for that resource. In this way, security principals establish the security context in which they operate. This context defines what security principals— Users, Groups, Computers, and Services—are allowed to do, right down to what privilege level the application threads run under.

As we said before, when a resource is requested, the access token is presented as the credential to allow access. If requesting a file on an NTFS partition, for example, the access token is compared to the ACL for the file. Part of what the ACL contains is a list of SIDs and their permissions for the resource, whether Read, Write, or Full Control, for example. That means the SIDs of the access token are compared to the SIDs in the ACL, and access is granted based on this comparison.

Table 6-4 shows what is contained in an access token and therefore the definition of the security context.

Name	Description
User	This is the user's SID and does not apply to groups, since a group cannot log on. It does apply to users, computers, and services. The SID will be Local or Domain, depending on which type of account is used to log on. It cannot be affected to any great degree other than logging on as a different user.
Groups	All SIDs from all security groups the user is a member of, including all nested groups, are collected here. This applies to users, computers, and services. This list can be directly affected to meet security requirements.
Privileges	For our purposes, the privileges are the user rights and security options contained in Local or Domain group policies. Rights and privileges can be directly edited by Administrators to meet security requirements.
Owner	When a security principal creates or takes ownership of an object, there is a default behavior to determine which user or security group actually is the owner. Table 6-2 shows this placeholder as value S-1-3-0. The default behavior in Windows XP is for the individual creator to become the owner. This creator SID is included in the token, replacing the S-1-3-0 value, and attached to the created object. Even if the creator is a member of the Administrators or Domain Admins group, this is still the default behavior. Members of the Administrators group are always able to take ownership of any object.
Primary group	By default, normal users, as created, are members of the Users group. The Users group is set as the Primary group. If you have applications that create users, and you don't want those users to be in the Users group, you have to specifically assign an alternate group as the Primary group before removing the user from the Users group.
Default Discretionary Access Control List (DACL)	When an object is created, permissions must be set for access to it. The defaults are Creator Owner and System Full Control, but remember that inheritance rules are in effect. You can indirectly influence this by editing inheritance rules, generally applicable to files and directories.
Source	Processes cause access tokens to be created, and their identities are included in the token. Processes such as Remote Procedure Calls (RPC), LAN Manager, or Session Manager are examples. This cannot be influenced to any great degree in a way that will affect security requirements.
Type	Type distinguishes between a primary token and a token used for impersonation. As an example, you can call `ImpersonateAnonymousToken` before a particular API call in order to force anonymous credentials to be used. When enumerating shares and users, this can actually be quite powerful, as normal users will most likely not have access to NetUserGetInfo calls, but the null user will.
Impersonation Level	The degree to which a service can adopt the security context of a client represented by this access token.
Statistics	This is internal operating system information relating to the token. This cannot be affected to any great degree.
Restricting SIDs	Some processes can create threads that have less privilege than their parent process, as a security measure. Internet Explorer versions 5 and later have this capability. Web pages from untrusted sites can be executed with less privilege than the currently logged-on user. This can be greatly affected to meet security requirements, for example, by using Security Zones in Internet Explorer.
Session ID	Distinguishes a Terminal Services token from other tokens. Short of logging in via Terminal Services, this cannot be affected to any great degree.

Table 6-4.   Access Token Contents

OWNERS AND OWNERSHIP OF OBJECTS

When a security principal creates or takes ownership of an object, a default behavior determines which user or security group the owner actually is. The default behavior in Windows 2000 is for members of the Administrators group or the Domain Admins group to become the owner.

As an example, suppose that in Windows 2000 a member of the Administrators group with a username of Bill creates a folder to contain all the payroll records of his organization. The actual owner of the folder is the SID of the Administrators group, so all group members have equal ownership. Bill can modify permissions on this folder by virtue of his membership in the Administrators group. Later, he changes roles in the company and is removed from the Administrators group. At this point, Bill no longer has ownership rights to this folder because his token no longer matches the access list.

The same scenario in Windows XP turns out quite differently. Since Bill created the folder, the actual owner is Bill, *not* the Administrators group. In this case, even when Bill is no longer a member of the Administrators group he is still the owner of the folder, and as such has the ability to change permissions on the folder. The default Windows XP setting is less secure than it could be.

 SECURITY ALERT   Be aware of this default behavior when an object is created or ownership is taken. Windows XP makes the individual creator the owner, not the group, even when the creator is in the Administrators group. If the creator leaves the Administrators group he or she retains ownership, and thus can easily regain full control of the object. This behavior can be controlled through the "System objects: Default owner for objects created by members of the administrators group" security option, as described in Chapter 1.

On .NET Server, this policy is labeled "Not Defined," but in fact the Administrators group is the default owner, which is the opposite of Windows XP and is a more secure design.

USERS

There are several new user accounts and some other user idiosyncrasies in Windows XP. Some accounts are great improvements in security, but others are more than suspect. In this section we will note the new *built-in accounts* and their characteristics. Of particular note is First User Created on Default Install. When performing a workgroup-based installation, the First User Created account, at least locally, is inherently insecure because it is given a blank password automatically. On top of that, you are allowed to create up to five additional user accounts, all of which are automatically added to the local Administrators group and given blank passwords.

You do not need to fear this insecure functionality in a domain environment, however, as that installation is completely different than a workgroup install. During installation, you are asked whether or not to join a domain before any user accounts are created.

Once joined to a domain, you are asked to enter a password for the local administrator account (which, of course, you could choose to leave blank). After this point, you are asked which domain users you want to add to local security groups.

While a remote connection to the Windows XP system is not allowed when using a blank password, console access still is. Also, recall from our discussion on security principals that all accounts are issued SIDs when created and have access tokens created when they log on.

Built-in Accounts

There are several new built-in accounts for Windows XP, most notably Support_388945a0 (or another OEM-added support account), HelpAssistant, LocalService, and NetworkService. The first two are designed to aid in enterprise help desk services. The third and fourth are actually considered groups that enhance security. They have some user characteristics, including profiles and the ability to be used to start services (we will discuss them in detail in the "New Accounts in Windows XP" section). For the purposes of discussion, we have added the First User Created on Default Install account to the list of built-in accounts. While it is not a built-in account in the strict sense, it is a required account and is inherently insecure when created as part of a workgroup installation. Table 6-5 shows the basic characteristics of these accounts/security principals.

HelpAssistant Account

The HelpAssistant account is for use during Remote Assistance sessions. It has limited user rights and is used for the initial remote assistance logon after the "novice" user requests assistance from the "expert." The initial connection gives the expert view-only

Built-in Account	Important Characteristics
HelpAssistant	Default built-in account on Windows XP only, for use with Remote Assistance. Enabled by default.
Support_388945a0	Default built-in account on Windows XP only, for vendor use with the Help and Support Service. Disabled by default.
Local Service	Default built-in account on Windows XP only, for local services not requiring extensive Local System privileges and few or no network privileges. Has a hidden local profile.
Network Service	Default built-in account on Windows XP only, for network services not requiring extensive Local System privileges but requiring more extensive network privileges. Has a hidden local profile.
First User Created on Default Install	Not a default built-in account but a default account that must be created on install. It is a member of the Administrators group. When the account is installed as a workgroup computer (as opposed to a domain member), auto logon is enabled by default and the password is blank.

Table 6-5. Built-in Security Principals

access, but if the novice agrees to give the expert remote control of the desktop, then the expert inherits the rights of the novice's logged-on user account, and HelpAssistant is no longer needed. At this point, the expert essentially becomes the user, similar to a pcAnywhere remote connection.

The randomly generated password makes HelpAssistant difficult to compromise, but be aware that users can change this password. The HelpAssistant account is disabled by default, and is enabled only when Remote Assistance sessions are being set up, at which point its credentials are actually authenticated by the Microsoft GINA, as any other account would be. Once a Remote Assistance ticket has expired, the account will once again be disabled.

NOTE The HelpAssistant account has Auto Logon enabled when used with Remote Assistance, and can log on interactively from the console and connect to shares. It is a member of the Users group and is disabled by default, but temporarily enabled by the OS when it is needed.

Support_388945a0 Account

The Support_388945a0 account, like Guest, is assigned the following user rights:

- Deny access to this computer from the network
- Deny logon locally

It is a member of the Help Services group. It is also given the user right to log on as a batch job. It is disabled by default. We recommend that you do not enable this account except in specific circumstances. Once you do, you must edit its user rights to make the account useful.

First User Account

During the installation of Windows XP, you are first asked whether the computer is a domain or workgroup member. If you choose to install a workgroup computer, then you go through the process of adding local users. You can create up to five users and are given no choice as to their password or group membership. They will all be members of the local Administrators group, and will each have a blank password. You can only change group membership and passwords after installation is complete and you boot into Windows XP.

 SECURITY ALERT Beware of workgroup-based installations. When performing a workgroup-based installation, the First User Created on Default Install account, by default, has a *required* blank password. It is also a member of the Administrators group and has Auto Logon enabled. You will also have the option to create up to five additional accounts, each of which will have these same characteristics, except that Auto Logon will be disabled. This constitutes a severe risk if the computer is physically accessible.

Fortunately, this is not the functionality that is in operation when you are joining the computer to the domain during installation. With a domain-based installation, the user account creation is much more secure, since you can manually set a password during the install.

GROUPS

There are six new group accounts in Windows XP along with a few group peculiarities. Most of the new groups are improvements in capabilities and features. In this section we will note new built-in groups and briefly discuss some differences from Windows 2000. For example, a major security enhancement has been added to the Everyone built-in group. We will also define and explain two unique new accounts, Local Service and Network Service, which have user as well as group characteristics and perform unique security tasks. We also include a brief listing of user rights.

Built-in Groups

Built-in groups come in two flavors: those you can directly affect membership in and those you cannot. You can simply change the membership of such groups as Administrators and Guests. Other built-in group memberships, such as Local or Interactive, change as a user's role and activities change. The former you see and can manage in Local Users and Groups. The latter you do not see there, and you can only indirectly and dynamically affect membership.

For example, an administrator cannot add users to the Interactive group, but if a user logs on at the console, the group SID for the Interactive group will be added to their access token, and they are considered to be in that group. It works the same way for the Batch group. An Administrator can allow a user to become part of the Batch group by granting the "Log on as a batch job" user right, thus indirectly affecting that group's membership. When the user logs on using the Scheduler service, for example, the Batch group SID will be added to their access token, and they will be considered in that group.

Table 6-6 shows all the built-in groups in Windows XP. The first six groups listed are new and found only in Windows XP. All other groups can be found in both Windows 2000 and Windows XP. We will discuss the six new groups in more detail. The "Direct or Indirect" column indicates whether that group's membership can be directly or only indirectly affected.

User Rights

We discuss user rights in the "Groups" section of this chapter for a simple reason: best practice dictates that group accounts be used when assigning privileges and permissions.

Group Name	Direct or Indirect	Important Characteristics
Local Service	Indirect	Account/group on Windows XP only, for local services not requiring extensive Local System privileges and few or no network privileges. Has a hidden local profile.
Network Service	Indirect	Account/group on Windows XP only, for network services not requiring extensive Local System privileges but requiring more extensive network privileges. Has a hidden local profile.
Remote Interactive Logon	Indirect	Group on Windows XP only that allows users to log on using Remote Desktop Connection.
HelpServicesGroup	Direct	Group on Windows XP only that can use helper applications to diagnose system problems. Vendor support can use it to access the computer from the network and to log on locally.
Network Configuration Operators	Direct	Group on Windows XP only that can configure networking features, such as IP address assignment.
Remote Desktop Users	Direct	Group on Windows XP only that has the right to log on remotely using Remote Desktop Protocol.
Everyone	Indirect	Group containing all users who access the computer, including Guests and Users from other domains. On Windows XP does not include anonymous logons.
Authenticated Users	Indirect	Group including users who are authenticated locally by a trusted domain controller. Guest account is not included in this group.
Anonymous Logon	Indirect	Group assigned to network logons with no credentials.
Batch	Indirect	Group for batch processes accessing a resource on the computer.
Creator Owner	Indirect	Group that is a placeholder in an inheritable ACE.
Creator Group	Indirect	Group that is a placeholder in an inheritable ACE.
Dialup	Indirect	Group that accesses the computer over a dial-up connection.
Interactive	Indirect	Group of users who log on locally.
Network	Indirect	Group of users who log on over the network.
Service	Indirect	Group of services.
System	Indirect	Group that is the operating system. Also known as Local System.
Terminal Server User	Indirect	Group of users who access the computer by using a terminal server session.
Administrators	Direct	Group where members have total control of the local computer.
Backup Operators	Direct	Group that can back up and restore files on the computer, regardless of the permissions that protect those files.
Guests	Direct	Group that is denied access to the application and system event logs. They have the same access rights as members of the Users group.

Table 6-6. Default Built-in Groups

Group Name	Direct or Indirect	Important Characteristics
Power Users	Direct	Group that has less system access than Administrators but more than Users.
Replicator	Direct	Group that replicate files across a domain.
Users	Direct	Group with limited access on the system.

Table 6-6. Default Built-in Groups *(continued)*

TIP To minimize the number of permissions that must be managed, use the UGLR rule (pronounced "uglier") for user and group management: Users are placed into Global groups, which are placed into Local groups, which are given access to Resources.

Table 6-7 summarizes user rights from the Group Policy MMC snap-in and compares default Windows 2000 to default Windows XP rights. (Remember that these were enumerated by the Whoami utility as part of the access token.) There are several new rights and changes to existing rights in Windows XP, as indicated in the table. From a security standpoint a few are important, each of which was discussed in detail in Chapter 1. These key rights are "Deny access to this computer from the network," "Deny logon locally," and "Logon as a batch job."

User Right	Default Groups in Windows 2000 Workstation	Default Groups in Windows XP Professional
Access this computer from the network	Administrators, Backup Ops, Power Users, Users, Everyone	Administrators, Backup Ops, Power Users, Users, Everyone
Act as part of the OS		
Add workstations to the domain		
Adjust memory quotas for a process (new to XP)		Local Service, Network Service, Administrators
Allow logon through Terminal Services (new to XP)		Administrators, Remote Desktop Users
Backup Files and Directories	Administrators, Backup Ops	Administrators, Backup Ops
Bypass Traverse Checking	Administrators, Backup Ops, Power Users, Users, Everyone	Administrators, Backup Ops, Power Users, Users, Everyone
Change system time	Administrators, Power Users	Administrators, Power Users
Create a Pagefile	Administrators	Administrators

Table 6-7. User Rights Summary

User Right	Default Groups in Windows 2000 Workstation	Default Groups in Windows XP Professional
Create a Token Object		
Create Permanent Shared Objects		
Debug Programs	Administrators	Administrators
Deny access to this computer from the network		SUPPORT_388945a0, Guest
Deny Logon as a Batch Job		
Deny Logon as a Service		
Deny Logon Locally		SUPPORT_388945a0, Guest
Deny Logon through Terminal Services (new to XP)		
Enable computer and user accounts to be trusted for delegation		
Force shutdown from a remote system	Administrators	Administrators
Generate Security Audits		Local Service, Network Service
Increase Quotas	Administrators	
Increase Scheduling Priority	Administrators	Administrators
Load and Unload Device Drivers	Administrators	Administrators
Lock Pages in Memory		
Logon as a Batch Job		SUPPORT_388945a0
Log on as a Service		Network Service
Logon Locally	Administrators, Backup Ops, Power Users, Users, Guest	Administrators, Backup Ops, Power Users, Users, Guest
Manage audit and security logs	Administrators	Administrators
Modify firmware environment variables	Administrators	Administrators
Perform volume maintenance tasks (new to XP)		Administrators
Profile a single process	Administrators, Power Users	Administrators, Power Users
Profile system performance	Administrators	Administrators
Remove Computer from a Docking Station	Administrators, Power Users, Users	Administrators, Power Users, Users
Replace a Process-Level Token		Local Service, Network Service
Restore files and directories	Administrators, Backup Ops	Administrators, Backup Ops
Shut down the system	Administrators, Backup Ops, Power Users, Users	Administrators, Backup Ops, Power Users (Users group not a default in XP)
Synchronize Directory Service Data		
Take ownership of files or other objects	Administrators	Administrators

Table 6-7.   User Rights Summary *(continued)*

As you can see in Table 6-7, some things have changed since Windows 2000, including the following:

- The "Deny access to this computer from the network" and "Deny logon locally" rights added the SUPPORT_388945a0 and Guest accounts. Windows 2000 has no accounts assigned these rights by default. Once you enable these accounts they are not useful until you change one or more of these rights depending on whether you need network or local access. The default settings provide a good security posture.

NOTE   Guest and SUPPORT_388945a0 accounts can be enabled easily but are still not useful until user rights have been edited to allow local or network access. This helps prevent accidental Guest or SUPPORT_388945a0 access to resources.

- The "Logon as a batch job" right is given to the SUPPORT_388945a0 account. If you enable this account, think carefully about what this right allows. In Windows 2000 it is normally only given to Local System.

- The "System Objects: Default owner for objects created by members of the administrators group" setting is given by default to the object creator, more commonly known as Creator Owner. Under certain circumstances this can be a security risk. See the "Security Principals" section and Chapter 1 for a complete discussion.

NEW ACCOUNTS IN WINDOWS XP

Network Service and Local Service are new accounts to Windows XP. They are designed to reduce the risk of compromise and to reduce the damage should they be compromised. Network Service has more extensive rights on the network and very limited rights on the local machine. On the other hand, Local Service has some rights on the local machine and very limited rights on the network. Essentially, the Local Service account is a null user while the Network Service is a machine account. They are built-in accounts but, like LocalSystem, you will not see them in Local Users and Groups.

Local Service Account

The Local Service account is a default built-in group on Windows XP only, and it can be only indirectly affected by an Administrator. It is designed for local services that need fewer local privileges than the Local System account, and for limited network access. This account has no password. When a service using this account is started by the Service Controller it presents credentials to the LSA for authentication just like any other account. The advantage is that Local System credentials are not used. When dealing with the local machine the LocalService account is equivalent to a member of the Users group. This service is equivalent to the local Users group for local tasks and to Anonymous users for network access.

Local Service accesses network resources as a null session with no credentials. If one of the services using this account is compromised on the local machine, the chances of severe network compromise are much less than if a service using Local System is compromised. Ten local services use this account by default:

- Alerter Service
- Application Layer Gateway Service
- Remote Registry
- Smart Card
- Smart Card Helper
- SSDP Discovery Service
- TCP/IP NetBIOS Helper (called Lmhosts during service enumeration)
- Uninterruptible Power Supply
- Universal Plug and Play Device Host
- WebClient

The equivalent services in Windows 2000 all run as Local System. This account has user characteristics and has a hidden profile in \windows\documents and settings.

Network Service Account

The Network Service account is a default built-in group on Windows XP only, and it can only be indirectly affected by an Administrator. It is designed for network services that need fewer local privileges than Local System but network access equivalent to Local System. When a service using this account is started by the Service Controller it presents credentials to the LSA for authentication just like any other account. Four network services use this account by default:

- Distributed Transaction Coordinator
- DNS Client
- Performance Logs and Alerts
- Remote Procedure Call (RPC) Locator

The equivalent services that exist on Windows 2000 all run as Local System.

The Machine account, instead of null credentials (Local System), is used when accessing network resources, and the local Users group credentials are used when accessing local resources. This account has user characteristics and has a hidden profile in C:\Documents and settings.

A quick way to see which context a process is running in is to use the Windows XP `tasklist` and `qprocess` commands. In the following listing, note that the results of `qprocess` show Svchost.exe running as Local Service with PID 984 and as Network Service with PID 876. The results of Tasklist show that PID 984 is handling four services, and PID 876 is handling Dnscache, which is the DNS Client service.

```
c:\>qprocess "local service"
  USERNAME                SESSIONNAME        ID    PID   IMAGE
>local service            console            0     984   svchost.exe
c:\>qprocess "network service"
  USERNAME                SESSIONNAME        ID    PID   IMAGE
>network service          console            0     876   svchost.exe
C:\>tasklist /SVC /FI "PID eq 984"
Image Name                       PID Services

======================= ====== ======================================
svchost.exe                      984 LmHosts, RemoteRegistry, WebClient
 C:\>tasklist /SVC /FI "PID eq 876"
Image Name                       PID Services
======================= ====== ======================================
svchost.exe                      876 Dnscache
```

Note that this output does not include other users, such as the one currently logged on, and the System account. To see all the processes that are launched in the context of local System, just execute

```
qprocess * /SYSTEM
```

Remote Interactive Logon

Remote Interactive Logon is a Windows XP default built-in group that can be only indirectly affected by an Administrator. It includes all users who log on to the computer using Remote Desktop Protocol (RDP). Because it is a subset of the Interactive group, access tokens that contain the Remote Interactive Logon SID also contain the Interactive SID.

HelpServicesGroup

HelpServicesGroup is a Windows XP default built-in group that can be directly affected by an Administrator. It is designed to use helper applications to diagnose system problems. Vendor support personnel can use it to access the computer from the network and to log on locally. By default this group has one member, Support_388945a0, and minimal rights and access. Actually it does nothing until given members, rights, and permissions.

Network Configuration Operators Group

Network Configuration Operators Group is a Windows XP default built-in group that can be directly affected by an Administrator. It allows specific users to configure networking parameters as follows:

- Change any TCP/IP parameters including IP address
- Rename, enable, or disable LAN connections
- Modify, delete, or rename RAS connections
- Use IPconfig.exe to release or renew commands

This is an excellent account for delegation of networking tasks. If for security reasons you choose to operate your computer as a regular user rather than as an Administrator, you can retain control of network parameters without using the `runas` command. Basically these rights are made possible by giving the Network Configuration Operators Group rights to many of the appropriate registry keys.

Remote Desktop Users

Remote Desktop Users is a Windows XP default built-in group that can be directly affected by an Administrator. Members of this group have the right to log on remotely. This group has the "Allow logon through Terminal Services" user right by default. Once a user in this group logs on, the SID of the Remote Interactive Logon group is attached to the user's access token. Even if you are not running as an Administrator, you can add yourself to this group for remote access to your computer.

NETWORK LOGONS—
ANONYMOUS VS. AUTHENTICATED

Windows XP performs logon functions much the way Windows 2000 does, but there are some differences and improvements. In this section we will discuss anonymous logons, what they are and how they differ from Windows 2000. These logons present null credentials and expect to be given access. Authenticated logons, on the other hand, are those that present credentials other than null, have them verified by a security authority, and expect to be given access.

In Windows 2000 the Everyone group by default *is* included in the Anonymous Logon access token. In Windows XP, the Everyone group by default *is not* included in the Anonymous Logon access token. This essentially means that any object granting the Everyone group rights will not be allowing Anonymous Logon rights at the same time.

In Windows XP, under Security Options in Group Policy there is a setting that will allow Anonymous Logon back into the Everyone group, as described in Chapter 1. "Network Access: Let Everyone permissions apply to Anonymous users" will give Everyone permissions to users logging on anonymously.

SECURITY ALERT   If you allow Anonymous Logon into the Everyone group you open your computer up to the possibility of enumeration of vital information. Many times, this information is the beginning of a complete compromise.

Some older legacy applications might require Anonymous Logon to be in the Everyone group, or equivalent permissions, to function properly. In that case, you could enable this policy setting. Otherwise, the extra security provided should stop many attackers from all but the most peripheral enumeration of your network.

RestrictAnonymous

As in Windows 2000, you can successfully connect with a null session to Windows XP by typing the following command at the prompt:

```
C:\>net use \\10.0.2.10\ipc$ "" /u:""
The command completed successfully.
```

Using the Resource Kit tool Local.exe, you can compare results of null session connections. See the listings that follow: the first IP is to a Windows 2000 machine, and the second to a Windows XP machine. If the Anonymous Logon is allowed to enumerate users, then we should get a listing of the Administrators group members from the following command. If not, then we should get "access denied." First we establish a null session with each machine, then type the commands shown here:

```
C:\WINNT>local administrators \\10.0.2.20
CORPXPPRO\Administrator
CORPXPPRO\gumby

C:\WINNT>local administrators \\10.0.2.10
Access Denied.
```

The first IP, 10.0.2.20, is a default Windows 2000 Professional install, and gives us two members of the local Administrators group. The second IP, 10.0.2.10, is a default Windows XP Professional install and denies us access. Other enumeration tools that rely on null sessions, like SomarSoft's DumpSec (http://www.somarsoft.com), do not work on default Windows XP installs. We can anonymously log on to Windows XP, but we cannot access anything. This is a great improvement over Windows 2000.

In Windows 2000, the registry setting RestrictAnonymous could be set with a value of 1 or 2. A value of 1 was supposed to stop user account enumeration, but a value of 2 actually did.

NOTE   In Windows 2000, it was often thought that a RestrictAnonymous setting of 1 was good enough to prevent anonymous user/group account enumeration. However, that belief was challenged when tools like UserDump.exe and UserInfo.exe (available from www.hammerofgod.com) came to town. This type of tool used an API call that could override the RestrictAnonymous setting unless it was set to 2. Setting RestrictAnonymous to 2, however, was found to break many applications, especially domain controllers. Armed with this information, Windows comes equipped with a new security option called "Network Access: Allow anonymous SID/Name translation disabled," defending against tools that could previously beat RestrictAnonymous set to 1.

In Windows XP, the single RestrictAnonymous registry setting was replaced with four settings, each of which corresponds to a new value in the Security Policy, as noted in Table 6-8. As you can see, what previously equaled RestrictAnonymous set to 1 (in Windows 2000), now equals RestrictAnonymousSam set to 1 (in Windows XP). Similarly, what was RestrictAnonymous set to 2 (in Windows 2000) is now sort of like RestrictAnonymous set to 1 (in Windows XP). Windows XP has made a drastic improvement, however. In retrospect, it seems that Microsoft used RA = 2 as a simple stop mechanism in Windows 2000, which blocked null sessions from being created remotely. In Windows XP, the RA design is much more sophisticated and doesn't prevent a null session from being established (as it did in Windows 2000), which ended up breaking things like down-level client connectivity and domain trusts. The ability to restrict anonymous access has also been expanded to include the two new settings mentioned, which are discussed more in Chapter 1.

Registry Setting	Security Policy
RestrictAnonymous	Network Access: Do not allow anonymous enumeration of SAM accounts and shares
RestrictAnonymousSam	Network Access: Do not allow anonymous enumeration of SAM accounts
(No registry value is mapped, as this setting is implemented by the UI)	Network Access: Allow anonymous SID/Name translation
EveryoneIncludesAnonymous	Network Access: Let Everyone permissions apply to anonymous users

Table 6-8.   The New Windows XP Settings to Restrict Anonymous User Enumeration

> ## CHALLENGE
>
> On one of Foundstone's security consulting engagements with a Fortune 100 company, the null session capability enabled a server compromise. During an internal security review, we were told the company was very security conscious and we should target specific servers. Those servers offered no easy avenue of attack. They were members of a domain, and one of the DCs allowed null sessions with RestrictAnonymous set to 0, meaning to allow anonymous user and group enumeration. The Anonymous Logon was a member of the Everyone group. This allowed null session connections and the use of tools like DumpSec to be used against the DC. By running DumpSec (or any similar tool) important user and group information can be discovered that most Administrators believe is only available to other Administrators.
>
> No passwords were discovered immediately, but there were comments for specific accounts, user and group details including SIDs, logon hours, last logon time, and so on. One of our target computers and the administration password for that computer was typed into the comments field of a certain user. The comments even said "admin password for server X". Obviously server X was quickly compromised. Unfortunately, it was multihomed into an undocumented test-and-development subnet. That subnet was soon compromised as well. In real life, overlooking small security measures can lead to large server or larger domain compromise.

PASSWORD MANAGEMENT

In this section we discuss some new Windows XP password management tools designed to make administrators' lives easier and help users work more efficiently. Using these tools also poses significant security risks that should be thoroughly considered. There is no doubt that auditing passwords on a network is good security practice; however, you don't want to send those passwords across the Internet or store them in a file in plain clear text. We will also discuss a security setting that will, over a period of time, remove the vulnerable LAN Manager hashes from the SAM and Active Directory and thus nullify the effectiveness of popular password auditing tools.

Credential Management—Stored User Names and Passwords

A new feature of Windows XP is the ability to store multiple credentials for network connections and other resources. This feature is also available on .NET servers, including domain controllers. This solution is Microsoft's attempt at a single sign-on solution, and managed appropriately it actually works quite well.

Open Control Panel and click User Accounts to access the interface. It is slightly different if you are in a domain than otherwise. NTLM, Kerberos, Microsoft Passport, and SSL authentication can all be stored here. You specify a resource such as a domain name, a server, or server and share name, and a username and password for that resource. Once entered, they are encrypted and stored in the user's local profile under the \Documents and Settings\Username\ Application Data\Microsoft\Credentials directory.

The next time you attempt to connect to a network resource, your current credentials are presented. If those fail, then the Stored User Names and Passwords cache is checked and the appropriate credentials are sent.

These credential-management features can be a great time-saver for both users and network administrators who access their computers as a normal user but require administrative or other credentials to access domain resources. The Administrator can specify their entire domain using *.*domainname* and their domain administrative credentials. When they attempt to connect to a domain resource, these credentials will be presented. My Network Places could easily be used to store these connections for later use.

SECURITY ALERT   Realize that if a computer is compromised, then an attacker can gain access to all resources that have credentials stored.

If a machine is compromised, stored credentials can be used by the attacker to gain access to other parts of the network. The attacker need not know those usernames or passwords to complete this attack. Network connections using My Network Places are stored in a hidden directory called NetHood under \Documents and Settings\Username\ and could be viewed by the attacker. If the attacker gained a remote shell and changed to this directory he would be able to determine which connections might be vulnerable. Using the compromised machine and compromised username and password, any of these resources could be automatically accessed if the credentials were stored. A net use connection would be crafted to first try the compromised user's credentials and then to search the stored usernames and passwords for valid credentials.

NOTE   There is a Group Policy setting on Windows XP and .NET Server that can prevent this behavior. In Group Policy, go to Computer Configuration → Windows Settings → Security Settings → Local Policies → Security Options and choose "Network Access: Do not allow storage of credentials or .NET Passports for network authentication."

Prevent Forgotten Passwords

Windows XP allows users to create a password-reset disk for use if the password is forgotten. This can only be used on local accounts on the local machine, not on domain accounts. First, log on to your local machine SAM using local credentials. Next, from Control Panel choose User Accounts and then Prevent a Forgotten Password. You must supply the currently logged-on user's password and a blank, formatted floppy. You will be prompted for a new password for that account, and you can add a hint to help you remember the new password.

You can also follow these alternative steps to create the disk:

1. Press CTRL-ALT-DELETE.
2. Click Change Password.
3. Click Backup to access the Forgotten Password wizard.

A public key is created and used to encrypt the user's password. This self-signed certificate, including the user's SID, is then stored on the local hard drive. The certificate and private key is stored on the floppy. Once the process is completed, you are prompted to label this floppy "Password Reset" and advised to keep it in a safe place. Now you can reset your password if you forget it. You can even change your password multiple times and still use the same Password Reset disk to gain access to your machine. Or you can change your password to a blank password. The public and private key pair will be validated before passwords are changed.

NOTE   If you reset a user account, settings such as web page credentials, file share credentials, EFS-encrypted files, or Certificates with private keys (SIGNED/ENCRYPTed e-mail) may be lost.

If an attacker used a password-reset disk to compromise a machine in a domain, the damage would be lessened, as only local accounts would be compromised. Password-reset disks can also be copied and used successfully. So if an attacker discovered a password-reset disk, copies could be made for later use, providing the disks are matched to the correct machines.

 SECURITY ALERT   By capturing the password-reset disk an attacker can gain access to a local machine. This disk is much like a user writing their password on a Post-it note and sticking it on their monitor.

Limit Use of Blank Passwords

Windows XP will not allow network access to accounts with blank passwords as a default security measure. The security option "Accounts: Limit local account use of blank passwords to console logon only" is enabled by default. Careful reading of this security option reveals that it only applies to local accounts and not domain accounts. Further, the Guest account is exempt from this restriction. Therefore, domain accounts with blank passwords can connect over the network. If the Guest account is enabled and removed from the user right "Deny access to this computer from the network," then Guest with a blank password could also connect over the network. The Administrator, with a blank password, could not. This is one more very good reason not to use the Guest account.

 SECURITY ALERT   As noted in Chapter 1, as a default security option, accounts with blank passwords are not allowed network access to Windows XP machines. *This does not apply to domain accounts or the Guest account.*

Change Passwords from the Command Line

You can change a *domain* user's password at the command line. If you are the Administrator in a domain, you can issue the following command to change the password:

```
net user <user_name> * /domain
```

At the password prompt, type the new password and confirm it at the next prompt.

You can also use the following command to change the password for a *local* user account:

```
net user <user_name> <new_password>
```

No LMHash

Windows XP, like Windows 2000 Service Pack 2, has the ability to clear the LAN Manager hash from the SAM or Active Directory. Each password must be changed before the hash is removed, so some time and effort will be involved to fully implement this setting. The LAN Manager hash is much weaker than NTLM, NTLMv2, or Kerberos, and it is used mainly for backward compatibility with down-level clients like Windows 95/98. On networks that are all NT and above, this setting will enhance security without requiring significant effort.

Enabling the Group Policy security option "Do not store LAN Manager hash value on next password change" clears the LAN Manager hash value the next time a password is changed. This policy is disabled by default. Similarly, setting a password of 14 characters or more will also clear the LM hash, and will do so immediately. This works in both Windows 2000 (no Service Pack needed) and Windows XP. This setting can help prevent password sniffing and cracking tools like L0phtCrack from being effective. When L0phtCrack is used on these hashes, it reports them as No Password and is unable to crack them. On the other hand, Administrators will not be able to use such tools to audit their passwords and password policy either. Also, some legacy applications that rely on LAN Manager authentication may not function properly.

CAUTION   If your network has no down-level clients, we recommend configuring Windows 2000 and Windows XP to prevent storing the LAN Manager hashes. This ensures that only the NTLM password hashes are used, providing an effective security measure against password-cracking tools.

TOOLS OF THE TRADE

Most of the tools used in this chapter come from the Resource Kit or are native to Windows XP. Otherwise they are freely available on the Internet.

Tasklist.exe   A new tool in Windows XP, Tasklist displays running processes in a number of ways. Using `tasklist /svc` you can dump out the process list with running services by process.

Whoami.exe   From the Windows 2000 Resource Kit, Whoami displays the access token contents of the currently logged-on user, including the user SID and all SIDs of groups the user belongs to. Using the `/all` switch includes a user rights listing as well.

Local.exe   Also from the Windows 2000 Resource Kit, Local displays the local group members of a specified group. Requires a null or authenticated session with target machine.

Qprocess.exe   Another new Windows XP tool, Qprocess displays processes running on a local or remote machine and includes the username associated with the process. To display all viewable processes, just run `qprocess.exe *`.

DumpSec   A GUI enumeration tool, DumpSec (available from http://www.somarsoft.com) displays the contents of User Manager, including usernames, groups, shares, and policies. DumpSec requires that you set up a null or authenticated session connection with the target machine.

User2sid and Sid2user   Available from http://www.chem.msu.su/~rudnyi/NT, these are command line tools for querying and translating SIDs to their corresponding usernames and vice versa. They take advantage of well-known SIDS. Both require that you set up a null or authenticated session connection with the target machine. These tools even get around the RestrictAnonymous = 1 setting.

L0phtCrack   This password-auditing and -cracking application utility is available from http://www.atstake.com. It is in version 4 at the time of this writing. L0phtCrack also has SMB packet capture ability, to capture LANMAN hashes off the wire.

CHECKLIST: USER AND GROUP MANAGEMENT

In this chapter we explored security principals: what they are, how they are created, and how they function through SIDs, RIDs, access tokens, and security context. All of these relate to how users and groups work in Windows XP, with some differences from Windows 2000.

We discussed new accounts and explored their functions and uses. Then we also explored some new tools for displaying processes and services, enumerating user and group information, and auditing password strength. Regardless of how you manage your users and groups, it pays to fully understand how things work so that you can make informed security decisions.

Be sure to check the following user- and group-related settings and configurations on your Windows XP machines:

☐ Windows XP's default behavior for determining an object owner is not the same as Windows 2000's. Understand whether it is the Administrators group or the Creator of an object who takes ownership by default. Under Group Policy, check Computer Configuration → Windows Settings → Security Settings → Local Policies → Security Options → "System Objects: Default owner for objects created by members of the administrators group."

☐ The HelpAssistant account is disabled by default and only temporarily enabled by the OS when it is needed for Remote Assistance.

☐ Beware of workgroup-based installations, and assign a password to the first user created in a default install *immediately*. If more users are created on install, assign them passwords right away as well. Be sure you really want these users in the Administrators group.

☐ A better option during installation is to join a domain before any user accounts are created, which provides more secure behavior than the workgroup-based installation.

☐ Both Guest and Support_388945a0 have the following user rights assigned: "Deny access to this computer from the network" and "Deny Logon locally." Do not remove these rights from these accounts unless you are sure there is a real requirement to do so.

☐ Do not enable the security option "Network Access: Let Everyone permissions apply to Anonymous users" unless you understand the security risk. Vital system information can be needlessly exposed if it is enabled.

☐ Be sure you fully understand the use of Stored User Names and Passwords and how it can, under certain circumstances, turn a one-machine compromise into a domainwide compromise. Remember that there is a Group Policy setting available to disable this functionality.

☐ Be sure you and your users know the importance of protecting password-reset disks, even though they apply only to local machine logons and not to domain logons.

☐ Windows XP does not allow network access with blank passwords. But be aware of two caveats: This does not apply to the Guest account. This also does not apply to domain accounts. Local accounts only are subject to this default setting.

☐ If you choose not to store LAN Manager hashes, then password-auditing tools you may have come to rely on will most likely not work like you expect.

Windows XP Professional Security Blueprints

Table of Contents

Network Map

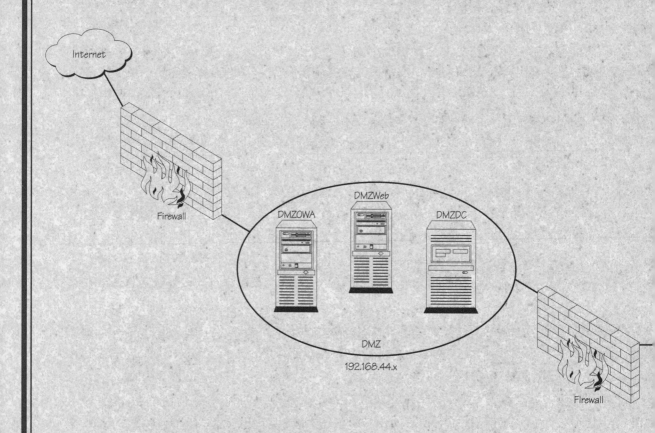

This is a sample network to use as a reference throughout the book. The main network has three network segments, each separated by a firewall to provide the basic perimeter defenses. The other pages of blueprints provide close-ups of the various parts of this network map.

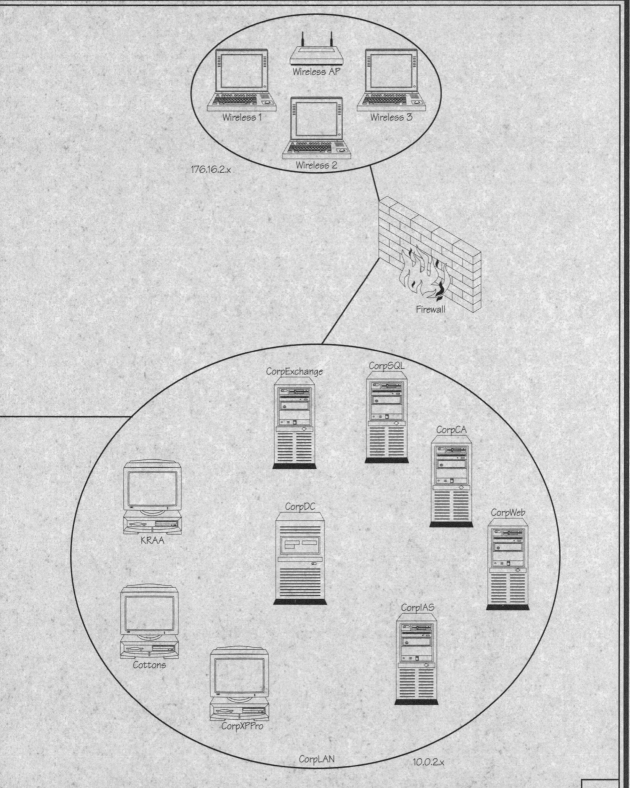

Wireless AP

Wireless 1

Wireless 3

Wireless 2

176.16.2.x

Firewall

CorpExchange

CorpSQL

CorpCA

KRAA

CorpDC

CorpWeb

Cottons

CorpIAS

CorpXPPro

CorpLAN

10.0.2.x

3

Active Directory Forest

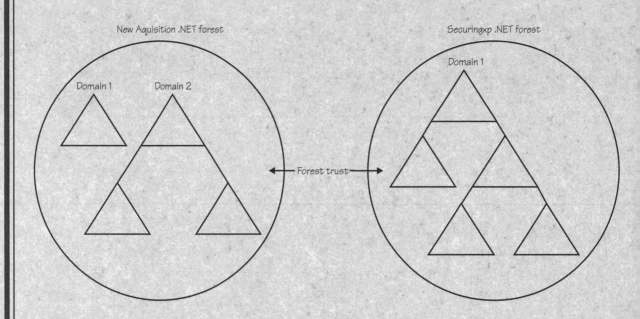

A forest is a collection of domains that are not necessarily a part of the same contiguous namespace. Just as within a tree, all domains within a forest have a two-way transitive trust by default. So in the New Acquisition forest, there are two separate domains and two-way trusts between all domain and child domains.

This diagram does not depict the inner forest trusts, but only the forest namespace hierarchy. It does depict the two-way trust between both forests, indicated by the arrow in the center. Remember that cross-forest trusts are only possible in a Windows .NET Active Directory infrastructure. For more details, see Chapter 11.

Active Directory Tree

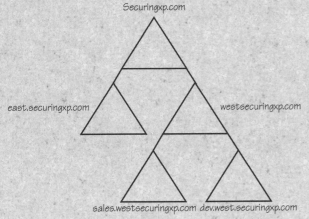

Securingxp.com

east.securingxp.com

westsecuringxp.com

sales.westsecuringxp.com dev.west.securingxp.com

In Active Directory, a tree is a logical collection of a root domain naming context and all child domains. In this case, the root domain is Securingxp.com, and the child domains include east.securingxp.com, west.securingxp.com, and so forth. These domains do not have to line up with the actual DNS zones, but life is much simpler when they do.

All the domains in a tree share a contiguous namespace as well as a common schema, configuration naming context, and global catalog as AD data is replicated throughout the tree.

A default two-way transitive trust is set up between each pair of domains in the tree, although this diagram only depicts the hierarchical namespace relationships.

Active Directory Organizational Units

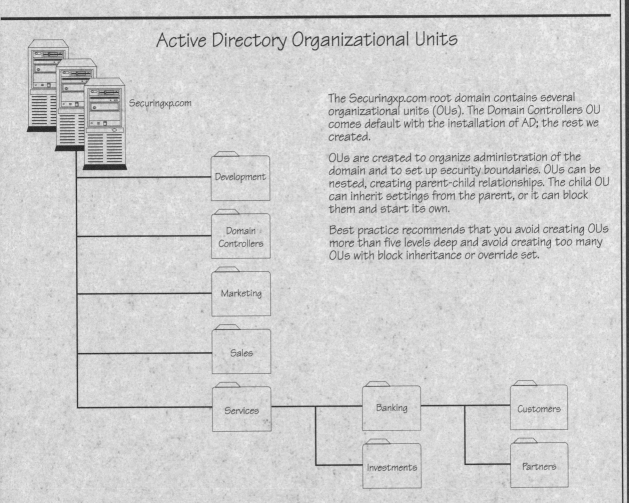

Securingxp.com

Development

Domain Controllers

Marketing

Sales

Services

Banking

Investments

Customers

Partners

The Securingxp.com root domain contains several organizational units (OUs). The Domain Controllers OU comes default with the installation of AD; the rest we created.

OUs are created to organize administration of the domain and to set up security boundaries. OUs can be nested, creating parent-child relationships. The child OU can inherit settings from the parent, or it can block them and start its own.

Best practice recommends that you avoid creating OUs more than five levels deep and avoid creating too many OUs with block inheritance or override set.

5

Wireless Ad Hoc (Peer-to-Peer) Network

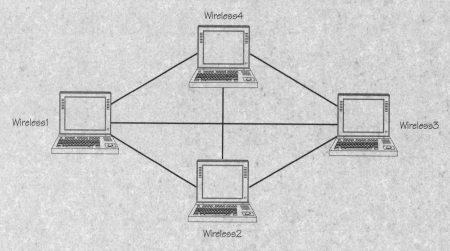

A pure peer-to-peer type of network, wireless ad hoc does not use an access point (hub) to link each wireless client. Instead, each client connects directly to the other clients in a mesh type of design, with no dependence on a central hub.

Wireless Infrastructure Mode Network

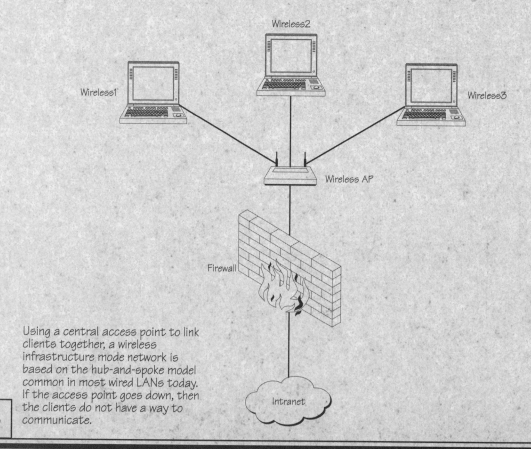

Using a central access point to link clients together, a wireless infrastructure mode network is based on the hub-and-spoke model common in most wired LANs today. If the access point goes down, then the clients do not have a way to communicate.

Wireless Network with 802.1x

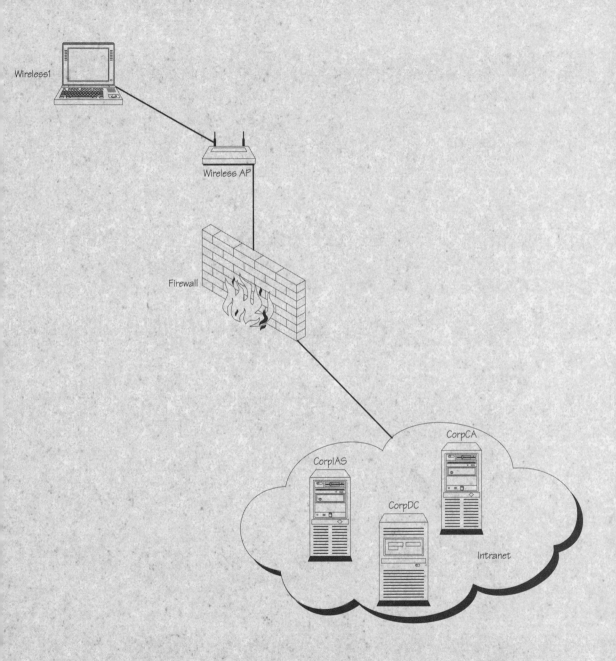

Not to be confused with the 802.11x standards for wireless networking, 802.1x provides standards for data link layer authentication. Authentication at this layer protects even basic access, or connectivity, to the local network by requiring client certificates (for example) before allowing a connection. In this way, the 802.1x standards protect a wireless network by preventing any anonymous user or computer from connecting to it.

Wireless Network with IPSec VPN

Another secure wireless network design uses an IPSec VPN at the perimeter of the intranet. While anonymous connections to the wireless network itself will still be allowed, only authenticated connections to the intranet will be. Once a client is authenticated with the VPN gateway, strong encryption can be used to secure all traffic sent over the airwaves.

PART II

Network Security

CHAPTER 7

IP Security

This chapter covers network security using IP Security (IPSec), which by now most administrators have at least heard of, and most hackers have grown to hate. Our coverage of IPSec here is focused on IPv4, even though IPSec support is present in IPv6, where its roots actually live. In general, the concepts provided in this chapter will apply to both IPv4 and IPv6.

The security problems with TCP/IP are numerous, ranging from unencrypted and unauthenticated traffic to replay, man-in-the-middle, and denial of service attacks. The solution is IPSec, a name given to a set of protocols that work to secure *unicast IP traffic* (traffic between two computers). Operating at the network layer, IPSec starts by protecting the IP layer and providing the following security services to IP and upper layer protocols:

- Authentication
- Confidentiality
- Integrity
- Antireplay protection

These four security services will be discussed throughout this chapter. They are also referenced throughout this book. For example, IPSec is presented as a secure solution for 802.11x wireless networks in Chapter 9. Mutual authentication is performed before and during IP communications. Confidentiality is achieved through packet encryption. Integrity is maintained for each IP packet by identifying modified or spoofed traffic. IP sessions cannot be replayed because every IPSec communication channel is uniquely identifiable.

NOTE IPSec operates at the network layer, allowing higher layer protocols such as TCP and UDP to benefit transparently from its security. The greatest benefit perhaps is that application developers can rely on IPSec for securing network transactions, rather than trying to build security into each application.

In this chapter we will present you with all the terminology that makes IPSec possible. Remember that IPSec consists of a set of protocols as illustrated by the following equation:

IPSec = IKE + (AH or ESP)

IPSec consists of the IKE (Internet Key Exchange) protocol for authentication, plus either the AH (Authentication Header) or the ESP (Encapsulating Security Payload) protocol for packet protection.

Don't get lost in the language though; the four security services mentioned are what it is all about. We will bring you up to speed on what is new in Windows XP and then delve right into the Windows and IPSec architectures, explaining the protocols—IKE, ESP, AH, and so on. We will talk briefly of how IPSec and L2TP can be used together to form a secure VPN solution for remote access clients. Then we will explore your logging options and the inherent risks. You will learn about the *default exemptions* in Windows XP, a potential security risk that you absolutely must be aware of. Finally, we will present the tools available for administering and troubleshooting IPSec in Windows.

One important point to realize about IPSec filters in Windows is that they can essentially serve as a personal firewall. A personal firewall is basically created with an IPSec policy that blocks all traffic and permits only that which you allow. This is not to be confused with ICF (covered in Chapter 8), which in no way implements IPSec to perform its firewall function.

WHAT'S NEW IN WINDOWS XP/.NET

Native support for IPSec was first introduced in Windows 2000. Its development was a joint effort between Microsoft and Cisco, with the two main goals being integration with both Cisco's ISAKMP/IKE and Active Directory. IPSec functionality has been improved with Windows XP and Windows .NET.

Some new tools are available in Windows XP, including the command line Ipseccmd.exe from the support tools package and the IPSec Monitor MMC snap-in. Both are discussed later in this chapter and in the "Tools of the Trade" section.

In Windows .NET, several new designs and features are planned for release. There will be support for the NAT-Traversal IETF proposal currently in Internet draft form. This proposal provides a method for IPSec to work through gateways performing Network Address Translation (NAT). In this case, the IPSec packets are UDP-encapsulated before transmission.

With L2TP over IPSec, NAT-Traversal will enable a remote client computer to connect through a NAT gateway to a VPN server that can itself sit behind a NAT gateway. Of course the remote client must be able to support NAT-Traversal. As we were writing this, new L2TP/IPSec client software for legacy Windows (9x/Me/NT) systems was released, and plans were to eventually include this support for Windows 2000/XP clients as well.

Other Windows .NET server IPSec enhancements will include:

- IPSec integration with Network Load Balancing
- Support for Resultant Set of Policy (RSoP)
- Configuration support for Diffie-Hellman 2048-bit keys in IKE for L2TP/IPSec connections
- Netsh.exe command line tool support for IPSec policy configuration

LOCAL POLICY AND ACTIVE DIRECTORY POLICY

IPSec policies can be defined either locally or as a group policy object that is applied to computers through Active Directory. Locally, IPSec policies can be configured by using the following tools:

- IP Security Policies MMC snap-in
- Ipseccmd.exe command line tool

In Active Directory, IPSec policies are defined in the normal manner, using the Group Policy editor or GPO editor and the IP Security Policies container.

In either case, IPSec policies are defined by creating rules and filters. If you open Secpol.msc through Start → Run and click IP Security Policies on Local Computer, you will see a screen similar to Figure 7-1.

Only one IPSec policy can be active at any given time. Each IPSec policy can consist of many rules. Each rule can contain many IP filters, but only one authentication method and one filter action (traffic is either permitted, blocked, or secured). Depending on how complex your needs are, you could have a policy with many rules applied, and each rule could contain many IP filters.

Firewall Rules

Let's say that you want to administer the computer DMZDC from your administration workstation CorpXPPro (refer to the network map in the "Blueprints" section of this book). DMZDC is a Windows 2000 domain controller running Terminal Server on the standard TCP port 3389. A Telnet server is running on the standard TCP port 23. To create this IPSec policy you can set up one rule that contains two IP filters with one authentication method and one filter action each.

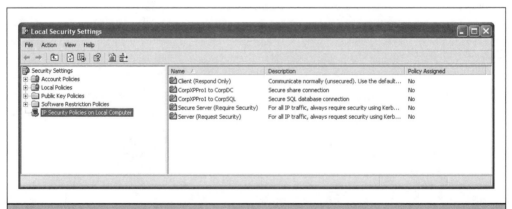

Figure 7-1.   IP security policies in the Local Security Settings UI

Application Traffic

For the firewall setup, you first need to allow TCP ports 23 and 3389 only from your computer to DMZDC. That takes care of the remote administration capabilities. Now you need to add two rules for the raw IP protocol IDs 50 and 51. These represent ESP and AH respectively.

Authentication Traffic

IPSec supports the following three methods of authentication:

- Kerberos
- Certificates
- Preshared key

Regardless of which method you are using for authentication, IKE will be responsible for initiating the exchange. To allow IKE traffic through, you will need to add a rule for source and destination port UDP 500.

If your DMZDC computer was in the same domain as CorpDC, then you could just use Kerberos authentication and enable a rule to let UDP/TCP port 88 through. Since the setup we are describing, however, uses certificates for authentication, we are assuming that the CA is reachable by each computer and handled by IKE, so no additional rules need to be configured. The specifications for reaching a Certificate Authority are stored in its certificate.

Certificate Authentication

Certificates provide one of the strongest means of authentication. IKE is used only to negotiate the certificate parameters; the Cryptographic API (CAPI) is used to actually validate the certificates. As far as IPSec is concerned, CorpXPPro merely needs to be configured with the Certificate Authority for DMZDC's certificate. Likewise, DMZDC needs to be configured with CorpXPPro's CA. The CA's certificate must exist in each computer's list of trusted CAs. When the authentication begins, the computer's personal certificate will be checked against the CA.

In addition to your default and other firewall rules, DMZFW's firewall ruleset would have entries as shown in Table 7-1. This is assuming that DMZFW is a *stateful firewall*, meaning that it will know to allow the return traffic from DMZDC to CorpXPPro.

Source Host	Destination Host	Protocol	Source Port	Destination Port
CorpXPPro	DMZDC	TCP	Any	23
CorpXPPro	DMZDC	TCP	Any	3389
CorpXPPro	DMZDC	UDP	500	500
CorpXPPro	DMZDC	IP protocol ID 50 (ESP)	—	—
CorpXPPro	DMZDC	IP protocol ID 51 (AH)	—	—

Table 7-1.   Firewall Ruleset to Allow the IPSec Traffic

IPSec Policy

Now you have to set up IPSec policies on each machine that will secure all Telnet and Terminal Server traffic. As an example, let's discuss the IPSec policy for CorpXPPro, since you can assume that DMZDC will have a mirror copy. The policy on CorpXPPro has one rule with two filters defined. The first filter is defined for traffic to TCP port 23, and the other filter is defined for traffic to TCP port 3389. The rule is set to use CAs for authentication and require strong security. The following matrix illustrates the policy in detail.

IPSec Policy Name	CorpXPPro to DMZDC
Rule Name	Telnet and Terminal Server traffic
Filter Action	Require security
Authentication	Certificate
Filter 1:	
Mirrored	No
Description	Telnet from CorpXPPro to DMZDC
Protocol	TCP
Source DNS Name	CorpXPPro
Source Port	Any
Source Mask	255.255.255.255
Destination DNS Name	DMZDC
Destination Port	23
Destination Mask	255.255.255.255
Filter 2:	
Mirrored	No
Description	Terminal session from CorpXPPro to DMZDC
Protocol	TCP
Source DNS Name	CorpXPPro
Source Port	Any
Source Mask	255.255.255.255
Destination DNS Name	DMZDC
Destination Port	3389
Destination Mask	255.255.255.255

Our CorpXPPro to DMZDC policy is set up with just one rule, which contains two filters. As mentioned, however, a single policy can contain many rules, which can each contain many filters. Only one policy can ever be active at a time.

THE WINDOWS ARCHITECTURE

This gives a brief overview of the framework that provides IP security in Windows. Throughout the rest of the chapter we will be referencing this architecture, so it will become clearer as you read on.

The Windows implementation of IPSec is built on open industry standards. Three main components responsible for IPSec functionality in Windows are

- Policy Agent
- IKE module
- IPSec driver

These three components interact with other Windows components such as the TCP/IP driver, the crypto API, and the registry.

The *Policy Agent* is started as a service, appropriately named *IPSEC Services* in Windows XP. Although we recommend setting this to manual when it is not being used (see the appendix to this book), this service will need to be set to automatic and started before IPSec will work. Its job is to acquire and distribute the IPSec policies that you have defined, which will exist either as local policies or Active Directory policies. The appropriate parts of the policy are then distributed among the IKE module and the IPSec driver.

NOTE   Once acquired, Active Directory IPSec policies are written to the local registry, where they are cached for future use in the event of an unreachable domain controller.

As you will see in upcoming sections, the *Internet Key Exchange (IKE) module* has the most complex job. It negotiates the security associations (SAs) that are used to identify and manage secure IPSec channels. As you will see, a security association is like a contract with the negotiated terms of communication. These contract terms are determined by the security settings that the Policy Agent delivers.

The *IPSec driver* is like a stateful inspection firewall. Responsible for the statefulness of connections, it inspects packets, comparing them to the filters distributed by the Policy Agent. The IPSec driver actually determines which packets are permitted, blocked, or secured.

THE IPSEC ARCHITECTURE

IPSec is a set of protocols that work to secure TCP/IP traffic. At a minimum, IPSec will always use IKE to perform the initial handshake and secure channel negotiations. After that point, you have the choice of using either AH, ESP, or both. Each protocol provides a security service, as shown in Table 7-2.

Security Service	Protocol
Authentication	IKE
Confidentiality	ESP
Integrity	AH, ESP
Antireplay protection	IKE, AH, ESP

Table 7-2. Security Services Provided by IPSec Protocols

We will look at each of these protocols in more detail in the following sections. For the authoritative documentation, check the IETF's RFCs:

- Security Architecture for the Internet Protocol: http://www.ietf.org/rfc/rfc2401.txt

- IP Authentication Header: http://www.ietf.org/rfc/rfc2402.txt

- IP Encapsulating Security Protocol: http://www.ietf.org/rfc/rfc2406.txt

- Internet Security Association and Key Management Protocol (ISAKMP): http://www.ietf.org/rfc/rfc2408.txt

- The Internet Key Exchange (IKE): http://www.ietf.org/rfc/rfc2409.txt

- Oakley: http://www.ietf.org/rfc/rfc2412.txt

Transports vs. Tunnels

IPSec filters operate in either *transport* or *tunnel mode*. Transport mode is designed for host-to-host protection, while tunnel mode is designed for gateway-to-gateway traffic protection. For example, if you want to set up IP security between an IIS and a SQL server on your LAN, you would use a transport mode filter that defines the security settings you want. In transport mode, the original IP headers are used and only protected when using AH's authentication.

In tunnel mode, the original IP datagram is encapsulated inside a new set of IP headers. Tunnel mode is meant mainly for connections between two routers, or gateways, otherwise known as *tunnel endpoints*. When in tunnel mode, the original IP headers are moved inward and protected completely by either ESP or AH, and a new set of IP headers is wrapped around the encapsulated datagram. These packets are illustrated in the "Encapsulating Security Payload" and "Authentication Header" sections, later in the chapter.

Internet Key Exchange—The Means of Authentication

The Internet Key Exchange (IKE) is the first protocol used when an IPSec channel is initiated. It is the most complex of the protocols because it performs a lot of work.

IKE is actually a combination of the Internet Security Association and Key Management Protocol (ISAKMP) and the Oakley Key Determination Protocol (Oakley). IKE borrows from pieces of these protocols to build security associations using a secure Diffie-Hellman key exchange and Kerberos, certificate, or preshared key authentication.

When CorpXPPro initiates communication with DMZDC on TCP port 3389, it sees that an IPSec filter is supposed to be applied. At this point the IKE module becomes active, as a two-phase negotiation process is kicked off. The first phase is called Main Mode, which performs the authentication and sets up a secure channel for the second phase, called Quick Mode. Quick Mode, as the name implies, is faster because it has less work to do; it negotiates a secure channel for the IP addresses and ports defined in the rule's filters.

Security Associations

IPSec would not happen without security associations, which are fundamental. Security associations (SAs) can be defined as the negotiated terms of security between two hosts. SAs are always established before any IPSec channel is set up. You can think of an SA as a temporary contract. If CorpXPPro and DMZDC cannot agree on the terms of contract, then negotiations fail and communications stop. Otherwise, they will talk back and forth until some agreeable terms can be reached.

Take a Quick Mode example: As the initiator, CorpXPPro might say, "I will talk to you under these conditions: you use 3DES and MD5." As the responder, DMZDC might reply, "Well, I can't do that, but I can do DES and SHA1." Then CorpXPPro would finish the exchange either by agreeing and setting up the secure IPSec channel, or by disagreeing and stopping further communications.

SAs are *unidirectional,* meaning that if a secure channel has been set up between two computers, they will each have a unique SA to manage that channel. A unique security association is created for each host during each IKE phase. So for Main Mode you will end up with one inbound SA (from DMZDC) and one outbound SA (from CorpXPPro), each being unique. The same goes for Quick Mode.

As mentioned, security associations have finite lifetimes. By default, in Windows 2000 and XP, Main Mode SAs live for 8 hours, and Quick Mode SAs live for 15 minutes. Actually, this configuration is completely configurable, and even more granularly: lifetimes can be set on the number of bytes transferred as well.

IKE Phase I—Main Mode

Main Mode, as the name implies, is where the main IKE negotiations happen. This is where authentication takes place; if it fails, then Quick Mode will never even happen. At the conclusion of a successful Main Mode negotiation, each host will have an ISAKMP SA set up to last for 8 hours.

Main Mode is where the master key material is generated and computer identities are securely authenticated. Identities are encrypted when using certificate or preshared key authentication, but Kerberos computer identities are sent in clear text.

To modify Main Mode SA lifetimes for an IPSec policy, click the key exchange Advanced button under the General tab for that policy. If you continue on and click the Methods button under Key Exchange Settings, you will reach the Key Exchange Security Methods screen, where you can configure the encryption and hashing algorithms that IKE will use for SA negotiations, the Diffie-Hellman key strengths, and the preference order to be negotiated with.

IKE Phase II—Quick Mode

Quick Mode is where SAs are created for the policy rule filters. In this last phase of IKE negotiations, security protocols and parameters are exchanged.

Consider our example policy for CorpXPPro and DMZDC. The policy contains a rule with a filter action set to "Require security." As shown in Figure 7-2, "Require security" actually means that encryption and hashing algorithms will be negotiated between the hosts. As shown in the figure, several terms can be configured in order of preference.

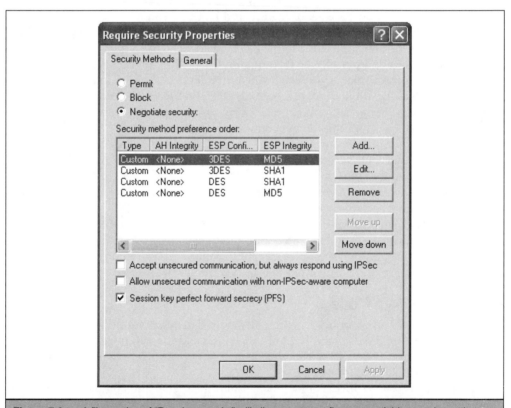

Figure 7-2.   A filter action of "Require security" will allow you to configure negotiable security settings.

Our example shows that the highest preference is for the 3DES encryption algorithm and the MD5 hashing algorithm. Our lowest acceptable preference is for DES encryption and the MD5 hashing algorithm.

Once IKE has finished with phase I and II negotiations and SA creation, it passes off the encryption key and SAs to the IPSec driver for secure communications to begin.

Authentication Header—Integrity

When you choose the "Require security" option in your IPSec rule, you can choose the Authentication Header (AH) protocol to provide integrity and antireplay protection. AH does not provide encryption of data. You would use AH instead of ESP in cases where you are only concerned with authenticating hosts before establishing communication channels, and you do not care if network traffic is encrypted. AH will provide for your authentication needs without the extra overhead of using encryption algorithms.

As shown in Figure 7-3, the original IP headers are signed in transport mode, using either the HMAC-MD5 or HMAC-SHA1 hashing algorithms (configurable through the IP Security Policies snap-in: Policy Properties → Rule → Filter Actions tab).

Even in tunnel mode, AH will sign the endpoint IP header, as shown in Figure 7-4.

Encapsulating Security Payload—Encryption and Integrity

Experience shows that most people choose IPSec for its encryption capabilities, and therefore choose ESP as the preferred protocol. ESP provides the same protection that AH does, including authentication, integrity, and antireplay protection, but it also encrypts the encapsulated upper layer headers and data. ESP does not protect the original IP headers directly, as AH does.

As shown in Figure 7-5, a transport mode ESP packet is protected with authentication (or HMAC signing) just after the original IP header, and encrypted starting just after the ESP header.

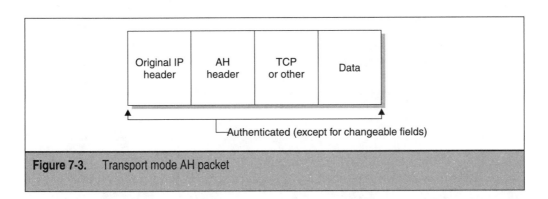

Figure 7-3.   Transport mode AH packet

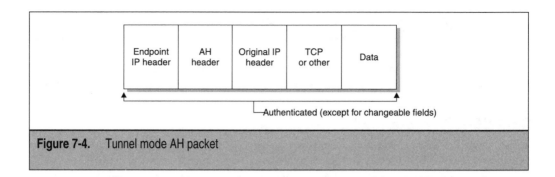

Figure 7-4. Tunnel mode AH packet

In tunnel mode, as shown in Figure 7-6, the original IP datagram, IP headers and all, is actually encapsulated and protected with both ESP authentication and encryption. The endpoint IP headers are not directly protected, but the ESP integrity check will fail if they are modified.

NOTE AH and ESP both provide authentication, integrity, and antireplay protection of IP datagrams. They differ in that AH signs the entire IP datagram with a hashing algorithm, while ESP encrypts the datagram payload.

L2TP/IPSEC FOR A VIRTUAL PRIVATE NETWORK

L2TP can be used over IPSec to create one of the most secure VPNs available. Many vendors, such as Cisco, provide products to support a solution that works with Windows clients. Previously, L2TP/IPSec support only existed in the Windows 2000/XP operating system. However, as we were writing this book, Microsoft released software that brings

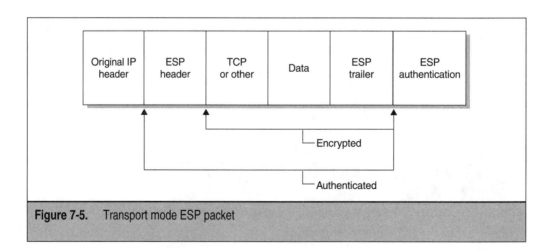

Figure 7-5. Transport mode ESP packet

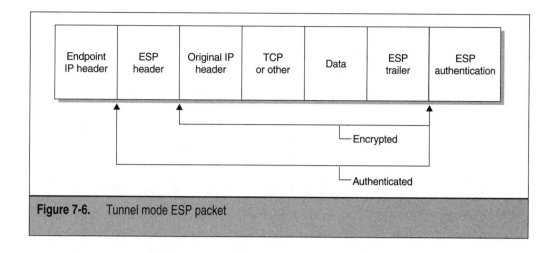

Figure 7-6.   Tunnel mode ESP packet

L2TP/IPSec support to Windows 9x/Me/NT clients. This VPN client even has support for the NAT-Traversal Internet draft currently being proposed in the halls of the IETF.

NOTE   Microsoft has released L2TP/IPSec VPN client software for Windows 9x/Me/NT clients, available from http://www.microsoft.com/windows2000/server/evaluation/news/bulletins/l2tpclient.asp.

Windows 2000/.NET server can natively serve as a VPN gateway for L2TP/IPSec remote access clients. However, Windows .NET is planned to include support for NAT-Traversal as well, when acting as a VPN gateway. At the time of this writing it was planned that Windows .NET Server will also provide configuration support for Diffie-Hellman 2048-bit keys in IKE as well.

NOTE   When using certificates with L2TP/IPSec, the trusted root CA must be the same for both the local computer and the remote gateway.

ADVANCED LOGGING

Much of IPSec's work is recorded in the event logs. For example, event ID 541 will show up in the Security log when a security association is successfully established. For troubleshooting and security monitoring purposes, you will want to keep an eye on some of the other event IDs as well, as listed in Table 7-3.

All the events in Table 7-3 are IKE-related events. As mentioned, IKE is where the action happens because the juicy negotiations for authentication and confidentiality take place in the ISAKMP exchanges.

Event ID	Description
541	IPSec security association established.
542	IPSec security association ended. Mode: Data Protection (Quick Mode)
543	IPSec security association ended. Mode: Key Exchange (Main Mode)
544	IPSec security association establishment failed because peer could not authenticate.
545	IPSec peer authentication failed.
546	IPSec security association establishment failed because peer sent invalid proposal.
547	IKE security association negotiation failed.

Table 7-3. IPSec-Related Event IDs

The Oakley Log

If you crave even more detail on what is really happening behind the scenes, you have a registry key at your disposal. To aid in troubleshooting IPSec connectivity, an Oakley log can be generated by creating the `EnableLogging` registry DWORD value set to 1 in the following key:

```
HKLM\System\CurrentControlSet\Services\PolicyAgent\Oakley\
```

The key and value must both be created, as they do not exist by default. Upon the next restart of the Policy Agent, a log file will be created in the %SYSTEMROOT%\Debug folder. All ISAKMP Main Mode and Quick Mode negotiations will be logged to the file along with such granular details as the SA and the SPI number and associated IP addresses.

SECURITY RISKS

To recap, IPSec provides end-to-end security for IP datagrams, including authentication, confidentiality, integrity, and antireplay protection for every packet. So where is the risk in that? The risk is in the exceptions.

Quite simply, IPSec starts its protection at the network layer, meaning that IP traffic and associated higher layer protocols like TCP and UDP are protected. What is not protected includes

- Lower layer protocols (e.g., ARP)
- Higher layer application flaws (e.g., web server buffer overflows)
- Non-IP traffic (e.g., AppleTalk, IPX/SPX)

IP security is just that—protection for IP traffic. Be aware that these other types of protocols are not protected. Also, if you haven't patched your SQL or IIS server for the latest buffer overflow or denial of service attack, then IPSec will not be able to protect against the clients that you allow through.

Preshared Keys

In addition, there is a danger when using preshared keys for authentication. Microsoft specifically recommends that preshared keys be used only for testing and not in a final live implementation. Preshared keys are stored in clear text in the registry, where they are readable by anyone with administrative rights. Also, they are stored in Active Directory where they are readable by Authenticated Users by default. Lastly, preshared key authentication just does not stack up to the level of secure authentication that certificates and Kerberos provide.

Default Exemptions

The Microsoft implementation of IPSec defaults to exempt several types of traffic from your filters. So even if you have a filter set up to block all IP traffic, the following types will still be permitted to pass with no security applied to them (by default):

- **Broadcast traffic**   Traffic from one sender to many receivers on the same subnet

- **Multicast traffic**   Traffic from one sender to many receivers in the address range of 224.0.0.0 to 239.255.255.255

- **Resource Reservation Protocol (RSVP) traffic**   IP Protocol ID 46, used for Quality of Service (QoS) of IP traffic

- **Internet Key Exchange (IKE) traffic**   Crucial to IPSec functionality, uses UDP port 500

- **Kerberos**   The core authentication protocol of a Windows 2000/XP domain, travels over TCP/UDP port 88

 SECURITY ALERT   By default, if you set up a filter to block all IP traffic, the exempt traffic will not be blocked. For example, this means that an attacker could trick your computer into permitting traffic just because the attacker's packet has a TCP source port of 88.

These exemptions are enabled by default to facilitate most normal network operations. In other words, broadcast traffic is necessary to many networking operations. In addition, IKE is crucial to IPSec functionality, and Kerberos traffic is standard in a Windows 2000/ XP domain.

NoDefaultExempt

Microsoft has provided a configurable registry key to disable some of these default exemptions and enable IPSec protection for these traffic types. Add the NoDefaultExempt DWORD value in the following key:

```
HKLM\SYSTEM\CurrentControlSet\Services\IPSec\
```

The default exemptions can be controlled with the following settings:

- 0 = Exemptions are still active
- 1 = Disable the exemption for RSVP and Kerberos traffic

A reboot is required in Windows XP after NoDefaultExempt is changed, but only a service restart is needed in Windows 2000.

TOOLS OF THE TRADE

Some new tools are available to monitor and get details about IPSec policies and connections.

Ping A simple ICMP echo request packet provides a fair bit of aid to verifying or troubleshooting IPSec connections. If there was a filter that required security for all ICMP traffic between a computer named Cottons and DMZDC, you would see the "Negotiating IP Security" message when you first tried to ping, as in the following output:

```
C:\WINDOWS\system32>ping 192.168.44.132
Pinging 192.168.44.132 with 32 bytes of data:
Negotiating IP Security.

Reply from 192.168.44.132: bytes=32 time<1ms TTL=128
Reply from 192.168.44.132: bytes=32 time<1ms TTL=128
Reply from 192.168.44.132: bytes=32 time<1ms TTL=128

Ping statistics for 192.168.44.132:
    Packets: Sent = 4, Received = 3, Lost = 1 (25% loss),
Approximate round trip times in milli-seconds:
    Minimum = 0ms, Maximum = 0ms, Average = 0ms
```

IP Security Monitor (MMC Snap-In) This monitoring tool replaces the IPSecmon.exe tool from Windows 2000. It provides much more detailed information through an MMC snap-in. Use this tool to get the details of current Main Mode and Quick Mode filters and Security Associations. Figure 7-7 shows an example of the Main Mode SA created between COTTONS and DMZDC after IP security was negotiated.

Netdiag.exe   Netdiag.exe installs with the Support Tools package available from the /Support folder of the Windows XP installation CD. It is a scriptable tool that runs from the command prompt. Netdiag performs a wealth of network-related diagnostic tests, one of which happens to be IPSec. To get the most verbose and detailed information about the assigned IPSec policies on a host, run **netdiag /test:ipsec /v /debug** and, toward the end of the tests, you will see output similar to the following:

```
IP Security test . . . . . . . . . : Passed
    Service status  is: Started
    Service startup is: Automatic
    Local IPSec Policy Active: 'CORPXPPRO to DMZDC'
    Description: 'Secure telnet and terminal server connection
for remote administration.'

    Last Change (Timestamp): Tue Jul 30 23:59:42 2002
    Policy Path:
HKLM\SOFTWARE\Policies\Microsoft\Windows\IPSec\Policy\Local\
ipsecPolicy{c5d3c11f6-49e6-40fc-9664-e633bc57f0}
    Note: run "ipseccmd /?" for more detailed information

The command completed successfully
```

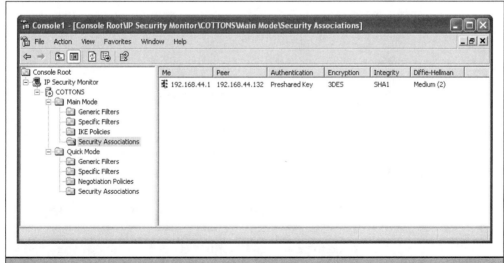

Figure 7-7.   IP Security Monitor MMC snap-in showing Main Mode SA

IPSeccmd.exe   Also from the Support Tools package, IPSeccmd.exe is a multifunction tool that will provide you with a mountain of options to both configure and query IPSec policy information. With this command line tool, you can script up IPSec policies from scratch. IPSeccmd.exe will let you define an entire policy, with rules, filters, authentication methods, and filter actions, all from the ground up. Essentially, everything that can be done from the GUI can be done from the command line, and more.

IPSeccmd.exe provides nearly the same functionality that IPSecpol.exe from the Windows 2000 Resource Kit provided. For example, dynamic mode policies (those that persist only until reboot) can be created for Windows 2000 machines (Windows XP does not support dynamic mode). Otherwise, standard static mode policies can be created as well.

An enormous amount of policy information can be queried. Type **ipseccmd.exe show all** to display policies, filters, IPSec usage statistics, and IKE SAs. The information displayed is different from what Netdiag shows because it is much more detailed and focused on IPSec.

IPSecScan.exe   As an IT professional you may very well want to know which computers on your network are IPSec enabled. IPSecScan.exe from Arne Vidstrom is available at http://www.ntsecurity.nu, and it is one of the only IPSec scanners available. You run it from the command prompt: just give it an IP range, and IPSecScan.exe will scan for IP protocol ID 50 and 51, as well as UDP 500, which is where IKE runs, in an attempt to identify computers running IPSec.

CHECKLIST: IP SECURITY

IP security has many important uses. An IPSec policy can be designed on a single host to essentially act as a personal firewall, blocking all traffic except that which you specifically permit. Policies can be used in transport mode between two hosts to provide end-to-end authentication, confidentiality, and integrity of each IP packet. In tunnel mode, policies can provide security for encapsulated IP packets between two gateways.

Some important chapter highlights to remember include:

- ☐   IP Security (IPSec) is made up of several protocols, including IKE for authentication and AH or ESP for packet protection.
- ☐   In Windows, only one IPSec policy can be assigned at any given time.
- ☐   An IPSec policy can consist of many rules, each of which can consist of many filters.
- ☐   An IPSec rule can either permit the defined traffic, block it, or negotiate security for it.
- ☐   Use IPSec tunnel mode to protect all IP traffic between two gateways.
- ☐   Use IPSec transport mode to secure host-to-host communications.

☐ Authentication methods available include certificates, Kerberos, and preshared keys.

☐ L2TP can be used with IPSec to create a remote access VPN solution.

☐ Advanced logging can be set up to get extended Oakley information.

☐ The default exemptions that exist in Windows will permit certain types of traffic even if you have a policy that specifically denies them.

☐ Preshared keys should only be used for testing, and not in production, as they are stored in clear text in both the registry and Active Directory.

☐ Set the `NoDefaultExempt` registry key to 1 to disable the Kerberos and RSVP exemptions.

☐ New tools in Windows XP include IPSeccmd.exe and the IP Security Monitor MMC snap-in.

☐ New tools in Windows .NET include those in Windows XP plus Netsh.exe support for IPSec.

☐ New designs and features added to Windows .NET include support for the NAT-Traversal IETF Internet draft proposal, support for Network Load Balancing (NLB), support for Resultant Set of Policy (RSoP) processing, and configurable Diffie-Hellman key sizes in IKE with L2TP/IPSec.

CHAPTER 8

Firewalls

F*irewalls!?! We don't need no stinkin' firewalls!*
If only that were the case, life would be much simpler. The reason you need a firewall is rather obvious by now. If you don't know, you probably shouldn't be reading this book.

In this chapter we will focus on your options regarding built-in firewall and access control capabilities in Windows XP Professional. The ability of anyone with a computer to become a hacker and target unsuspecting systems on the Internet has led to many robust features in the latest operating systems from Microsoft. The built-in firewall features add to your *defense-in-depth* strategy, which utilizes several layers of defenses.

Up until recently, firewalls were typically used to protect just networks. The advent of the personal firewall for each computer has really strengthened the overall security architecture of most companies. Host-based firewalls have brought security controls to the end user's system. In this chapter we will examine firewall options in general and Internet Connection Firewall (ICF) and Internet Connection Sharing (ICS) in Windows XP in particular.

FIREWALL BEST PRACTICES

There are lots of implementation configurations you can do with just about every firewall out there, whether they are network- or host-based. ICF can be used as a host or network firewall. Key concepts and practices you want to utilize are shown in Table 8-1.

Practice	Reason
Drop traffic that is not specifically allowed.	Denying packets sends information back to the attacker and lets the attacker know what some of your filter rules may be.
Restrict services that are not specifically allowed.	By using only allowed rules, you decrease the likelihood of misconfigurations and complex filter rules.
Consider how different types of firewalls work best in the different locations of your network.	ICF may be inappropriate as your Internet gateway firewall but may serve in a DMZ or in the CorpLAN. ICF is not meant to replace a robust firewall such as ISA or Checkpoint Firewall-1.
Disable ICMP responses.	Why let attackers know your systems are even alive? Multiple layers of defense are needed in a defense-in-depth strategy.
Enable any feature that will prevent IP spoofing if it is not already on by default.	This is a fundamental feature in most firewalls.
Autoblocking of attacking IP addresses should be enabled if the firewall has the functionality. Unfortunately ICF cannot do this, yet.	This active response to an attack can strengthen your security posture. If unmanaged, however, active response can also cause problems when, for example, a friendly computer is mistaken as an attacker.

Table 8-1. Firewall Best Practices

Practice	Reason
Utilize any Denial of Service prevention functionality that may be part of the firewall.	The more features you put in play against DoS attacks the better. Router access control lists alone will not be enough.
Enable egress filtering if the functionality is available. Unfortunately, ICF does not do egress filtering.	Trojans, worms, and malicious code take advantage of outbound connections once they have compromised a system. Block unnecessary outbound traffic to minimize the propogation of such attacks.

Table 8-1. Firewall Best Practices *(continued)*

DENIAL OF SERVICE (DOS) PREVENTION STEPS

With a defense-in-depth strategy, you have multiple places to try and stop DoS attacks. In our network diagram (see the "Blueprints" section of the book), we have two firewalls where we can set up filter rules to block certain types of DoS attacks. On the individual machines in the DMZ and CorpLAN, we can implement operating system features and personal firewall features to further increase our ability to stop DoS attacks.

The three basic forms of DoS attacks are

- Consumption of scarce, limited, or nonrenewable resources
- Destruction or alteration of configuration information
- Physical destruction or alteration of network components

In Windows 2000 and XP, we can use the following registry keys, described further in Chapter 3, to help protect the operating system from attack:

- HKLM\SYSTEM\CurrentControlSet\
  Services\Tcpip\Parameters\synattackprotect=1 REG_DWORD

- HKLM\SYSTEM\CurrentControlSet\
  Services\Tcpip\Parameters\\tcpmaxconnectresponseretransmissions=2
  REG_DWORD

- HKLM\SYSTEM\CurrentControlSet\
  Services\Tcpip\Parameters\\tcpmaxdataretransmissions=3 REG_DWORD

- HKLM\SYSTEM\CurrentControlSet\
  Services\Tcpip\Parameters\\enablepmtudiscovery=0 REG_DWORD

Windows XP and Windows 2000's implementation of "raw sockets" allows programs to manipulate the TCP/IP data packets, thanks to the inclusion of the IP_HDRINCL option. With this ability, it is possible for a Trojan or "zombie" program that is installed on a Windows XP system to be used to launch spoofed DoS attacks against other systems. This is not a Windows XP–specific problem, of course, as many other operating systems have this capability (earlier versions of Windows have this capability thanks to third-party drivers such as WinPCap), but it is something to be aware of when protecting your systems from falling victim to, or participating in, DoS attacks.

To help secure your systems from being "DoSed," you can take the following steps:

- Implement router filter rules that can restrict flooding attacks, both inbound and outbound.

- Implement any patches to the operating systems that can restrict TCP SYN flooding attacks.

- A service cannot be attacked if it is not running, so disable unused network services.

- Take advantage of quota functionality in the network devices and operating systems if possible.

- Minimize your points of failure by having redundancy built into the architecture.

- Develop operating metrics to allow you to quickly identify out-of-the-ordinary activity.

- Establish and maintain regular backup schedules and policies, particularly for important configuration information.

- Use network-based intrusion detection systems (IDS) to monitor traffic and get detailed packet information.

- Larger organizations may be able to gain the assistance of their ISP in modifying router rules for ISP-owned routers.

GROUP POLICY

Group Policy settings that allow the use of ICS, ICF, and Network Bridge are determined by the domain administrator in most corporate environments. The group policy in a corporate network can be used to restrict or disable networking functionality. Operating in a corporate environment with the capabilities of ICF and ICS can cause network problems.

When connecting to a corporate domain, the group policy can be used to restrict networking services using the location-aware Group Policy settings. Group Policy configurations can be set for groups of users and computers to restrict functions and can be used with Active Directory containers. A group policy object (GPO) can be a local computer GPO or a domain-based GPO.

The Group Policy Microsoft Management Console (MMC) snap-in is used to create GPOs. You can access the Group Policy editor through Start → Run → gpedit.msc. Group Policy settings include "User Configuration specific" and "Computer Configuration specific." The Winlogon service polls for changes every 90 minutes by default (but every 5 minutes for domain controllers). When a change is detected in the computer configuration, an update is performed. Manual updates can be executed with Gpupdate.exe /target:computer on a Windows XP computer and Secedit.exe /refreshpolicy machine_policy on a Windows 2000 computer.

For ICF and ICS purposes, the default Group Policy settings for Windows XP and .NET (found under Computer Configuration → Administrative Templates → Network Connections) set the Computer Configuration Group Policy as follows:

- **Prohibit use of Internet Connection Sharing on your DNS domain network**   Not configured

- **Prohibit use of Internet Connection Firewall on your DNS domain network**   Not configured

- **Prohibit installation and configuration of Network Bridge on your DNS domain network**   Not configured

- **IEEE 802.1x Certificate Authority for Machine Authentication** Not configured

Because these GPOs are set to "Not configured" by default, there is no prohibition on the use of ICS and ICF, and no CA configured for machine authentication. (Note that these GPO settings are not available in Windows 2000.) The administrator can change these settings using the Group Policy snap-in; as shown in Figure 8-1, where all are Enabled.

While we demonstrate enabling all of these settings, your needs may vary. You would, for instance, choose to disable the "Prohibit use of Internet Connection Firewall on your DNS domain network" setting when you are utilizing ICF in your network.

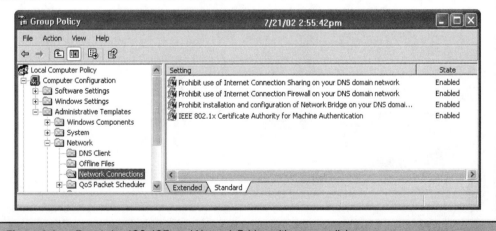

Figure 8-1.   Restricting ICS, ICF, and Network Bridge with group policies

Within the registry, the keys associated with these Group Policy settings are the following:

- `HKLM\SOFTWARE\Policies\Microsoft\Windows\Network Connections\NC_AllowNetbridge_NLA`

- `HKLM\SOFTWARE\Policies\Microsoft\Windows\Network Connections\NC_PersonalFirewallConfig`

- `HKLM\SOFTWARE\Policies\Microsoft\Windows\Network Connections\NC_ShowSharedAccessUI`

The User Configuration Group Policy settings in the User Configuration → Administrative Templates → Network → Network Connections node can also be modified. Using the Group Policy snap-in, you can modify the settings to either give or restrict a user's ability to view and modify the computer's network connections and properties, as shown in Figure 8-2.

In Figure 8-2, we enabled the following settings to restrict the domain users' ability to modify network connections.

- Prohibit TCP/IP advanced configuration

- Prohibit access to the Advanced Settings item on the Advanced menu

- Prohibit Enabling/Disabling components of a LAN connection

- Ability to change properties of an all user remote access connection

- Prohibit access to the New Connection Wizard

- Prohibit access to the Dial-up Preferences item on the Advanced menu

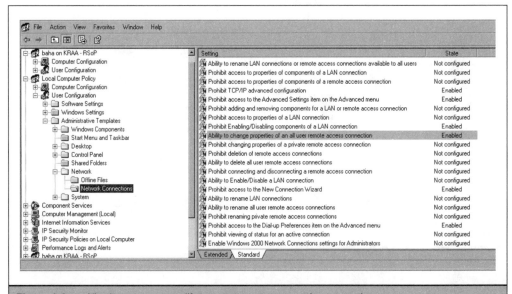

Figure 8-2.   Allowing users to modify remote access connection properties

You should note that some of these settings can be overridden by other GPO settings. For instance, if you have set the "Enable Windows 2000 Network Connections settings for Administrators" setting to "Disabled" or "Not configured" while the "Prohibit TCP/IP advanced configuration" setting is enabled, then Administrators will still be able to modify advanced TCP/IP configurations. Likewise, you could enable this setting to prevent even Administrators from modifying network connections.

There are a couple of different ways to manage these Windows XP–specific GPO settings in a Windows 2000 domain. You can either launch the Group Policy MMC snap-in from a Windows XP computer (as explained in Chapter 11), or you can export the .ADM file from a Windows XP computer to a Windows 2000 domain controller. The first option will be the easiest to manage, but if you want to update the DC to use the Windows XP core Group Policy settings, use the file System.adm. On your Windows XP system:

1. Copy *systemroot*\Inf\System.adm to the Windows 2000 domain controller as System_xp.adm in *systemroot*\Inf.

2. In Administrative Tools → Active Directory Users and Computers, right-click the container to apply the Windows XP core Group Policy settings, and select Properties → Group Policy → Edit.

3. In the Group Policy snap-in, select Computer Configuration → Administrative Templates → Add/Remove Templates, click "system" under Name, and click Remove.

4. Select Add/Remove Templates → Add → Policy Templates, choose the file System_xp.adm, and click Open.

Repeat these steps for each domain controller.

INTERNET CONNECTION FIREWALL (ICF)

ICF is available for local area network (LAN), Point-to-Point Protocol over Ethernet (PPPoE), VPN, or dial-up connections. Windows XP includes native support for PPPoE, which is geared toward broadband connection users. ICF cannot, however, be enabled on the Internet Connection Sharing (ICS) private adapter, a member of the Network Bridge, the Network Bridge, or incoming connections. The two basic scenarios in which you will most likely use ICF are these:

- Securing a single PC connected to the Internet, either directly or indirectly in a LAN

- Securing a single PC on an untrusted corporate intranet

ICF does not support the following transport protocols:

- IPX
- NetBEUI
- IPv6

> **NOTE** ICF will not work with custom dialer software such as that from AOL or ATT. It will only work with MSN 8. A set of APIs is available within the Platform SDK to enable independent software vendors (ISVs) to utilize ICF, however, so these problems will probably be addressed in the future.

ICF falls in the stateful packet filter category, because it keeps a table of active connections. Once a connection is terminated, the state information is removed from the table. ICF uses the following rules when filtering:

- If a connection is established, a packet matching that connection is allowed.

- A packet sent from the host will create a new connection in the table if it does not match any of the current connections.

- If a packet is received but doesn't match a connection already in the table, it will be compared against the filter rules to decide whether it is allowed or dropped.

Built into ICF is the ability to drop packets with impossible flag combinations, such as SYN and FIN set on a single packet, which can help defend against DoS attacks.

Configuration

By default, ICF is not turned on for each connection. You can enable ICF either through the Network Setup wizard or through manual configuration. Both means allow the user to eventually configure each component of the network connection.

Network Setup Wizard

The Network Setup wizard will enable the ICF on all Internet connections. The default firewall rules will be enabled. These settings basically restrict all inbound connections that have not been initiated by an outbound connection from the local host. In addition to blocking unsolicited incoming traffic, the ability to ping the local host is also restricted. The wizard does not set up logging by default.

The wizard can also set up the Network Bridge, shared files and printers, and computer names for systems. Basically, you use the floppy disks created by the wizard to set up other systems on the network that will be using the ICF host as a gateway. This is really more of a home networking feature. During the wizard setup, you can create a network floppy to allow you to run the setup wizard on other systems in your network that will use your ICF gateway. The wizard can be run on other systems (such as Windows ME, Windows 98, and Windows XP) from a floppy or CD.

You run the setup wizard from Start → Control Panel → Network Connections and select "Set up a home or small office network." Once the wizard begins, select the connection type, either direct to the Internet or through another computer, as shown in Figure 8-3.

Change the hostname and workgroup through the next several screens as needed. Once you have finished you can create a network setup disk to run on

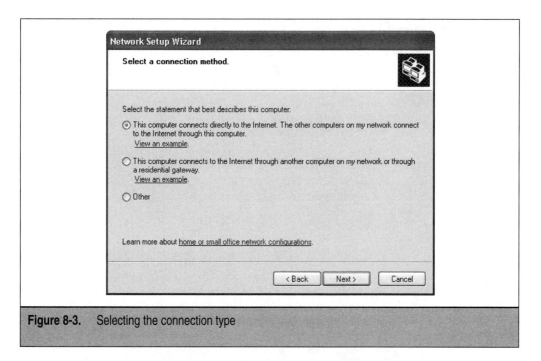

Figure 8-3.   Selecting the connection type

Windows 98/Me/2000/XP or just complete the setup on the current computer, as shown in Figure 8-4.

Figure 8-4.   Creating a network setup disk

Manual Configuration

You can also choose to manually configure ICF. To select the adapter you wish to run ICF on, go through Start → Control Panel → Network Connections. Select the properties of the adapter, click the Advanced tab, and select the ICF check box, as shown in Figure 8-5.

In the Settings window, you can modify the default allowed or disallowed services (all are off by default). For network services you have running on your computer, you can use ICF to allow or disallow access. Even though all services may be running, ICF will control access to those ports mapped to the running services. In Figure 8-6, we are disallowing all inbound access to running services except FTP. The FTP port 21 will been seen as open on an external port scan. All other unsolicited inbound access to running services will be blocked by ICF.

Port Mapping

By default, ICF has a number of service rules that can be turned on or off. You can set up custom port mapping that can be shared by both ICS and ICF if both are running. The built-in port mappings are turned off by default, making a default install secure. Even ICMP is disabled by default.

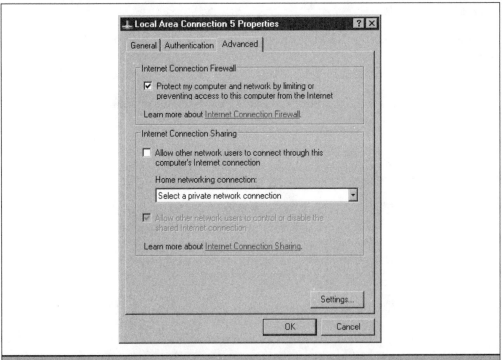

Figure 8-5.   Turning on ICF manually

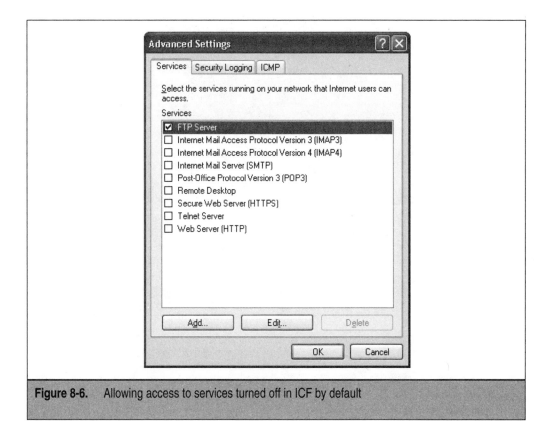

Figure 8-6. Allowing access to services turned off in ICF by default

NOTE   One convenient—though perhaps bad—feature about ICF port mapping is that an application can automatically install its own port mappings and enable them. An example of this is Windows Messenger. With most applications, trying to modify the ICF rules triggers a warning message letting the user choose to allow or disallow the modification. But some Microsoft applications, such as Windows Messenger, will not warn the user at all. Beware.

To add your own specific service, go through Start → Control Panel → Network Connections. Select the properties of the adapter, select the Advance tab, and click the Settings button. Then click the Add button to create a service, as shown in Figure 8-7.

As an example, on our system we have a TCP network service called Kraagen running. We need to allow access to this service through the firewall. In Figure 8-7, we created a rule called Kraagen Custom Service, which runs on port 27201. The external port number would be seen from the Internet side, and the internal port number will be the actual port number on your computer. We can now see the service turned on in the list of services, as shown in Figure 8-8.

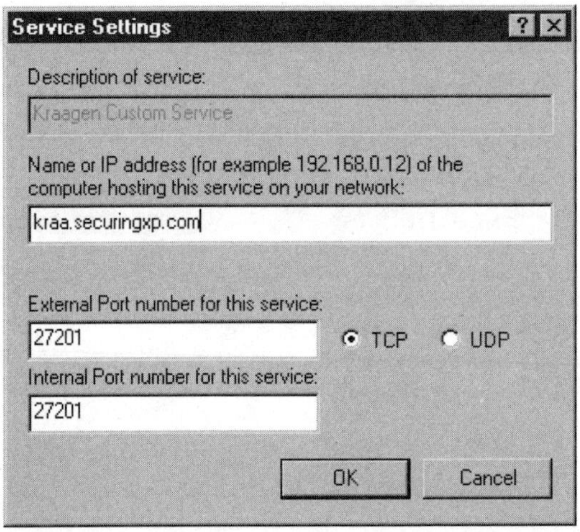

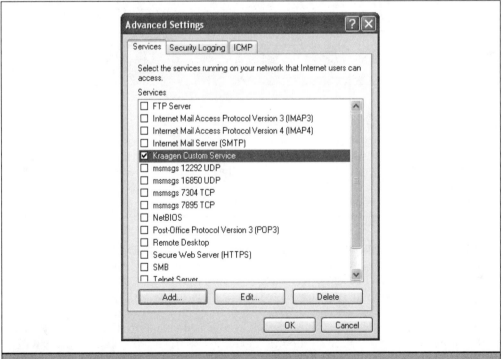

Figure 8-7.   Custom service and port setup

Figure 8-8.   Custom network service, Kraagen, is now allowed through the firewall.

If we were going to use a stand-alone system on the company's network, we could have whatever services we want running on the desktop/laptop such as Web and FTP, and allow them through the laptop firewall by selecting the appropriate ruleset.

Internet Control Message Protocol (ICMP) Options

By default, ICF drops externally initiated inbound ICMP traffic. To modify the ICMP options, go through Start → Control Panel → Network Connections. Select Properties of the adapter, select the Advanced tab, and click the Settings button. From here, select the ICMP tab, and you will see that by default none of the options are checked, as shown in Figure 8-9.

The defined rules allow you to modify nine different types of ICMP traffic, as shown in Figure 8-9.

Application Programming Interface (API)

Several APIs are provided to allow third-party applications to interact with ICF. An administrator can use the designed APIs to customize a configuration editor for ICF through one of the .NET programming languages. Several of these APIs are listed in Table 8-2.

NOTE   When a method either enables or disables ICF, a dialog box is opened, warning the user.

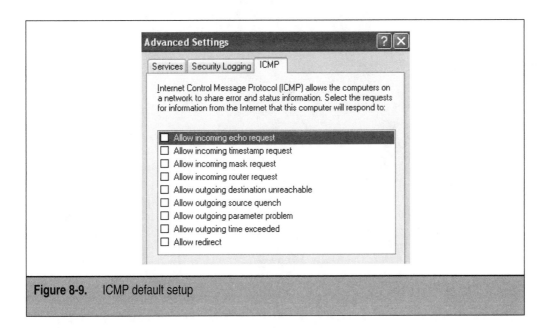

Figure 8-9.   ICMP default setup

Function	API
Determine an interface for a connection	INetSharingManager::get_INetSharingConfigurationForINetConnection
To check if ICF is enabled	INetSharingConfiguration::get_InternetFirewallEnabled
To disable ICF	INetSharingConfiguration::DisableInternetFirewall
To enable ICF	INetSharingConfiguration::EnableInternetFirewall
Enumerate port mappings	INetSharingConfiguration::EnumPortMappings
Add a port mapping to an interface	INetSharingConfiguration::AddPortMapping
Remove a port mapping from an interface	INetSharingConfiguration::RemovePortMapping

Table 8-2. APIs for Interacting with ICF

Logging

By default, logging is not enabled. You can enable logging and set up the file-size limit for the log file. Logging is limited to dropped packets and successful connections (both inbound and outbound), as shown in Figure 8-10. The default filename is %systemroot%\pfirewall.log. You may want to change this to something else by simply specifying a different file location and name.

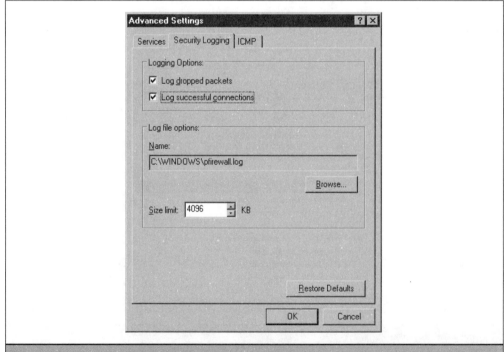

Figure 8-10. Logging functions in ICF

Logs are generated in World Wide Web Consortium (W3C) Extended Log Format, which can be used by log analysis programs. The log shown in the following output shows dropped inbound packets and successful inbound and outbound connections (the output is wrapped to fit the page).

```
#Version: 1.0
#Software: Microsoft Internet Connection Firewall
#Time Format: Local
#Fields: date time action protocol src-ip dst-ip src-port dst-port size tcpflags
 tcpack tcpsyn tcpack tcpwin icmptype icmpcode info
2002-04-21 22:29:15 OPEN UDP 192.168.44.130 10.0.2.101 137 137
2002-04-21 22:29:24 DROP ICMP 10.0.2.101 192.168.44.130 - - 60 - - - - 8 0
2002-04-21 22:30:49 OPEN UDP 192.168.44.130 192.168.44.1 68 67 - - - - - -
2002-04-21 22:31:14 DROP TCP 10.0.2.101 192.168.44.130 1035 445 48 S 3873330287
 0 16384
2002-04-21 22:31:25 DROP ICMP 10.0.2.101 192.168.44.130- - 60 - - - - 8 0
2002-04-21 22:31:29 OPEN-INBOUND TCP 10.0.2.101 192.168.44.1301037 21
2002-04-21 22:31:36 OPEN TCP 192.168.44.130 10.0.2.101 20 1039
2002-04-21 22:31:50 CLOSE TCP 192.168.44.130 10.0.2.101 20 1039
2002-04-21 22:34:20 OPEN TCP 192.168.44.130 10.0.2.101 3504 445
2002-04-21 22:34:20 DROP TCP 10.0.2.202 10.0.2.101 3505 139 48 S 3265931610
 0 16384
```

The log includes the information shown in Table 8-3.

Item	Description	Example
#Version	Internet Connection Firewall version	1.0
#Software	Security software	Microsoft Internet Connection Firewall
#Time	Timestamps	Local
Action	Action taken based on filter rules	Open
Date	Date of log entry	2002-04-21
Time	Time of log entry	22:31:36
Protocol	Protocol of logged entry	TCP
Src-IP	Source IP address	192.168.44.130
Dst-IP	Destination IP address	10.0.2.101
Src-port	Source port	20
Dst-port	Destination port	1039
Size	Packet size in bytes	60
TCPflags	TCP control flags from the TCP header of an IP packet	Syn
TCPsyn	TCP sequence number in the packet	145362721
TCPack	TCP acknowledgment number in the packet	0
TCPwin	TCP window size in bytes in the packet	63728

Table 8-3. List of log fields

Limitations

As mentioned earlier, the most significant weakness of ICF is its inability to filter *egress* (outbound) traffic. With constant attacks from viruses and worms, egress filtering has taken on more importance in your firewall functionality. Logging is probably the second major weakness of ICF. It is rather limited, and does not notify you when activity is occurring, such as when packets are being dropped.

Other problems with ICF include:

- Incoming broadcast or multicast traffic is not blocked.

- If a remote assistance request is created, and ICF is started after the request is made, the request cannot be answered. The request must be reissued.

- Service Redirection does not apply to ICF (see Microsoft Knowledge Base article Q297942).

- There is no notification when the system is being attacked.

- To redirect traffic to other ports, ICS is needed.

- ICF enables a Lightweight Directory Access Protocol (LDAP) proxy on port 389 and appears to accept connections when nothing actually happens. LDAP is part of the firewall service. A Telnet connection to 389 will show a successful connection even though no listening service is running on the port. This can also occur with ports 21, 1002, and 1720. This quirk shows up when you run a port scan from a system running ICF, in which case the private side of the FTP or LDAP proxy (these protocols use dynamically opened ports) responds with an Ack, without checking where the Ack is coming from. It appears as a valid connection. Since ICF and ICS are implemented as one service, this will occur even when you don't have ICS enabled.

- ICF prevents browsing the network by means of the Windows NetBIOS protocol. You have to set specific rules to allow NetBIOS communications. Ports that need to be set up include:
  - TCP/UDP 135 RPC/DCE Endpoint mapper
  - TCP/UDP 137 NetBIOS Name Service
  - UDP 138 NetBIOS Datagram Service
  - TCP 139 NetBIOS Session Service
  - TCP/UDP 445 Microsoft SMB/CIFS

- Port ranges cannot be specified, only specific ports.

- Some Microsoft applications, such as Windows Messenger, can install custom ports and filters without notifying the user. To check this, you must look at the filter rules.

- ICF does not check for applications launching, as other personal firewalls now do. Such functionality could be helpful for stopping Trojans or worms from launching applications on your system.

> ## CHALLENGE
>
> In your corporation, you have power users. These folks are masters of their own laptops. As you know, in today's connected world remote access is a must-have. Road warriors wield their laptops like a sword in battle. The problem with swords, however, is that if you are not careful, you can cut yourself instead of the enemy.
>
> The challenge you face as an administrator is that when you send out laptops with these road warriors, you lose the ability to protect them. How do you secure your internal network from perhaps-dangerous laptops, and protect them when they are out of the office? When they come back, these laptops can create havoc on your internal network if they set up their own server services, such as DHCP or DNS. How do you manage these powerful laptops on your network?
>
> The answer is that you must use Group Policies to push protections onto your road warriors. First off, think about how to protect them when they are out of the office. The simplest solution—assuming you want to avoid the costs of third-party firewall software—is to set up ICF on their laptops. By implementing ICF, you can easily turn on a very simple firewall that power users can understand and learn to modify as necessary. If you need to remotely administer these laptops, set up appropriate rulesets in ICF to allow you to connect via Remote Desktop and Remote Assistance.
>
> Second, you have to consider how to integrate these users back into the corporate network when they return to the office. This can be easily controlled once they log in to the domain at the office. Using your GPO, you can force their laptops to shut down ICF and ICS. This makes their machines available for you to remotely administer and keeps them from doing any kind of network bridging or hiding from your port scans by blocking ICMP. Assuming you protect your internal users, you shouldn't have to worry too much about them not running a personal firewall when logged into the corporate domain.
>
> Unfortunately, Microsoft did not include many GPO settings that control ICF, other than a couple that allow or prohibit its use. You can still get creative with logon and logoff scripts, however, to control the behavior of ICF, until a future update is provided that offers more GPO settings.

INTERNET CONNECTION SHARING (ICS)

ICS is used to allow one computer (host) to share its network connection with other computers on the network. Computers (clients) behind the ICS host will be protected from direct connections to the Internet by the host computer. The host handles all traffic in and out of the network as well as Network Address Translation (NAT) and DHCP. The host also handles Domain Name Service (DNS), because a local DNS resolver is built in.

An ICS host on an UPnP (Universal Plug and Play) network broadcasts its status periodically. UPnP is used by Windows XP ICS clients to detect and locate ICS hosts. Information such as connection status, uptime, and statistics are broadcast using UPnP. UPnP is used to connect or disconnect ICS, to list network address translation port mappings, or to create or modify port mappings.

 SECURITY ALERT   While UPnP provides great remote discovery functionality and ease of use, it is a broadcast medium, and problems may arise with it in the future. One critical vulnerability has already been discovered, as listed in Microsoft Security Bulletin MS01-059. We recommend you disable the UPnP service if you have no need for it.

Location-Aware Group Policy in ICS

Like ICF, ICS has the location-awareness Group Policy ability. When connected to a domain, the domain policy can be pushed down to the computer and thus protect it, using the security controls that are in place for the corporate network. You will not need to run ICS to share a connection, because you will be using the corporate network. When you are not connected to a domain, the ICS policy will automatically take over, and your computer can then become the ICS host again.

In your Group Policy editor, modify the setting through Computer Configuration → Administrative Templates → Network → Network Connections. Change the setting "Prohibit use of Internet Connection Sharing on your DNS domain network" to Enabled.

Configuration

To use ICS, the host system needs two network connections. The external adapter typically connects to the Internet, and the internal adapter is used to connect to the internal LAN. ICS must be enabled on the external connection. The connection is shared by all the other computers. Computers connecting through the ICS host should use DHCP to request an address from the internal network adapter. In the following output, the IP address we are using for the internal network is called "pcmcia card"; it has an address of 192.168.44.101. The external adapter has the address 10.0.2.133. Systems on the internal network will have an address on the subnet 192.168.44.X.

```
C:\>ipconfig
Windows IP Configuration
Ethernet adapter dell internal:
        Connection-specific DNS Suffix  . :
        Autoconfiguration IP Address. . . : 10.0.2.133
        Subnet Mask . . . . . . . . . . . : 255.255.255.0
        Default Gateway . . . . . . . . . : 10.0.2.1

Ethernet adapter pcmcia card:
        Connection-specific DNS Suffix  . :
```

```
Autoconfiguration IP Address. . . : 192.168.44.101
Subnet Mask . . . . . . . . . . : 255.255.255.0
Default Gateway . . . . . . . . :
```

When ICS is enabled on the external adapter, the internal adapter cannot have ICS turned on, as shown in Figure 8-11.

When you enable ICS, the local area network connection is given a new static IP address and configuration. Consequently, TCP/IP connections established between the internal LAN and the ICS host computer at the time of enabling ICS are lost and need to be reestablished. You must configure client machines on your LAN to use DHCP. Client computers running Windows 98, Windows 98 Second Edition, and Windows ME need to have the Network Setup wizard run to enable ICS Discovery and Control. Internet Explorer version 5.0 or later must also be installed.

The client computer may be disallowed from controlling the ICS connection, but the clients can always check the status of the shared connection by selecting the network connection and using the "View status of this connection" option under Network Tasks. To disallow clients from controlling the ICS connection or even disabling it, do not check the box labeled "Allow other network users to control or disable the shared Internet connection" on the Advanced tab when setting up the ICS connection.

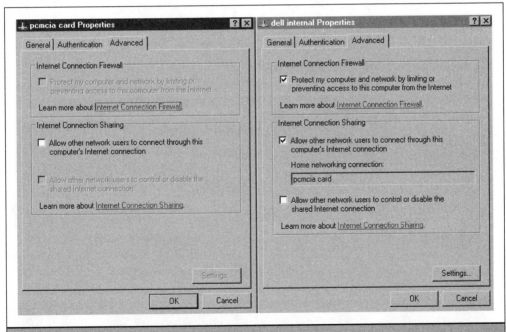

Figure 8-11. ICS enabled on the external adapter

To enable ICS, go through Start → Control Panel → Network Connections, and select the network connection that will be shared. Select properties for the connection, or select "Change the settings for this connection" from the Network Tasks list, and click the Advanced tab. Figure 8-12 shows that the ICS option is selected on the Internet-facing connection. "Home networking connection" is a drop-down list of the connections that you will use to connect to your private network of computers. In Figure 8-12, our network connection is named Local Area Connection 7.

If your computer is a client using another computer for ICS connectivity, you can configure it to look for the ICS computer. Through Control Panel → Internet Options → Connection, select "Never dial a connection," and then click LAN Settings. Under LAN Settings, clear the "Automatically detect settings" and "Use automatic configuration script" check boxes. When you set up ICF, you created the network setup disk to run on other computers. Using this disk, you can run the wizard on other computers in your network to allow them to use the ICS host. You can run the Netsetup.exe program to execute the wizard.

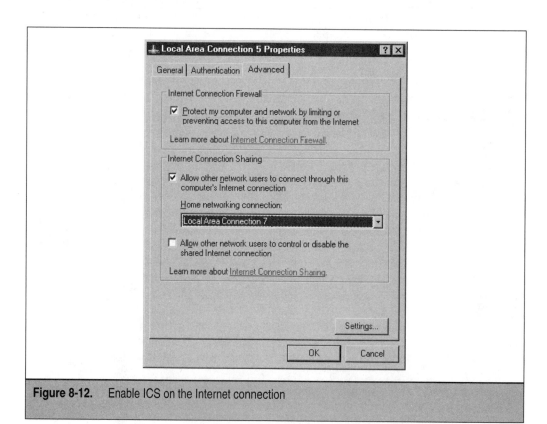

Figure 8-12. Enable ICS on the Internet connection

QoS for ICS

Networking Quality of Service (QoS) is used to prioritize types of traffic or applications in a network environment. The QoS in Windows XP can be used to speed up Internet Connection Sharing. If there is a mismatch between a fast and slow link, a bottleneck can arise because the fast link is pushing traffic faster than the slow link can handle. So when one network is connected to another, slower network, QoS can be used to maximize the throughput.

A Windows XP system running ICS can control the speed of traffic to accommodate different link speeds. By minimizing the problems with queuing up packets, packet loss can be reduced and transmissions made more stable. The QoS packet scheduler makes adjustments automatically for slower links.

Limitations

As a gateway, ICS performs well for small environments. But there are several limitations, including:

- No specific ICS logging functionality. While ICF logging is available for the firewall ruleset, connections through ICS cannot be tracked.

- No granular control of connecting systems. Each system using the Windows XP system as a gateway can do so without the permission of the ICS host.

- No ability to restrict internal systems or specify IP address or ranges.

- No control over DHCP. Any machine can acquire a DHCP address from the ICS host on the network.

- A host running ICS in stand-alone mode connected to a corporate network may disrupt legitimate DHCP service and network connectivity.

- Using the bridging capability between networks on a corporate network may cause broadcast and multicast traffic problems, as well as circumvent network connectivity restrictions.

NOTE   Internet Connection Sharing, Internet Connection Firewall, Discovery and Control, and Network Bridge are not available on Windows XP 64-Bit Edition.

NETWORK BRIDGING SUPPORT

Traditionally, connecting networks together would require configuring multiple IP address subnets and routers. The Network Bridge enables a Windows XP system to act as a bridge for these multiple network mediums. When multiple network connections are added to a Windows XP system and the Network Setup wizard is used to configure the system, the Network Bridge will automatically bridge the networks for you.

This makes it easy to connect multiple network segments and mediums. The Windows XP Network Bridge will route traffic to the correct network. For example, if your ICS host is connected to two different networks, 192.168.2.x and 10.0.2.x, you can use the Network Bridge to connect the two. To enable the bridge, select Start → Settings → Control Panel → Network Connections. Then select the two adapters that are the gateways for the two networks. Once they are selected, right-click the selected adapters and use the Bridge option. You will see Windows XP making the bridge, as shown here.

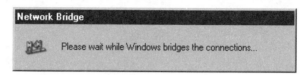

NETWORK DIAGNOSTICS FEATURES

Windows XP has added several network diagnostics features to help analyze and fix problems. New options include the following:

- **The network diagnostics web page and NetSh helper**   Executed from the Network Connections folder and the Tools option in Help and Support, this option lets you gather information about the local computer and the network. It can perform various diagnostic tests to find and fix problems. In addition, a NetSh helper DLL can be used to execute more tests from the command line. Use the command **netsh diag** to access the options for network diagnostic tests.

- **Network Connections Support tab**   Each network connection has a Support tab that provides information about the connection. This option replaces IPconfig and Winipcfg.exe, although you can still run Ipconfig.

- **Network Connection Repair**   On the Support tab of each network connection, the Repair button will perform a DHCP lease renew, flush the ARP cache, run Nbtstat –R, run Nbtstat –RR, flush the DNS cache, and register the DNS name.

- **Task Manager Networking tab**   The Networking tab in Task Manager shows networking statistics for each adapter.

- **Updated command line network diagnostics tool**   Netdiag.exe is a command line diagnostics tool provided with the Support Tools on the Windows XP install CD.

TOOLS OF THE TRADE

There weren't too many tools discussed in this chapter. Let's briefly recap the main ones you need to remember.

Internet Connection Firewall (ICF)   This built-in function is used to provide basic firewall features for a single computer or small network.

Internet Connection Sharing (ICS)   This function is used to share one network connection with multiple computers in a small network.

Netdiag.exe   This tool, installed through the support tools in Windows 2000 and Windows XP, is a command line diagnostic tool used to troubleshoot networking and connectivity problems.

Netsh.exe   This built-in command line script utility is used to display or modify the network configuration of your system, either locally or remotely.

CHECKLIST: FIREWALLS

Firewalls have made their way from network border defenses to personal computer defenses—and rightfully so. The functionality of personal firewalls such as ICF has increased over recent years to provide a secure yet convenient end user experience. Be aware of the convenient features of ICF, and utilize it only when you have a defined action plan for implementation and management of its functionality.

- ☐ Use the built-in registry keys to assist in stopping some forms of DoS attacks.
- ☐ Use router ACLs and enterprise firewalls to prevent DoS attacks, rather than relying on ICF.
- ☐ When in stand-alone mode or when in a remote environment (home, hotel, wireless airport connectivity), ICF should be turned on.
- ☐ Only enable rules that allow necessary functionality of inbound services. By default, all unsolicited inbound connections are dropped.
- ☐ Do not allow ping to the host. By default, ICMP rules are not enabled.
- ☐ Turn on logging and check log files periodically.
- ☐ Rename the ICF log file to something innocuous, and move it to a different directory than the default.

☐ Use group policy objects to control whether or not ICF and ICS can be used on the Windows XP clients in your network

☐ Configure services that you allow through the firewall securely, such as inbound FTP and HTTP.

☐ If you install any network services, such as Windows Messenger, check your ICF rules for any changes that you were not explicitly notified about.

☐ Investigate more robust personal firewalls for functionality that ICF does not have.

☐ Do not bridge your corporate network to outside connections such as a dial-up. This may provide a back door past your corporate firewall through your laptop/desktop machine.

☐ Use group policies in the corporate network to disable ICS on client systems.

☐ Enable QoS for ICS hosts.

CHAPTER 9

Wireless Networking
Security

Wireless technology releases us from copper wires. A user can have a notebook computer, PDA, Pocket PC, Tablet PC, or just a cell phone and stay online anywhere a wireless signal is available. The basic theory behind wireless technology is that signals can be carried by electromagnetic waves that are then transmitted to a signal receiver. But to make two wireless devices understand each other, we need protocols for communication.

In this chapter we will first take a look at what Windows XP Professional has promised to bring to you in wireless technology. Then we will discuss the current security problems with wireless networks and your options for dealing with them. Last, we will present two methods that you can use to secure your wireless networks.

You will see two concepts heavily reinforced: *authentication* and *encryption*. These concepts will be the glue for our two recommended methods of secure wireless networking. If you just cannot wait, the first method is a solution using an IPSec VPN located on (or behind) a dedicated firewall that separates the wireless network from an intranet. The other method uses a combination of 802.1x authentication with a back-end Internet Authentication Server and dynamic WEP keys for encryption. Both methods use strong authentication, which can be based on client certificates. For a clearer understanding, read on.

NOTE Refer to the "Blueprints" section of this book for network maps of the two recommended wireless network architectures.

It is easier to understand wireless technologies by categorizing them into three layers, as shown in Table 9-1. The three layers are *device, physical,* and *application and service* (protocol).

In the device layer (mobile devices) are gadgets ranging from the smallest cell phone to PDAs and notebook computers. These devices use wireless technologies to communicate with each other. The physical layer contains different physical encoding mechanisms for wireless communications. Bluetooth, 802.11x, CDMA, GSM, and 3G are different standards that define different methods to physically encode the data for transmission across the airwaves. In this chapter, we will focus on networks built upon

Layer	Technologies
Application and service	Wireless applications: WAP, i-mode, messaging, Voice over Wireless network, VoIP, location-based services
Physical	Wireless standards: 802.11a, 802.11b, 802.11g, AX.25, 3G, CDPD, CDMA, GSM, GPRS, radio, microwave, laser, Bluetooth, 802.15, 802.16, IrDA
Device	Mobile devices: PDAs, notebooks, cellular phones, pagers, handheld PCs, wearable computers

Table 9-1. Different Layers of Wireless Technologies

the 802.11x and Bluetooth standards. The application and service layer, also referred to as *ISO layers 2 to 7*, contains the protocols that enable wireless devices to process data in an end-to-end manner. Protocols like Wireless Application Protocol (WAP), Voice over IP (VoIP), and i-mode reside in this layer.

Many security problems can be traced back to the end user in wired networks. Wireless networks are no exception, and it is typically the IT department's responsibility to protect the end user. Before your enterprise adopts the latest wireless network technologies, you will need to

- Understand the capability of current products
- Understand your networking needs
- Understand the potential risk you are facing
- Find a solution tailored to your environment

WINDOWS XP'S SUPPORT FOR WIRELESS TECHNOLOGIES

Wireless Infrared Data Association (IrDA) devices have been supported across many Windows operating systems, including Windows 9x/NT/2000. Windows 2000 natively supports some 802.11 wireless network devices, such as the original Lucent Wavelan card. Windows XP continues the support of IrDa and enhances the support of 802.11b (Wi-Fi) wireless network devices natively. Bluetooth support might be enabled in the near future.

There are two categories of wireless technology, distinguished by the distances they can cover: *wireless personal area network* (WPAN) and *wireless local area network* (WLAN), as discussed in the following sections.

WPAN

As the name "personal area network" suggests, such a network is small—in the range of about 10 meters (30 feet). Infrared Data Association (IrDA) and Bluetooth are the main WPAN wireless technologies; they exist in the physical layer (see Table 9-1). The devices that take advantage of a WPAN include PDAs, printers, cameras, cell phones, and access points, to name a few. The support of IrDA enables a user to transfer data between a computer and another IrDA-enabled device for data synchronization, file transfer, or device control. The speed for IrDA is up to 4 Mbits per second (Mbps) and the distance is usually less than 30 feet in an unobstructed line of sight.

Bluetooth uses radio waves to transmit data and therefore doesn't have the line-of-sight restrictions of IrDA. Bluetooth also supports higher data transmission rates (11 Mbps) and uses the 2.4 GHz ISM bandwidth. Support for Bluetooth, however, has not yet been integrated into Windows XP.

WLAN

The range of a wireless local area network (WLAN) is, of course, greater than that of a WPAN. For example, most 802.11b implementations will have a speed of 1 Mbps and a range of about 500 meters (1500 feet). With a closer proximity to the access point (AP), speeds of up to 11 Mbps can be reached. Windows XP supports the IEEE 802.11b standard natively; this standard uses Direct Sequence Spreading Spectrum (DSSS) to transmit the data in the bandwidth of 2.4 GHz—the *ISM band*. Since this bandwidth is free for public use, other devices such as cordless phone can cause problems and interference.

Windows XP's native support for 802.11x simplifies the implementation process for hardware and software vendors. As we will demonstrate later in this chapter, one of the most secure designs for a wireless network has users perform mutual authentication with a back-end server like Internet Authentication Service (IAS) before they are authorized to use the wireless network.

For questions about Windows XP hardware support, you can always consult the detailed Hardware Compatibility List (HCL) at http://www.microsoft.com/hcl. The next step is to figure out what other products and services you will need to set up your wireless network. Before we delve into solutions, however, let's have a look at the potential problems.

CHALLENGE

Your manager demands the integration of a wireless network into your existing corporate network. You have spent years perfecting the security of your wired network. Now you have to integrate a new technology that has new holes popping up all the time. What choices can you make that will keep your wired and wireless networks secure yet usable? Can you anticipate future attacks against wireless and be prepared for them?

Any new technology poses challenges in security. In this regard, wireless networks have to be treated the same as wired networks. There is some security built in to 802.11x, but as we've seen with wired technologies such as OSs and applications, the standard security always needs beefing up.

One option is to implement peripheral technologies such as IPSec with mutual authentication and encryption to make your wireless network secure. Another strong solution is to require client certificates in combination with dynamic WEP encryption keys. It's easy to allow unauthenticated access to wireless networks, and most people actually do. There are also other, more insecure methods of authentication for wireless networks, which end up being the same as letting anyone plug into your corporate LAN. Restrict your wireless as you would your wired networks.

CURRENT SECURITY PROBLEMS IN WIRELESS

The most mature wireless network technology today is 802.11b, which is what we will focus on. Let's briefly go over the IEEE 802.11b standard.

IEEE 802.11b makes use of the 2.4 GHz ISM band and provides speeds from 1 Mbps up to 11 Mbps, with the range about 1500 feet. (Although in reality, you are hard-pressed to get this range out of products on the market today.) This standard uses Direct Sequence Spread Spectrum (DSSS) to encode data before transferring it. IEEE 802.11, 802.11a, 802.11b, and 802.11g use Carrier Sense Multiple Access/Collision Avoidance (CSMA/CA) as the protocol in the data link layer.

There are two names you need to know in a wireless network:

- Station (STA)
- Access point (AP)

STA is a wireless network client—a desktop computer, laptop, or PDA. The AP is the central point (like a hub) that creates a basic service set to bridge a number of STAs from the wireless network to other existing networks.

There are two different modes of wireless networking:

- Ad hoc mode, or independent basic service set (IBSS)
- Infrastructure mode, or basic service set (BSS)

Ad hoc and infrastructure modes are illustrated in the network blueprints. The ad hoc mode is equivalent to peer-to-peer networking. That means an ad hoc wireless network does not have an AP to bridge the STAs together. Every STA in an ad hoc wireless network can communicate with any other STA in the same network directly.

The infrastructure mode will have at least one AP to form a BSS. If there are multiple APs, they will form an extended service set (ESS). All traffic from or to an STA will go through the AP first. The AP in turn could be connected directly to another network, such as your wired intranet. In such a case, we recommend placing a firewall between them, as we describe in more detail later.

Almost every protocol set has some mechanism to protect the data, and the same is true for IEEE 802.11b. An encryption mechanism called Wired Equivalent Privacy (WEP) protects the data as it travels through the airwaves.

 SECURITY ALERT   After the WEP encryption mechanism was released, it was proved (by Nikita Borisov, Ian Goldberg, and David Wagner, in 2001) to be vulnerable to multiple forms of attack. WEP uses the symmetric cryptography system called RC4 with a user-specified key (64 bits and 128 bits) to protect the data. As a result, WEP alone is not enough to protect your data, and coming sections will address this fact with practical solutions such as dynamic WEP, IPSec, and 801.1x authentication.

The problems we focus on concern how a hacker could attack your network. The attack methodology is as follows:

- **Footprint the wireless network**   Locate and understand your target.

- **Passive attack**   Analyze the network traffic or break the WEP.

- **Authentication and authorization**   Determine what methods are enforced and how they can be circumvented.

- **Active attack**   Launch denial of service (DoS) attacks.

Footprint the Wireless Network

Attacking a wireless network begins with finding it, and that hinges on the interaction between the STA and AP. This section introduces the interactions between an STA and AP and then goes on to the methods for discovering and footprinting the wireless network in an active or passive way.

The Interaction

Because there are no physical wires between an STA and AP, they have to establish what is termed an *association* (a virtual wire) to communicate. The procedures are

1. Make sure an AP is available.

2. Authenticate with the AP.

3. Establish an association with the AP.

The first requirement is to identify the BSS provided by the AP. The service set ID (SSID) is the identifier that serves the purpose of identifying a BSS or IBSS. Then an STA can use the SSID to establish an association with an AP. So how does an STA know which SSID to join? There are two ways:

- **Active method**   In the active method, the STA sends out a *probe request* with the SSID inside to see if an AP responds. If the STA doesn't have the SSID in the beginning, the STA will send the probe request with an empty SSID. The empty SSID is useful, because most APs will respond to it with their own SSID in a *probe response* packet. At this point the STA knows the correct BSS with which to associate. You can think of it as walking into a house and yelling "Anyone home?"— the people in the house might respond with their names. Luckily, an AP can be configured to ignore a probe request with an empty SSID.

- **Passive method**   An attacker can still use the passive way to detect the existence of an AP by sniffing the packets from the airwaves, which will reveal the AP, SSID, and STAs that are live.

The Trace

The passive way to identify an SSID is to sniff the network traffic and look for three kinds of packets. The first one is called a *beacon*. An AP sends out a beacon periodically, usually once every 100 milliseconds. With this beacon, the STA will know there is an AP available. The beacon could contain the SSID as part of its information. The second packet is the *probe request and response*, and the third packet is the *association request and response*. All of these packets contain an SSID to identify a BSS or IBSS nearby. As long as the hacker is within the proper range, you basically cannot hide your wireless network. Some extreme methods do, of course, exist, such as surrounding the perimeter with metal or other substances that contain the wireless signals.

The Tools

Windows XP supports the active method of finding a nearby AP. Just open the property of your wireless network card, and click the Wireless Network tab, where you should see a list of currently available wireless networks. From there you can choose any available access point to connect to.

There are also other tools you can use specifically for the purpose of discovering wireless networks, such as NetStumbler (http://www.netstumbler.com). For the passive method of discovering a wireless network, you can use AiroPeek (commercial software found at http://www.wildpackets.com) to sniff the traffic and find nearby wireless networks. After you identify a wireless network, you then proceed with traffic analysis. Traffic analysis allows you to determine which attacks to launch against the wireless network.

Passive Attack

A *passive attack* is the method of analyzing the intercepted network traffic and extracting useful information from the collected raw information. The common tool we use for this is a sniffer such as AiroPeek. Due to the physical properties of a wireless network, you can perform traffic capture at any location as long as the signal reaches your system. You probably have heard of a "parking lot attack" or "war driving." As you might guess, these methods illustrate that people can perform traffic analysis in a car by either parking near your building or just driving the surrounding streets.

Clear Text Traffic

Probably the best scenario for a hacker and the worst for you, the system administrator, is *clear text traffic*. If there is no protection on the data being transmitted over wireless, then an attacker can easily sniff the traffic and perform protocol or data analysis later to crack into your information gold mine: credit card information, passwords, and personal emails. If the data is not protected, then the odds are high that the rest of the network setup is also insecure.

Problems with WEP

If the wireless network has WEP enabled, the hacker's game is still not over. The following problems exist in the WEP algorithm, and can potentially be exploited.

Brute Force Attack   WEP makes use of a symmetric cryptography system called RC4. The user can use a shared secret key. The real key to encrypt the data with RC4 algorithm is generated by a pseudo random number generator (PRNG). But flaws in PRNG can cause the real key space to be less than 64 bits or 128 bits. The flaw actually reduces the key space of the 64-bit key to 22 bits. Therefore, it is possible for an attacker to collect enough information to try to discover the key offline.

Duplicate IV   Initiation vector (IV) is a 3-byte random number generated by the computer. It is combined with a key chosen by the user to generate the final key for WEP encryption/decryption. The IV is transmitted with the encrypted data in the packet without any protection so that the receiving end knows how to decrypt the traffic. When your wireless network is using the same user-chosen key and duplicate IV on multiple packets, you might be in trouble. The attacker would know that all those packets with the same IV are being encrypted with the same key, and can then build a dictionary based on the packets collected. By knowing that the RC4 cryptography system uses the XOR algorithm to encrypt the plaintext (user data) with the key, the attacker can find the possible value of the packets. The attacker can do this because the XOR result of two different plaintext values is the same as the XOR result of two ciphertext-encrypted values with the same key. If the attacker can guess one of the plaintext packets, then they can decrypt the other packet encrypted with the same key.

Chosen/Known Plaintext   On the other hand, if you know the plaintext and ciphertext of a WEP-protected packet, you can determine the encryption key for that packet. There are several methods of determining the key, including sending an email or generating ICMP echo request traffic (ping). An attacker who knows the corporate intranet pretty well could send in an email to the network. Knowing the contents of that email, the attacker could then capture the traffic on the wireless side, identify the packets related to the email, and find out the key, eventually building a dictionary for a real-time decryption attack.

Weakness in Key Generation   A weakness in the random key generator of the RC4 algorithm used in WEP can permit an attacker to collect enough packets with IVs that match certain patterns to recover the user-chosen key from the IVs. Generally, you would need to sniff for millions of packets to get enough "interesting" IVs to recover the key, so it could take days, if not weeks, to crack a moderately used wireless network. This is just a very basic attack, with several tools available to do the sniffing and decoding for you. Airsnort is the famous one: it runs on Linux and tries to break the key when enough useful packets are collected.

Bit-Manipulation Attack   WEP doesn't protect the integrity of the encrypted data. The RC4 cryptography system performs the XOR operation bit by bit, making WEP-protected packets vulnerable to bit-manipulation attack. This attack requires modification of any single bit of the traffic to disrupt the communication or cause other problems.

Authentication and Authorization

Once the attacker knows information such as the SSID of the network, MAC addresses on the network, and maybe even the WEP key, they can try to establish an association with the AP. There are currently three ways to authenticate users before they can establish an association with the wireless network.

Open Authentication

Open authentication usually means you only need to provide the SSID or use the correct WEP key for the AP. It can be used with other authentication methods, for example, using MAC address authentication. The problem with open authentication is that if you don't have other protection or authentication mechanisms in place, then your wireless network is totally open, as the name indicates.

Shared Secret Authentication

The *shared secret authentication* mechanism is similar to a challenge-response authentication system. It is used when the STA shares the same WEP key with the AP. The STA sends the request to the AP, and the AP sends back the challenge. Then the STA replies with the challenge and encrypted response. The insecurity here is that the challenge is transmitted in clear text to the STA, so if someone captures both challenge and response, then they could figure out the key used to encrypt it.

802.1x Is Not 802.11x

Not to be confused with the 802.11x wireless standards, the *802.1x authentication standard* handles the authentication process and key management while utilizing Extensible Authorization Protocol (EAP) to integrate with other back-end servers for authentication, authorization, and accounting (AAA). Wireless network users must authenticate themselves to the authentication server (e.g., a RADIUS server) at the other end of the wireless network to get authorization. The only known security problem is that if there is no mutual authentication (only the server authenticates the user), then the whole protocol is vulnerable to the famous "man in the middle" (MITM) attack. That means someone can intercept the traffic between the STA and AP, steal the authentication information, and use the wireless network. If there is mutual authentication between the user and the server (EAP-TLS or EAP-MD5), then 802.1x can be one of the most secure means of authentication available.

Active Attacks and Denial of Service

We just introduced most of the security problems using passive attacks; however, there are some active attacks to consider, too. One of the most interesting attacks is to set up a fake access point and let valid users establish associations, then collect information or perform a MITM attack. In a corporate environment, if a malicious employee installs a rogue AP on the corporate intranet, then they are creating a security hole—someone in the parking lot can easily hook on and surf your intranet. Another known attack is to try and steal the key for WEP from a wireless network user's laptop. A tool called Lucent

Orinoco Registry Encryption/Decryption (http://www.cqure.net/tools.html) can break the encryption and extract the WEP key for Lucent Orinoco card users from the registry.

If an attacker tried all the above methods and failed, then the final choice might be denial of service attacks. Such attacks might bring down the wireless network and disrupt the service. We will describe the attacks from two different levels: physical level and protocol level.

Physical Level

There are two ways to disrupt the service of a wireless network physically:

- **Physical destruction**   To physically destroy an AP, you have first to locate the AP. You can also try to find the antenna, since destroying the antenna probably has the similar effect as destroying the AP.

- **Interference**   Even if the attacker does not have an electromagnetic pulse gun, that doesn't mean you are safe from such attack. Remember we mentioned that 802.11b uses the 2.4 GHz ISM band, which is open and free for public use. So the signal of the 802.11b wireless network can be disrupted by the microwave in the kitchen or the new 2.4 GHz digital cordless phones.

Protocol Level

An attacker can disrupt service from the protocol level. Remember that we talked about establishing associations to use the wireless network? If you can build an association, then there must be a way to disassociate. If you can authenticate, then there must be a way to unauthenticate. Unfortunately, in the IEEE 802.11b standard, both methods exist, and both methods do not require any authentication in the message. That means the attacker can send out a disassociate or unauthenticate message to an arbitrary wireless network user and disconnect them. This is a bad design from the protocol's perspective.

From the Wired Side

Do not assume that just because a hacker cannot get access to the wireless network that there is no other way to attack it. Suppose you have a wireless network connected to the intranet and configured only for a few users. Another employee in the company discovers the AP from the internal network and accesses the management interfaces on the AP. He breaks in through a default SNMP community string and changes the configuration, so he is now part of the list of allowed users.

This situation points out a problem: every AP has its own management interface(s). The most commonly seen management interfaces are Telnet, FTP, web, and SNMP. If any of these management interfaces are not secured, there is always a chance that someone can take advantage of the default setup.

CURRENT COUNTERMEASURES TO WIRELESS INSECURITY

Before you decide to convince your boss not to build a wireless network for your intranet, think through how you can solve the problems we have outlined. The problems may be scary, but that's why you are reading this book. Once you know the methods a hacker can use to attack the wireless network, you can protect yourself by closing those holes. If you have read *The Art of War* by Sun Tzu, then you should know this saying: "If you know the enemy and know yourself, you need not fear the result of a hundred battles."

The rest of the chapter focuses on principles that you can adopt when designing your wireless network. But the single principle you should bear in mind at all times is "Defense in Depth"—the philosophy that you should never depend on a single mechanism to protect your valuable assets. Now that we have used the obligatory Sun Tzu quote, we can discuss several options for protecting your wireless network:

- **Change the SSID.**   A wireless STA uses the SSID to identify the wireless network. There is currently no way to hide that from a potential attacker. The only thing you can do is change the SSID so it doesn't make immediate association to your company. For example, if you work for IBM, do not name the SSID "IBM_WN20." This technique is more obfuscation than protection.

- **Configure the AP correctly.**   Make sure you change the default SSID, default password, and SNMP community string, and close down all the management interfaces properly.

- **Do not depend on WEP.**   Use IPSec, VPN, SSH, or other substitutions for WEP. Do not use WEP alone to protect your data. You know it is broken!

- **Adopt another authentication/authorization mechanism.**   Use 802.1x, VPN, or certificates to authenticate and authorize your wireless network users. Using client certificates can make it nearly impossible for an attacker to gain access.

- **Segment the wireless network.**   The wireless network should be treated as a remote access network and separated from the corporate intranet. A firewall, packet filter, or similar device should be in between the AP and the corporate intranet. This can prevent the damage caused if the wireless network gets broken into.

- **Prevent physical access.**   You can use directional antennas on your APs to restrict the directions of the signal. Shield your building or facility from electromagnetic interference as well. These methods can protect your wireless network and other electronic devices, but must often be weighed against the actual risk. MAC address filters can be implemented, but by sniffing the wireless traffic, the allowed list of MAC addresses can be easily determined.

Now you are ready to enter the next phase—designing a secure wireless network with Windows technologies for your corporate intranet.

DESIGNING A SECURE WIRELESS NETWORK

This section goes into detail about the design of two different security architectures using Windows technologies. There are similarities between the two; for example, both rely on client certificates and both use WEP to some degree. Here we assume that you are using an environment full of Windows 2000/XP/.NET machines and with Windows 2000 domain controllers to manage your forest, although Windows .NET DCs would work just as well.

The first method simply uses an IPSec VPN, while the second uses the 802.1x Extensible Authentication Protocol (EAP). The purpose of both is to guarantee the user authentication and authorization and to protect the data's confidentiality and integrity.

Both of these architectures are illustrated in the "Blueprints" section of this book. Table 9-2 lists some of the pros and cons of each method.

In the rest of this chapter, we first look briefly at the IPSec VPN architecture. Then we'll delve into the details of setting up the 802.1x architecture.

IPSec VPN: A Simple and Secure Method

Referring to the "Blueprints" section of this book will help you picture the architecture we are describing here. The basic structure is this: the wireless clients, or STAs, connect to the open wireless AP and then authenticate with the IPSec VPN for access to the organization's protected intranet.

Method	Pros	Cons	Notes
IPSec VPN	Controls access to the intranet Strong encryption Strong authentication Simple design Less server setup	Does not control access to the Wireless LAN Can be expensive to scale (bigger hardware, more devices) Doesn't support dynamic WEP	IPSec authentication starts at the network layer.
802.1x EAP	Controls access to the intranet Controls access to the wireless LAN Strong encryption through dynamic WEP Strong authentication	Requires more servers (CA, IAS/RADIUS, DC) More complex design	802.1x authentication starts at the data link layer.

Table 9-2.   IPSec VPN Versus 802.1x with EAP

This scenario provides an easy-to-manage, secure solution with strong authentication and encryption of network traffic. The downside is that authentication happens at the network layer with IPSec, meaning that the lower layers are still unprotected. Essentially, the wireless network will be wide open, while the intranet will only be accessible with strong authentication and encryption. This may be a fair trade-off for someone looking for a good solution with less overhead.

Architecture

Start this design by placing a firewall on the perimeter of your intranet, to securely segment the wireless network. At this point the intranet is considered to be "behind" your firewall. Then you need to decide whether to run an IPSec VPN on the firewall or on a system behind the firewall.

You can configure your firewall to deny all traffic going outbound to the wireless LAN except that which originated from the wireless side. Of course, if you need to access management interfaces, you will need to add appropriate rules. The firewall will serve to minimize broadcast traffic and prevent intranet users from poking around at the wireless AP and STAs.

IPSec can be used to build up security associations between a wireless client (STA) and the internal network/intranet. The method for authentication can be either Kerberos (which is easier to implement and manage) or client certificate-based authentication (which is more difficult to set up but more secure). In our example diagrams we use client certificates for authentication.

Authentication, data confidentiality, and packet integrity are provided through IPSec's industry standard protocols, such as IKE and ESP, described in detail in Chapter 7. Because broadcast traffic is not protected by IPSec, we recommend also using WEP.

 SECURITY ALERT!   As noted in Chapter 7, broadcast traffic is exempt from IPSec filters, so WEP must still be used with this method to protect broadcast traffic.

L2TP/IPSec VPN

When setting up your VPN gateway, be sure to configure your clients and gateway to negotiate strong encryption. You can use a Windows 2000/.NET server as the VPN, or you can choose a server from another vendor. As noted in Chapter 7, L2TP is the protocol that must be used to provide a remote access VPN solution with IPSec. The L2TP headers will be encapsulated and encrypted when using IPSec ESP, and the outer IP headers and lower layer headers will transmit unencrypted.

While we were writing this book, Microsoft released public beta software that allows legacy Windows 9x/Me/NT machines to use the L2TP/IPSec protocols. This means that all your Windows clients can now be outfitted for the secure VPN. The software and Microsoft's L2TP/IPSec implementations are based on industry standards and should work well with other vendors' VPN solutions. However, you could just as easily implement the remote access VPN on a Windows 2000 server behind the firewall. As a plus, Microsoft's L2TP/IPSec VPN client software also provides support for traversing NAT. Download the Microsoft L2TP/IPSec VPN client from http://www.microsoft.com/windows2000/downloads/tools.

NOTE Several of the upcoming sections can be applied to this IPSec VPN architecture. For example, if you decide to use client certificates for authentication, then the "Certificates" and "Certificate Service" sections will apply. Also, for most IPSec VPN deployments, the "Wireless Zero Configuration" section will apply, as well as the sections on network policies and Active Directory.

802.1x—Secure Authentication Through EAP

Another strong wireless solution uses 802.1x with EAP-TLS and machine certificates to authenticate both the STA and the server. It also manages the WEP key by periodically and automatically sending a new key, to avoid some of the known WEP key vulnerabilities. The data confidentiality will be protected by these dynamic WEP keys.

To use 802.1x, both the Internet Authentication Service and Certificate Authority are needed to provide authentication and authorization. Refer to the "Blueprints" section of the book for the architecture utilizing 802.1x.

Architecture

Similar to the IPSec VPN solution, 802.1x gives you a wireless network separated from the intranet by a firewall/packet filter. Behind the firewall/packet filter is a network that contains a domain controller, Certificate Authority, and Internet Authentication Service. You can put all these services on a single machine or, more preferably, put them on separate machines with additional backup or standby servers. It really depends on your need for scalability. Again, the purpose of this architecture is to use certificates (computer or user) and the 802.1x protocol to authenticate to the IAS server in the back end and provide the security of dynamic WEP keys and secure communications.

A new WEP key will be periodically transmitted from the AP to the STA and encrypted by the public/private key pairs contained in the certificates. The frequency of change to a new key depends on the configuration of the AP. Of course, the AP has to support the dynamic WEP keys (e.g., Cisco AP 350) and the client has to support them as well (Windows XP does so natively). You just need to check the option to receive the WEP key from the AP when configuring your wireless network card on Windows XP. You can also set your group policy to allow certain users intranet access only while other users have Internet access on your IAS server.

WEP

You know that WEP doesn't protect your data well enough, but if you remember the "Defense in Depth" principle, you still want to enable WEP. To configure your WEP securely, follow these suggestions:

- **Use the highest security available**   If your devices support 128-bit WEP, then use it. It is extremely hard to brute-force a 128-bit WEP key. If you cannot dynamically change WEP keys, then set the 128-bit policy and change the key periodically. The length of this period depends on how busy your wireless network traffic will be.

- **Use dynamic WEP keys**   If you are using 802.1x, you should also use dynamic WEP keys if possible. Some of the wireless network device vendors also implement their own solutions similar to dynamic WEP keys. Evaluate them before you deploy.

NOTE   Using dynamic WEP keys will provide a higher level of security and will counter some of the known WEP insecurities. To use dynamic WEP, however, you must purchase an access point that can provide them and use clients that support them. Luckily, Windows XP provides this support natively when you check the WEP option "This key is provided for me automatically."

- **Use MIC when available**   We also mentioned that the WEP key does not protect the integrity of the packet. Currently IEEE is working on 802.11i both to fix the problem in WEP and to implement 802.11x and Message Integrity Checksum (MIC) for data confidentiality and integrity. MIC will generate checksums for the encrypted data to ensure the integrity of the data. To date, however, no product supports this capability.

Authentication/Authorization

Because of the limited functionalities of an AP, wireless network users do not usually authenticate themselves to the AP directly. The SSID serves only to identify the access point and does not identify the user or machine connecting to it. The information for authentication and authorization has to be processed by a server on the back end of the wired network.

802.1x supports Extensible Authorization Protocol (EAP). It can be combined with TLS (EAP-TLS) or MD5 (EAP-MD5) to provide high security during the authorization procedure. The wireless network user uses a certificate to authenticate himself to an authentication/authorization server in the back end of the AP. The AP that supports EAP will forward the messages from both ends. The communication between the wireless STA and the backend authentication server will be encrypted by the public keys on the user certificate and server certificate.

The backend authorization server (usually RADIUS, as with IAS) then authorizes an authenticated user to use a port of entry. In a wireless network, a *port* means establishing an association (virtual network cable) between the STA and the AP. So users must first authenticate themselves to the backend authorization server to be able to use the wireless network. In our example network, we will authenticate via a user certificate from the Certificate Authority of your enterprise.

Certificates

In order to let your users use certificates to authenticate themselves, you have to build your own certificate infrastructure that is capable of generating "user" certificates. Machine certificates would actually work just as well. The choice of whether to tie authentication to a machine account or a user account is yours. We will cover both types of certificates here. If you don't have a third-party CA installed already, you can install the Certificate Authority service available with Windows 2000 Server. Make sure you do the following things (assuming the CA and IAS are on the same machine):

- Generate your enterprise root certificate.
- Generate the computer certificate and user certificate with their private key.
- Verify that the computer certificate includes the FQDN name of the computer.
- Verify that the computer certificate is installed in the local computer certificate store.
- Verify that the user certificate is installed in the local user certificate store.
- Verify that the root CA certificate is installed in the Trusted Root Certification Authorities store.

You can also use group policies to perform these functions automatically. With all these things done, you can let your users use the certificate (user or computer) to authenticate, using 802.1x to communicate with your intranet.

As mentioned in Chapter 5, a secure method of distributing certificates is to give users smart cards and enable autoenrollment on the certificate server.

Wireless Zero Configuration

Wireless Zero Configuration is necessary for the method we are describing, and luckily, Windows XP supports it natively. *Wireless Zero Configuration* refers to the capability of Windows XP to use information broadcast from the AP to automatically configure the client side.

NOTE In general, we recommend that you turn off Wireless Zero Configuration as part of a baseline build. However, based on your needs, services should be turned on or off, and in this case it must be turned on.

To enable Wireless Zero Configuration, just open your Network Connections and select Properties for your wireless network connection. Then click the Wireless Networks tab and check the "Use Windows to configure my wireless network settings" option, as shown in Figure 9-1. As we are writing this, this feature is not yet working for all wireless network cards. For example, if you are using Prism II chip-based cards (made by Linksys, SMC, D-Link, and other OEM vendors), you will need to do extra work to make the device work under Windows XP. (A guide to making Prism work correctly is available at http://www.frars.org.uk/cgi-bin/render.pl?pageid=1084.)

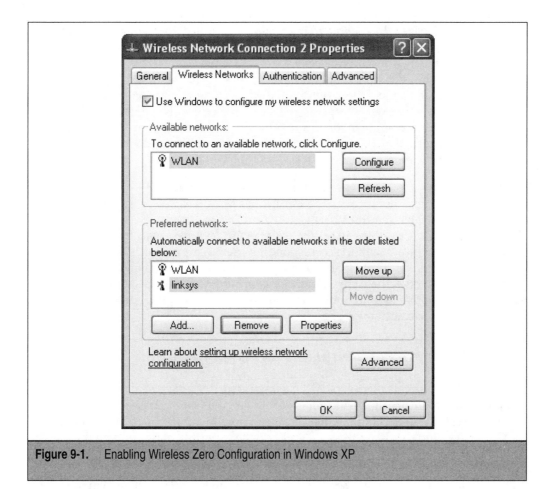

Figure 9-1. Enabling Wireless Zero Configuration in Windows XP

Authentication

As we have stated again and again, you will need certificates to authenticate your users. In this section, we are going to cover the main procedures for configuring your certificate server and other related services to build your own authentication infrastructure. First, we begin with the Certificate Services on your Windows 2000 Server. Second, we will go through what you should do with your Internet Authentication for 802.1x-based security. Third, we will discuss the configuration of Active Directory and several policy issues.

Certificate Service

We will start by looking at the installation of the Certificate Service and the generation of a certificate for your users. Next, we'll go through how to import and export those certificates. Lastly, we will walk through how to use the certificate for authentication.

Install Certificate Service   In general, to install the Certificate Service on your Windows 2000 Server, go to Settings → Control Panel → Add/Remove Program → Add/Remove Windows Components, and then select the Certificate Services check box. Choose this CA to be your Enterprise Root CA. Enter the appropriate names and information to identify your organization. After you install the Certificate Service, you can generate a root certificate for your own enterprise, and this certificate will be the root of every other certificate you generate in the future. The installation can be more complicated than this. We suggest that you read Microsoft's documentation and white papers on setting up a Certificate Server.

Generate Certificates   You can have certificates generated directly by having the user request a certificate, either through the Certificates MMC snap-in or through the intranet at http://*your_ca*/certsrv.

You still need a copy of the user certificate public key (no private key needed) as a file to map the certificate with the corresponding user account. This is because you will need to associate the certificate to that user or computer account under Active Directory. To do that, simply open the Active Directory Users and Computers snap-in, choose the user, right-click on that user account, and then click Name Mapping. Map the saved user certificate to this user account.

NOTE   Note that for Name Mapping to be available, you must first select Advanced Features on the View menu.

Import Certificates   After the certificate is generated, you need to transfer it to the user in some way. If the user generated the certificate from the Certificates MMC snap-in or the CA's web interface, then the user should do the exporting and send you the certificate public key.

If you generated the certificate for the user, you can export it from the certificate store on the CA and save it to a file. Then the user will have to import it to their Windows XP computer. To do this they simply right-click on the certificate file (we assume it's a .pfx file for personal information exchange format) and choose Install PFX, as shown here.

If the certificate is generated via a group policy, you can just view it from the server (or from any Certificate Authority MMC plug-in), and invoke the Export Wizard from the Copy to File button.

As a user, you can choose a passphrase to protect your private key. Whenever you need to use the certificate for authentication, you will be prompted for your password, which is used to unlock the private key and encrypt/decrypt information. You can also allow the private key to be exported again for backup purposes—however, managing security of backup certificates can get out of control. Figure 9-2 shows protection of the private key with a password.

The next step is to save the certificate to the current user's certificate store. You can just accept the default option to automatically let the software choose a certificate store for you, as shown in Figure 9-3.

That's it. Now you have a user certificate on your computer. If you want to install computer certificates automatically, nearly the same process can be used, but you would import the certificate to the local computer's certificate store rather than the user's store.

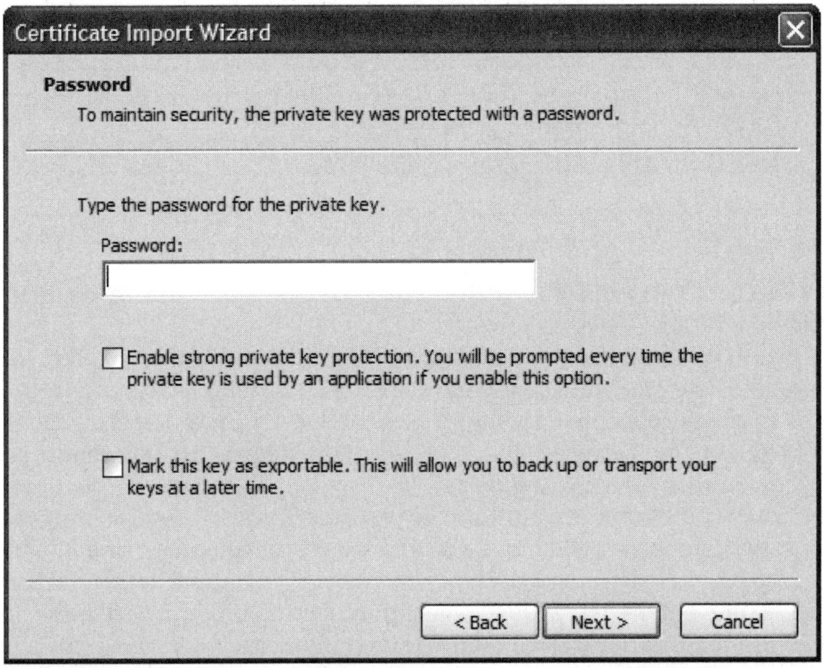

Figure 9-2. Choosing a password to protect a private key

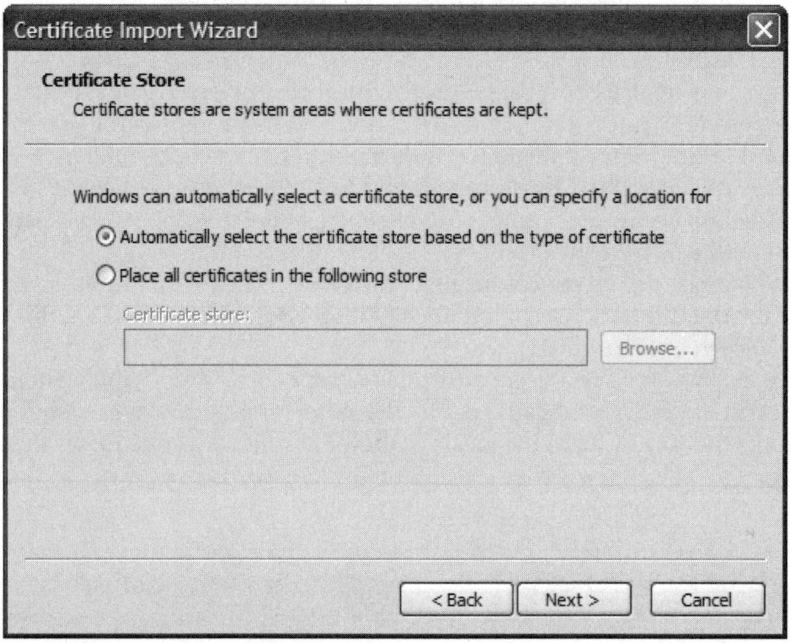

Figure 9-3. Automatically choosing a certificate store to save a certificate

Configure a User Certificate with EAP With the certificate installed, you are ready to begin authentication with the wireless network.

Even though we don't discuss the setup of IAS until later in this chapter, we are going to assume here that you already have both your AP and IAS configured. The first step now is to open Properties for your wireless network connection. You should see your preferred network. Next click the Authentication Method tab; you should see 802.1x enabled by default, as shown in Figure 9-4.

On the EAP type, choose "Smart Card or other Certificate." You can also click the Properties button and then choose "Use a certificate on your computer" and "Validate the server certificate." These options will allow you to perform mutual authentication with your server, to prevent the MITM attack mentioned earlier. If you choose these options, you should also choose your trusted domain name and trusted root certificate authority.

Now you are ready to use the wireless network by authenticating via 802.1x with the IAS, which is finally covered in the next section.

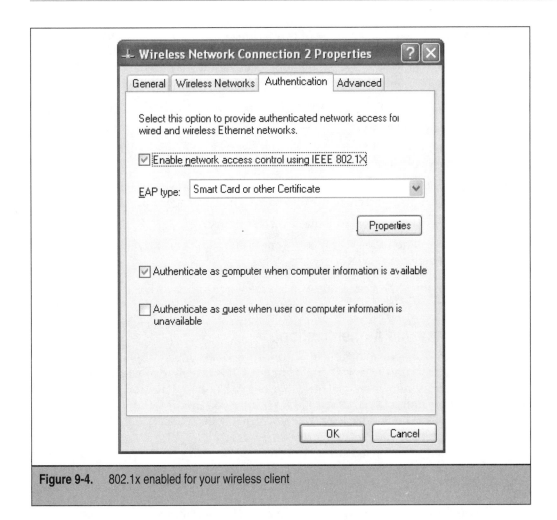

Figure 9-4.   802.1x enabled for your wireless client

Internet Authentication Server

To use 802.1x authentication, you begin by setting up the Internet Authentication
Server (IAS) on a Windows 2000 Server. Quite simply, IAS provides authentication and
authorization service for remote access. (See the "Blueprints" section of this book for
the network architecture.)

First you install IAS through Add/Remove Programs in Control Panel. Then in
Add/Remove Windows Components, highlight Networking Services, then click
Details, and select the Internet Authentication Service check box. Install Service Pack 2

and apply hotfix Q304697 (at the time of this writing). After you install IAS, you need to decide where the service will be in your network architecture. With our example, you can choose either to have a separate domain outside your intranet or to just use an IAS as your current domain. After you figure this out, do the following:

- Enable IAS to read objects in the Active Directory by registering the IAS to your Active Directory.

- Turn on file logging for accounting and authentication events. It could help you when you need to do some troubleshooting.

- Use the Internet Authentication Service snap-in to the MMC to add your AP as a client of your IAS and configure the shared secret between your AP and your IAS.

- Use the snap-in to create a Remote Access policy.

- Set up a backup IAS server if you want to enhance the survivability of your wireless network service.

IAS is now ready to process requests from the wireless network users for 802.1x authentication.

Active Directory and Authentication

Active Directory manages all objects in a "forest," and lets you apply policies at the Domain level, and at the Organizational Unit level. It is therefore a critical component in our network of Windows technologies. For our 802.1x-based method of security, you will need to apply hotfix Q306260 and Q304347 after you install Windows 2000 Server Domain Controller with Service Pack 2, or you can just install Service Pack 3. You are almost ready to deploy your secure wireless network.

Now you need to do the following:

- Design different groups and organizational units for access from wireless networks to either intranet or Internet. For example, you might have a group name "Wintrausers" for users allowed access to your intranet, and "Winterusers" for users allowed Internet access.

- Ensure every wireless network user belongs to at least one group.

- Ensure every computer has a computer account.

- Ensure every user account maps to the corresponding certificate.

- If a user is allowed to use wireless networks, they should be granted remote access rights, an option on the Dial-in tab.

We will discuss Active Directory in more detail in Chapter 10. The only thing not yet prepared is the policy. The next section will describe what kind of policy you should set up for your wireless network users. Remember that the policy will not be useful if it does not conform to your organization's requirements.

Wireless Network Policies

If we had to make a single recommendation for whether to use the IPSec VPN or the 801.x infrastructure for a secure network, it would be to use both. Perhaps the best solution is to combine both architectures. This would mean that your wireless network would be protected at the low data link layer through 802.1x authentication, and access to your organization's intranet or Internet gateway would be strongly authenticated and encrypted at the network layer by the IPSec VPN.

Before we discuss specific policies, and before you set up your own policy, ask yourself two questions: What are the goals of these policies? and How do I enforce them? A policy without enforcement is useless.

Important Policies to Configure

In devising good network access policy, you want to make sure that you think about the "4W1H" rule: who, where, when, what, and how. You need to configure the following:

- Restrict access by user or computer identity (e.g., Joe has access while Jane does not).

- The domain or group the user belongs to (e.g., set up Wireless_Intranet and Wireless_Internet user groups and organizational units).

- Where you want to restrict connections, the authentication services behind the firewall should only allow connections from the AP.

- When the user is allowed to access resources, what access do you want your user to have: intranet only, Internet only, or both?

- How do you want your network traffic to be secured: with dynamic WEP, using IPSec, or with no protection?

After you decide what restrictions you need and turn them into policy, you are ready to define them in your Active Directory.

Define Active Directory Group Policy or IAS Policy

You can define group policies in Active Directory or IAS to control various things, including

- Wireless Network (802.11) configurations
- IPSec policies
- User accounts
- Groups
- Remote access rights
- EAP type
- Access time
- Authentication methods
- Encryption grade

Make sure that you design your policy well, and make use of the full capability of Windows 2000 and Windows XP. There is a new Group Policy setting in Windows .NET called Wireless Network (IEEE 802.11) Policies. You can use this to configure the wireless client settings for Windows XP computers such as 802.1x and preferred SSID networks and apply them to an entire organizational unit of your wireless computers. At the time we are writing this, a Windows .NET domain controller is necessary to create these policies and implement them through AD.

Remember to apply these Windows XP–specific GPO settings to an organizational unit that contains only Windows XP computers. (In most cases, GPOs should be separated for Windows 2000 and Windows XP computers, as described in Chapter 11.)

TOOLS OF THE TRADE

In this chapter, we have discussed the many security issues of wireless networks. Let's review the tools you can use to secure and test your wireless network.

AiroPeek   WildPackets' AiroPeek (available from http://www.wildpackets.com) is a commercial sniffer for wireless networks. It uses the passive technique we spoke of earlier for identifying wireless networks.

NetStumbler   NetStumbler (http://www.netstumbler.com) is a free and publicly available tool. It runs on Windows platforms. In the "Footprint the Wireless Network" section of this chapter, we talked about two different ways to identify a wireless network. NetStumbler uses the active method: sending out "probe requests" with an empty SSID, expecting the AP to respond with its SSID. You can also hook up a GPS device to the computer, and NetStumbler will be able to read the signal to associate the coordinates with the AP. There are actually a lot of people using such information to build a database of publicly accessible APs. Figure 9-5 shows NetStumbler in action.

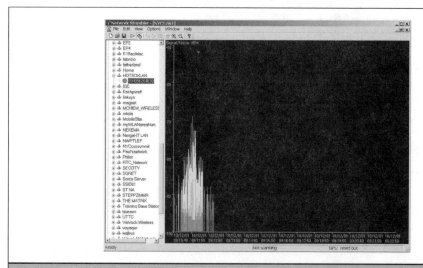

Figure 9-5.   NetStumbler

.NET Wireless Monitor   Wireless Monitor is the new functionality added into the Windows .NET server beta builds we used. Hopefully, it will make it to final release. It is capable of monitoring two targets: AP and client. To monitor an AP, the wireless monitor acts like NetStumbler, and it keeps a record of APs that respond with SSIDs. The wireless monitor also catches the signal strength for your information. On the client side, the wireless monitor is capable of showing you the action your wireless network client is performing. "Action" here means Probe, Associate, Authenticate, and other related actions defined in the standard. It is a good tool for helping you identify problems in your wireless network. To use it, open your MMC and add the Wireless Monitor snap-in.

CHECKLIST: WIRELESS SECURITY

In this chapter, we described various wireless technologies and focused on designing secure wireless networks using either IPSec or 802.1x authentication. You can create an even better design, albeit more complicated, by combining both 802.1x and IPSec. As you know by now, the key words throughout this chapter have been *authentication* and *encryption*.

You should know what Windows XP supports in the field of wireless technologies, and stay aware of the current security problems in the IEEE 802.11b wireless network (Wi-Fi). This chapter has provided you with questions and answers for planning to work with and implement wireless technologies, as well as steps for securing Windows XP in a wireless world.

We have also illustrated two scenarios that can be used separately as secure wireless network solutions, or together for an even stronger solution. A network built on 802.1x authentication will maintain authorized access at the data link layer, while IPSec will provide even stronger authentication and encryption at the higher network layer.

- ☐ Answer important planning questions before setting up a WLAN: Do you really need a wireless network? What is the purpose?
- ☐ Understand Windows XP's support for wireless technologies.
- ☐ Understand the current security problems of 802.11b/Wi-Fi.
- ☐ Understand the types of attacks that can be made on wireless networks: active and passive, WEP, authentication, client side, and DoS.
- ☐ Decide whether to use IPSec or 802.1x for client authentication (or a combination of both).

☐ To use IPSec for wireless security, set up an IPSec gateway that connects wireless clients to the intranet with strong authentication and encryption. The gateway can be either behind the perimeter firewall or a part of it.

☐ To use 802.1x to protect your wireless network, set up dynamic WEP with the strongest keys possible (128-bit), use Message Integrity Checksum (MIC) when available, and use client certificates for authentication. Configure the server with RADIUS and IAS for back-end authentication, and use Certificate Server for creation and management of client certifications. Use Wireless Zero Configuration for clients' wireless cards.

☐ With either IPSec or 802.1x: Physically protect your AP. Configure your AP well, changing its SSID and default settings (SNMP strings and usernames). Secure your wireless clients (use the rest of this book to harden your Windows XP client operating systems). Separate your wireless network with a firewall between the AP and wired network—and don't allow wired intranet users to poke around at the management interfaces.

☐ Specify policy for your wireless network: Design different groups and organizational units for access from wireless networks to either intranet or Internet. Enforce a group policy for use of IPSec and 802.1x.

CHAPTER 10

Remote Administration and Patch Management

Remote administration is a problem that has plagued mankind for eons. OK, maybe not eons, but surely for a decade or two. There are many methods of approaching remote administration, including everything from ADSI and WMI scripts to third-party software such as VNC (www.uk.research.att.com/vnc). Recognizing the need, Microsoft has continued to improve built-in Windows features such as Remote Desktop, Terminal Services, and Telnet Server.

Patch management goes hand in hand with remote administration. Pushing out patches to a large installed base can turn into a management nightmare if it is not thoughtfully planned and deployed. But take heart, some of the new tools from Microsoft are making this easier, especially for larger organizations. New options such as Automatic Updates make things a bit easier.

In this chapter we will cover how you can utilize the new features of Windows XP and Windows .NET for remote administration and discuss the several options you have for managing patches on your networked systems. Specifically, we will cover

- Remote Desktop
- Remote Assistance
- Telnet Server
- Terminal Services
- HFNetChk
- MBSA
- Automatic Updates
- System Update Service
- Systems Management Server

REMOTE ADMINISTRATION

You have several different options for remote administration. The various options include remotely controlling a desktop, logging into remote terminal servers and making outbound client connections for help requests, and remotely connecting to a command shell. In this section we will discuss Remote Desktop, Remote Assistance, Terminal Services, and Telnet Server.

Remote Desktop

The remote control function in Windows XP Professional is called Remote Desktop. This is by far the most powerful remote administration tool available to Windows XP administrators. It uses RDP (Remote Desktop Protocol) over TCP 3389 (by default), similar to Terminal Services. Remote Desktop works between Windows XP/.NET; however, it is disabled by default on Windows XP Professional. The client software included with Windows XP/.NET is backward compatible with Windows NT/2000 Terminal servers. Likewise, the Terminal Services client for Windows 2000 will work to connect to a Windows XP computer. You can also download the client software separately from http://www.microsoft.com/windowsxp/remotedesktop/ if you want to install it on pre–Windows XP systems.

NOTE For systems running anything from Windows 95 through Windows 2000, you can download the file program Msrdpcli.exe from Microsoft to install the remote desktop client.

Remote Desktop is based on the Terminal Services feature in Windows NT/2000. To access the client application use Start → Programs → Accessories → Communications to get to the Remote Desktop Connection dialog box, shown in Figure 10-1. Console users get locked out when a connection is made with the same user account, and remote desktop sessions will be disconnected when the local user decides to log back onto the desktop.

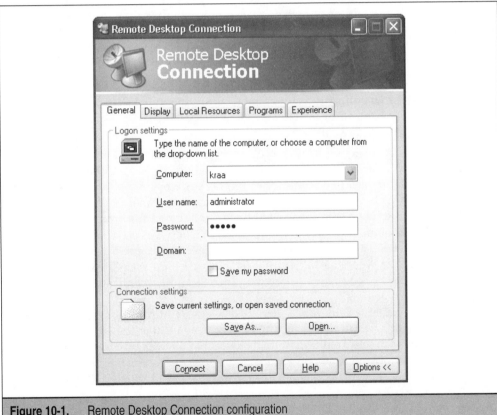

Figure 10-1.   Remote Desktop Connection configuration

SECURITY ALERT!   If you choose to save your password in the Remote Desktop Connection client on a physically insecure computer, an attacker who has compromised your machine will be able to launch a remote connection and access that system. We recommend that you do not save the password.

Configuration

Remote Desktop is fairly easy to configure. To configure Remote Desktop to accept connections go to Control Panel → System and click the Remote tab. Select the "Allow users to connect remotely to this computer" check box. You then have to select which users are allowed to connect. Remember from Chapter 8 that if you are using ICF, you will have to create a rule to allow Remote Desktop to operate. Do this by clicking the Settings button in the ICF configuration and selecting the Remote Desktop check box under Services.

Since the default port is known for Remote Desktop, we recommend you change it to some unique value. Once it is changed, you can access the remote system by appending the port number to the hostname with a delimit colon as in "corpxp.securingxp.com:4433." To change the listening port, run Regedit.exe and modify the following registry key (as described in Chapter 3):

```
HKEY_LOCAL_MACHINE\System\CurrentControlSet\Control\TerminalServer\
WinStations\RDP-Tcp\PortNumber
```

Then click the Decimal option and enter a new port number.

Remote Desktop Web Connection

Another method of connecting to a remote system is to use the Remote Desktop Web Connection. This is essentially a safe-for-scripting ActiveX control/COM object that lets you use a web browser to connect to the remote system. On the target system, you have to install the Web Connection option through Control Panel →Add Remove Programs → Add/Remove Windows Components → Internet Information Services → Details. In the Subcomponents of Internet Information Services list, select World Wide Web Service → Details → Remote Desktop Web Connection. Using the Internet Services Manager, expand the Web Sites folder to \Web Sites\Default Web Site\tsweb → Properties → Directory Security → Anonymous access and authentication → Edit and select "Anonymous access."

To access the remote system from a client, just browse to http://remotesystem/tsweb. You will get a login prompt; you do not even have to connect to the original target remote system but can select a different target system in the web browser login window. The connection window is shown in Figure 10-2.

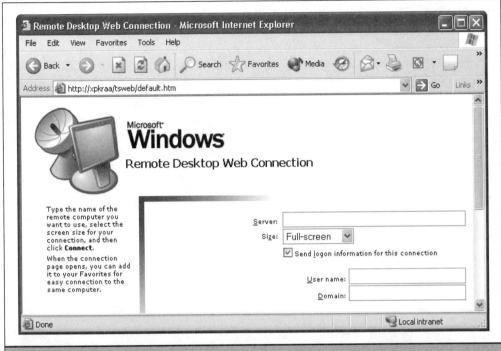

Figure 10-2.   Connecting to a remote system via Remote Desktop Web Connection

Auditing and Logging

There is no real way to log what takes place during a Remote Desktop session. If you have Audit Logon Events enabled, then you will see several records in the event logs indicating a Remote Desktop logon and logoff.

Other than that, you have only some very basic options for checking access. First, as the local or remote user, you can check Task Manager to see who is logged in and what programs are running. Second, if you use the Web Connection, you can check your log files of the web server to see logged HTTP requests.

You can use Performance Monitor (Perfmon.msc) to view some useful statistics related to the sessions. If you choose the option to add counters, and select the Terminal Services or Terminal Services Session object, you will have a useful list of counters that can be added, such as Active Sessions.

Remote Desktop MMC (TSmmc.msc)

The Remote Desktop MMC can be used to manage multiple remote desktop sessions from a single interface. First, you have to download Adminpak.msi for Windows XP Professional from Microsoft's web site. The Adminpak has the TSmmc.msc GUI, which is a powertoy for any administrator.

TIP TSmmc.msc is one of the most useful MMCs for Windows XP Professional administrators, despite some shortcomings. It will even allow you to connect back to Windows NT/2000 terminal services. Its biggest feature is that it allows you to preconfigure and group all your Remote Desktop connections under one roof. All the computers you want to connect to will be listed on the left, and on the right you will see the console for whichever one you are currently connected to. Its shortcoming is rather important: it does not let you modify the remote port number to connect to. As a result, any connection will be assumed to be accessible on the remote TCP port 3389.

Once you execute the Remote Desktop MMC, you can set up multiple connections, as shown in Figure 10-3.

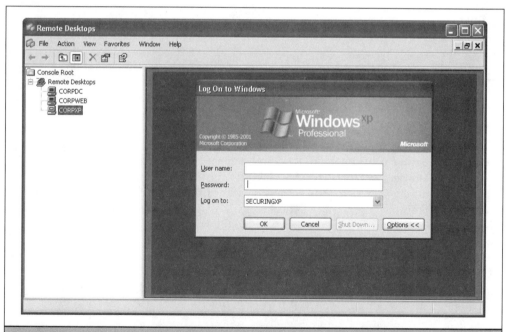

Figure 10-3.   Setting up remote connections using MMC

Group Policy

As we discussed in Chapter 1, group polices make administration of a large network much easier. From a hacker's perspective, allowing someone to remotely control your computer means "Let the games begin." If you wanted to restrict this ability in your network, you can apply a group policy object at the site, domain, or organizational unit level.

To use the remote desktop GPO settings, click Start → Run → and type **gpedit.msc**. Then go to Expand Computer Configuration → Administrative Templates →Windows Components and select the Terminal Services container. There are many settings you can use to control Remote Desktop behavior. You can even modify the encryption level: go to Computer Configuration → Administrative Templates → Windows Components → Terminal Services → Encryption and Security, and change the "Set client connection encryption level" option to High Level.

Credential Manager

In Chapter 6 we discussed credential management. The stored username/password feature maintains multiple sets of different credentials that have been used on the system, making single sign-on a reality. A remote desktop connection adds a temporary default credential whenever a dial-up or VPN connection is established. This credential contains the username and password. You can manage the user information using the Stored User Names and Passwords functionality.

CHALLENGE

As an administrator you have to manage multiple servers, perhaps on the level of 5,000 to 10,000 systems. So far we have discussed host security in various ways. How can you remotely manage all these servers and desktops?

Large environments are addressed by the various remote options. The Group Policy settings are always necessary for managing large numbers of computers in a domain, and your clients and server will be more accessible when they are part of a domain.

Your first step would be to set up group policies that configure your clients and servers to allow remote access and remote assistance. The settings in this chapter that can be pushed out by a GPO will be very helpful in managing your enterprise.

Your second step is to use the right tools to manage your servers. The Remote Desktop, Terminal Services, and Remote Assistance programs allow you to easily manage and configure clients and servers.

Last, you have to keep your enterprise up-to-date with the latest patches and hotfixes. You can set each client to automatically update itself with Automatic Updates, push updates using the SUS or SMS server, or manually manage systems one at a time using the remote administration options.

What's New in Windows .NET

Remote Desktop is much the same on Windows .NET servers as it is on Windows XP clients. On a Windows .NET server, you can remotely connect to the console and interact with "session 0," which is the login at the physical console. You can connect to the console in several ways:

- Via the Remote Desktop MMC console (TSmmc.msc)
- By executing the Remote Desktop Connection (Mstsc.exe) program with the /console switch
- By creating Remote Desktop Web Connection pages that set the ConnectToServerConsole property

Remote Assistance

Windows XP has expanded the terminal service functionality with Remote Assistance. What this does is allow an expert computer/user to be contacted by a novice computer/ user in a request for help. The connection allows the expert to view or even control the novice system to provide help. As an administrator you should control the ability of your users to issue these requests. Security measures have been built into the functionality through explicit permission requests; the user has to issue the help request, and the expert can answer the request as time permits.

The main difference between Remote Desktop and Remote Assistance is that the latter provides a view-only feature combined with some help desk–type support. Both the expert and novice can see the screen, and the expert can take control of the mouse and keyboard.

Configuration

To configure Remote Desktop on the remote system, as the Administrator, go to Control Panel → System, click the Remote tab, and select the Remote Assistance check box. On the Advanced tab you can set the amount of time an invitation should remain open. We recommend you set it to no more than 30 minutes.

To send a request for help, go through Start → Programs → Remote Assistance. You can send a request via Messenger, e-mail, or a file.

TIP   When using the File option for the Iivitation, use the password option to protect the invitation. When using the e-mail option, you can use PGP or S/MIME to encrypt the message for further security.

When using the File option, the file rcBuddy.MSRcIncident is created, which can easily be e-mailed to the expert. It is an XML file that contains the connection information, so it deserves its own security. When e-mailing, you should use encryption, such as provided by PGP or S/MIME, if possible. Session keys make sure one RA token can't be used for a different request session. The expert receives the file, saves it to the hard drive, and opens it. If a password is on the invitation, a password box will appear. You should send the password via a different route than the e-mail containing the invitation file.

We will use Messenger to display an example of the invitation. Figure 10-4 shows the invitation for assistance the expert user receives. They can accept or decline the invitation.

Once the expert system accepts, the novice gets a message asking them to allow the expert to connect. The first connection is in Screen View mode only, at which point the expert can ask to take control of the novice's system. The novice's system receives a dialog box for granting approval. Control or acceptance is not assumed in any step without explicit permission.

Because an end user may be susceptible to "social engineering" and allow an unauthorized person to gain access to their system, we recommend you restrict Remote Assistance using the Group Policy options described in the upcoming section.

Audit and Logging

As with Remote Desktop, there are few logging and auditing options aside from events written to the event logs and performance counters that you can monitor. The same option of checking Task Manager is available to you, as it is in Remote Desktop, but you also have one other option. To see outstanding invitations, use Start → Help and Support, select "Invite a friend to connect to your computer with Remote Assistance," and click View Invitation Status.

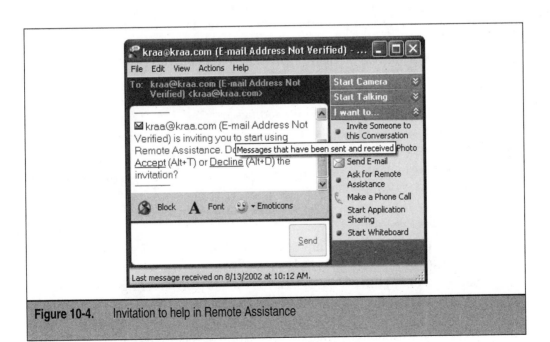

Figure 10-4.   Invitation to help in Remote Assistance

Group Policy

As with Remote Desktop, you can use GPOs to manage your user systems. Launch the Group Policy editor and modify the Computer Configuration → Administrative Templates → System → Remote Assistance → Solicited Remote Assistance option. By default, it is not configured. Users can configure Remote Assistance via the Control Panel. Enabled, this GPO allows users to send a request to you for assistance and allows you either remote-control or view-only capabilities. Otherwise, you can disable the ability to request help altogether.

The second option for GPO administration is Offer Remote Assistance, which has similar options. This would allow the expert to request control of the user system without the user first sending the invitation. The user still has to explicitly give permission. Be careful with this—users can be conned into thinking a valid administrator is asking for access to their system. User awareness of this type of attack is very important.

Terminal Services

Terminal Services is separate from Remote Desktop, and can allow multiple user desktop sessions to run simultaneously on a Windows 2000/.NET server. You can add the "Terminal Server" functionality using the Windows Components option in the Add/Remove Programs wizard in the Control Panel. The options you have with Terminal Services include

- **Group Policy**   You can use GPOs to manage Terminal Services. Use the GPO to set up various properties of multiple servers, such as profile path and screen resolution.

- **Windows Management Instrumentation (WMI) Provider**   WMI lets you script Terminal Services settings.

- **Active Directory Service Interfaces**   ADSI can be used to give programmatic access to Terminal Services profile settings.

- **Terminal Services Manager**   Updated functionality allows for managing multiple servers.

- **Single Session Policy**   A connected user can be limited to a single session. This can be very important if you are using Internet-reachable systems.

- **Client Error Messages**   Increased error messages make it easier to troubleshoot problems.

- **Remote Desktop Users Group**   You can set up a Remote Desktop Users (RDU) group to allow access to Terminal Services.

- **Security Policy Editor**   The SPE can be used to assign user rights without having to be part of the Remote Desktop Users group.

- **128-Bit Encryption**   The default setup uses 128-bit, bidirectional RC4 encryption when the client supports this form of encryption.

There are certain steps you can take with Terminal Services to increase security. We recommend that you do the following:

- Use Remote Administration mode in most cases. If you do use Application Server, do not install it on a domain controller, and restrict available applications with Windows XP/.NET software restriction policies (see Chapter 2).

- Restrict the RDP-TCP settings by setting the encryption to High, disconnect sessions after one day, disconnect idle sessions after 15 minutes, disable client connection settings, and disable mapping functions.

- Allow only Windows 2000 or later client connections.

- Monitor and log all traffic on TCP and UDP port 3389.

Telnet Server

Telnet comes built in with Windows XP, in manual start mode. Running Telnet on a server allows you to connect remotely to the server and perform administration tasks from the command line. Since there is no GUI, the speed is greatly increased over Remote Desktop and Terminal Services. However, unlike with Remote Desktop, you cannot use applications through Telnet administration.

On Windows XP, you can have two simultaneous connections. You can connect with a local Windows username and password or via a domain account. Telnet is an unencrypted transmission, so if you do not use the NTLM option for authentication, your username and password will be flying across the network in the clear just waiting for someone to capture it. With NTLM authentication enabled, the Windows XP security context for authentication is used, and the username and password are encrypted across the network. Of course, the rest of your Telnet session will still be transmitted in clear text.

NOTE   Since the session information is transmitted across the network in the clear, you should consider the following alternatives:

- Use IPSec to encrypt all Telnet traffic including the login (native to Windows).
- Use SSH as an alternative remote administration protocol (requires third-party software).

Both methods will provide encryption and strong authentication.

Configuration

By default, access to Telnet is available to users in the Administrators group. If you want users to access the Telnet Server, create a local user group on your server called TelnetClients. Users in this group can access the Telnet Server. In the following output, you can see that NTLM authentication failed and you have to connect manually. This will send the information in clear text.

```
Telnet server could not log you in using NTLM authentication.
Your password may have expired.
Login using username and password
```

```
Welcome to Microsoft Telnet Service
login: chris
password: (valid password entered)
Access Denied: Specified user is not a member of TelnetClients group.
Server administrator must add this user to the above group.
Telnet Server has closed the connection
```

In this output, we entered the correct password, but the account was not in the TelnetClients group, so authentication failed. Once you put the user in the correct group, a valid login will put you in the user's directory in C:\Documents and Settings. Type **exit** to disconnect.

Using Login.cmd

The program Login.cmd is run whenever someone logs into the Telnet Server. You can edit the login.cmd file to change the text that appears when someone logs on, and you can use Login.cmd to run other programs. When Windows Services for Unix is installed, the program is copied to %SystemRoot%\system32\login.cmd. This is what it looks like:

```
@echo off
rem
rem  Default global logon script for the Telnet Server
rem
rem  In the default setup, this command script is run
rem  when the initial command shell is invoked. It, in
rem  turn, will try to invoke the individual user's
rem  logon script.
rem
echo
*=====================================================
echo
Welcome to Microsoft Telnet Server.
echo
*=====================================================
cd /d %HOMEDRIVE%\%HOMEPATH%
```

You can put whatever you want in the file, and it will be executed when someone logs in. We recommend you remove the banner describing the server, at a minimum. You can manage the Telnet Server options with the command tlntadmn. As an administrator logged into the Telnet Server, run this command by itself to see the options as shown here:

```
C:\Documents and Settings\Administrator>tlntadmn
The following are the settings on localhost
Alt Key Mapped to 'CTRL+A'   :   YES
Idle session timeout         :   1 hrs
Max connections              :   2
```

```
Telnet port                 :    29
Max failed login attempts   :    3
End tasks on disconnect     :    NO
Mode of Operation           :    Console
Audit logs                  :    +eventvwr
Authentication Mechanism    :    NTLM, Password
Default Domain              :    securingxp.com
Audit Settings              :    Login(admin)
State                       :    Running
```

We recommend that you change the port number to something other than the default port, 23. This puts another roadblock in place for attackers. While a good attacker will check all open ports, simple modifications such as changing banners and default port numbers will make harder the easy access scenarios. If you really don't need Telnet, disable the service altogether.

Auditing and Logging

Fortunately, the Telnet Server does allow you to audit events. Using the `tlntadm` command, you can set the log file, filename, size of the log file (we recommend 80 MB), set auditing for both the log file and event log, and log user access, failed attempts, and administrator access.

PATCH MANAGEMENT

Let's move on to one of the biggest administration concerns, keeping your systems up-to-date. Several different options are available for updating your systems with the latest patches and hotfixes. You can do it manually, on a host-by-host basis, by visiting the Windows Update site and configuring the Automatic Updates feature, if you wish (see the "Automatic Updates" section). Or you can push patches out to your client systems. The following list gives an idea of when the different update options should be used. Home users and small businesses with small networks will usually be fine using the Windows Update site or the Automatic Updates features. Medium-size enterprises with up to 500 computers will probably want to explore the Microsoft Software Update Services (SUS). Large enterprises of more than 500 computers might want to use SMS for distribution.

- **Small business** Windows Update, 1–50 users
- **Medium enterprise** SUS, 1–500 users
- **Large enterprise** Microsoft SMS, 500+ users

Updating your system with patches is not the only step you should take. Looking for security weaknesses in your environment should also be part of your update process. In Chapter 14, we describe a methodology that you can use for penetration testing on your network. Pen-testing is essentially the concept of trying to break into your own machines.

To aid you with patch and security management, Microsoft has enhanced several tools. The two we will discuss in detail are HFNetChk and Microsoft Baseline Security Analyzer.

HFNetChk

HFNetChk is a simple command line tool that helps you identify installed and missing patches on your systems (Windows NT 4.0, Windows 2000, and Windows XP). Rather than having to go to the Windows Update web site all the time to check for patches, you can use HFNetChk. This program uses an XML .cab file that is updated by Microsoft. The first run of HFNetChk sends a request to Microsoft to get a copy of the latest XML file. The digitally signed .cab file is downloaded and decompressed. You can run HFNetChk against either your local system or remote systems that you have rights to administer. HFNetChk analyzes

- Windows NT 4.0/2000/XP

- Microsoft applications, including Internet Information Server 4.0, 5.0, and 5.1

- SQL Server 7.0 and 2000

- Internet Explorer 5.01 and later

HFNetChk can be run from Windows NT 4.0, Windows 2000, or Windows XP systems.

The more robust commercial versions, HFNetChkPro and HFNetChkLT, are available from Shavlik Technologies (http://www.shavlik.com). These powerful versions will answer many of your patch-management concerns by extending you even more options. HFNetChkLT is actually a lighter version of HFNetChkPro, but both include the capability to push patches and service packs out across the network. HFNetChkLT is free, like HFNetChk; HFNetChkPro is not, but it includes many more features, such as support for Exchange server, to name just one.

Microsoft Baseline Security Analyzer

The Microsoft Baseline Security Analyzer (MBSA) is a new tool licensed to Microsoft by Shavlik that goes way beyond being a hotfix checker. As the name implies, it is also focused on analyzing the security of your systems. It looks for problems on your system relating to the following:

- Windows operating system security
- IIS security
- SQL security
- Hotfixes installed and missing
- Password security

The hotfix check that is performed by MBSA is based on HFNetChk. The password checks are limited to looking for blank and easy-to-guess passwords. You may want to use a third-party password-checking tool if one of your major goals is password controls.

Configuration

To configure MBSA, you first have to download it from Microsoft. Once it is installed, you have the option of turning checks on or off as shown in Figure 10-5. Administrative rights are required on the systems you want to scan. You can scan your local computer or a range of computers. If you are an administrator on the domain and scan computers in the domain, you will get valuable information back.

Once the scan is completed, the report is saved to a file in the C:\Documents and Settings\Username\Security Scans folder, and displayed on the screen. The output of a scan is shown in Figure 10-6. For each problem, there is a solution with detailed information and links to exact fixes.

CAUTION   Be aware of the depth of the password checking of MBSA. It checks for blank passwords, usernames as passwords, and other seemingly easy passwords. Do not rely on its password-checking ability beyond these very minor checks.

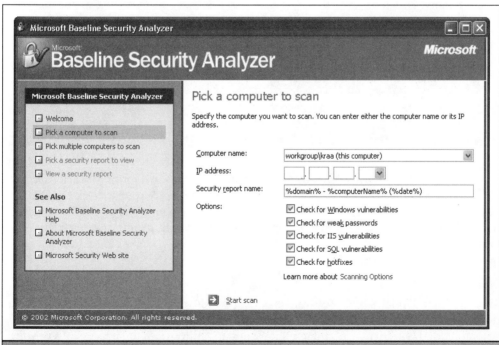

Figure 10-5.   Options for scanning with MBSA

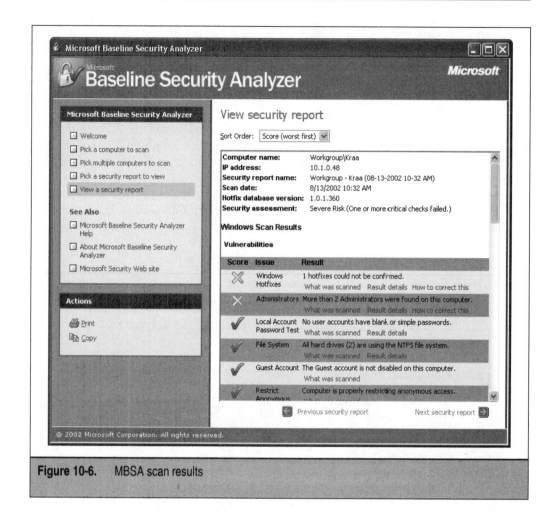

Figure 10-6. MBSA scan results

MBSA can also be run from the command line using the program Mbsacli.exe.

If you like MBSA's functionality but need more power and features, check out Shavlik Technologies' EnterpriseInspector (http://www.shavlik.com). This is the mega version of MBSA, with more features that will prove useful in medium-to-large heterogeneous environments.

Automatic Updates

The Automatic Updates client software is new to Windows XP/.NET, and is available as a download for Windows 2000 (http://www.microsoft.com/windows2000/downloads/recommended/susclient/default.asp). It essentially automates the process of visiting the Windows Update site. The Windows 2000 download is available as an MSI installer package that can be distributed via the Software Installation (a.k.a. Intellimirror) functionality of Active Directory Group Policy. The Windows Update site's functionality has improved with each release and has now become more than just a place to download patches. The update site has become an integral part of the desktop security for Windows operating systems, and it is now integrated with the Automatic Updates feature.

Configuration

To configure Automatic Updates options, go to Control Panel → System and select the Automatic Updates tab. You can either disable Automatic Updates altogether or choose from one of the three options in the GUI, as shown in Figure 10-7.

- "Notify me before downloading any updates and notify me again before installing them on my computer"

- "Download the updates automatically and notify me when they are ready to be installed"

- "Automatically download the updates, and install them on the schedule that I specify"

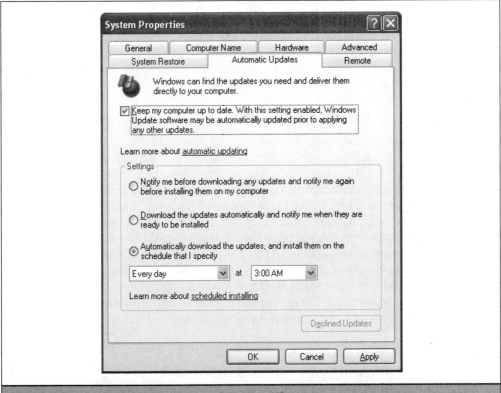

Figure 10-7. Automatic Updates feature of Windows XP

NOTE When an update is available, the steps in the process for releasing the update include

- Associated Security Bulletin
- Updated MSSecure.XML file for HFNetChk and MBSA
- Security patch available through Windows Update
- An updated catalog for Software Update Services

Group Policy

There are some very useful new GPO settings in the Administrative templates of Windows XP/.NET. Windows XP comes with only one setting, located in User Configuration → Administrative Templates → Windows Components → Windows Update. Here you can choose to either completely enable or disable the Automatic Updates feature for Windows XP computers. It is an all-or-nothing choice: if you choose to allow Automatic Updates, users will have the ability to configure it on their own systems.

Windows .NET provides some more granular controls, in the Computer Configuration → Administrative Templates → Windows Components → Windows Update container. Here you have two options to completely control the behavior of Automatic Updates on Windows XP SP1, Windows 2000 SP3, and Windows .NET computers. Your options are to configure Automatic Updates and configure an intranet server to be used as the update service location.

Microsoft Software Update Services (SUS)

If you want to make updates available to a server that does not have an Internet connection, you can set up your own in-house web server to act as the update server. You can download various operating system updates from the Windows Catalog site (http://v4.windowsupdate.microsoft.com/catalog/en/default.asp) and put them on this internal SUS server. Using SUS, you can update Windows 2000/XP/.NET systems utilizing the Automatic Updates client software. The SUS server software runs with a web site component on Windows 2000 Service Pack 2 or later, or Windows .NET server (see http://www.microsoft.com/Windows2000/downloads/recommended/susserver/default.asp). Computers running the Automatic Updates client software can then be configured to contact your internal SUS server. Microsoft has provided an excellent Software Update Services Deployment Guide, available at http://www.microsoft.com/windows2000/windowsupdate/sus/susdeployment.asp.

Server Features

The SUS server has several features that address security and functionality, including:

- SUS automatically installs under the current server web site or will create a new web site if one if not running.
- The administrative pages are restricted to local administrators.

- Digital certificates are used to validate downloads.
- NTFS is required on the SUS server.
- IIS Lockdown and URLScan are installed.
- Updates are not available to clients until approved by the administrator.
- An administrative web interface is available over SSL.
- Content can be scheduled to be automatically synchronized from Windows Update using HTTP from the Windows Update web site, a local parent server running SUS, or a local distribution point.
- Network Load Balancing is supported.
- Server-side logging of Synchronization XML logs shows what was synchronized, and an approval XML log shows which items were approved.

Client Features

The clients that connect to your SUS server can be configured with several different options, including:

- Prompt for approval before automatic download and install
- Schedule time for download and installs
- Registry-based policy support
- Automatic updates feature is available as an MSI installer package and also included in Windows 2000 SP3 and Windows XP.
- Content synchronization with the public Windows Update service

Properly implemented, the SUS architecture can add a high degree of administrative relief and security, by providing consistent, automatic patch and service pack updates across an entire network. In a small site of about 500 clients or less, the SUS architecture is fairly simple, consisting of a single server. You can set up this SUS server in a DMZ, where it can automatically synchronize with the Microsoft update site. The server is configured and managed through an SSL-protected HTTP interface. Once the server setup is complete, corporate Windows 2000/XP/.NET servers and clients can be configured to automatically pull updates from the SUS server. You can even centrally manage this configuration through Group Policy or a script that configures the appropriate registry keys on the clients, as detailed in the Microsoft Software Update Services Deployment Guide. Figure 10-8 shows a basic SUS setup.

Systems Management Server (SMS)

When your organization gets too large to use SUS for update distribution, you can turn to SMS. SMS provides a lot more functionality other than update distribution. In the past, SMS was used more for inventory and software management, Remote Desktop

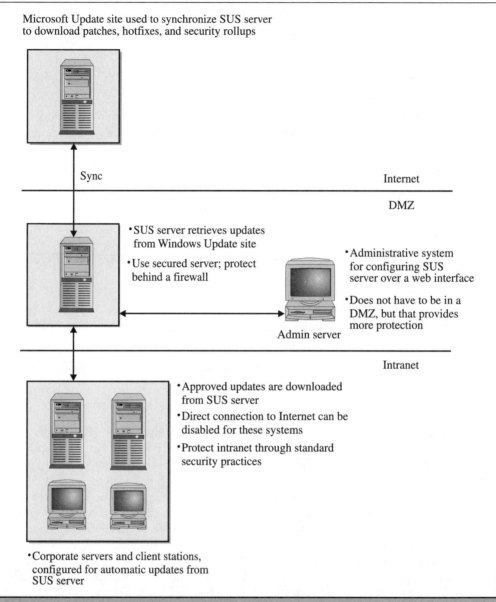

Microsoft Update site used to synchronize SUS server
to download patches, hotfixes, and security rollups

Sync

Internet

DMZ

- SUS server retrieves updates
  from Windows Update site
- Use secured server; protect
  behind a firewall

- Administrative system
  for configuring SUS
  server over a web interface
- Does not have to be in a
  DMZ, but that provides
  more protection

Admin server

Intranet

- Approved updates are downloaded
  from SUS server
- Direct connection to Internet can be
  disabled for these systems
- Protect intranet through standard
  security practices

- Corporate servers and client stations,
  configured for automatic updates from
  SUS server

Figure 10-8. SUS server basic architecture

control, and security and virus-protection distribution. Several key functions of using SMS today include

- HFNetChk will be integrated with Systems Management Server as part of the Systems Management Server Value Pack.

- HFNetChk can be deployed to enterprise systems, and scan results can be collected for SMS inventory.

- SMS collects information on client systems and can run automatically to update systems.

- Data can be stored in a central repository and used for inventory purposes.

- Unlike SUS, SMS supports Windows NT 4.0.

- SMS can be used to push out Service Packs, Windows updates, and Microsoft Office updates.

- Detailed logging and status reporting are available for installation on client computers of patches and hotfixes.

- A web interface for SMS administration is built in.

- Software distribution can be scheduled.

- Deployment of the Security Tool Kit can be done with Systems Management Server.

- Windows XP and Windows .NET server packages can be pushed out using SMS.

TOOLS OF THE TRADE

All the tools we have discussed make it much easier to keep your system up-to-date with the latest security patches. Remember to consider the dangers that enabling remote administration can open up, and carefully evaluate the remote patch management options available to you.

Remote Desktop   The new functionality of Remote Desktop makes it very easy to use. Remember to use encryption where possible and restrict who can actually remotely connect to systems. Use TSmmc.msc from the Adminpak.msi installer for Windows XP. This awesome utility lets you set up multiple systems for your Remote Desktop needs and connect to each of them through a single interface.

Remote Assistance   Remote Assistance is very helpful in troubleshooting problems for your users. Before deploying it, you should educate users on how it works. Otherwise, you can disable it on user desktops through GPOs.

Terminal Services   You should be familiar with Terminal Services through previous versions of Windows. Continue to use good security practices that have been developed for Terminal Server. Take advantage of the new software restriction policies (see Chapter 2), instead of the old Appsec.exe, to control what software your users can and cannot run.

Telnet Server   Telnet is inherently insecure because all traffic is sent in clear text. If you are not using NTLM for authentication, then your login credentials will be sent in clear text as well. If you do use Telnet Server, modify as many of the default settings as possible, and restrict access to the server. Use IPSec to encrypt the Telnet traffic whenever possible.

HFNetChk   Use HFNetChk to analyze and identify missing hotfixes on Windows computers across your network. Use the commercial version to keep your systems up-to-date by using its automatic patch push technology. You can analyze all the systems in your domain very easily, and should do so on a scheduled basis.

MBSA   MBSA provides a wealth of information about missing patches and inadequate security settings. Use it on a regular basis. As with HFNetChk, you can scan a range of systems all at once or one at a time. If you need the industrial-strength version, check out EnterpriseInspector from Shavlik Technologies.

Automatic Updates   Windows 2000/XP/.NET systems can be set up to automatically update by downloading the latest patches and hotfixes from your own managed Software Update Server. The client software is included with Windows XP/.NET, and can be downloaded for Windows 2000 from http://www.microsoft.com/ windows2000/downloads/recommended/susclient/default.asp. It's very simple to keep numerous systems up-to-date with the Automatic Updates feature. If you use a Windows .NET member server in a Windows 2000 domain, you can even apply some very helpful GPO settings that control the behavior of Automatic Updates.

SUS   SUS provides you with more control over the patch-distribution functionality by letting you bring the process in-house. If you have systems that are not connected to the Internet, then SUS is a good solution for distributing patches and updates across your intranet.

SMS   Large organizations have a good alternative for distributing patches and applications. You can define your own packages to push out service packs, patches, and other software to thousands of systems.

CHECKLIST: REMOTE ADMINISTRATION AND PATCH MANAGEMENT

Throughout this chapter we have discussed some important administration concerns for any environment. To manage a large environment efficiently with your remote connectivity and patch management options, be sure to do the following:

☐ Restrict access to your critical servers' remote connection software by IP/computer name, and use IPSec where appropriate.

☐ Utilize encryption options of the remote connectivity software.

☐ Restrict end users from issuing Remote Assistance requests if you do not trust them to make informed decisions about who can remotely manage their system.

☐ Use SSH as an alternative to Telnet, or use IPSec to protect the Telnet traffic.

☐ Monitor traffic for remote connectivity ports, and review event logs for successful and failed connection attempts.

☐ Use Automatic Updates if at all possible, to minimize administrative effort spent updating client systems.

☐ Use HFNetChk to identify missing hotfixes on a network of systems, or use HFNetChkPro, which will manage the whole process of identifying and pushing out hotfixes.

☐ Use MBSA to identify security weaknesses across your network, or use EnterpriseInspector if your needs are more complex.

☐ Use SUS or SMS to push updates to your client systems, to ease administration as well as to minimize the risk of systems' connecting to the Internet.

PART III

Active Directory, .NET Framework, and Internet Services

CHAPTER 11

Active Directory and Group Policy

This chapter is about two things, Active Directory and Group Policy. We will start with a crash course in Active Directory and then cover some of the new features scheduled with the release of Windows .NET server. Then we will discuss Group Policy, which provides the most powerful way to manage and securely configure a network of Windows XP computers. Next we will discuss how the new Windows XP group policy settings, such as software restriction policies and the new Administrative Templates, can be deployed in a Windows 2000 domain. And last, but definitely not least, you will learn what the caveats are when you need to apply GPOs to both Windows 2000 and Windows XP computers.

Let's first revisit some of the terminology and acronyms that will be used. These terms will be explained throughout this chapter:

- AD = Active Directory
- DC = domain controller
- Domain = the root domain
- Forest = a collection of domains
- GC = Global Catalog, provides the index of the AD
- GPO = group policy object
- MMC = Microsoft Management Console
- NC = naming context
- OU = organizational unit, a subdivision of a domain
- Site = a logical representation of the physical network, usually considered a collection of IP subnets with fast reliable connections between them
- Tree = a domain and its collection of subdomains

You may be wondering whether this chapter focuses on administration or security. The fact is that security in a Windows 2000/XP domain is dependent on the design and management of an entire security infrastructure. The security infrastructure in a Windows environment consists of Active Directory, Group Policy, software restriction policies, IPSec, Certificate Services, smart cards, EFS, 802.1x, and more.

Understanding Active Directory and Group Policy is absolutely essential to understanding security in Windows 2000/XP/.NET. With that in mind, let's get started.

CRASH COURSE IN ACTIVE DIRECTORY

In Windows 2000, Active Directory replaced the Windows NT domain SAM and created a major technology change that required a new way of thinking for Windows NT administrators. Centralized administration became a reality, transitive trusts were a given, and Windows NT's support for 40,000 user objects was blown away by AD's support for millions.

AD provides the foundation for a Windows 2000/XP/.NET domain. Somewhat similar to Novell Network Directory Services (NDS) or UNIX Network Information System (NIS), the Active Directory is a database that provides central directory services and resource management. Physically, the Active Directory comes down to a file, named NTDS.DIT; the extension stands for "directory information tree." This file is located by default in the C:\Winnt\NTDS directory on a Windows 2000 DC, or C:\Windows\NTDS on a Windows .NET DC. The file contains the database, which contains all the user objects, computer objects, passwords, and much, much more.

A Windows 2000/.NET server must be promoted to a domain controller using Dcpromo.exe before it can even create or receive a copy of the Active Directory. Also, the DNS is central to an AD infrastructure, and must be used in place of or in addition to the legacy WINS for name-to-IP translation.

Your Active Directory domain naming context (NC) does not have to match your DNS scheme, but your life will be a whole lot easier if it does. For example, DNS names will map more intuitively to universal principal names (UPNs), e-mail addresses, and your DNS zones.

DCs Everywhere

When multiple domain controllers exist in the same domain, the AD database will be replicated between them so that they each maintain a full copy of the database. In this way, the domain infrastructure becomes more resilient, because even if many of the DCs go down, the domain will still function as long as one is standing.

In a larger or globally distributed enterprise, many domains can exist, and the DCs can be spread out and configured to only replicate the parts of the database that are necessary to their location. For instance, domain-specific data is not replicated between DCs in different domains but is instead replicated only between DCs of the same domain. In either case, the Global Catalog server is used as an index, and only maintains a portion of the AD database. A GC knows which data in the database it needs because that data is specially marked for indexing by a GC.

More Than Just Trees—A Forest Has Domains

A forest in the Windows 2000/.NET AD infrastructure is a logical collection of domains. A domain represents a tree when it contains subdomains (or *child domains*). As depicted in the "Blueprints" section of the book, a tree is a collection of domains along the same contiguous namespace. So for example, while securingxp.com is the root domain, the child domains such as west.securingxp.com and dev.west.securingxp.com exist within the same contiguous namespace, and the whole thing makes up a tree.

NOTE   By default, a two-way transitive trust exists between each domain within a tree, and each domain within a forest. Therefore, each domain inherently trusts user and computer accounts from the other.

Organizational Units

A domain is a security boundary in the Active Directory. It is also a replication boundary. OK, technically a site is a security boundary too, as GPOs can be applied to a site; however, our focus is on the domain, where such things as users, groups, computers, and OUs are created and managed.

OUs are actually one of the most important logical management containers, because you have the flexibility to create any OUs you want and to add group resources into them, such as computers, users, and printers. Once your OUs are created, you manage their contents by applying group policies to them.

Nobody uses a Windows 2000/XP domain without implementing OUs to segment resources. In fact, the OU model introduced in Windows 2000 has nearly replaced the trusted domain model of Windows NT. In the Windows NT world, separate domains had to be created to establish security boundaries to group resources within. In the Windows 2000/XP world, a single domain can be used with many organizational units providing security and management boundaries.

In the "Blueprints" section of this book, there is a diagram of the organizational units we created for the root domain securingxp.com. Our choices represent needs for our particular domain—yours will be quite different. Some people choose to design an OU structure based on organizational structure, geography, operating systems, public and private services, Internet-facing hosts, and much more. The OU design provides a logical management structure and is completely flexible, limited only by your imagination.

To get an idea of how OUs are used as containers in parent-child relationships, zoom into the Services OU, which we decided to use for our imaginary public services offerings. The Banking and Investments OUs are each children of the parent, Services OU. Likewise, Customers and Partners are children of Services.

OUs are containers used for managing resources in a domain. It is not something you would apply permissions to, like a user or group. Instead you can apply Group Policy to an OU and every object it contains. For administration purposes, you can even delegate authority to a specific group responsible for managing the OU.

Delegation of Control

You can delegate control at the site, domain, and OU level. If, for example, you want a certain group of people to be responsible for the daily administration of the Marketing OU, you would create a global or universal security group and place their user accounts into it. Then you just right-click on the Marketing OU and select Delegate Control. The wizard will pop up, asking you to choose the group for delegation and the tasks you want them to be allowed to do. Your control here is very granular, and you have many prebuilt common tasks you can assign rights for. If you don't like the built-in tasks, you can even create your own custom-built ones based on properties in the Active Directory.

CAUTION You should always use the Delegation of Control wizard when assigning management rights to a site, domain, or OU. This wizard will set all the correct permissions on objects in the Active Directory, whereas setting them by hand will increase your risks of misconfiguration.

Users, Computers, and Groups

You have a lot of flexibility in designing a security infrastructure with AD. User accounts are, of course, created as members of the Domain Users group by default. You can then add a user to any one of the built-in groups to organize their rights in the AD. The Domain Admins group has full control of the domain, while the Enterprise Admins group has full control of the forest. You will probably create most user accounts as less-privileged Domain Users first, and then assign more rights from that point.

Computers also have accounts in the AD. Once joined to the domain, a computer is given a randomly selected password, which is changed automatically every 30 days. You can assign computer accounts to groups just as you can assign users to groups, which opens up a great amount of potential for designing security.

You can create security groups anywhere in the domain or OU structure, and use those groups to organize user accounts and computer accounts in any way that you need. For example, in the chapter challenge, you will see one way that security groups are useful in separating computer accounts by operating system—one group for Windows 2000 and another group for Windows XP. This makes it easier to configure exactly when GPO settings are applied.

So Just What Is Active Directory, Again?

The Active Directory is a name given to a collection of several elements that provide the security infrastructure central to a Windows 2000/.NET network. Essentially it is a central directory database stored in a file named NTDS.DIT, and it consists of three major partitions, or *naming contexts:*

- **Domain naming context** contains domains and organizational units.
- **Schema naming context** contains the blueprint of the AD database.
- **Configuration naming context** contains sites, subnets, replication transports, and trusts.

The Active Directory provides a centralized structure for resource management in a Windows 2000/XP domain. Combined with organizational units and GPOs, it gives you the flexibility to create your own logical management structure and wield its powerful controls.

What's New in Windows XP and Windows .NET

Originally released with Windows 2000, Active Directory provided one of the biggest technological advances for Microsoft technologies. With the release of Windows .NET, Active Directory moves into its second generation, with many improvements and enhancements, but the same core concepts and objectives.

NOTE   You will need the AdminPak.msi from Microsoft's web site (http://www.microsoft.com/windowsxp) in order to use the new features of Windows XP described in this section. The AdminPak contains many useful tools for administering a domain from your Windows XP workstation, including the Dsa.msc Active Directory Users and Computers MMC snap-in. At the time of this writing, the AdminPak was in beta 3.

Assuming you have AdminPak.msi installed, the Active Directory Users and Computers MMC snap-in can be launched using Start → Run → dsa.msc after. Immediately noticeable are the GUI enhancements in Windows XP. In fact, you will see that you can now perform useful drag-and-drop operations and have the new Saved Queries feature available through the familiar Active Directory Users and Computers MMC snap-in.

Saved Queries for the AD Users and Computers Snap-in

As Figure 11-1 shows, Windows XP comes with a new container called Saved Queries, which is part of the Active Directory Users and Computers MMC snap-in. This is a great new time-saver for administrators. The figure shows this snap-in being run from Windows XP to manage a Windows 2000 domain.

Some examples of queries you can create and save include:

- Identifying all disabled user accounts
- Identifying all Windows 2000 Professional computers
- Identifying all Windows XP Professional computers

Of course you could get a lot more imaginative than this if you wanted to.

NOTE   You can use the new Saved Queries feature in a Windows 2000 domain by simply running Dsa.msc (Active Directory Users and Groups MMC snap-in) from a Windows .NET member server.

If you were running a pure Windows .NET domain, you could select multiple objects (e.g., users) to edit at the same time, and would have many additional new features available. The following sections briefly discuss some of the most notable improvements.

The Global Catalog Is Not Required for Logon

With Windows .NET AD, a reachable GC server is no longer required for login, as it was in Windows 2000. With a Windows 2000 domain, GC servers needed to be placed

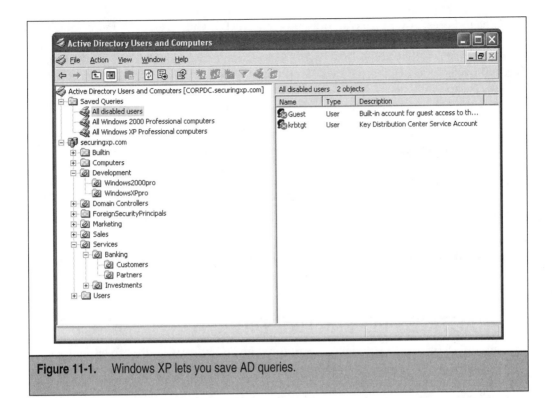

Figure 11-1.   Windows XP lets you save AD queries.

at remote offices so that there wouldn't be any logon failures if the link to the main organization was disconnected.

New Trusts, Authentication, and Authorization

As mentioned, two-way transitive trusts are created between every domain in a tree and every tree in a forest. Some major new enhancements will be made in this area with the release of Windows .NET, including new cross-forest trusts.

Easy Trust Creation Through a New Trust Wizard   A new Trust wizard has been included with Windows .NET, along with a new API that makes doing the following things simple:

- Create a new trust link.
- Validate a trust link.
- Deploy resource forests.

Cross-Forest Trusts in Windows .NET   Now trusts can be created between forests, either one-way or two-way. When a forest trust is created in Windows .NET, it means that all domains in Forest A will trust all domains in Forest B, and vice versa if you set up a two-way trust. Something to keep in mind is that trusts are not transitive between three or more forests, as they are with domains. For example, if Forest A trusts Forest B, and Forest B trusts Forest C, there is no default trust created between Forests A and C.

This is especially useful in organizations containing independent business units that may not trust each other but need to share information. A one-way trust solves the problem.

Cross-Forest Authentication   Along with cross-forest trusts comes cross-forest authentication, which basically allows Kerberos or NTLM to be used for authenticating accounts between forests. Essentially providing a single–sign on solution between forests, secure authentication can be used as long as the Netlogon RPC channels are open between forests.

Cross-Forest Authorization   Windows .NET allows you to include users and groups from trusted forests into groups or ACLs from the trusting forest. Logically, this is something you would want to do after creating the trust.

BEST PRACTICES FOR ACTIVE DIRECTORY

The amount of flexibility you have in designing an AD infrastructure can either help you or hurt you. Make sure you approach any AD deployment or upgrade with a solid and well-documented plan that defines groups, permissions, OUs, and delegation. Remember you can always go back and change things, but it may not always be the smoothest operation. You will be much happier if you start with the simplest plan and build slowly from there. Keep in mind the following rules:

- Assign permissions to groups, not users.
- Assign the least amount of privilege possible to enable a group to perform its task.
- In a large environment with distributed domains and many administrators, it will be necessary to plan a group infrastructure and document it.
- You are free to design your own logical management structure based on OUs.
- Before implementing an OU structure, have a plan. Do not merely try to mimic your corporate structure—that is not what OUs are for, although that is commonly assumed.
- Start with the default OUs and only redesign as you need.
- Plan and document a delegation structure for who controls which domain and OU.
- Give the appropriate group power to administer an OU, using the Delegation of Authority wizard.
- Use OU inheritance as much as possible.

GROUP POLICY

As we started out saying in the beginning of this book, Group Policy is the single most comprehensive and useful feature for managing security in a Windows domain. By implementing Group Policy, you can organize the management and security of your domain and decrease the total cost of ownership (TCO) for your company. After all, security does affect the bottom line in more ways than one, but being prepared with security can lower costs over a longer period of time.

The idea behind Group Policy in a domain is simple, although the configuration and management of it can be complex. There are literally hundreds of security settings that need to be set on a Windows XP computer, and luckily, they do not all have to be set manually. By exercising Group Policy in conjunction with Security Template .inf files (as described in Chapter 5), secure configurations can be repeatedly distributed across a network, automatically.

Group Policy depends on an Active Directory infrastructure; however, local group policy settings can be applied to a local computer as well. The basic steps to creating and applying Group Policy are

1. Create a GPO with the settings of your choice.

2. Link the GPO to a site, domain, or OU.

3. Configure the Security permissions on the GPO.

When a Windows computer boots up, it will query AD to find out which GPOs apply to it and in what order of priority. The policies that are applied can do a lot of things, such as causing the computer to download and run scripts from the DC's SYSVOL share. The following list describes just *some* of the things you can do with Group Policy:

- Install service packs (and other .msi files).
- Apply security templates (.inf files).
- Configure password and account lockout policies.
- Configure scripts to be run (logon/logoff scripts run in the context of the user, startup/shutdown scripts run as SYSTEM).
- Set software restriction policies.
- Configure event log settings.
- Configure auditing and other security settings.
- Set IPSec, Kerberos, and PKI policies.
- Configure registry values.
- Configure NTFS permissions and auditing settings.
- Set up wireless security policies (Windows .NET only).

- Configure Folder Redirection.
- Control user desktops and control panels.
- Configure ACLs on system services.
- Configure Internet Explorer and Windows Update.

There are more than 200 new GPO settings available in the Windows XP/.NET Administrative Templates alone. And that's not to mention the new security options, software restriction policies, and wireless security settings we have listed in other chapters. Some of the more important Administrative Templates settings you will want to consider using are listed in the next section. All of these are available to Windows XP and do not require Windows .NET.

Administrative Templates in Windows XP

The familiar Administrative Templates from Windows 2000 have only grown to include more settings with Windows XP. This is the only category of settings in Group Policy that actually applies a certain level of quality assurance. Basically, the options for the Administrative Templates are stored as ASCII-based .adm files in the %SYSTEMROOT%\system32\GroupPolicy directory. They can be edited with Notepad, to modify or add your own custom settings. Each setting is listed with the operating system version or application version that supports it (e.g., Windows 2000, Windows XP, Windows Media Player 8) so that you know exactly which one is appropriate for your GPO. This information is displayed in the new Web View.

Administrative Templates Web View

An extremely useful new feature of the Group Policy MMC snap-in on Windows XP/.NET is the Web View, which is only available for the Administrative Templates. As shown in Figure 11-2, you will now see an "extended" pane on the right-hand side, which displays an explanation of the selected GPO setting. More important, this view will let you know the exact OS and service pack that the selected setting can be used on, for example Windows 2000, Windows 2000 SP3, or Windows XP.

New Administrative Templates Settings

As mentioned earlier, there are more than 200 new GPO settings in Windows XP, which are located in the Administrative Templates container.

The original Windows 2000 Administrative Templates categories still exist with Windows XP, but they have been enhanced to include many new settings. What is more exciting, however, is the containers listed here that are brand new to Windows XP. These can be found under Computer Configuration → Administrative Templates, and will offer you some powerful controls:

- System\Net Logon
- System\Net Logon\DC Locator DNS Records

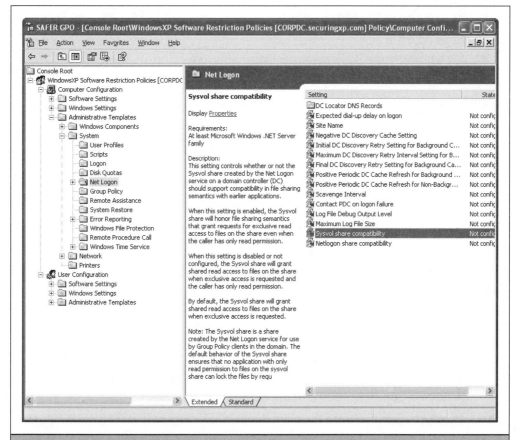

Figure 11-2. The extended view now shows which OS is required for the GPO setting.

- System\Remote Assistance
- System\System Restore
- System\Error Reporting
- System\Error Reporting\Advanced Error Reporting settings
- System\Remote Procedure Call
- System\Windows Time Service
- System\Windows Time Service\Time Providers
- System\Network
- System\Network\QoS Packet Scheduler

- System\Network\QoS Packet Scheduler\DSCP value of conforming packets
- System\Network\QoS Packet Scheduler\DSCP value of non-conforming packets
- System\Network\QoS Packet Scheduler\Layer-2 priority level
- System\SNMP
- Windows Components\Windows Messenger
- Windows Components\Terminal Services\Client/Server data redirection
- Windows Components\Terminal Services\Encryption and Security
- Windows Components\Terminal Services\Licensing
- Windows Components\Terminal Services\Temporary Folders
- Windows Components\Terminal Services\Session Directory
- Windows Components\Terminal Services\Sessions

It doesn't stop there, either. Even in the User Configuration, under the Administrative Templates section of Group Policy, there are many new settings, and brand-new containers:

- Control Panel\Display\Desktop Themes
- Shared Folders
- Windows Components\Microsoft Management Console\Restricted/Permitted snap-ins\Group Policy\Resultant Set of Policy snap-in extensions
- Windows Components\Terminal Services
- Windows Components\Terminal Services\Sessions
- Windows Components\Windows Messenger
- Windows Components\Windows Update

Be sure to run GPedit.msc and look through the detailed Web View explanations for each of these new settings and categories, as you will surely find some that you want to apply. Remember, best practice recommends keeping separate GPOs for the computer configuration and user configuration settings.

What's New in Windows .NET

You will want to be aware of what is planned for the final release of Windows .NET server, as there are many new enhancements designed to provide more control over your distributed Windows network. If you decide to implement a native Windows .NET Active Directory domain, you will have powerful controls, including Wireless Network Policies and WMI filters.

Wireless Network (IEEE 802.11) Policies

Available only in a pure Windows .NET domain, the Wireless Network Policies appear in the Security Settings container under Computer Configuration → Windows Settings. By creating a new policy, you can configure the Wireless Zero settings for Windows XP, such as 802.1x authentication and network SSID. An example of this was discussed in Chapter 9.

WMI Filters

Windows Management Instrumentation is one of the most intriguing management interfaces for Windows 2000/XP computers. WMI exposes a lot of the underlying hardware and software functionality through APIs that interact directly with the registry and the operating system. One way to use WMI is through a simple VBScript. You can run a WMI query to get a list of running processes, find the operating system version, list the user accounts on a computer, and a whole lot more.

When you decide to move to a pure Windows .NET Active Directory, you will have the option for applying group policy objects based on a WMI filter that you define. Right-click on a site, domain, or OU and select its properties, and you will see a new WMI Filter tab when you select the properties of a GPO.

GPOs, Links, and Order of Precedence

Visualize a GPO as an independent object, not a property of a domain or OU, for example. A GPO is linked to a site, domain, or OU through the MMC snap-in, at which point its settings are applied to that container's objects, according to the security permissions on the GPO, as described in the following note. The most important thing to remember is that a single GPO is created just once and can be linked to many OUs. Once a change is made to that single GPO, it is changed in all OUs that it is linked to.

NOTE GPOs also have individual security settings, much like a file or any other object in AD. The GPO permissions are special, and two that we are concerned with are Read and Apply Group Policy. There are other permissions too, like Full Control and Write, but the two mentioned are the ones that determine whether or not a GPO is applied to a user or group. If, for example, we allow Domain Users both the Read and Apply Group Policy permissions, they will receive the GPO. If we instead deny Domain Users these two permissions, they will not receive the GPO. By creating groups with user and computer accounts, you can finely tune your GPO deployments not only to specific OUs but to specific groups as well.

If you start applying many GPOs to the same OU, or you start nesting OUs and GPOs, you will need to understand the order of precedence, as well as a couple of options called No Override and Block Inheritance.

When multiple GPOs are applied throughout the Active Directory structure, say, one GPO at the site level, one GPO at the domain level, and one GPO at the OU level, you have to ask, in what order each GPO is applied. That is, while each GPO will certainly be applied eventually, it happens in a specific order, as shown here.

Levels and Precedence of Policy

NT 4.0

Local

Site

Domain

OU

Windows NT 4.0 system policies are supported in a Windows 2000 mixed-mode domain, and will be applied first. Local group policy will be applied next, if it is configured. Following that will be Site, then Domain, until finally the OU containing the computer or user object applies its settings. In general, the order goes from least specific to most specific, with the exception of Local since it is applied early. In this way, the OU containing the object has the final "say" as to what Group Policy settings should be applied.

So what happens when a computer or user object is deeply nested in a child OU somewhere and, say, multiple OU-level GPOs are applied? Let's illustrate the answer using the Customers OU from the "Blueprints" section of this book, which is a child of the Banking OU. Consider that we have GPOs applied at the domain level and at each OU, as shown in Table 11-1.

Starting at the top level, there is a domain GPO named Default Domain Policy that will be propagated down through the domain structure. As a parent OU, Services inherits the Default Domain Policy and applies one of its own GPOs, Services Computer Policy, to its own objects and its child OUs. Notice that Services User Policy is *disabled*, meaning that it will not be used at all.

Banking is a child OU of Services, and a parent of Customers. Banking inherits both Default Domain Policy and Services Computer Policy. After applying those two GPOs,

Level	Name of GPO Applied	Inheritance/Setting
Domain: Securingxp.com	Default Domain Policy	
Parent OU: Services	Services User Policy Services Computer Policy	Disabled
Child OU: Banking	Banking Policy	No Override
Child OU: Customers	Banking Customer's GLB Policy	*Block Policy Inheritance

Table 11-1. An Example of GPO Precedence and Inheritance

the Banking OU has its own Banking Policy GPO to apply. Notice that this one is set to No Override, a very powerful setting, meaning that all child OUs have no way to block inheritance of the GPO.

That brings us to the innermost OU, a child named Customers which is set up to Block Policy Inheritance. This setting has an asterisk by it in Table 11-1 because it is applied at the OU level, and not at the GPO level like Disabled and No Override. When Block Policy Inheritance is set on an OU, it will refuse to inherit any GPO that doesn't have No Override set. In our example, the Customers OU will block inheritance of both the Default Domain Policy and the Services Computer Policy, but will not block inheritance of the Banking Policy because it is forcing its way through with the No Override setting.

BEST PRACTICES FOR GROUP POLICY

Experience has shown many caveats and best practices for using Group Policy. In general, don't be disorganized with it. Go ahead and draw out some plans, even if they are just outlines, and figure out how your enterprise can best be divided into security boundaries. You are free to use any combination of OUs and domains to draw the lines by operating system, user group, geographic location, organizational department, service, network segment, or whatever else you want. Here are some guidelines:

- In Windows 2000/XP integrated domains, create separate security groups and GPOs for each OS. By using security groups for computer accounts, you can link a GPO to one OU with mixed computers and use the GPO permissions to control which computers it is applied to.

- Link GPOs to the parent OU and use inheritance as much as possible. Linking GPOs to deeply nested child OUs can quickly create a complex and confusing design.

- On the same note, avoid using too many Block Inheritance and No Override directives.

- Document the "group infrastructure" for your organization, mapping out Universal and Global security groups.

- Apply GPO permissions to groups instead of users.

- Import *.inf security template files into a GPO's Security Settings container for repeatable distribution of security.

- Use Group Policy at the domain level to restrict administrative MMC snap-ins.

- Use OU inheritance whenever you can, and avoid using the Block Inheritance and No Override GPO options, as your structure will become confusing if you do.

RESULTANT SET OF POLICY

It is now possible to determine the ultimate effect of all GPOs applied to an object such as a user or computer. This is useful in many cases, including our earlier example of the Customers child OU. For example, consider that there is a user named Rochelle and a computer named CorpXPPro in the Customers OU. You want to know exactly what the effect of Rochelle logging on to this computer would be.

With the AdminPak.msi from Microsoft installed, you can launch an MMC and add the Resultant Set of Policy snap-in, or alternatively, just launch the prebuilt console RSOP.msc. You can select from two modes for running RSOP, either logging mode or planning mode. Logging mode will process every GPO and setting that was applied to a computer and user and display the results in an MMC that looks similar to GPedit.msc. The difference is that you will see the enforced settings along with the source GPO, as shown in Figure 11-3.

In addition, you can right-click on either the Computer Configuration or User Configuration container and select Properties. From this window you can view a list of all the GPOs that affected this OU, and whether or not they were applied. Figure 11-4 shows the Computer Configuration Properties window.

Look back at Figure 11-3, and notice that the GPO with the highest priority is listed at the top of the list, Banking Policy. Banking Policy has the highest priority because it

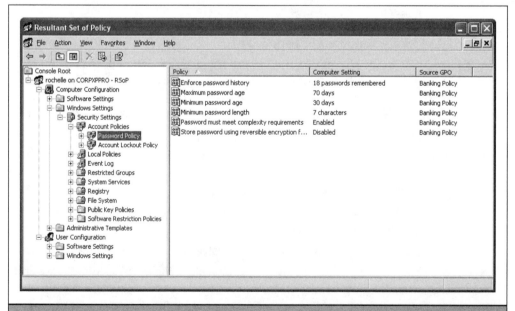

Figure 11-3.   The Resultant Set of Policy MMC snap-in calculates the effect of all applied GPOs.

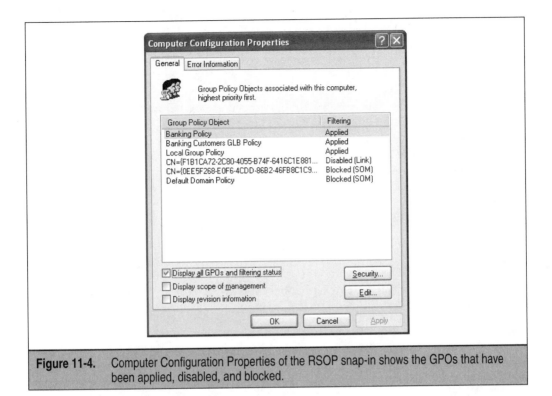

Figure 11-4.   Computer Configuration Properties of the RSOP snap-in shows the GPOs that have been applied, disabled, and blocked.

was set to use the No Override option. Next, the Banking Customer's GLB Policy has priority because it is specifically linked to the Customers OU of which CorpXPPro is a member. Then Local Group Policy is listed with preference above the other three GPOs (including Default Domain Policy) because each of the three was not applied. One was disabled per its own setting, and the other two were blocked by the Customers OU's Block Policy Inheritance setting.

An alternative to the RSOP snap-in is the command line tool GPresult.exe, which we discussed a bit in Chapter 2. This is installed by default with Windows XP, and provides the same information as RSOP.msc, but delivers text-based output.

USING WINDOWS XP GPOs IN A WINDOWS 2000 DOMAIN

If you were to ask us whether it's possible to manage Windows XP GPOs in a Windows 2000 domain, the short answer would be, "Yes of course, but there are some serious gotchas you need to consider first." We can't tell you how to design your Active Directory and Group Policy infrastructure, because it all depends on your organizational needs. We can, however, tell you that managing Windows XP in a Windows 2000 domain is extremely useful, provided you do it thoughtfully.

Windows XP–specific GPO settings can be applied in a Windows 2000 domain simply by managing a GPO from your Windows XP workstation with GPedit.msc. It doesn't even matter whether the GPO was first created on the DC or the Windows XP computer.

Before you say, "Cool, I can't wait to try that!" you need to be aware of exactly what it means. Consider this warning first: if you create a GPO with Windows XP–specific settings, and the GPO is then applied to a Windows 2000 computer, that computer will receive the settings, regardless of whether or not it supports them. The same is true of the reverse, where a GPO with Windows 2000–specific settings will write those settings to a Windows XP computer that may not support them.

Let's use the following example to illustrate this key point. Say that you open up the Default Domain Policy GPO on your Windows XP workstation, and set the following setting to Enabled:

```
Network access: Let Everyone permissions apply to anonymous users
```

If you saved the GPO and opened it up on your Windows 2000 DC, you wouldn't even see this setting because there is no inherent way for Windows 2000 to map it back to a UI option. However, you know that this setting exists in the GPO, and that it maps to the following registry value:

```
HKLM\SYSTEM\CurrentControlSet\Control\Lsa\everyoneincludesanonymous
```

When enabled, this registry value equals 1, and when disabled it equals 0. But who cares, because the point is that this value doesn't exist and isn't understood on a Windows 2000 computer. However, if you were to apply this GPO to a Windows 2000 computer, this value would sure enough be created on it.

Let's try it another way. This time, open up the Default Domain Policy GPO from Windows 2000 and set the following Security Option to "No access without explicit anonymous permissions":

```
Additional restrictions for anonymous connections
```

This setting is RestrictAnonymous = 2 and is understood by Windows 2000 but not by Windows XP, which understands only a RestrictAnonymous value equal to 0 or 1 (well, not quite, as we explain in a minute). However, if you open up this GPO in a Windows XP Group Policy console, you will see that the following option is set to Enabled:

```
Network access: Do not allow anonymous enumeration of SAM accounts and shares
```

This indicates that the UI checks for a Boolean value where 0 equals false, but any other value means true. This is the identical behavior of the registry key as well, since when you apply this GPO to a Windows XP computer, you can look in its registry and see that RestrictAnonymous is indeed set to 2, a setting which is not supposed to be understood. However, when you test it out by using an anonymous connection to enumerate users, you do in fact get an access-denied message; hence, this key is working even with an improper value.

The bottom line here is that you need to be cognizant of this behavior when configuring GPOs for multiple Windows OSs. You can try to logically map out how each setting will apply to the different OSs, and take the chance that things will work as you hope. Or you can go with the more foolproof option of creating a GPO for each OS, as in one for Windows 2000 and one for Windows XP. You can get very imaginative with this. If, for example, you know that some settings match up directly on each OS, then you can create a third GPO that contains the bulk of the shared settings, in addition to the Windows 2000–specific and Windows XP–specific GPOs. The fact is, while there are several exceptions, many of the settings do map up with no problem. For example, the Security Options listed in Table 11-2 are just some examples that will work identically in each OS.

Windows XP	Windows 2000
Audit: Audit the access of global system objects	Audit the access of global system objects
Audit: Audit the use of Backup and Restore privilege	Audit use of Backup and Restore privilege
Devices: Prevent users from installing printer drivers	Prevent users from installing printer drivers
Devices: Restrict CD-ROM access to locally logged-on user only	Restrict CD-ROM access to locally logged-on user only
Domain member: Digitally encrypt or sign secure channel data (always)	Secure channel: Digitally encrypt or sign secure channel data (always)
Domain member: Require strong (Windows 2000 or later) session key	Secure channel: Require strong (Windows 2000 or later) session key
Interactive logon: Do not require CTRL+ALT+DEL	Disable CTRL+ALT+DEL requirement for logon
Interactive logon: Message text for users attempting to log on	Message text for users attempting to log on
Microsoft network client: Digitally sign communications (always)	Digitally sign client communication (always)
Microsoft network client: Digitally sign communications (if server agrees)	Digitally sign client communication (when possible)
Microsoft network client: Send unencrypted password to third-party SMB servers	Send unencrypted password to connect to third-party SMB servers
Microsoft network server: Digitally sign communications (always)	Digitally sign server communication (always)
Microsoft network server: Digitally sign communications (if client agrees)	Digitally sign server communication (when possible)
Network security: LAN Manager authentication level	LAN Manager Authentication Level
Shutdown: Clear virtual memory pagefile	Clear virtual memory pagefile when system shuts down

Table 11-2.   Security Options Mappings Between Windows XP and Windows 2000

NOTE You can add, delete, or modify settings that show up in the Security Options container of any supported MMC snap-in, such as Secpol.msc or GPedit.msc. This is done by modifying the C:\Windows\inf\sceregvl.inf file, where all the Security Options settings are stored, as both registry values and strings for the UI to display. Once you customize this file with your modified settings, you need to register it with the OS by running `Regsvr32 Scecli.dll`. When you get the message "DllRegisterServer in Scecli.dll succeeded" you can open up one of the snap-ins to see your modified settings. Be careful, as editing this file is not supported by Microsoft, and your syntax needs to be perfect for everything to work as you expect.

You may still be wondering how exactly you can use Windows XP GPO settings in a Windows 2000 domain, so let's walk through the steps on our own network to help explain. Referring back to the "Blueprints" section of this book, CorpXPPro is a Windows XP Professional workstation and CorpDC is a Windows 2000 DC running SP2.

1. On CorpXPPro, open the MMC (Start → Run → MMC).

2. Now add a new Group Policy snap-in to manage a GPO from your DC by clicking File → Add/Remove snap-in.

3. When prompted to select a Group Policy Object, select Browse to choose your GPO from one in the list, as shown in Figure 11-5, or choose to create a new one.

4. Click your way through to accept the snap-in and get back to the MMC.

5. That's it, you will now see the GPO with all available categories, such as Software Settings, Windows Settings, and Administrative Templates.

6. At this point you can configure any settings you want for the GPO, including Software Restriction Policies, Event Log settings, File System ACLs, Security Options, and everything else.

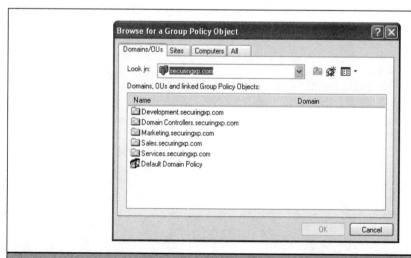

Figure 11-5.   Selecting a GPO to manage through the Group Policy snap-in

So managing Windows XP GPOs in a Windows 2000 domain is literally as simple as editing the GPO from your Windows XP computer.

CHALLENGE

Returning back to the challenge of Chapter 1, remember that your work is not finished. You designed the security settings to use, but have not deployed them. There are still a couple of questions.

- How can you create a security policy that will only apply to the development department?

- How can you ensure that Windows 2000 and Windows XP settings do not get mixed together?

The answers are not easy, and as you will see, there are some caveats to guide how you implement your GPOs.

There are several ways to approach these problems; we are presenting just one here.

Knowing that this department doesn't have any dependencies on legacy operating systems and software, you decide to group all the computer accounts into an Active Directory organizational unit (OU) called Development. This answers the first question, but remember, *you shouldn't mix Windows 2000 and Windows XP Group Policy Objects* containing security options. Refer to the "Blueprints" for an illustration of this OU.

Then you create Security groups, one for each OS. You create the first as a security global group called Dev Windows 2000, and add all the Windows 2000 computers from the Development OU. You create the second as a security global group called Dev Windows XP, and add all the Windows XP computers from the Development OU. Having these two security groups of computer accounts will let you control which OS receives the GPO settings by modifying its Apply Group Policy permission.

Now it's time to create the GPOs and link them to the Development OU. The first GPO is called Development Default and gets configured with your organization's requirements for Account Lockout Policies and Password Policies for the Development department. These settings match up nicely between Windows XP and Windows 2000 computers, so there is no problem creating one GPO to share between them. You link the Development Default GPO at the parent-level Development OU, and you build Development Secure Windows XP with more secure settings. For this GPO you set the Apply Group Policy permission according to the following table:

Development Secure Windows XP GPO	
Security Group	Apply Group Policy Permission
Dev Windows XP	Allow
Dev Windows 2000	Deny

CHALLENGE (continued)

You then build the "Development Secure Windows 2000" GPO with similar settings that are specific to Windows 2000 computers. You set the Apply Group Policy permission for this GPO according to the following table:

Development Secure Windows 2000 GPO	
Security Group	Apply Group Policy Permission
Dev Windows XP	Allow
Dev Windows 2000	Deny

To recap this challenge, you have created one OU named Development, two security groups (one for Windows 2000 and one for Windows XP computers), and three GPOs. The first Development Default GPO gives you a fallback, or safety net. That is, if you run into problems with the other two GPOs you can unlink them and troubleshoot based on the Development Default GPO. Most importantly, by separating out the OS-specific GPOs, you can ensure that only the proper settings are being applied.

What's the catch? It may be a chore now for you to keep up with changing OS configurations. For instance, what happens when one of the computer accounts in the Dev Windows 2000 security group is upgraded to Windows XP? At that point you will have to manually move it to the Dev Windows XP security group. This is when the WMI filters slated for Windows .NET's release will come to the rescue. Instead of having to apply GPOs based on group memberships, you can apply the GPO based on a WMI query that determines the OS build. And that is just one of thousands of possible uses for WMI.

It is important to realize that this isn't the only option you have for dealing with OS-specific GPOs. You may want to take an alternate approach. Instead of creating security groups for each OS, you could create two separate organizational units—one for Windows 2000 computers and one for Windows XP. At that point you could link the OS-specific GPOs to the appropriate OU, and take it a step further by delegating control of each OU to the appropriate Windows 2000 or Windows XP administrator. Remember, be creative and look for the solution that best suits your organization.

TOOLS OF THE TRADE

Many tools are available for the Active Directory and Group Policy. As an administrator, you will definitely want to download and install the AdminPak.msi, and make good use of GPupdate.exe.

AdminPak.msi   As mentioned earlier, you will definitely want to download and install the Administration Tools Pack from Microsoft. It contains most of the tools that you need to remotely administer Windows 2000 servers and domains, including many MMC consoles, such as the Active Directory Users and Computers snap-in, the Cluster Administrator, DNS, WINS, and DHCP snap-ins, the Network Load Balancing snap-in, the very handy Remote Desktops snap-in, and many more.

GPupdate.exe   Installed by default with Windows XP, the Group Policy update command line tool replaces the old Secedit.exe from Windows 2000 for the task of refreshing group policy. When run with no specific parameters, GPupdate.exe will update only the policy settings that have changed for both the user and computer. When you use the /force switch, GPupdate will reapply all settings, regardless of whether they have changed or not.

GPresult.exe   This command line tool is installed by default with Windows XP, and calculates the Resultant Set of Policy information for a user, computer, or both. The tool works on local or remote computers, and actually goes beyond the RSOP snap-in by providing you the /V and /Z switches, which provide verbose and superverbose information, respectively. The superverbose switch details specific settings that have been applied with a precedence of 1 and higher, so you can see if a setting was applied in more than one place.

Ldp.exe   Installed from the Support tools package of the Windows XP installation CD's \Support directory, Ldp.exe is an LDAP client. This is a useful tool for connecting to a domain controller and expanding its containers and objects. You will get a very raw display with Ldp.exe, not prettied up like the MMC snap-ins. Instead, every container and object is listed by its common name. When you first run Ldp.exe you need to connect to a domain controller running LDAP on TCP port 389, which is all of them by default. Click Connection → Connect and fill in the server name or IP address and the port number. When you first connect, you are not using any credentials, but you are able to expand the base DSA information, which will be shown on the right-hand side of the tool's window.

When you are ready to go further and see the juicy information such as OUs and user accounts, you will need to authenticate by clicking Connection → Bind and providing credentials as we have done in Figure 11-6. You will be authenticated, at which point you need to click View → Tree and enter the distinguished name for the container you want to view. In our case, we authenticated as "administrator" and set the Tree to "DC=securingxp, DC=com" which represents the root domain.

As Figure 11-7 shows, the display of Active Directory containers is similar to what you would see in an MMC snap-in; however, the information is much more raw, showing the distinguished names of each object and each associated object property. For example, you can see details such as the primaryGroupID property for the Administrator user account set to 513, which is a RID corresponding to the Domain Users group.

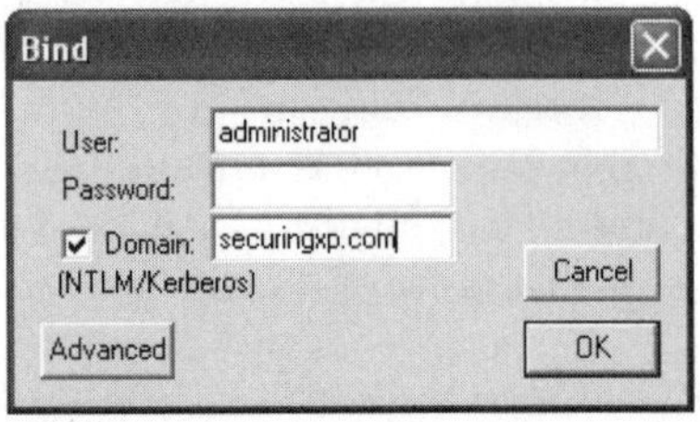

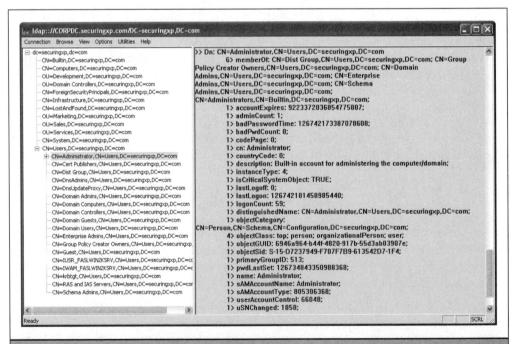

Figure 11-7. Binding to the directory with Ldp.exe

Despite the seeming simplicity of the Ldp.exe tool, it is actually quite advanced. You can search, query, and modify objects in the Active Directory through its cryptic interface. You can also enable TLS to secure the network traffic.

Adsiedit.msc Adsiedit.msc is another tool installed from the Support tools package. It is similar to Ldp.exe in that it gives a raw display of content in the Active Directory; however, it uses the Active Directory Services Interfaces instead of LDAP to access it, which connects via RPC channels. The tool is actually quite handy at accessing raw object information for queries, searches, or modifications.

Figure 11-6. The Ldp.exe LDAP client displays raw information about objects in the Active Directory.

CHECKLIST: ACTIVE DIRECTORY AND GROUP POLICY

Active Directory and the Windows forest-domain model provide a method for businesses to completely organize their information resources into logical units and manage security in them through Group Policy. This chapter was designed to highlight some of the security-related information you will want to know. Remember, however, that these topics run deep with features, options, and best practices that can be best explored through other resources. That said, here are our recommendations:

- ☐ Plan and document a solid AD design before implementing any changes.
- ☐ Use OUs as security boundaries, but don't nest more than five deep, as this can get confusing and hinder performance.
- ☐ Use the Delegation of Control wizard to assign rights over a site, domain, or OU.
- ☐ Plan and document a security group infrastructure, with groups for both user and computer accounts.
- ☐ Use OU inheritance as much as possible.
- ☐ Use the new AD features for Windows .NET, which will most likely include new cross-forest trusts and minimal needs for a GC.
- ☐ Plan and document a Group Policy infrastructure.
- ☐ Avoid using the Block Inheritance and No Override GPO options except when absolutely necessary.
- ☐ Be very thoughtful when designing a GPO that applies to both Windows 2000 and Windows XP computers, remembering that many settings do not match up between the two, even though the GPO will seem acceptable.
- ☐ Use new Group Policy features for Windows .NET, which will most likely include Wireless Network Policies and WMI filters.

CHAPTER 12

.NET Framework for Administration

In this chapter we will focus on understanding the concepts behind .NET Framework and the way .NET Framework implements policies across managed code. Let's start by taking a look at the Microsoft .NET family. The .NET family is the next generation of platforms after Windows 2000 workstations and servers.

- **The server operating systems** for this series are .NET Web Server, .NET Standard Server, .NET Enterprise Server, and .NET Datacenter Server.

- **The workstation operating systems** are Windows XP Home and Windows XP Professional.

- **The tools** for developing applications for these environments are Visual Studio .NET, which includes Visual Basic .NET, Visual C++ .NET, and Visual C# .NET (a new language developed specifically for .NET).

Third parties are also currently developing—or in some cases have already developed—translators for languages that are as old as COBOL and Pascal, as well as for Perl, Python, and Java.

The .NET Framework is Microsoft's initiative to simplify application development, support multiple programming languages, and streamline management and deployment of applications and web services. It is the *programming model* (the tools for developing applications) of the .NET platform.

NOTE   The .NET servers are completely different from the .NET Framework. The .NET Framework is the development environment that can run on most Windows operating systems, whereas the .NET servers are Microsoft's new operating systems release.

The basic components of the .NET Framework include the *common language runtime* (CLR) and the .NET Framework *class libraries*.

The common language runtime is the engine that runs and manages code execution. In essence the CLR is an agent that manages code at execution time and prevents the code from behaving unexpectedly. It provides core services such as memory management, thread management, and also different forms of code accuracy to ensure security and robustness.

The .NET Framework class libraries are a collection of reusable code. The class libraries can be used to develop command line applications, graphical user interface (GUI) applications, or web-based applications. The classes implement many important security features, including *permissions* (the right to access one or more system resources), authentication mechanisms, and cryptographic protocols that help ease the process of secure application development.

OVERVIEW OF .NET FRAMEWORK

Let's take a look at how .NET Framework fits in with the operating system. Figure 12-1 gives a high-level view of the .NET Framework. As you can see, there are two main

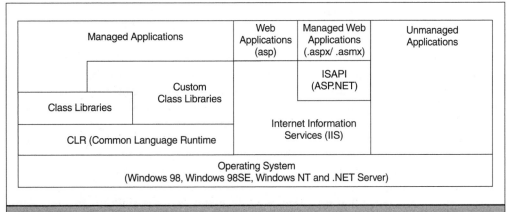

Figure 12-1.   The .NET Framework overview

types of applications: managed applications and unmanaged applications. *Managed applications* are applications that are written using class libraries (prewritten code). The CLR (common language runtime) manages these applications, hence the term *managed applications* or *managed code*.

The applications that have been traditionally written (pre .NET/Visual Studio) cannot be managed by the CLR, hence the term *unmanaged applications* or *unmanaged code*. Let's try to understand these building blocks—CLR and class libraries—a little better.

Common Language Runtime

The CLR is a sandbox that provides a number of services, including but not restricted to:

- Code management (loading and execution)
- Application memory isolation
- Conversion of Microsoft Intermediate Language to native code
- Access to metadata
- Managing memory for managed objects
- Enforcement of code access security
- Exception handling
- Support for developer services (profiling, debugging, etc.)

From a security perspective, the CLR enforces the .NET Framework's restrictions on executing code and prevents code from behaving unexpectedly.

The CLR is built upon a single common language, Microsoft Intermediate Language (MSIL, or just IL), into which different languages are compiled. The MSIL is then converted into platform native code just before it is required for execution; this is called *just-in-time (JIT) compilation.* The JIT compiler provided by .NET Framework will compile and link the MSIL for execution when an object is needed. The advantages of JIT include smaller footprint (since unused classes are not compiled) and code portability (hardware independent). When the code is compiled it still produces EXEs and DLLs, and metadata is still used to describe the classes used and what they can do.

Metadata describes information about the methods, fields, properties, and events associated with a class. In the pre-.NET environment, metadata was stored either in the registry or in the type libraries. In the .NET environment, metadata is held in the same file as the component itself.

It is important to note that today much of the code we use is still unmanaged code, thus the traditional program flaws (buffer overflows or application crashing) still exist. The CLR is designed for the software of the future; however, it also supports software that has already been developed in existing environments. This support for traditional, unmanaged code enables you to use the necessary COM components (EXEs and DLLs) from the existing environment in the .NET framework. Software development for the .NET framework can be performed on operating systems from Windows 98 on.

NOTE The list of supported operating systems and the .NET Framework Software Development Kit are available for download from Microsoft's web site at http://msdn.microsoft.com/netframework/default.asp.

So why is managed code so important? One of the main problems with existing code is that programmers have to deallocate memory they have dynamically allocated, which (among other problems) also leads to buffer overflows or application crashes. The CLR implements memory management through *garbage collectors,* so the programmer is no longer responsible for deallocating memory. Instead, the CLR manages memory, and when there are no programs referring to an object in memory, the garbage collector deletes it.

Memory management and garbage collection are big advantages of moving toward managed code. In languages such as C#, Visual Basic, and Jscript, data is managed by default. Data from C# can be marked as unmanaged (meaning that it will not use the class libraries of the framework) through the use of special keywords. Visual Studio .NET C++ data is unmanaged by default (even when using the /CLR switch), but when using Managed Extensions for C++, a class can be marked as managed by using the "__gc" keyword.

Another advantage of managed code is flexibility: you can use any of the supported languages to write applications.

NOTE An up-to-date list of available translators can be found at Microsoft's web site at http://msdn.microsoft.com/vstudio/partners/language/default.asp.

For managed code functionality to be implemented successfully Microsoft decided to standardize all the types with Common Type Specification (CTS) and Common Language Specification (CLS). CLS is a subset of .NET Framework features that is supported by a broad set of compliant languages and tools. Code written in one language can inherit implementation from classes written in another language; exceptions can be thrown from code written in one language and caught in code written in another. Thus, developers using class libraries are no longer limited to libraries developed for the programming language they are using.

Class Libraries

The .NET Framework class libraries are a collection of reusable classes that developers can use to write programs that will execute in the common language runtime. These implement many important security features, including permissions, authentication mechanisms, and cryptographic protocols, as well as other common programming tasks. Developers can implement security in the majority of their applications by simply using the System.Security namespace with no specific security code required.

Namespaces are a way to organize classes into a hierarchy. Namespaces are similar to packages in Java, without the link to the full path. The System.Security namespace helps accomplish tasks such as permission management, policy management, and assignment of type of managed code policy level.

Apart from tasks such as string management, database connectivity, and security of the application, the .NET Framework class libraries also enable you to build applications for specialized scenarios such as the following:

- Console applications
- Scripted or hosted applications
- Windows GUI applications (Windows Forms)
- ASP.NET applications (Web Forms)
- XML web services
- Windows services

Console applications support a set of classes that allow you to develop command line applications.

Windows Forms support a set of classes that allow you to develop Windows-based GUI applications—facilitating drag-and-drop GUI development and providing a common, consistent development interface across all languages supported by the .NET Framework.

Web Forms and services include classes that enable you to rapidly develop web-based GUI applications.

XML web service classes support the development of lightweight distributed components. XML classes enable XML data manipulation and XML searching and translations.

ADO.NET is part of XML web services and Web Forms and supports persistent data management. It includes SQL classes for manipulating persistent data stores through a standard SQL interface.

Assemblies

Assemblies are another important part of the .NET Framework. In fact, assemblies form the fundamental part of deployment, version control, reuse, and security permissions. The CLR gets all the type implementation information (interfaces and classes) from assemblies (EXE or DLL). Assemblies can be either dynamic or static.

Dynamic assemblies are run directly from memory and are not stored on the disk. However, they can be saved to the disk after they have been executed.

Static assemblies include types (interfaces and classes) as well as resources (resource files, image files, etc.) for the assembly. Static assemblies are stored in PE (portable executable) files on the drive. The PE file is an executable that can be executed on most processors, including x86, Alpha, and Power PC.

Each assembly has a version number as part of its identity; thus, multiple versions of the same assembly could potentially exist. It is both an advantage and disadvantage that multiple versions of the assemblies can exist. The advantage of multiple versions existing is that if two different applications needed two different versions of the same assembly to run, this functionality would facilitate the implementation of the different versions. The drawback is that if an application improperly uninstalls, it could leave unwanted versions of the assemblies on the system.

Let's take a look at the version number, which is physically represented as a four-part number in the following format:

```
<major version>.<minor version>.<build number>.<revision>
```

The assemblies are stored either in the global cache and/or in the application directory or subdirectories. The global assembly cache, which is the machinewide code cache, is installed on the machine once the CLR is installed. The Global Assembly Cache tool can be run from the command line (Gacutil.exe). This tool can be used to view, add, or delete assemblies (as shown in the following code listing) from the global assembly cache. The global assembly cache mainly contains the assemblies that are to be used by server applications. The assemblies for individual applications are installed in the application directories or subdirectories, which can be accessed only by the application, and not by the server application.

```
C:\> gacutil /l

Microsoft (R) .NET Global Assembly Cache Utility.   Version 1.0.3705.0

Copyright (C) Microsoft Corporation 1998-2001. All rights reserved.

The Global Assembly Cache contains the following assemblies:
```

```
Accessibility, Version=1.0.3300.0, Culture=neutral, PublicKeyToken=b03
f5f7f11d50a3a, Custom=null

IEExecRemote, Version=1.0.3300.0, Culture=neutral, PublicKeyToken=b03f
5f7f11d50a3a, Custom=null

IEHost, Version=1.0.3300.0, Culture=neutral, PublicKeyToken=b03f5f7f11
d50a3a, Custom=null

mscorcfg, Version=1.0.3300.0, Culture=neutral, PublicKeyToken=b03f5f7f
11d50a3a, Custom=null

System, Version=1.0.3300.0, Culture=neutral, PublicKeyToken=b77a5c5619
34e089, Custom=null

System.Configuration.Install, Version=1.0.3300.0, Culture=neutral,
PublicKeyToken=b03f5f7f11d50a3a, Custom=null

System.Data, Version=1.0.3300.0, Culture=neutral, PublicKeyToken=b77a5
c561934e089, Custom=null

System.Design, Version=1.0.3300.0, Culture=neutral, PublicKeyToken=b03
f5f7f11d50a3a, Custom=null

System.DirectoryServices, Version=1.0.3300.0, Culture=neutral,
PublicKeyToken=b03f5f7f11d50a3a, Custom=null
```

Assemblies can be signed either with a strong name (using Sn.exe) or using signcode. Using the strong name to sign an assembly would add a public key encryption to the manifest. An assembly manifest contains the version requirements and all the metadata needed to define the scope of the assembly. All assemblies contain a collection of data that describes how the elements in the assembly relate to each other. This ensures prevention of spoofed assemblies; however, there is no way to prove that it is published by a particular publisher.

A *signcode* (also referred to as *Authenticode*) requires a publisher to prove their identity to an authority (someone like VeriSign), obtain a certificate, and then sign the code. If the code has been tampered with since it was published, a warning message is received. (Using Code Access Policy, this can be changed to deny execution or bypass warning message.)

One last thing to know about assemblies is that, by default, assemblies try to bind with exactly the same version of assembly that the application was built with. However, administrators can override this by configuration file settings using the Framework Configuration tool (Mscorcfg.msc). A more detailed description of the tasks that can be performed with the Framework Configuration tool is provided in the next section, ".NET Framework Security."

.NET FRAMEWORK SECURITY

There are three main components to the .NET Framework security:

- Evidence-based security
- Role-based security
- Code access security

Evidence-based security combines evidence with policy to compute permissions granted to an assembly. Evidence associated with assemblies would be either strong names or signcode (Authenticode). Evidence associated with the environment would be the origin of the code (URL, site, security zones).

Role-based security, also referred to as the *authentication and authorization process,* lets you check the identity of the current user based on the user ID and the role that the user is currently adopting. It either permits or denies that identity access to the particular resource. This is done using SIDs in Windows XP, Windows 2000, and Windows NT.

Code access security is used to ensure that the assembly code does not access resources and operations that it doesn't have permissions to access. The developers can use the `System.Security.CodeAccessPermission` namespace to implement code access security. When a managed code assembly is accessed by a resource, the `System.Security.CodeAccessPermission` namespace would be used by the CLR to determine the set of permissions to grant the assembly. The CLR, to determine which set of permissions to grant to an assembly, initiates a *stack walk*. The stack walk checks each assembly in the chain for the appropriate permissions and returns the results to the CLR, thus either allowing or disallowing access to execute the particular assembly.

Traditionally, permissions would be assigned by an administrator of the local machine for directories and subdirectories on DLLs and EXEs. An executable could then, if required, make a call to any other DLL or EXE.

Microsoft has taken a slightly different approach with .NET. Apart from the assignment of permissions by administrators, assemblies can also notify other executables of the permissions required. When the stack walk is initiated, the assemblies in the chain notify the permissions they need to be executed. For this notification to take place, the permissions have to be predefined by the developer for the assemblies (EXEs and DLLs). The permissions that can be defined are Required, Optional, or Refused. Thus, when the CLR requests permission to execute an assembly, each assembly in the chain of the stack walk can provide a list of required permissions to complete the successful execution of the assembly.

 SECURITY ALERT The code developer, when writing code for the assembly, should always define the permissions (Required, Optional, or Refused) for the assemblies in the stack walk. If no permissions are defined, the default permissions would allow access to all the assemblies in the stack walk.

The designers of .NET Framework also came up with the idea of *code groups*, which is analogous to the concept of groups of users. Just as users belonging to a certain group have a certain level of permissions, so do assemblies. An assembly can belong to one or more code groups.

NOTE A default set of code groups exists. More code groups can be created depending upon need.

Let's take a closer look at what happens when a particular action is requested by an assembly:

1. The CLR looks at a code group's security policy every time an assembly requests that an action be taken.

2. The security policy dictates whether the CLR allows or disallows the action.

3. When an action is requested by the assembly, to determine if that action is allowed, the CLR looks at the security policy of the code group and either allows or disallows the action requested.

The security policies for the code groups can be defined at different levels:

- **Enterprise policy** applies to all managed code in an enterprise setting.
- **Machine policy** applies to all managed code on a local machine.
- **User policy** applies to all applications and resources for a particular user.
- **Application Domain policy** applies to any application that hosts the CLR. It is defined by the runtime host.

The Enterprise policy, Machine policy, and User policy are specified by the administrator; the User policy can also be specified by the user. An *application domain* is a secure unit of processing that the CLR can use to provide isolation between applications. The Application Domain policy is defined by the application domain host code. When granting permissions to application domains, the CLR uses the Enterprise policy, Machine policy, and User policy to compute the actual permissions. We will take a look at how to calculate permissions in the section "Computing Permissions," later in this chapter.

Default Security Policies

Assemblies and applications come with a default set of policies. Let's look at the different policies and how they are set up. To understand these policies, first you need to know the different types of permission classes that exist and what functionality each of them pertains to. Then we will look at the default set of policies in .NET Framework. The default permission classes are as follows:

- **DnsPermissions** Controls rights to access Domain Name System (DNS) servers on the network

- **EnvironmentPermission**   Controls access to system and user environment variables

- **EventLogPermission**   Allows control of code access permissions for event logging

- **FileDialogPermission**   Controls the ability to access files or folders through a file dialog box

- **FileIOPermission**   Controls the ability to access files and folders

- **IsolatedStoragePermission**   Represents access to generic isolated storage capabilities

- **PrintingPermission**   Controls access to printers

- **ReflectionPermission**   Controls access to metadata

- **SecurityPermission**   Describes a set of security permissions applied to code

- **UIPermission**   Controls the permissions related to user interfaces and the clipboard

- **WebPermission**   Controls rights to access an HTTP Internet resource

CHALLENGE

The cutting-edge company you work for wants to develop secure code using .NET for your web site and other client software. You have been running Windows 2000 Domain Controller, and your development platform includes Visual Studio 6.0. Fortunately, Visual Studio 7.0 (currently still in beta) is the development platform for .NET Framework.

You would benefit from the security enhancements in the .NET Framework, such as protection from buffer overflows and use of class libraries. The .NET Framework would also allow you, as an administrator, to roll out policies on the code that is being installed on the server by using the .NET Framework wizard. And you can maintain control at the desktop to allow or disallow a user from trusting code.

Remember to

- Apply security policy on all code.

- Ensure the use of managed code on your production systems.

- When using the sample deployment package, ensure the security permissions on all the code that is being deployed by using the Permview tool before creating the package.

The security policy that will be created can be deployed on most Windows operating systems including Windows XP, Windows 2000, and Windows NT.

The default policies are applied to each zone. Security zones were initially implemented in Internet Explorer 4.0, and they have since come to play a much more important role. In the .NET Framework, each code base is classified into a specific security zone. On the basis of this zone, the CLR decides if the code should or should not have access to the permission classes described. The security zones are My Computer, Local Intranet, Internet, Trusted Sites, and Untrusted Sites. Table 12-1 describes the default policies that apply to each zone. My Computer contains all the applications on the local computer; the default setting is Low. Local Intranet is Medium-Low. Internet (Trusted Sites) is Medium, and Internet (Untrusted Sites) is High. Permissions are classified into one of these four categories. We will look at configuring the zones in the ".NET Framework Wizard" section.

Let's look at how to access and modify these permissions. These permissions can be viewed via either command line using the Code Access Security Policy tool (Caspol.exe) or the .NET Framework Configuration snap-in to the MMC (Mscorcfg.msc).

Permissions	My Computer	Local Intranet	Internet (Trusted Sites)	Internet (Untrusted Sites)
DNS	Unrestricted permissions	Unrestricted permissions	–	No access
Environment	Unrestricted permissions	User name and temp environment variables (TEMP, TMP)	–	No access
EventLog	Unrestricted permissions	Instrument (write-only)	–	No access
FileDialog	Unrestricted permissions	Unrestricted permissions	Read-only access to files	No access
FileIO	Unrestricted permissions	Read (to share of origin)	–	No access
Isolated storage	Unrestricted permissions	Assembly isolation by user; unrestricted quota	Domain isolation by user quota: 10,240 bytes and 365 days	No access
Printing	Unrestricted permissions	Default printing	Safe printing	No access
Reflection	Unrestricted permissions	ReflectionEmit	–	No access
Security	Unrestricted permissions	Execution, remote configuration, and assertion	Execution	No access
User Interface	Unrestricted permissions	Unrestricted permissions	Safe top-level windows; own clipboard	No access
Web	Unrestricted permissions	Connect (site of origin)	Connect (site of origin)	No access

Table 12-1.   Default Policy of Security Zones

NOTE .NET Security can be turned off by setting the following key: `HKLM\SOFTWARE\` `Microsoft\.NETFramework\Security\Policy\GlobalSettings"00 00 00` `1F"` The only reason to disable the security would be to increase performance. In the absence of this registry key, security is enabled; thus the CLR will read the policy and determine the permissions allowed.

TOOLS FOR THE .NET FRAMEWORK

As an administrator or user, you will need to view, edit, or delete permission sets or permissions. Two main tasks can be performed using the .NET Framework Configuration tool (Mscorcfg.msc) and Code Access Security Policy tool (Caspol.exe): configuring code groups and configuring permission sets. This section looks primarily at some of the actions that can be performed using Mscorcfg.msc, which provides a graphical interface through the MMC. The Caspol.exe tool is the command line equivalent of that tool; it would be useful when you are using scripts to implement the configuration and permissions across a number of machines. It's used as follows:

```
<drive>:\ Winnt\Microsoft.NET\Framework\<runtime version number>\Caspol.exe
```

The command `Caspol.exe -help` displays all the possible help options.

The following command will bring up the MMC snap-in shown in Figure 12-2:

```
<drive>:\Winnt\Microsoft.NET\Framework\<runtime version number>\Mscorcfg.msc
```

Expanding on My Computer → Runtime Security Policy (in the left pane of Figure 12-2) causes three main policy-level subtrees to become visible: Enterprise, Machine, and User. (Each level can have a policy defined.) By selecting any one of these, you can view the code groups, permission sets, and policy assemblies for that tree.

In the Code Groups subtree, the root level is All_Code, which grants all code full trust. There are subcode groups at Machine level: My_Computer, LocalIntranet, Internet_Zone, Restricted_Zone, and Trusted_Zone. (In the ".NET Framework Wizard" section, later in the chapter, we look at how to access the security zones.) Thus, all the code would reside in one of the subcode groups of the root level (All_Code). Depending on the code groups that the code belongs to, and depending upon the permission set assigned to the code, the code can access those subroutines. By right-clicking the code group and selecting Properties, the membership condition and permission set can be viewed.

In the second subtree, Permission Sets, there are seven main permissions by default: FullTrust, SkipVerification, Execution, Nothing, Everything, LocalIntranet, and Internet. To create a new permission, right-click Permission Sets and select New. This enables you to create a new permission set or modify a permission set. Selecting the permission set and selecting Change Permissions allows you to change the particular permissions. The third subtree, Policy Assemblies, contains assemblies used during policy evaluation.

Thus, an assembly (DLLs and EXEs) could belong to more than one code group. The membership conditions would determine the conditions that an assembly would need to meet to belong to a particular code group. And that group would have

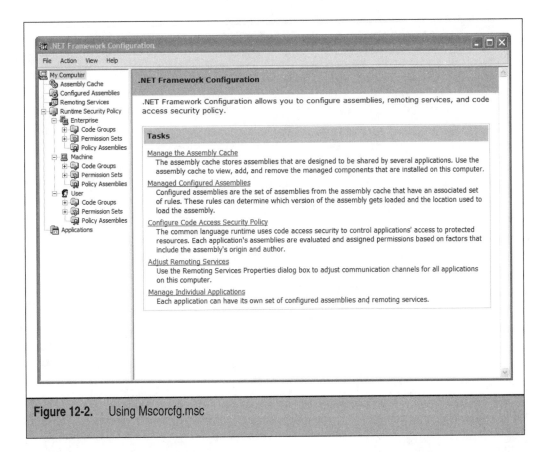

Figure 12-2.   Using Mscorcfg.msc

permissions determined by the permission set specified for it. An important point to note is that all assemblies would belong to the All_Code group, and the All_Code group, by default, has no permissions at all.

Working with Permission Sets

Most of the basic code groups and permission sets have already been defined for you. However, new code groups and new permission sets can be created to fulfill specific needs.

Creating a Permission Set

To create a new permission set, right-click the desired Permission Sets tree and select New. The dialog box shown in Figure 12-3 appears, in which you can enter a name and description for the new permission set. Then click Next.

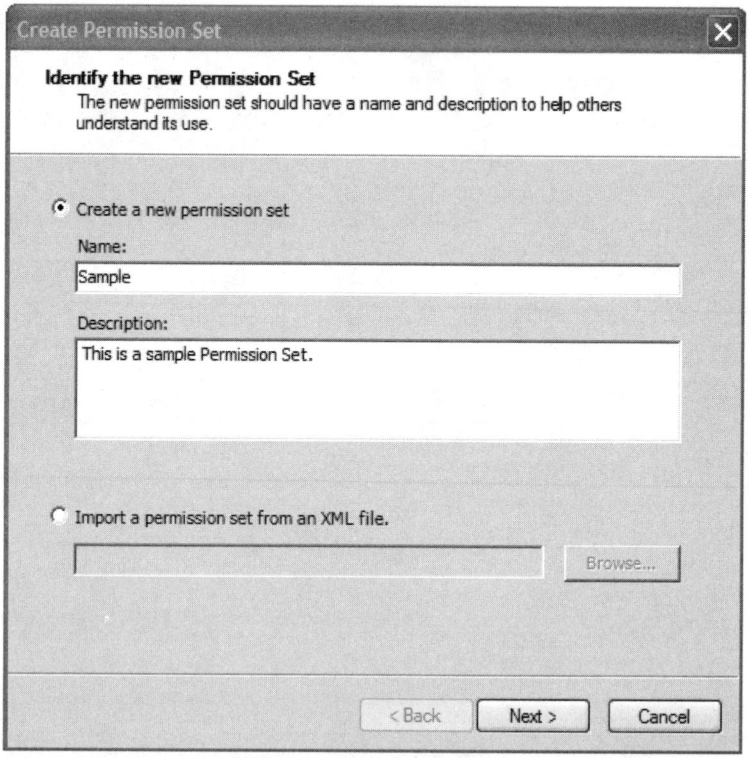

Figure 12-3. Creating a permission set

Adding Permissions

When you click the Next button, you will be prompted to assign individual permissions to the permission set from the Available Permissions list. Highlight the desired permission and click the Add button. In Figure 12-4, we have selected Security. You can then make additional permission settings.

It is important to note that each permission in the list of available permissions has a different subset of possible permission settings. In the Permission Settings box (shown

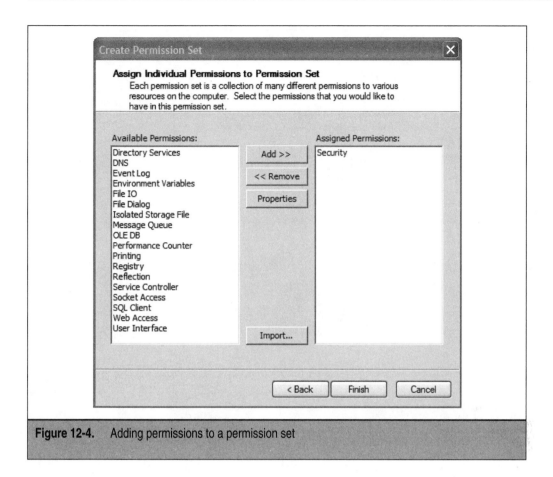

Figure 12-4. Adding permissions to a permission set

in Figure 12-5) you use the radio buttons to select either "Grant assemblies unrestricted access to all security permissions" (at the bottom of the box) or "Grant assemblies the following security permissions." (restricted access). In the latter case, you would then use the check boxes to select the desired permissions from the list. In Figure 12-5, we have selected restricted access and the permission "Enable assembly execution." To finish creating the permission set, click OK.

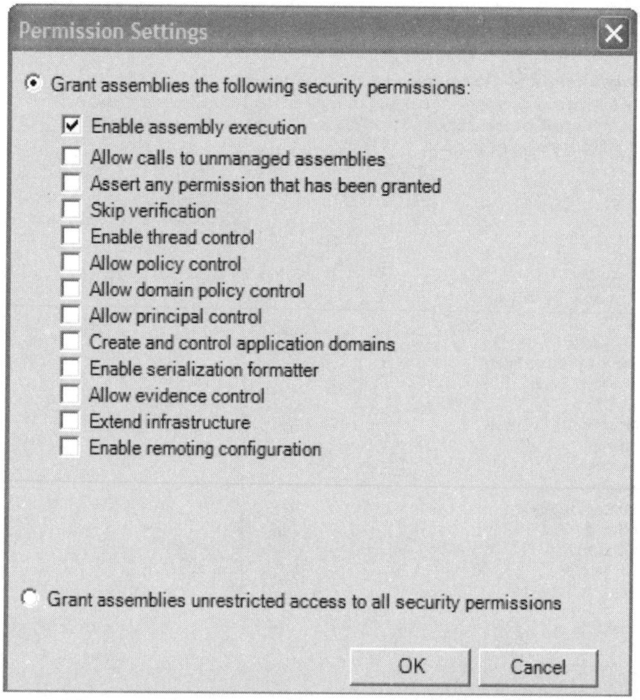

Figure 12-5. Setting permissions while creating a permission set

The permissions in the permission set can be modified at any time. To view or change the assigned permissions, right-click the permission set and select Edit. To then modify a permission's properties, select that permission set in the Assigned Permissions list, and select Properties.

Creating a Code Group

Now that you have created a permission set, you can create a code group and assign the code group the same permissions. To create a code group, right-click All_Code (or any subtree of All_Code) and select New. Enter a name for the group; in Figure 12-6 we entered "Sample Code Group."

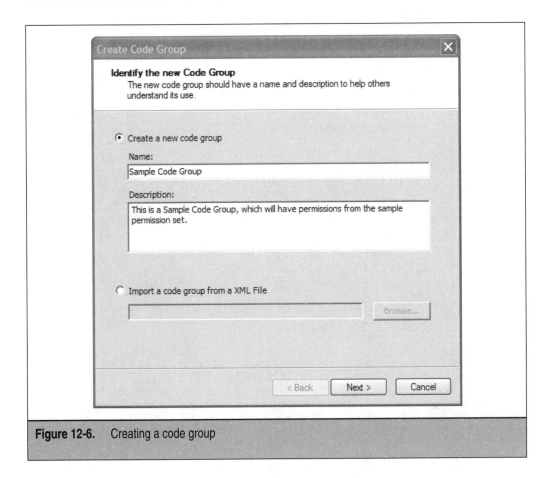

Figure 12-6. Creating a code group

Click Next, and you will be prompted for the membership condition, as shown in Figure 12-7. Select a condition type and click Next. You will then be prompted to select the permission set. Choose the appropriate permission set, and select Next and then Finish. This completes the creation of the code group.

NOTE If you at some point try to delete a permission set that is in use by a code group, you will be notified of that fact and will have to close the permission set to delete it.

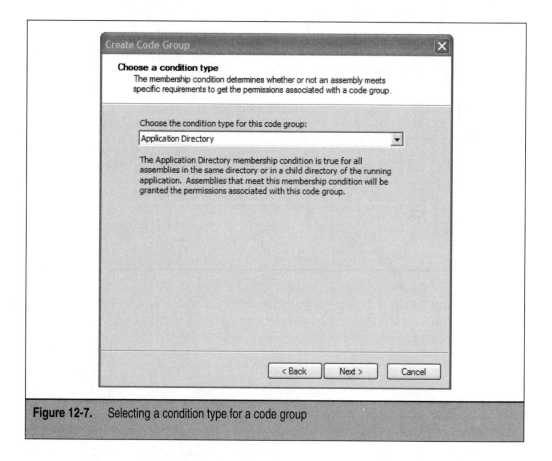

Figure 12-7.   Selecting a condition type for a code group

Saving and Deployment of Security Policy

After making all appropriate changes to the security policy, either by adding, modifying, or deleting the code groups or permission sets, the policy can be saved and deployed across the Enterprise, Machine, or User level. This can be done by creating a simple deployment package.

To create the deployment package, right-click Runtime Security Policy and select Create Deployment Package. You will be prompted to select the security policy level that you would like to deploy (Enterprise, Machine, or User) and the path and filename for the installer package you are creating. (As an installer, it will get an .msi extension.) The package can be deployed to the Windows clients using Group Policy or Systems Management servers, or simply by double-clicking the filename; for example, the file is called SampleDeploymentPackage.msi in Figure 12-8.

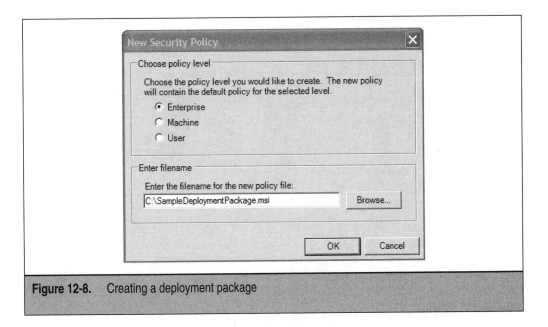

Figure 12-8. Creating a deployment package

NOTE A white paper on .NET Framework Security has been written by Foundstone and is available at http://www.foundstone.com/knowledge/white_papers.html.

.NET Framework Wizard

Another utility provided with .NET Framework is the .NET Framework wizard; it is another MMC snap-in for the .NET Framework. This snap-in can be accessed by going to the MMC console (select Start | Run and navigate to MMC.exe) and selecting the .NET Framework wizard (File → Add/Remove Snap-in → Add → .NET Framework Wizard). The .NET Framework wizard contains three main tools:

- Adjust .NET Security
- Trust an Assembly
- Fix an Application

NOTE The .NET Framework wizard is the only way to change the level of trust for assemblies. Although the Adjust .NET Security tool can be accessed by right-clicking Runtime Security Policy, that version is equivalent to read-only mode.

The Security Adjustment wizard can be used to reset to the default settings or change the general settings of each zone, as shown in Figure 12-9.

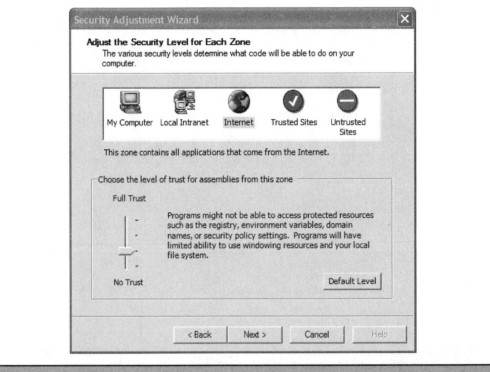

Figure 12-9. Security Adjustment wizard

Computing Permissions

The policy levels (Enterprise level, Machine level, and User level) and code groups (My_Computer_Zone, LocalIntranet_Zone, Internet_Zone, Restricted_Zone, and Trusted_Zone) help the CLR determine the permissions on each assembly. The permission-granting process can involve one or both of the following:

- Compute the allowed permission set
- Determine the granted permissions

To compute the allowed permissions, the CLR does this:

1. Uses the identity information to determine the groups the code belongs to.
2. Combines all the permissions received (using union).
3. Repeats this process at all three policy levels, resulting in three main sets of "unioned" permissions. The CLR then uses intersect to merge these permissions.

The result is a set of allowed permissions for the application domain or assembly. To compute the granted permissions, the CLR does this:

1. Computes the allowed permissions, as described above.

2. Compares the set of allowed permissions with the permissions the assembly requested, determining the granted permissions.

3. It then looks at the permission set (Required, Optional, or Refused), and if no permissions are present, the assembly is granted the permission set.

If one of the three permission sets exists (Required, Optional, or Refused), the CLR does the following:

1. Determines whether the set of required permissions is a subset of the allowed permission set (using intersect).

2. Uses union to extract the results from the minimum requested permissions.

3. Subtracts the result from any permission that is refused.

The result is the final set of granted permissions for the assembly.

WINDOWS 2000/XP AND .NET FRAMEWORK

The .NET policies that you create can be applied to machines running Windows 2000 or Windows XP. However, to apply these policies you will have to install either the redistribution package or the SDK for Windows platform. Either of these would enable you to run applications that are developed for the .NET Framework (managed applications) on the Windows 2000 and Windows XP platforms.

The configuration for the .NET Framework for Windows 2000 can be accessed using the MMC in the same manner as it is accessed on the .NET platform:

1. Bring up the MMC console up: select Start | Run and navigate to MMC.exe.

2. Choose File → Add-Remove Snap-in → Add.

3. Select .NET Framework → Add → Close → OK.

TOOLS OF THE TRADE

There are many tools that the .NET Framework uses, but here is a list of the main tools that would be required from an administrator's perspective:

Caspol.exe   The Code Access Security Policy tool enables users and administrators to modify security policy for Enterprise, Machine, and User policy levels.

Signcode.exe   The File Signing tool signs a portable executable (PE) file—which can be either a component or assembly—with an Authenticode digital signature.

Permview.exe   The Permissions View tool is used to view permission sets requested by an assembly (Required, Optional, or Refused).

Sn.exe   The Strong Name tool helps sign assemblies with strong names. This tool provides options for signature generation/verification and key management.

Mscorcfg.msc   The .NET Framework Configuration tool is a MMC snap-in that allows you to manage and configure assemblies and adjust code access security policy.

CHECKLIST: ADMINISTERING .NET FRAMEWORK

All code is classified as one of two types: managed or unmanaged. The code can reside on any recent Windows operating system (Windows 98 and later). Managed code or managed applications can be written in any language that can be interpreted by Microsoft Intermediate Language (MSIL). All the languages can access the same types and libraries; this is made possible by using CTS and CLS in the class libraries. All of this sits on top of the common language runtime (CLR), which allows or disallows any or all of these applications, code, and assemblies to execute.

Assemblies are classified into different security zones, depending on the origin of their code. The policies for the code, which are a set of configurable rules, can be assigned by user, by machine, or enterprisewide. Microsoft has provided an MMC snap-in and command line utility to perform these tasks.

The CLR, depending upon the origin and zone for the code, determines the assembly's permissions to access a resource. Keep the following checklist in mind when designing your .NET Framework:

☐ Use either the MMC snap-in (Mscorcfg.msc) or the command line utility (Caspol.exe) to add, modify, and delete permissions.

☐ Create a sample deployment package to deploy policy across your enterprise network.

☐ Since the registry no longer plays an important role in storing an application's configurations, you can simply copy application files across your enterprise network.

☐ All code should have explicit permission sets assigned to it—either Required, Optional, or Refused.

CHAPTER 13

Internet Services

W e have covered a good deal of information in this book so far. In this chapter we will cover some of the more fun things in Windows, Internet Services. Well, trying to lock down these services is not fun for you, but they sure are fun for someone trying to break into your systems. If you are on the Internet, you are vulnerable if you have any service running. What will you typically have running? Most likely you will have web services, ftp services, mail service, and perhaps some special services unique to your organization.

In this chapter we will cover the following:

- Security configuration of Internet Information Services (IIS) 5.1 on Windows XP Professional
- Security configuration of IIS 6.0 on Windows .NET
- Configuring Internet Explorer more securely

INTERNET INFORMATION SERVICES

IIS 5.1 for Windows XP and IIS 6.0 for Windows .NET Server have gained in functionality and security. However, since no software product these days is inherently secure, you have to put a little effort into making it so. We shall discuss configuration and security of IIS in the next several sections.

IIS does not mean the World Wide Web Publishing Service (W3SVC), although the terms are often used interchangeably. The fact is that IIS provides a framework for Internet services such as the web server (HTTP), Network News Transport Protocol (NNTP), File Transfer Protocol (FTP), and Simple Mail Transport Protocol (SMTP). As we delve into this chapter, we will often use the term IIS as a catchall for whatever service we are talking about at the time, although we are largely focused on the web server.

Authentication Methods

IIS 5.1 and 6.0 have different methods of access control. Each of them allows Anonymous access, where the anonymous user is impersonated by the IUSR_COMPUTER account created by IIS. The user browsing the site has no real interaction with this account.

Windows XP Professional's IIS 5.1 allows for the following four authentication methods:

- Anonymous authentication
- Basic authentication
- Digest authentication
- Integrated Windows authentication

Windows .NET's IIS 6.0 controls access to the server via one of five methods. Each method allows different functionality based on access permission. Authentication methods can be combined to offer different levels of security and authentication. The five methods of authentication are

- Anonymous authentication
- Basic authentication
- Integrated Windows authentication
- Digest authentication
- .NET Passport authentication

To authenticate a user, IIS will first try the Anonymous method (if enabled), then Basic (if enabled), Integrated Windows authentication, and finally the Digest authentication method (if enabled). If .NET Passport is enabled, it will be tried last.

Anonymous Authentication

Anonymous authentication is used when no authentication is required. It is most often used on informational-type web sites. The default usage of IIS is to require only anonymous access to retrieve requested information. If your computer name is KRAA, then the anonymous account used to access information will use the IIS-created user account called IUSR_KRAA, as shown in Figure 13-1.

 SECURITY ALERT! The permissions you give this account, which *should* be guest privileges only, will be granted to anyone accessing your web server.

The limited permissions of the IUSR account will protect your system files from being viewed. NTFS file-access restrictions will protect any data that you do not want anonymous users to access. Use this type of authentication for your information sites.

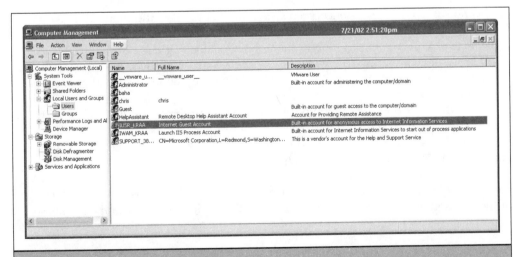

Figure 13-1.   Anonymous logon account

Basic Authentication

Basic authentication uses clear text HTTP authentication to provide some form of access control. The username and password are sent over the network in Base64 encoding, which is essentially clear text.

The Realm field added to IIS 5.1 is used to add additional security to Basic authentication. A realm can be set to require authentication. You can set different realms on different folders so that users have to authenticate when trying to access a different folder. If you have a public content folder in one realm and sensitive product information in another realm, setting permissions differently can require a logon by users to access the restricted information.

This type of authentication will require a username and password from the requesting client. The user account must be enabled on the server, or a domain user account must be enabled. The user must also have rights to log on locally, which raises security concerns in and of itself. There is no encryption of the login process or the data being transmitted. The authentication username and password are vulnerable to being captured and easily decoded. If you need to use Basic authentication, you should definitely use it over SSL to encrypt the password during transmission. Once logon is complete you can stop using SSL.

NOTE Users who need to use Basic authentication must have the "log on locally" user right described in Chapter 1.

Integrated Windows Authentication

Integrated Windows authentication is essentially the same as the Windows NT Challenge/Response authentication of earlier IIS versions. With this form of authentication, the username and password are encrypted when the client makes the connection. As with Basic authentication, a valid username must be on the server or a valid domain user must be enabled for web access, but the "log on locally" right is not required. If the client browser is not set up to log in with the same domain as the web server, such as in an intranet scenario, the user will be presented with a logon box, just as they would be for Basic authentication.

Using the Windows logon method does not transmit the password in clear text. The browser encrypts the password into a one-way hash. The hash is compared on the server side and allows access if the received hash and the server hash match. This is not as compatible with Netscape as it is with Internet Explorer.

Integrated Windows authentication can also use Kerberos 5.0 authentication. A site can be configured to communicate so that it supports Kerberos instead of NTLM authentication by setting the NT Authentication Providers property of the metabase.

Digest Authentication

Digest authentication, implemented in IIS 5.0 and IE 5.0, is a challenge-response authentication method. A client can authenticate securely to the server without a clear text password. The client creates a hash that is sent to the server. The server then performs the same calculation and allows access if the hash values match. Digest authentication can use Kerberos if the server is a member of a Windows 2000 domain.

.NET Passport Authentication

Available in Windows .NET only, Passport authentication is a cookie-based single sign-on service. When using Passport authentication, a token is created by the Local Security Authority (LSA) for the user and set by IIS for the HTTP request by the user. Passport is a forms-based authentication service to be used if your site needs to be compatible with Passport or you just want to take advantage of its credential infrastructure.

IIS 5.1 SECURITY

You should be very familiar with IIS 5.1 because it is not that much different from IIS 5.0. But as it is running on a client operating system, there will be some limitations such as connection limits. We will cover just the security configuration of IIS 5.1 on Windows XP, rather than running through all the features in descriptive detail. IIS 5.1 complies with the HTTP 1.1 standard.

IIS runs all applications separate from the IIS processes in pooled processes. This helps keep application errors from affecting the web service. As you will see in the section "IIS 6.0 Security," IIS 6.0 does a much better job of this. IIS 5.1 installs as a service of Windows XP Professional. The Microsoft Management Console (MMC) lets you administer IIS in a rather simple fashion. We will walk through the MMC in the following sections.

 SECURITY ALERT!   Previous versions of IIS had user code and ISAPI loaded into the core web server process Inetinfo. Failure of user code or an ISAPI filter caused an access violation, and as a result the World Wide Web Publishing Service (W3SVC) would crash, along with the Inetinfo.exe process. Since the Inetinfo.exe process was running with System level privileges, these types of access violations could cause serious security problems, such as remote buffer overflows that allowed attackers to run code to compromise access to the server.

Web Service Configuration

Like any application, your web server can be secure or insecure; it all depends on the time and effort you put into managing it correctly. The IIS Lockdown tool, which we mention later in this chapter, provides nearly all the security recommendations we are about to make.

We will assume you have installed the latest patches and service packs, and are ready to get down to the details of the web server configuration. To begin with, most default configurations of just about every application and operating system can be improved. IIS is no different.

Remove Samples

IIS comes with several default files and directories that need to be secured. If you upgraded from IIS 4.0 server, the IISADMPWD virtual directory will be created. You can remove this directory also. If you didn't upgrade, the .htr files will be located in Winnt\System32\Inetsrv\Iisadmpwd. Table 13-1 shows several samples that should be removed.

Most of the default files and programs that come with IIS 5.1 can be removed. The _vti_* directories should be examined to see what you really need and don't need for the purposes of your web site. If you are not using FrontPage directories, then you do not need the _vti_* and _private directories. In the web site properties under the Documents tab, you can remove the default pages that are listed and only leave the actual index page you will use, such as Index.htm.

Access Controls

Multiple layers of security are always needed. We can restrict access to programs and files on the web server and also access between servers in our DMZ. We can use file permissions, as discussed in Chapter 4. We can also use IPSec to restrict access between servers. For file permissions on web pages, set the permission to read only. If an attacker were to gain some form of access, they would not be able to modify the file very easily

Sample	Virtual Directory	Location
IIS samples	\IISSamples	C:\inetpub\iissamples
IIS documentation	\IISHelp	C:\winnt\help\iishelp
Data access	\MSADC	C:\program files\common files\system\msadc
Scripts	\Scripts	C:\inetpub\scripts
Printers	\Printers	C:\windows\web\printers
Terminal Server Web	\Tsweb	C:\windows\web\tsweb

Table 13-1. Samples That Need to Be Removed

File Type	Access Control Lists
CGI (.exe, .dll, .cmd, .pl)	Everyone (Read) Administrators (Full Control) System (Full Control)
Script files (.asp)	Everyone (Read) Administrators (Full Control) System (Full Control)
Include files (.inc, .shtm, .shtml)	Everyone (Read) Administrators (Full Control) System (Full Control)
Static content (.txt, .gif, .jpg, .html)	Everyone (Read) Administrators (Full Control) System (Full Control)

Table 13-2. Restricting Access to Various File Types

without first gaining full administrator privileges. Various file types can be stored in directories that you can lock down with NTFS permissions, as shown in Table 13-2.

To further restrict access to programs, we can remove the *script mappings,* which handle a request for a certain file type such as .shtml, if they are not used. You can do this by right-clicking on Web Sites in Internet Service Manager and selecting Properties → Home Directory → Configuration, as shown in Figure 13-2. Select the unused mappings, and click Remove. You can remove the mappings listed in Table 13-3.

A major culprit in allowing attackers to execute programs on your server is Cmd.exe. This was a huge headache in Windows 2000 and IIS 5.0, where IUSR had access rights to the System32 directory and, hence, Cmd.exe. In Windows XP, the default permissions on the System32 directory are somewhat stronger, giving Administrators and System Full Control rights, Power Users Modify rights, and Users Read & Execute rights. IUSR has no default permissions at all.

Mapping	Remove
Web-based password reset	.htr
Internet Database Connector	.idc
Server-side includes	.stm, .shtm, and .shtml
Internet printing	.printer
Index server	.htw, .ida, and .idq

Table 13-3. Files Mappings to Be Removed

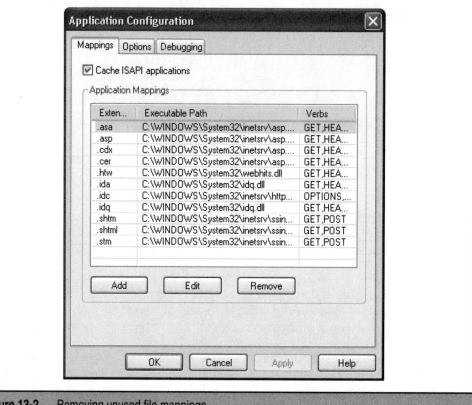

Figure 13-2. Removing unused file mappings

 SECURITY ALERT! Even though Windows XP has stronger default file system permissions that do not give IUSR access to the %SYSTEMROOT% directory by default, there is a caveat. If you are upgrading from Windows 2000, the weaker permissions will be retained.

The anonymous accounts IUSR_machinename and IWAM_machinename are created to allow nonauthenticated users access to web pages. You can restrict access to key directories such as %SYSTEMROOT%, Windows, or Winnt to deny access or further restrict from these accounts.

By default, each web site you have on the server will inherit the setting and access controls you set globally for the web server. Global rules can be set by right-clicking on the Web Sites folder and selecting Properties.

If you want to change individual web sites, select the web site and choose Properties → Server Extensions, and check Don't Inherit Security Settings. The three options you can modify here are

- **Log authoring actions**   Record information performed by an author and store the information in _vti_log/Author.log.

- **Manage permissions manually**   Disable the security-setting functions of FrontPage Server Extension administrative tools.

- **Require Secure Sockets Layer (SSL) for authoring**   Use SSL to authenticate web authors.

Further control over your application can be achieved by using the Application Protection control on the Home Directory tab. By selecting "High (Isolated)," you will run your application as an isolated process separate from other processes. This separation helps if a problem occurs in another application process.

Information Restriction

The host IP address is given out in the content-location header by default, providing an anonymous client excessive information about your internal network. You can restrict this information from being given out using the Adsutil program. At a command prompt in the inetpub\adminscripts directory you can issue the following command to have the server give the *fully qualified domain name* (FQDN). The default setting is False.

```
Cscript adsutil set w3svc/UseHostName True
net stop iisadmin /y
net start w3svc
```

File System Restriction

A good method of restricting access to the file system is to partition your drives to separate the system partition from the web root. For example, create a C:\ partition for the Windows system and boot files, and create a separate D:\ partition for the web server root directory (you can set the root directory under the Home Directory tab). Several recent vulnerabilities use directory traversal techniques to take the default paths and access system resources; however, partitioning the file system makes it nearly impossible for these techniques to work. By installing IIS on a nonsystem partition (i.e., one different from where you have \WINNT or \Windows installed), you gain another layer of security.

You might also be giving away excessive permissions if you enable parent paths and debugging information. A number of the directory traversal "../" exploits take advantage of the enabled parent paths. To disable parent paths, clear the Enable Parent Paths option under Application Configuration → Options. To disable debugging information, clear the Send detailed ASP error messages to client option under Application Configuration → Debugging.

Authentication Method

Once you have removed the basic default options, consider how you want clients to connect. This obviously depends on the role of the web server. Assuming that you are using it for a basic Internet web site, you will want to allow Anonymous authentication. You select the authentication method by right-clicking on Web Sites and selecting Properties. In the Properties box, select the Directory Security tab and click Edit next to the "Anonymous access and authentication controls" option. For this type of web server you select the Anonymous Access option, and deselect "Basic Authentication," "Digest Authentication," and "Integrated Windows Authentication."

NOTE   Digest authentication will not be an option on a Windows XP Professional system unless the computer is a domain member.

If you need to use Integrated Windows authentication, click the check box. When you browse the web site, you will see a pop-up login box.

Certificates

You can create a certificate using the Web Server Certificate wizard. This option is also accessed through the Directory Security tab. Click the Server Certificate button to install a server certificate. The wizard will let you obtain, configure, and renew server certificates. It can detect certificates and let you view them, reassign them, or replace them.

Using client-side certificates will provide the strongest authentication method possible. You can actually require a client certificate for a user to connect. First, however, you need to set up your server certificate. Once you have done that, right-click on Default Web Site and select Properties. Go to Directory Security and click Edit under Secure Communications. From here you can configure client certificate requirements.

Web Service Logging

The logging interface for IIS 5.1 is very granular if you select W3C Extended Log File Format. To access the logging options, select your web site (we are using the Default Web Site), right-click, and select Properties. Under the Web Site tab, you select the logging format, W3C Extended Logging Format, and then select Properties. In the Properties box, you can select the size of the log file or when the log should be created. You can have a new log created daily and select a log file directory other than the default. Preferably, use a nonsystem partition to store your log, as shown in Figure 13-3. Save your log files with your daily backups, because you never know when you will need to go back several weeks to investigate an incident.

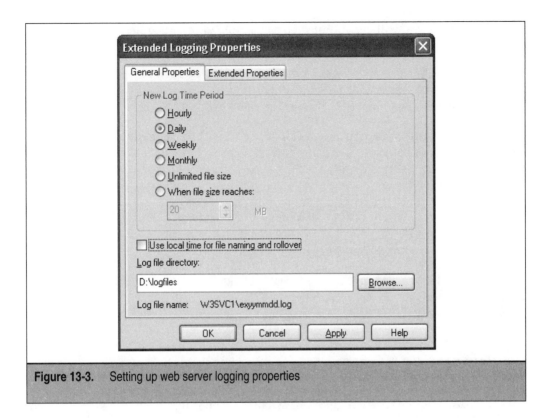

Figure 13-3. Setting up web server logging properties

Next select the Extended Properties tab, and select the options to log, as listed in Table 13-4.

Date	Time	Client IP Address	Protocol Status
User Name	Service Name	Server Name	Win32 Status
Server IP Address	Method	URI Stem	Host

Table 13-4. Fields to Log

In the log file, you will get output such as the following (Integrated Windows Authentication is used in this example):

```
#Fields: date time c-ip cs-username s-sitename s-computername s-ip
s-port cs-method cs-uri-stem sc-status sc-win32-status cs-host
cs(User-Agent)

2002-07-12 18:16:32 10.0.2.13 chris - W3SVC1 KRAA 10.0.2.12 80
GET / 401 5 kraa
Mozilla/4.0+(compatible;+MSIE+6.0;+Windows+NT+5.1;+.NET+CLR+1.0.3215;
+.NET+CLR+1.0.3705)

2002-07-12 18:16:36 10.0.2.17 joe W3SVC1 KRAA 10.0.2.12 80 GET / 401
5 kraa Mozilla/4.0+(compatible;+MSIE+6.0;+Windows+NT+5.1;
+.NET+CLR+1.0.3215;+.NET+CLR+1.0.3705)

2002-07-12 18:16:42 10.0.2.17 bill W3SVC1 KRAA 10.0.2.12 80 GET / 401
5 kraa Mozilla/4.0+(compatible;+MSIE+6.0;+Windows+NT+5.1;
+.NET+CLR+1.0.3215;+.NET+CLR+1.0.3705)

2002-07-12 18:16:51 10.0.2.17 chris W3SVC1 KRAA 10.0.2.12 80
GET /index.htm 304 0 kraa Mozilla/4.0+(compatible;+MSIE+6.0;
+Windows+NT+5.1;+.NET+CLR+1.0.3215;+.NET+CLR+1.0.3705)
```

In this example, we have two different machines connecting to the web server named kraa, 10.0.2.13 and 10.0.2.17. Several user names are trying to log in: chris, bill, and joe. When there is a login error, we see the return code 401. When login is successful, the web page index.html is returned.

This is a lot of data to sift through, but you can change the fields you want to log to cut down on some of the traffic. Reading through log files has never been pleasant, but it is a job you have to do. Under the Home Directory tab, make sure you have Log Visits checked. In your log files you will have such things as probes by the bots, spiders, crawlers, and normal visitors.

To restrict web-indexing programs, you can modify the file named robots.txt in the root directory of your site. Using the robot exclusion standard, indexing programs can be directed to the files you want indexed, or you can turn off all indexing by putting the following in your robots.txt file:

```
# Discourage all web indexing
User-agent: *
Disallow: /
```

File Transfer Protocol Configuration (FTP)

FTP is usually a must-have in Internet and intranet sites. For Internet sites you need to use a bit more caution. Using the IIS MMC snap-in, select the FTP Sites folder, right-click on it, and select Properties. Here you can set up anonymous FTP or set up a user account for FTP usage. You can use Anonymous connections or set up the account under the Security Accounts tab. Remember that FTP usernames and passwords are sent in clear text, so be careful when using a normal user account for FTP.

By default, the FTP directory is c:\inetpub\ftproot and has permissions of Creator Owner Full Control, Administrators group Full Control, System Full Control, and Users group Read and Execute. To lock down FTP directories at the command line, you can use the program Xcacls.exe (from the Windows 2000 Resource Kit). You can also do this through File Manager, by changing permissions on the folder. Using the IIS MMC snap-in, you can restrict the permissions through the Security Accounts and Home Directory tabs.

There are a number of other options you may wish to make use of as well:

- You can restrict the number of connections under the FTP Site tab.

- Under the Home Directory tab, you can set the home directory of your FTPRoot. In most cases you will want to allow only Read access to this directory.

- Be sure to select the Log Visits check box.

- You can see who is connected via the Current Sessions button, and disconnect a connection if necessary.

- Filling in the Message fields can provide some legal advantages, based on your network security policy.

FTP Logging   As with web service logging, you have some granular options for what you can log. On the FTP Site tab, check Enable Logging and select W3V Extended Logging File Format. Select Properties next to the logging option. You can modify where the log files are stored; be sure to use something other than the default. Select Log Daily and click Extended Properties. You should log the fields listed in Table 13-4.

SMTP Configuration

The default SMTP directory is c:\inetpub\mailroot. You can modify the folder permissions as you did with the FTPRoot folder, by selecting the properties of the folder and modifying the permissions. You can access the SMTP configuration by right-clicking the SMTP Virtual Server in IIS manager and selecting Properties. On the General tab you can set up the connectivity and logging. The access controls are set on the Access tab using the suboptions Access Controls, Secure Communications, Connection Control, and Relay Restrictions.

Configuring SMTP is a bit more than we want to go into, but since it exists as a service of IIS, some key points deserve discussion. That said, one key aspect of SMTP security you should adhere to is running SMTP on its own server. Having it on your web server can open up that server to more risk that you should be taking on.

Mail Relay   Another key point is that you do not want to allow mail relay, or spammers will use your server all day to send thousands of unsolicited e-mail messages. By default, mail relay is disabled, which means only users who authenticate can relay mail. To access the relay configuration, click the Relay button under the Access tab.

Authentication   The SMTP service has authentication options similar to the web and FTP services. Configure accordingly, but remember that you will have to leave "Anonymous access" enabled if you want anonymous Internet clients to send mail to your domain using your server.

You can also configure a server certificate to enable TLS encryption on SMTP sessions. If you really want to be secure, you can enable client certificates as well similar to how you would for the web service.

Messages   Under the Messages tab are several more controls. Here, several default restrictions are enabled to help prevent mail-flooding attacks. These restrictions include message size, session size, number of messages per connection, and number of recipients per message. The defaults provide adequate level of security.

SMTP Logging   As with service and FTP logging, you turn on logging in the General tab and select the W3V Extended Logging File Format. Select Properties next to the logging option to modify where the log files are stored. Be sure to use something other than the default. Also, click Log Daily, select Extended Properties, and opt to log the fields listed in Table 13-4.

IIS Lockdown Tool

A separate free tool has been provided by Microsoft to lock down IIS 4.0 and IIS 5.x web servers. The IIS Lockdown tool provides security templates you can apply to your web server to increase security. Once you execute the Lockdown tool, your first selection is from a list of templates. In the example shown in Figure 13-4, we are selecting a Dynamic ASP–enabled web server.

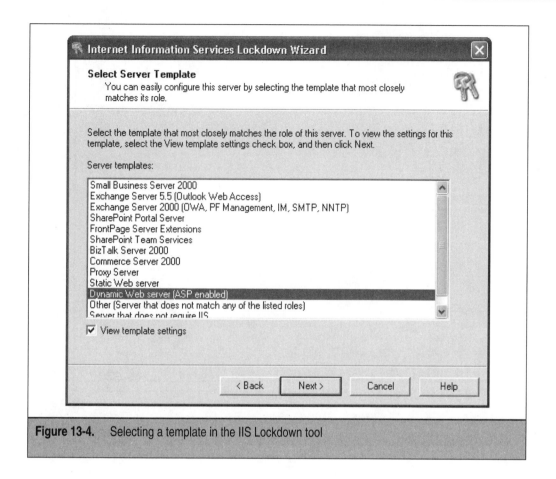

Figure 13-4. Selecting a template in the IIS Lockdown tool

The next selection is the services you want to run, web, FTP, or SMTP. After that you can automatically remove unused script mappings, as discussed earlier in the "Access Controls" section; see Figure 13-5.

Next you can remove samples, restrict utilities from being run, and restrict access, as shown in Figure 13-6. Lastly, you can use this tool to install URLScan on the server (see the following section).

As you will see in the "IIS 6.0 Security" section, the IIS Lockdown tool has changed in IIS 6.0. Most of its functionality is no longer needed, because the default installation of IIS 6.0 is more secure than previous versions.

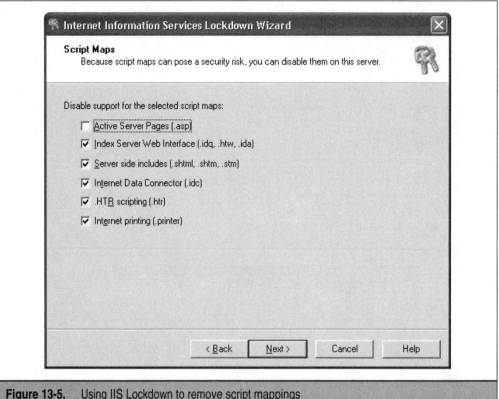

Figure 13-5. Using IIS Lockdown to remove script mappings

URLScan

Rules can be designed with URLScan to protect the server from incoming HTTP requests. URLScan attempts to stop invalid or malicious URL requests before they reach the server. Two options you have with URLScan are URLScan-SRP and Baseline URLScan. URLScan-SRP is different from Baseline URLScan in that it handles chunked encoding data transfers by default. Another difference is that uploads to the web server are restricted to 30MB per upload in Baseline URLScan.

URLScan can be installed using the IIS Lockdown tool. Once you have done that, you can download the latest version, URLScan 2.5, from Microsoft and install it. You should install the URLScan-SRP option.

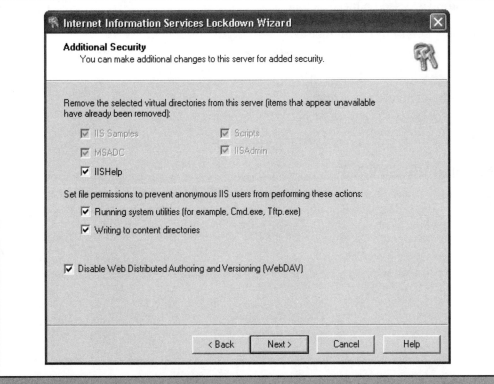

Figure 13-6. Removing samples and restricting access to utilities with IIS Lockdown

---

NOTE For the URLScan 2.5 installation to be successful, you must have a previous version of URLScan installed.

Several key features of URLScan include the following:

- Ability to change the log file directory.
- Ability to log long URLs.
- Ability to restrict the size of requests.
- MaxAllowedContentLength sets a maximum value to content length.
- MaxUrl sets limits on the length of the requested URL in bytes.
- MaxQueryString sets limits on the length of the query string in bytes; the default value is 4KB.

Filtering is based on these factors:

- Request of restricted methods
- Use-specific file extensions
- Use-suspect URL composition
- Use of non-ASCII characters in a URL
- Use of specific strings of characters in a URL
- Use of specific headers in a service request

Installing URLScan 2.5

URLScan 2.5 must be installed as an upgrade to either URLScan 1.0 or URLScan 2.0. To modify the setting of URLScan, open the Urlscan.ini file in \windows\system32\inetcrv\urlscan. Then add the following section to the Urlscan.ini file:

```
[RequestLimits]
MaxAllowedContentLength=30,000,000 (Urlscan-SRP) ; enforces a
maximum value to content-length
MaxAllowedContentLength=2,000,000,000 (Baseline Urlscan)
MaxUrl=16384 ;Restricts length of the request URL in bytes
MaxQueryString=4096 ;Restricts the length of the query string in bytes
```

Add the following entries to the options section:

```
LoggingDirectory= [set a logging directory]
LogLongUrls=1
```

In the DenyUrlSequences section, set the following values:

```
[DenyUrlSequences]
..          ; deny directory traversals
./          ; deny trailing dot on a directory name
\           ; deny backslashes in URL
:           ; deny alternate stream access
%           ; deny escaping after normalization
&           ; deny multiple CGI processes to run on a single request
/fpdb/      ; deny browse access to FrontPage database files
/_private   ; deny FrontPage private files (often form results)
/_vti_pvt   ; deny FrontPage Web configuration files
/_vti_cnf   ; deny FrontPage metadata files
/_vti_txt   ; deny FrontPage text catalogs and indices
/_vti_log   ; deny FrontPage authoring log files
```

In the DenyExtensions section, set the following values:

```
[DenyExtensions]
.asa      ; deny active server application definition files
.bat      ; deny batch files
.btr      ; deny FrontPage dependency files
.cer      ; deny x509 certificate files
.cdx      ; deny dynamic channel definition files
.cmd      ; deny batch files
.cnf      ; deny FrontPage metadata files
.com      ; deny server command-line applications
.dat      ; deny data files
.evt      ; deny Event Viewer logs
.exe      ; deny server command-line applications
.htr      ; deny IIS legacy HTML admin tool
.htw      ; deny Index Server hit-highlighting
.ida      ; deny Index Server legacy HTML admin tool
.idc      ; deny IIS legacy database query files
.inc      ; deny include files
.ini      ; deny configuration files
.ldb      ; deny Microsoft Access Record-Locking Information files
.pol      ; deny policy files
.printer  ; deny Internet Printing Services
.sav      ; deny backup registry files
.shtm     ; deny IIS Server Side Includes
.shtml    ; deny IIS Server Side Includes
.stm      ; deny IIS Server Side Includes
.tmp      ; deny temporary files
```

IIS 6.0 SECURITY

IIS has steadily improved with each new version. In this section we will cover the more important functions as they relate to security.

NOTE   At the time this went to press, Windows .NET and IIS 6.0 were still undergoing beta testing, so this information is subject to change.

IIS 6.0 comes with Windows .NET server but is not installed by default. Group policies can be used to restrict domain users from installing IIS. Microsoft has taken a very proactive step with IIS 6.0 by shipping it in a relatively locked-down configuration, compared to earlier IIS versions. Built-in ASP functions are run as a low-privilege account, and IIS will serve requests for only recognized file extensions. It has included support for various technologies such as XML, SOAP, and IPv6. You can run the IIS

You have been running IIS 5.0 for a while and you are comfortable with it. While it does have some known vulnerabilities, you have patched those and know how to keep updated. But your company is cutting edge. Your supervisor wants to move your web services to IIS 6.0 to benefit from its major performance enhancements, including the security of the Windows .NET platform. Since most of the features are the same and there is even more additional security, you feel like you won't have a problem using it. You also know how to use the additional security tools such as URLScan and IIS Lockdown.

But there are still some questions. How will you manage a server that is still in beta? How will you lock down a server that hasn't been in the public domain long enough to be subjected to hacker scrutiny? Will you *really* be secure with IIS 6.0?

If you follow the security guidelines as we have discussed so far, both on the operating system side and application side, any new operating system and application you bring online should be relatively secure; just remember to do the following:

- Lock down the operating system.
- Install IIS on a nonsystem partition.
- Unmap all unnecessary ISAPI extensions.
- Configure the necessary authentication methods.
- Enable your logging options.

snap-in manager through Start → Run → inetmgr. Additional security has been provided by the removal of a lot of default settings and samples that were part of earlier releases. Using Windows .NET Server, IIS provides among other things:

- Selectable cryptographic services
- Advanced digest authentication
- Configurable access control of processes
- Passport authentication
- Kernel mode HTTP service
- Web Administration Service
- Dedicated application processes

IIS 6.0 has given you more granular control for administering parameters such as connection limits, connection time-outs, application-pool queue lengths, bandwidth allocations, process accounting, and memory-based recycling. You can now disable and restart applications that cause a problem with fewer reboots, à la UNIX servers. As part of this functionality, configuration values are stored in a new-style XML-based metabase.

Remote administration can be done using the IIS MMC, through Remote Administration, which provides a web-based interface for managing your sites. While there are a lot of functionality improvements and performance changes, we will just focus on the security aspects.

Default Installation

Many samples and insecure default settings present in previous versions of IIS have been removed. A couple of default installations are the Web Administrative application and the Sharepoint application. The use of the IIS Lockdown wizard at the startup of the IIS MMC snap-in also greatly increases the security of a default installation.

The first thing you will notice is that the samples under the web root folder (inetpub/ wwwroot) are not there. The IUSR_machine account runs as a network service with lower-level privileges. A number of other changes will be discussed in the following sections.

SECURITY ALERT!   Remove the Web Administrative and Sharepoint default directories if you don't use them. As a rule of thumb, all default directories should be removed if unneeded, as they are publicly documented and have been known to open serious security problems in the past.

You should modify all the default options. The first thing you have to do in a default installation is run through the IIS Lockdown wizard.

IIS Lockdown Wizard

By default, the IIS Lockdown wizard runs when you first start up IIS manager. If you want to run it again, you can right-click on the computer name and select Security. It allows or disallows a list of ISAPI extensions and CGI executables to execute. You can add custom ISAPI extensions and CGIs to the list.

When you run the Lockdown wizard, the first thing you select are the features you want to run—FTP, web, SMTP, or NNTP—as shown in Figure 13-7. We have disabled NNTP and SMTP.

Next you can select CGIs and ISAPI extensions that you want to run, as shown in Figure 13-8. The Lockdown tool in IIS 6 is not as robust as the tool for IIS 4.0 and IIS 5.0, but it does make for a good baseline starting position to secure the server.

Web Site Properties

Most of the fields and security parameters we discussed earlier for IIS 5.1 configuration apply to IIS 6.0 as well. Refer to the "IIS 5.1 Security" section for information on authentication and access controls, information restriction, file system restriction, and logging.

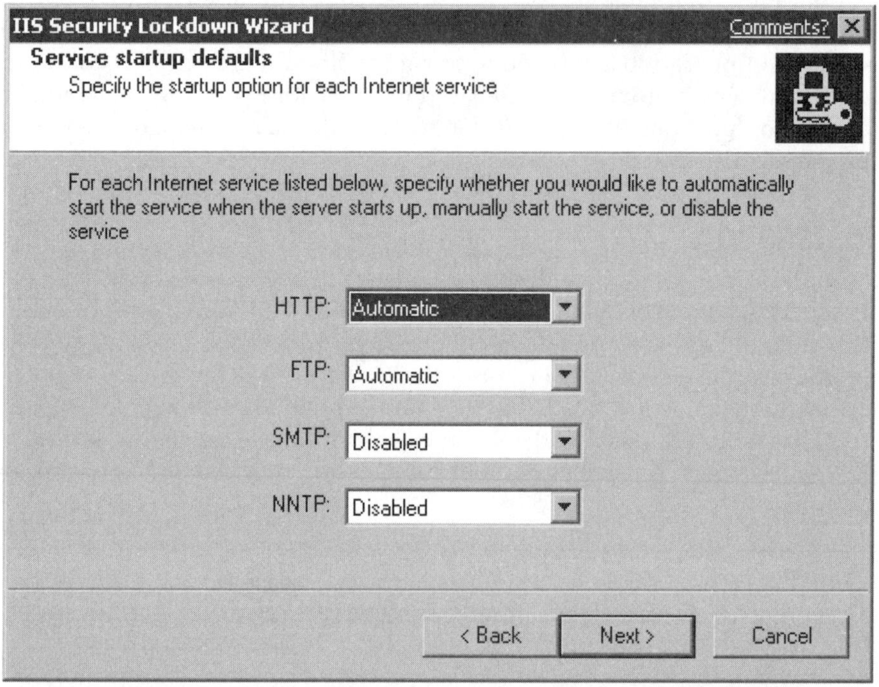

Figure 13-7. Selecting services to run with the IIS Lockdown tool

Some differences of note include these:

- **Operators tab** Specify user accounts that have Operator privileges and can make modifications. By default, Local Service, Network Service, and Administrators are in this list.

- **Service tab** Run the web site in IIS 5.0 isolation mode and set up application file compression. Isolation mode lets you run applications that can otherwise run only on IIS 5.X.

- **Performance tab** Scale back the bandwidth and number of connections.

The IIS 6.0 Authentication options also provide a change worth noting. Digest and Passport authentication are enabled on a .NET server. Passport single sign-on model authentication is now part of the core web server. A user that connects via Passport authentication can be mapped to an Active Directory account. By "mapped" we mean that you must have already created the account in your AD environment.

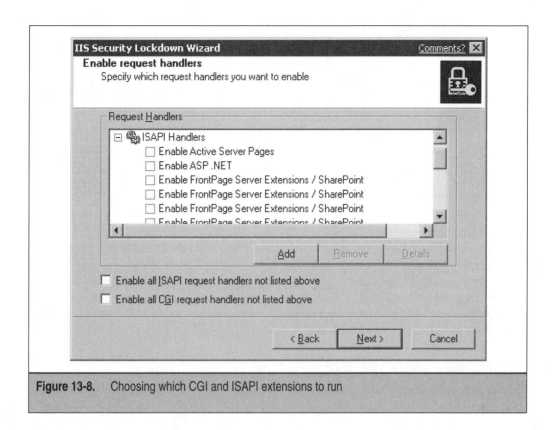

Figure 13-8. Choosing which CGI and ISAPI extensions to run

Metabase

The metabase contains all of the IIS configuration information for web, SMTP, and FTP services, such as directory structures and extension mapping. Changes to configuration are written to an XML text file, rather than a binary file (metabase.bin) as in previous versions of IIS. Two new files have replaced it: metabase.xml (which has configuration values) and mbschema.xml (which has default XML schema values). IIS reads in the values from these files, located in C:\WINDOWS*. The metabase is easily edited with a text editor, backed up, restored, and read, which can be a great troubleshooting aid. Old metabase binary files will be converted to XML when you upgrade your web server.

The metabase.xml file is stored in memory after being loaded at startup. You can interact with the metabase through several interfaces, including the IIS MMC snap-in, Active Directory Service Interface providers (ADSI), WMI providers, and COM-based software that uses ADSI or WMI. At startup, the Metabase Storage Layer manages the XML files and converts XML files to memory. The Metabase Storage Layer writes the in-memory version of the metabase to disk, where it can be stored permanently.

The admin base objects (ABOs) are COM objects that allow access to the metabase. ABOs are mapped to individual metabase key names, and the properties of the object represent the metabase properties. You can modify the METABASE.XML file and have the changes take place in EditWhileRunning mode and when the IIS service is stopped. You can find the EditWhileRunning check box on the Computer Name property page within IIS. To enable editing of the metabase while IIS is running, right-click on the computer name, select Properties, and check the box Enable Direct Metabase Edit.

CAUTION   If you make simultaneous updates to the metabase file via a manual update and a programmatic update, the last one to occur will take effect. This may cause configuration problems when making simultaneous changes.

Each modification of the metabase is kept with a new "history" feature. New metabase.xml files are tagged with a version number and saved to the history folder (%windir%\system32\inetsrv\history) and can be used for rollback. The version information is stored in the HistoryMajorVersionNumber and HistoryMinorVersion Number property. You can save the entire metabase and load it onto a separate computer. Backups are done securely with a password or in nonsecure mode without a password. Obviously, you should use a password.

Worker Process Isolation Mode

IIS 6.0 runs all application code in an isolated environment by routing HTTP requests to the correct application pool queue. Application pools are a set of applications that can share worker processes. Each application is separated by process boundaries. User mode worker-process requests are handled by the kernel. Separate web service processes allow you to administer each application separately. There is no need to stop the entire web service.

Work processes can be modified to run under a lower-privileged account. The LocalService account is used by default as a lower-privileged account. Worker processes can be run with the privileges of NetworkService. You can modify the account of each application service by right-clicking on the application (for example, Default Application Pool), selecting Properties, and clicking the Identity tab, shown in Figure 13-9.

You can also restrict access by applications by restricting the extensions of the files that can be sent to users. This is configured through the metabase as well. Restricting the ability of worker processes greatly increases the security measures of the server.

Kernel Mode Queuing

Kernel mode queuing is a major design change to IIS, which dramatically improves web server performance. The new functionality of Http.sys was once handled by the Inetinfo.exe process. In IIS 6.0, this bit of functionality is not handled directly by the kernel. The problem is that if something goes wrong here, you can bet there will be problems for the host.

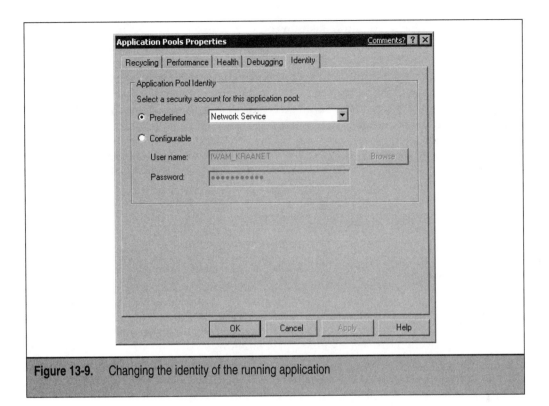

Figure 13-9.   Changing the identity of the running application

Http.sys is a kernel mode driver that handles all incoming HTTP requests on the IIS 6.0 server—such as connectivity, bandwidth management, and logging—all above the TCP/IP stack. Http.sys listens for HTTP requests and puts them on the appropriate queue. Requests for data are queued by Http.sys and mapped to the correct application pool. Since user applications do not run in Http.sys, problems based on user code are minimized. If a problem occurs within the user mode request-processing infrastructure, Http.sys continues to accept and queue requests until either no queues are available, no space is left on the queues, or the W3SVC is stopped.

Constrained, Delegated Authentication

Delegation is a term not to be confused with the delegation of control from Active Directory (see Chapter 11). With delegation, you can allow an application to act on behalf of a user or computer account in the domain. This is helpful if your application needs to interact and authenticate with other systems on behalf of the user account. Before Windows .NET and IIS 6.0 came along, delegation was either all or nothing. That is, once the application took on the identity of a user account, it had unrestrained access to any resource in the domain.

Constrained, delegated authentication comes along to secure this model a bit more, by helping domain administrators allow delegation to specific computers and services, because you do not want to allow an application to access any resource in the domain. For example, consider an e-commerce application that uses a COM object to perform some interaction with a backend SQL server. Because that COM object requires administrative-level access to the SQL server, the application impersonates a domain administrator user account and carries the context of that user account from server to server. Imagine that you could not control what that account was allowed to access, in which case it would have free rein over the entire domain. Constrained, delegated authentication lets you restrict the impersonated account's access to only that backend SQL server.

Command Line Administration

IIS 6.0 has taken a page from the UNIX world of web servers by increasing your ability to administer the web server from the command line. So if there are any UNIX administrators out there who have been having command line withdrawal symptoms, a remedy is at hand. Command line control is accomplished using Windows Scripting Host (WSH) scripts combined with ADSI and WMI—a type of functionality that has actually been around since Windows 2000 and IIS 5.0. While not all functionality can be accessed via the command line, you can perform the following tasks, to name a few:

- Enumerate and modify metabase settings
- Create, delete, start, stop, and enumerate web sites
- Create, delete, start, stop, and list File Transfer Protocol (FTP) sites
- Create and delete web virtual directories
- Create and delete applications
- Export and import IIS configuration
- Back up and restore IIS configuration

The scripts use ADSI and WMI to interface with IIS and the metabase. Adsutil.vbs is a favorite for accessing the metabase directly, and is located by default in inetpub\AdminScripts. The other scripts are located in %WINDIR%\system32 by default.

Using these scripts, the ADSI and WMI providers interact with the IIS metabase to make changes. Scripts that are built in include

- **Adsutil.vbs**   Enumerate and modify metabase settings
- **Iisweb.vbs**   Create, delete, start, stop, and list web sites
- **Iisftp.vbs**   Create, delete, start, stop, and list FTP sites
- **Iisvdir.vbs**   Create and delete virtual directories, or display the virtual directories
- **Iisftpdr.vbs**   Create, delete, or display virtual directories under a given root

- **Iiscnfg.vbs**   Export and import IIS configuration to an XML file
- **Iisback.vbs**   Back up and restore IIS configuration

Remote Administrative Interface

From the IIS MMC snap-in interface, you can connect to another web server and perform web server administration. From the Action menu, select Connect. Choose the server name you want to connect to, and connect as an account with privileges to modify the web server.

Once connected, you will have access to the remote machine and can perform administration on the web sites and other functions you have running on that web server, such as FTP, as shown in Figure 13-10.

Another method of remotely administering the web server is to use a browser. This duplicates the functionality of the IIS manager. The administration web application runs in a default install on port 8099. Be sure to do this all over SSL.

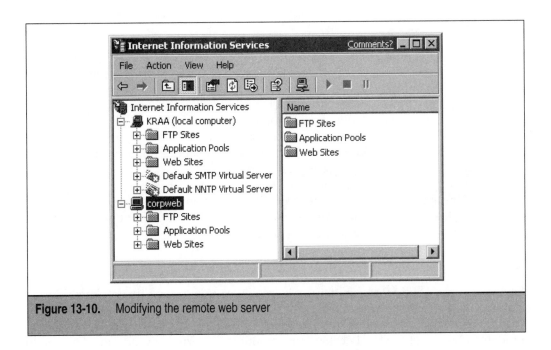

Figure 13-10.   Modifying the remote web server

> **NOTE**   If you are not going to perform administration through a web browser, you should definitely disable the Administrative web site.

Web Administration Service

The Web Administration Service (WAS) is used to configure Http.sys, start the service on demand and configure worker processes, and maintain the health-detection features. WAS periodically checks the worker processes for proper functioning (you can also check using the Health tab). The W3SVC service is used to start processes, and Http.sys can queue up requests as W3SVC starts new processes.

WAS reads the metabase information and initializes the Http.sys namespace routing table. With the information about each application in the table, Http.sys can request that a worker process be started for the application pool when needed. The web service configures Http.sys to accept requests for the new URLs and routing. WAS will start and recycle processes and block requests if they cannot be handled.

WAS ties together the application pools and the kernel mode queuing. WAS is not affected by user-mode code, unlike IIS 5.0, where code was shared by the web server process Inetinfo.

Recycling Processes

IIS can recycle application pools for applications that crash in user mode. A failed process is logged and restarted. The application can also be disabled if it continuously crashes using Rapid-Fail Protection, and Http.sys will return a "503 Service Unavailable" message. You can configure the recycle process based on elapsed time, number of requests served, scheduled times, memory usage, and on demand.

In the application pools, you can set up the recycle parameters. There are no hard-and-fast rules about what settings to use. If you have a major e-commerce site, you may want to recycle more often if memory gets used up quickly or if your application is so complex it may crash with too many users. You access the recycle properties by right-clicking on the application (for example, Default Application Pool), selecting Properties, and clicking the Recycle tab. You can set parameters for minutes of uptime, number of requests served, time of day, and memory used.

Site Health

Several features of IIS 6.0 concentrate on helping you monitor and fix problems. The Debugging tab can help you troubleshoot problems with worker processes. The Identity tab can be used to configure the worker processes to run with lower privileges other than LocalSystem. The LocalSystem account is low privilege and can allow you to let users upload programs without causing problems for the web server. The Health tab can be used to disallow Rapid Fail Protection. You access the health properties by right-clicking on the application, selecting Properties, and clicking the Health tab.

FTP Configuration

Additional security has been added to the FTP service. But once again, the logging capabilities have not been expanded. Use the same recommendations we made earlier in the chapter (see "IIS 5.1 Security"). The addition of the Directory Security tab expands the ability to grant or restrict access based on location. You can specify a specific site or a network range of addresses to allow or deny access.

Secure Sockets Layer and Transport Layer Security

Secure Sockets Layer (SSL) 3.0 and Transport Layer Security (TLS) provide a secure way to exchange information between clients and servers. In addition, SSL 3.0 and TLS provide a way for the server to verify who the client is before the user logs on to the server.

Server-gated Cryptography SGC, an extension of Secure Sockets Layer (SSL), lets financial institutions with export versions of IIS use strong 128-bit encryption. Although SGC capabilities are built into IIS 5.0, a special SGC certificate is required to use SGC. The Certificate wizard simplifies certificate administration tasks, such as creating certificate requests and managing the certificate life cycle. (A client certificate contains detailed identification information about the user and organization that issued the certificate.)

INTERNET EXPLORER SECURITY OPTIONS

With all the bugs that have been reported in Internet Explorer (IE), you really need to lock it down for a good sense of security when your network users are using Internet services and visiting web sites. IE has become an integral part of the operating system, and using it with Microsoft technologies is part of everyday life for most of us. In this section we will walk through the security zones and Group Policy settings available to administrators.

Security Zones

The security zones allow you to set up restrictions for different classes of functionalities for web sites. By default, the four zones—Internet, Local Intranet, Trusted Sites, and Restricted Sites—have different levels of restrictions. You access the zones through Tools → Internet Options → Security in IE. The default levels are

- **Internet** (Medium)   This setting will prompt you for some types of downloads and for unsigned ActiveX controls. This isn't all that secure, of course. You can make it more secure by actually disabling the download and scripting of ActiveX controls.

- **Local Intranet** (Medium-Low)   This setting is a bit more relaxed than that of the Internet default. It is meant for your local intranet sites, which you probably hope are secure and don't have malicious code to attack your users.

- **Trusted Sites** (Low)   Well, since you trust these sites, the Low setting makes sense. Here, all ActiveX content is allowed to download and be run. Be wary of what you consider a "Trusted Site" for your users.

- **Restricted Sites** (High)   This should definitely be High, because sites you add here are those you consider dangerous.

You can enhance the security settings of these zones through either the level setting or the Custom setting. Custom settings are sometimes the way to go. The Internet Zone is the one you really want to focus on. You can use the High setting, but that may be too restrictive. You have to balance functionality with security. To modify the Custom setting, the options that need changing in the Internet Zone are these:

- **Download Signed Active X controls**   Prompt
- **Download unsigned ActiveX controls**   Disable
- **Initialize and script ActiveX controls not marked as Safe**   Disable
- **Script ActiveX controls marked safe for scripting**   Prompt
- **Run ActiveX controls and Plug-ins**   Prompt
- **Access data sources across domains**   Disable
- **Drag and Drop or Copy and Paste Files**   Prompt
- **Software Channel Permissions**   High Safety
- **Active Scripting**   Prompt
- **Scripting of Java applets**   Prompt
- **Allow Paste Operation Via Scripting**   Prompt
- **Submit non-encrypted for data**   Prompt
- **User data persistence**   Disable
- **Logon**   Anonymous logon

NOTE   Placing a web site in the Restricted Sites security zone limits only the functionality of that site, such as ActiveX, applets, scripts, and downloads. Access to the site is still allowed.

Group Policy Settings

As we discussed in Chapter 11, you can push out group policies to your network users for various functions. For IE security zone settings, you can use a GPO to configure a myriad of Internet Explorer configurations such as zone information. Run GPedit.msc and navigate to Computer Configuration → Administrative Templates → Windows Components → Internet Explorer. Here you can configure the security zone settings and a whole lot more. The settings you should apply are shown in Figure 13-11.

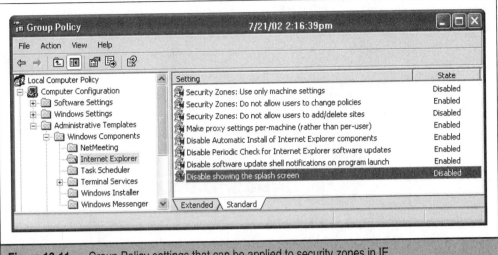

Figure 13-11. Group Policy settings that can be applied to security zones in IE

Privacy Options

The privacy options, which can be accessed through Tools → Internet Options → Privacy, are set to Medium by default. At a minimum, you should set this to Medium-High. This option will block a lot of third-party cookies. The High setting can also be used to further block cookies that do not ask for your consent to send out information. You can also modify the way cookies are handled with the Advanced option.

On the Content tab, you should disable the various AutoComplete options (Web addresses, Forms, User names and passwords). AutoComplete will store this type of information as you use it, so it can be remembered and reused later. You should also not set up a profile. The Profile option will transparently provide a web site your personal information, should it be requested.

The last set of security options that are worth looking into are on the Advanced tab. One thing that should be enabled is "Check for server certificate revocation." "Show friendly HTTP error messages" should be disabled. Also, the Use TLS 1.0 setting will need to be enabled if the computer is being configured with the "System cryptography: Use FIPS compliant algorithms for encryption, hashing, and signing" security option enabled, as described in Chapter 1. Scroll down to the Security section in the windows and modify these settings as shown in Figure 13-12.

TOOLS OF THE TRADE

To review, you can use the following tools to increase the security of the web server. There are also lots of third-party add-ons that you can get, but first make sure you have the tools provided by Microsoft.

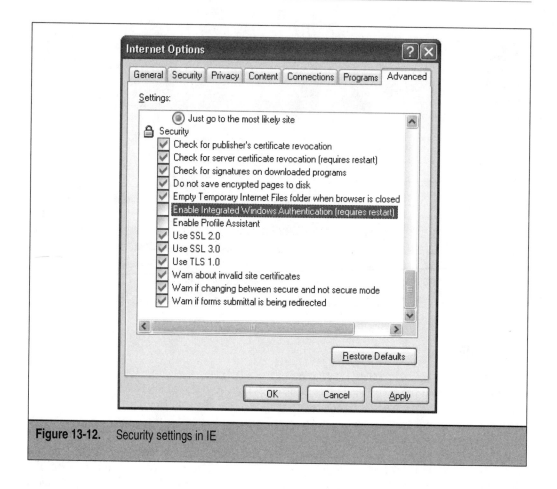

Figure 13-12.   Security settings in IE

URLScan 2.5   This tool makes increasing the security of your web server much easier. For different types of web servers, such as a Sharepoint server versus an e-commerce server, you will need different options. But making modifications to the URLScan.ini file is pretty simple.

IIS Lockdown Tool   The versions of IIS Lockdown differ between IIS 5.1 and 6.0, but both provide additional security to the web server. While the IIS Lockdown tool that runs on IIS 5.x and 4.x server may be more robust and offer templates for security, IIS Lockdown on IIS 6.0 does not have to do as much, because a lot of the default problems have been eliminated from IIS 6.0. Run the tool in both versions of the web server to add additional security controls.

CHECKLIST: INTERNET SERVICES

Your Internet-facing services are some of the most important to consider when implementing security, mainly because anonymous user access is allowed by default. Be sure to do the following:

- ☐ Install IIS on a nonsystem partition.
- ☐ Remove all default sample web sites and programs that are not needed from the web server.
- ☐ Disable or remove the Remote Administration and Sharepoint applications from your IIS 6.0 server.
- ☐ Unmap all IISAPI extensions that you are not using (typically you only need .asp).
- ☐ Install URLScan and configure it according to the needs of the web server.
- ☐ Install the IIS Lockdown tool and secure your server with it.
- ☐ Use ACLs to further restrict access to folders and programs.
- ☐ Modify permissions on command utilities such as Cmd.exe to be as restrictive as possible.
- ☐ Use SSL wherever you allow authentication or remote administration.
- ☐ Do not run SMTP on your web server if that is possible.
- ☐ Turn on logging for web and FTP access.
- ☐ Store log files on a different partition.
- ☐ Push down Internet security zone restrictions to your domain user computers.
- ☐ Do not use profile information in your web browser.

PART IV

Preparing for the Worst

CHAPTER 14

Penetration Testing

The past few years have seen the emergence of companies specializing in performing penetration assessments to test the integrity of your enterprise. In most cases, these companies will come in once a year to make a focused and concerted effort at breaking down your defenses by leveraging security weaknesses one point at a time until the entire IT organization falls. As far as they go, these assessments can be useful in identifying what is wrong with your implementation at that point in time from an unbiased third-party perspective. However, this effort must be ongoing. To ensure that you maintain security diligence, you must have an ongoing audit cycle of your environment to reduce the risk and keep improving network posture. Nothing is more frustrating than subsequent audits yielding a lower rating in the years following the initial third-party assessment.

So the question always comes up: "How do we protect and continue to ensure the integrity of the enterprise?" This answer goes back to the basics: "Audit your own network." Of course, management many times becomes concerned this may affect performance, or worse yet, fears the effects they may suffer if, in the context of your actions, you create a network or server outage. Never fear; if done properly this impact should be mitigated.

In the past, administrators have been focused on the availability of the systems to the end user, and various other factors were not taken into account. Today the world has begun to understand that security is an integral component, and not an afterthought, a premise echoed from the vendor to the CIO. Administrators responsible for the availability of these servers must fully understand how to secure them. For computers, much of the work of creating secure networks is done up front, during design and deployment, with updates for security and stability often "blurred" when released by the vendor. So, with that stated, it should be easy to go forward and create a new network with security as a key premise. Unfortunately, we do not live in a utopia, and legacy systems exist everywhere today, to complicate our lives.

The purpose of this chapter is to provide insight into how best to approach a security audit and the risks present in enterprises based on a Windows environment. While Windows XP has made leaps and bounds in making the lives of both users and administrators easier, very few organizations can take advantage of all the features in a domain today. As a result, attacking Windows XP from the network has not changed too much from the approach used prior to Windows XP. However, the product team has made some significant strides forward in the following areas:

- User account security
- Built-in host security options
- Default file and registry ACLs

More times than not in the past, hosts and domains have been compromised by a null administrator password, the lowest of all hanging fruit. Today, a blank password should get you nothing over the network, as the default local security policy restricts accounts with no passwords to console-only access. In addition, controlled network access in Windows XP is designed to grant only guest privileges when workstations are accessed from the network. However, in the real world this setting is not always enabled (depending on the installation choices) and should not be relied on as a "control" measure by a security-conscious professional. Finally, you have advanced features built in that can be taken advantage of relatively easily—such as the Internet Connection Firewall (ICF) used to thwart access unless specifically granted. The configuration, implementation, and full benefits of ICF are discussed in detail in Chapter 8. Unfortunately, ICF's features are best suited for use at home and on remote users' machines; they aren't easily implemented in most domains because there are no GPO settings available other than the one that sets it as enabled or disabled.

Since most people will implement Windows XP Professional in a domain environment that is heterogeneous, with Windows 2000 domain controllers installed and configured to be compatible with NT workstations, you must continue to perform security measures diligently. Needless to say, that adds to the confusion—which is what the rest of this book is designed to step you through. This chapter, however, is about running a penetration test, so let's get moving.

CAUTION   This chapter discusses active security testing on a network. Before you perform any of these activities you should be sure you have the appropriate approval and understanding from management. Also, you should first perform these activities in a test environment before directing them against production, to ensure that you understand every activity performed.

PLANNING

The success of any activity is dependent on the level and quality of planning. In performing a network assessment, start by defining your objective and the scope of the activity.

Objective

One objective of a network assessment traditionally is identifying where weaknesses exist. This allows you to later address the shortcomings in the most appropriate manner, whether they are individual findings or systemic issues that need to be addressed through policy and enforcement. For the purposes of this chapter, the objective is straightforward: identifying threats to your Windows-based hosts from the network. This objective allows you to focus on how to approach the audit, rather than becoming distracted by the various interactions among systems, applications, e-mail, and external points. Don't get us wrong—each of those is just as important to ensure a secure network; however, each could also be a separate chapter, and collectively they are outside the scope of this book.

Scope

Now that we have defined the objective, it makes sense to include within the scope all of the Windows systems on the network. The important thing to examine is whether you have a trust relationship built into your network that can allow access to the Windows hosts from the network by non-Windows hosts. Why is this important? Because many times database connections or backup software routinely interacts with Windows servers using the privileges of a local administrator, or in some cases a domain administrator. If this is the case in your environment, then these additional hosts should be addressed from the network as well. (We will not discuss the specifics here, since the different configurations are limitless when custom solutions are included.)

METHODOLOGY 101

The methodology of performing an assessment has many components as part of the process. As with any process, a list using a logical progression is one of the best tools to define what must be performed to achieve the goal. It is important to understand that even though you may know how to skip between the steps, an attacker will move through each step sequentially, working toward the end goal. Here is a compressed methodology used for "known" environments:

1. Identify the scope.
2. Perform reconnaissance.
3. Interrogate the targets.
4. Break the barriers.
5. Achieve local access.
6. Evaluate the impact.

More steps would be added if you were attacking with zero knowledge or had bad intentions.

To better grasp the concept of this list, let's run through the objective of each step as it pertains to the overall methodology.

Identify the Scope

During the planning phase, we identified the scope as the Windows network environment. At this stage we want to go into specifics and begin with the entire range of addresses the Windows hosts exist on to ensure complete saturation during our scans. In some organizations you can review the DHCP assignments to ensure you have all the IP addresses; in other organizations you identify the hosts within a DNS server. To make sure that all the hosts are accounted for, routing tables and ARP tables on routers should be reviewed so that all routable addressed space is accounted for in your organization. You can never be certain that a group of developers haven't created a new "test" network that leaves the rest of the enterprise vulnerable to attack.

Perform Reconnaissance

Once you have a range of targets defined, you will need to perform a network scan to determine what services are being offered in your environment to other hosts on the network. This will involve the first instance of running a utility against your network, which we will later describe in detail in the upcoming "Recon" section. For now, just understand that during this task each IP address will be systematically checked over the network to determine what services respond. Once these services have been mapped, you will begin to see what information can be obtained.

Interrogate the Targets

Interrogation is the art of obtaining information in the most subtle manner. Here you will attempt to retrieve information from a host, such as:

- Type of service running
- Version of service running
- Users on a system
- Information the host knows about a network
- Other seemingly benign information that is provided by network services

The strongest of security postures will provide limited information in this capacity; however, most networks virtually bleed information in order to make other systems aware of their existence and purpose—which is a viable design only if you possess blind faith.

Break the Barriers

Now you can begin to perform activities against the systems that you (as an attacker) may not be expected or invited to perform. Many of the actions are designed to be used by privileged users or as calls made between systems. Here, activities include methods that leverage known vulnerabilities, configuration weaknesses, or requests performed that are not designed to be part of an expected function. Ideally, you will go straight to administration. If not, you will need to continue: the only thing worse than someone gaining unauthorized access on a host on your network is someone gaining privileged access. If you are able to leverage the full power of XP, the attacker's goal of gaining administrative privileges may become very tiresome. However, should you fail or any level of host security fail, the worst-case scenario has occurred.

Achieve Local Access

Once you have a privileged account on a local system you are free to roam to your heart's content through files and directories on the system as well as, in most cases, any user-created files. Depending on the role of the host, the secrets may be limited to those the machine is aware of or—as we will discuss a bit later—might include some quite surprising ones.

Evaluate the Impact

This is the last step in the methodology of completing a penetration (pen) test, but in the real world it may only be the beginning of an attacker's feat. Depending on what domain you were able to compromise, there may be bigger fish to fry on your network. Imagine a critical domain for payroll or HR, where your initial scans failed to identify weaknesses. Once you have completed total domination on an adjacent domain, you may have obtained a key piece of the puzzle. Your new rights will allow you to review existing trust relationships or IPSec policies, which may provide a roadmap to additional domain compromises. Evaluating the impact is where you will begin to discover the value obtained from performing the pen test—the weaknesses that are important for you to address.

RECONNAISSANCE AND INTERROGATION

Here is the part you have been waiting for—the approach to assessing your network. The first thing you will need to do is compile a list of all the possible network ranges in your enterprise. Obviously, the size of this list can vary from a few thousand to millions of IP addresses. To make your job more manageable, it is often a good idea to break the scans down into manageable ranges. Obviously this is relative to the size of your network and host density, so you will have to make that decision.

If this is your first scan you will want to focus on some small target-rich ranges to ensure you have a solid understanding. Next you will need to perform the first enumeration scan of the targets. Fscan.exe (http://www.foundstone.com/knowledge/free_tools.html) is a command line utility for Windows environments that allows you to specify a variety of arguments. In the demonstration that follows, we will be scanning with a subset of TCP ports. Table 14-1 shows a list of common services available on a Windows network; you should place it in a file for ease of use.

Recon

At this point you should have a list of target hosts (e.g., targets.txt) and a list of ports to scan (e.g., ports.txt). We are now ready to begin the first enumeration. The following command will execute a port scan of the target hosts and save the output to a file:

```
Fscan -l ports.txt -f targets.txt -o target.output.txt
```

Port	Service
TCP 21	File Transfer Protocol (FTP)
TCP 25	Simple Mail Transfer Protocol (SMTP)
TCP/UDP 53	Domain Name Service (DNS)
TCP 80	WWW Hypertext Transfer Protocol (HTTP)
TCP/UDP 88	Kerberos
TCP 135	RPC/DCE Endpoint Mapper
UDP 137	NetBIOS Name Service
UDP 138	NetBIOS Datagram Service
TCP 139	NetBIOS Session Service
UDP 161	Simple Network Management Protocol (SNMP)
TCP/UDP 389	Lightweight Directory Access Protocol (LDAP)
TCP 443	HTTP over Secure Sockets Layer/Transport Layer Security
TCP/UDP 445	Microsoft Server Message Blocks/Common Internet File System (SMB/CIFS)
TCP/UDP 464	Kerberos kpasswd
UDP 500	Internet Key Exchange (IKE) for IPSec
TCP 593	HTTP RPC Endpoint Mapper
TCP 636	LDAP over SSL/TLS
TCP 1433	Microsoft SQL
UDP 1434	Microsoft SQL Monitor
TCP 3268	Active Directory Global Catalog
TCP 3269	Active Directory Global Catalog over SSL
TCP 3389	Terminal Services/Remote Desktop Protocol (RDP)

Table 14-1.   Windows Common Ports

The simplicity of this scan can easily be modified with additional arguments to tailor the scan time and rate to your optimum speed. The end result against our network hosts 10.0.2.10–12 will look similar to this:

```
Scan started at Tue Jul 09 19:32:23 2002
10.0.2.10          135/tcp
10.0.2.10          139/tcp
10.0.2.10          161/tcp
10.0.2.10          389/tcp
10.0.2.10          445/tcp
10.0.2.10          3268/tcp
10.0.2.10          3389/tcp
```

```
10.0.2.11          25/tcp
10.0.2.11         135/tcp
10.0.2.11         139/tcp
10.0.2.11         445/tcp
10.0.2.11        3389/tcp
10.0.2.12          80/tcp
10.0.2.12         135/tcp
10.0.2.12         139/tcp
10.0.2.12         443/tcp
10.0.2.12         445/tcp
10.0.2.12        1433/tcp
10.0.2.12        3389/tcp
 Scan finished at Mon Jul 09 19:32:24 2002
 Time taken: 54 ports in 0.54 secs (100.00 ports/sec)
```

We are now able to identify an Active Directory server, mail server, and web server. For simplicity in our testing, we will limit our discussion to these three hosts.

Interrogate

Now that we have identified our targets we need to attempt to verify what we are seeing. To accomplish this we can use a variety of tools. The first tool we will use is Fscan. As mentioned earlier, a variety of arguments can be passed, one of which is -b. The -b argument attempts to connect to open services and passes a "nudge" string to elicit a response. This method can leave a 400 error message, however, as seen below:

```
Scan started at Tue Jul 9 20:01:25 2002
10.0.2.12       80/tcp
HTTP/1.1 400 Bad Request[0D][0A]Server: Microsoft-IIS/5.0[0D][0A]Date:
Wed, 10 Jul 2002 03:00:14 GMT[0D][0A]Content-Type: text/html[0D][0A]
Content-Length: 87[0D][0A][0D][0A]<html><head><title>Error</title></head>
<body>The parameter is incorrect. </body></html>
Scan finished at Tue Jul 9 20:01:25 2002
Time taken: 1 ports in 0.230 secs (4.35 ports/sec)
```

A better method is to utilize the Netcat utility and make a legitimate request to the service. This will prevent an error from being generated and leave an entry of your activities that would draw interest. In the following example, we have connected to our target host on port 80 and issued a legitimate HEAD request with two carriage returns.

```
nc 10.0.2.12 80
HEAD / HTTP/1.0 <CR><CR>
```

The output is then provided as a 200 message from the web server, a valid connection request:

```
HTTP/1.1 200 OK
Server: Microsoft-IIS/5.0
Content-Location: http://10.0.2.12/index.html
Date: Wed, 10 Jul 2002 03:05:59 GMT
Content-Type: text/html
Accept-Ranges: bytes
Last-Modified: Tue, 09 Jul 2002 20:53:17 GMT
ETag: "6cbd53fb1c29c21:8e1"=
Content-Length: 12897
```

We can elicit identifiable responses from ports 25, 80, and 139. This information allows us to positively identify the type of service running by the protocol response. This will be used to target our activities when we try to break the barriers.

Other services will require more custom requests to get a positive identification. Fortunately, there are tools available to obtain this confirmation, as well as a plethora of more vital information. The first step up we will make is to obtain the shared information on the network host.

Given that Windows XP is new, you are sure to find some pre-XP hosts in your environment. In many cases the domain controllers will be around long after you have implemented Windows XP Professional and Windows .NET Server. If so, you can perform enumeration of the Windows hosts with traditional methods, with no restrictions for anonymous connections. The first command will utilize the Net.exe command. Though almost all users prefer the GUI, the command line utility allows you to explore your network at a level that gives you more granular host information.

Performing a "net view" will give you a list of domains or workgroups on the wire:

```
net view /domain
```

The next step is to use Nltest.exe (from the Windows 2000 Resource Kit) and substitute each domain name as the argument for domains. This will identify the domain controllers:

```
nltest /dclist:'domains'
```

If you have gotten this far, you don't have any restrictions to prevent you from easily harvesting accounts and shares from the hosts. Assume that Nltest.exe showed us the existence of a Windows 2000 domain controller after using the /dclist switch. We will want to start by harvesting user accounts on the DC, by first setting up a "null" session. This leverages the InterProcessCommunication feature of Windows Networking, by connecting to a remote compute as an anonymous, or null, user. This can be performed with the following syntax:

```
net use \\10.0.2.10\ipc$ """ /u:""
```

When you get the response "The command completed successfully," you know that RestrictAnonymous is set to either 0 or 1, because if it were set to 2 in Windows 2000, you would get an "access denied" message when attempting to connect. Of course, if you had credentials you could always use those instead of null.

For full details from the hosts you can execute a tool like DumpSec (http://www.systemtools.com) against the host. Or you can run a tool like Userdump.exe (http://www.hammerofgod.com), which can bypass RestrictAnonymous = 1 and still dump a list of users. By specifying a known user, such as Guest or Administrator, along with the number of user queries you want to run, you can harvest information about all the users on the system.

Recall that Windows XP's default settings do not allow anonymous enumeration of system information as Windows NT's and Windows 2000's do. Thus we are targeting a Windows 2000 domain controller here. With a list of all user accounts on the system, you can start brute-forcing passwords, as we will do in the next section, "Attack and Overcome."

Our final interrogation effort is to take advantage of SNMP over UDP 161. While we didn't include it in the original scans, a simple SNMP browser, such as that from Solarwinds (http://www.solarwinds.net), allows us to get critical information if a unique SNMP string has not been defined. Simply add the IP address of the target host and any community strings you want to include. The next step is to launch the tool to determine whether you have been able to guess the community string. The default read-only string is "public," and in many cases this is not modified.

ATTACK AND OVERCOME

Now that we have three known targets running multiple services we need to attack the network in a logical fashion. The next steps are breaking the barriers of the domain, gaining local access on the hosts, and finally taking a step back to evaluate the impact on the enterprise. These steps are considered intrusive by any measure, and it should be noted that some machines do not respond as expected all the time.

TIP These activities are best performed during nonpeak hours on critical hosts, to limit any type of negative result.

Break the Barriers

When dealing with a Windows environment we have multiple avenues of attack. The first avenue is direct attacks against the users. The next is attacks against services not properly updated. And the final avenue is attacks against improperly secured services.

Remember the list of users we were able to harvest? Well, if none of the practices mentioned are being followed it is only a matter of time before we obtain valid credentials. The first step is to create a script to systematically substitute the username and password in an ongoing loop. To make this easier, there are tools such as Nete, Enum, and Nat, which already have the ability to accept user and password lists as arguments. If you are able to guess a user account with administrative privileges, you can go to the next level. However, to do so would negate the purpose of this exercise. A pen test should be structured to test all aspects, regardless of the success or failure of earlier attempts.

NOTE Remember the original objective: identifying threats to your Windows-based hosts from the network.

Attacks against users are dependent on multiple factors that you as an administrator control. The lowest is that of password complexity. By forcing users to create strong passwords, you can reduce the risk of a scenario where an account is compromised as the result of a weak password. The next is to set an account-lockout policy to limit the number of unsuccessful attempts. The third is to perform routine audits against passwords, looking for easily guessable ones.

NOTE The security policies discussed in Chapter 1 are crucial to setting up this basic level of security in your domains.

The second avenue for attack concerns services running that are vulnerable as a result of not having current hotfixes installed. Lately, the majority of these have involved issues identified with IIS (see Chapter 13). IIS is now in its fourth iteration for Windows XP (version 5.1), yet there still appears to be no end to potential problems. Following its standard practice, Microsoft has made ease of use the primary goal. While that's a great tactic for marketing, it makes the administration of a production system much more difficult, as some companies are unsure about the level of functionality their current solutions require. Going forward with Windows .NET we see a much more secure default deployment in IIS 6.0, but for now attacks against IIS are the crux of Windows security concerns.

For an attacker to exploit these issues they have to find a vulnerable system. Fortunately for the attacker there is no lack of tools. One of the most widely distributed and used is a simple Perl script called Whisker (http://www.wiretrip.net/rfp/1/index.asp), which uses as its attack signatures an input file for "known" problem files on web servers. The simplicity of the tool is perhaps its greatest asset. As new vulnerabilities come out, the open source community continues to update and provide countless new checks.

Running Whisker requires Perl to be installed on the system you are scanning from (e.g., your workstation). The next step is to execute the command with the host as the argument. The result of a default scan will be the return of "potential" vulnerabilities that will need to be verified or, in most cases, exploited. There are multiple avenues for exploitation available for known vulnerabilities, and the likelihood you have an affected system is dependent on how current you are with vendor fixes. In April 2002, Microsoft released a patch addressing seven issues affecting IIS 4.0, 5.0, and 5.1. Attacks against this service can result in IUSR-level access or in some cases SYSTEM-level access.

The final avenue of attack is against improperly secured services. This is becoming as popular as attacks against services with vulnerabilities. For each service in your network running on top of the Windows operating system there are critical components you are responsible for configuring. Many of the freeware utilities available today for network monitoring come complete with web interfaces for management with default passwords. The problem with most of these is that you are not forced to create a strong password—nor are you truly made aware of the problems they can introduce. Take into account simulation packages for Xservers, or HTTP servers for remote connections. Many of these services are running independent of the security of Windows in the UI level, and if not properly secured, a weak password or the lack of a password altogether can be used to gain privileges. Depending on the context of the application running, leveraging these services can provide administrative access.

The most recently publicized and exploited example of this is the blank password set by default on SQL servers prior to SQL 2000. While many people are aware of the importance of setting the password for a full-blown production SQL server, many people still run the desktop component or test servers with a blank password. Enter SQLdict (http://ntsecurity.nu/toolbox/sqldict/). This utility allows you to specify the DBO user account, sa, and choose a password dictionary to use to guess passwords by brute force. The failed logins on this account will probably not be logged if mixed mode was selected, and the result will be the ability to run commands as a local administrator. Usage of SQLdict is shown in Figure 14-1.

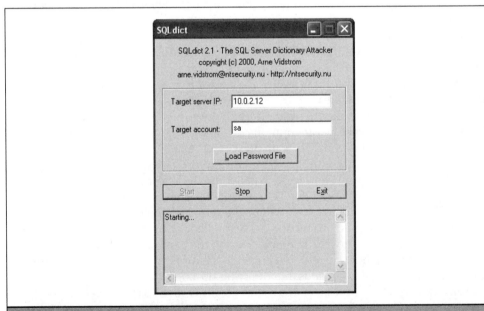

Figure 14-1. SQLdict running against a target

To be able to actually leverage this account, a SQL interpreter is required, as well as the extended stored procedures that are built in and probably still mapped for your convenience. A widely distributed exploit utility called SQLexec is available to do this; it requires no knowledge of SQL to perform attacks. Once it is launched against a system, any command can be issued as an administrator. Imagine the effects of these two commands on a system where the SQL services are running with local—or worse, domain—administrator privileges:

```
Xp_cmdshell 'net user bad mojo /ADD'

Xp_cmdshell 'net localgroup /ADD Administrators bad'
```

The commands will add a user named "bad" with a password of "mojo" to the Administrators group. At this point we have beaten down the door and positioned ourselves to come back to the host at any time in one fatal swoop.

CHALLENGE

You feel you have completed an internal assessment of a corporate subsidiary. You are satisfied you have exhausted all efforts at connecting to the "critical" servers and have not identified any high-risk issues that could be leveraged to compromise the network. Your own organization has recently undergone a similar outsourced review, which resulted in a domain compromise. Your supervisor is looking forward to similar results or definitive answers regarding the subsidiary. You feel that open shares, vulnerable services, and blank passwords do not exist on the domain controllers.

What is your next step? Should you complete your findings and recommendations for the network? Are you confident a third-party review would result in similar findings? Should you focus on a different approach or tactic to test the enterprise integrity?

Ideally, you have successfully performed the tasks you have engaged in against your network. In that case, your next goal is to attack the strong objective from the weakest point, the users. In a network, the people who work on the computers are not the only users. Users on a network extend to the workstations, which use the services in transparent fashion through the employees. Remember that workstations are integral parts of domains, each one joined in the trusted environment. A successful attack should focus on leveraging the potential for locally stored passwords, insecure services, and outdated configurations. The vulnerability on a domain workstation may provide the opportunity to establish a beachhead to launch a tactical strike not otherwise possible against the overall domain.

Achieve Local Access

You may not own the domain yet, but at this point you should have administrator-level privileges on a host. In this task, also known as "pillaging the box," you will be looking for clues to unlock the domain. In a *zero-knowledge* pen test, pillaging a box may include hiding your actions and obscuring the logs. However, we will skip that step here and go straight to searching the system for useful information.

To be truly effective at this you will need not only to search remote drives but to execute commands on the remote hosts. With local administrator privileges you can do this in many ways. One way is to leverage the Remote command from the Resource Kit. This requires you to perform multiple steps. To make life easier you should retrieve PStools (http://www.sysinternals.com), which has nearly a dozen utilities that allow you to run commands on remote systems by specifying legitimate user credentials. Remember the box we set up with "bad" and "mojo"? Let's see what happens in the following example when we want to get a remote command shell using the Psexec command.

```
C:\Tools\PSTools>ipconfig
Windows IP Configuration
Ethernet adapter Local Area Connection:
        Connection-specific DNS Suffix  . : securingxp.com
        IP Address. . . . . . . . . . . : 10.0.2.20
        Subnet Mask . . . . . . . . . . : 255.255.255.0
        Default Gateway . . . . . . . . : 10.0.2.1


C:\Tools\PSTools>psexec.exe \\10.0.2.12 -u bad -p mojo -s cmd
PsExec v1.24 - execute processes remotely
Copyright (C) 2001 Mark Russinovich
www.sysinternals.com
Microsoft Windows XP [Version 5.1.2600]
(C) Copyright 1985-2001 Microsoft Corp.



C:\WINDOWS\system32>ipconfig
Windows IP Configuration
Ethernet adapter Local Area Connection:
        Connection-specific DNS Suffix  . : securingxp.com
        IP Address. . . . . . . . . . . : 10.0.2.12
        Subnet Mask . . . . . . . . . . : 255.255.255.0
        Default Gateway . . . . . . . . : 10.0.2.1
```

As you see, we are not only able to run commands on the remote system, but we can obtain a remote shell back as well. We are now left with two choices. We can use Psexec to copy over our files we need to run, or we can map a share and copy them and run them from the command prompt we just got back. Either way we now have the ability to run commands in the context of the remote machine.

The first step to perform is to dump the passwords of the local host using Pwdump3e. This will provide you the hashes to start cracking with John the Ripper or L0phtCrack. There may be a local account of a user who has privileged domain access as well, and eight times out of ten, users keep the passwords the same between systems. With Pwdump3e you can run it remotely or locally. When run remotely, it encapsulates all the data using encryption, preventing anyone else on the network from seeing your activities.

Another step you will definitely want to perform is to dump the Local Security Authority (LSA) secrets. Among other things, the LSA stores credentials for services that need to start when the machine starts or services are run unattended. Many of these services include SQL and backup applications. Issuing the lsadump2 command will give you an output of the stored passwords. Ever wonder what the password was for the Remote Desktop Help account on your system? It's in there—no cracking necessary. Best of all, at this point you may have an account with domain administrator rights. Now sometimes there can be problems running this command, as you may not have rights. Using lsadump2 requires that you have the "Debug programs" user right, which by default is given to the local administrators group. To assure you do have rights, you can provide them to yourself using the NTrights.exe command line utility. This gives you the ability to set local policy without the need of a GUI.

 SECURITY ALERT   Service accounts pose one of the biggest security threats to a Windows domain. Consider an enterprise backup application that requires agents to run as services with domain admin accounts on every computer. All it takes is for one user on your network to get local administrator rights, dump the LSA secrets, and suddenly they have the domain admin password. Now ask yourself a few questions. Do you run services with domain admin accounts? Do you allow users on your network local administrator privileges—developers or researchers perhaps? If you answered yes to these questions, then you need to find a way to either downgrade those service accounts to domain users or prevent your users from having local administrator privileges.

A final big-ticket win you may be able to pull off is a clear text list of all the passwords. Windows XP does not create this, users do, and they do it more often than you would expect. If attacks against a domain controller fail, then people tend to look for easier targets. Workstations provide that, and none better than test boxes or administrative boxes. Too many times "golden eggs," also known as clear text lists of administrator passwords, are "safeguarded" on a workstation to facilitate account retrieval. Perhaps the most rewarding feeling is finding accounts and passwords stored in a clear text database file for some other use. Some companies have activities or bulletin boards on intranet sites that utilize separate authentication. In many cases, these applications do not have strong encryption methods for stored password values, and thus retrieval is much easier than brute-force guessing.

In any case, searching for clues can be rewarding and educational, as you will see much of the valuable information a company protects is used by end users who are not concerned with security and like to have copies of everything on their local computer in the event the servers or networks go down. Sometimes the biggest win isn't the domain administrator but the little test box that has copies of the source code for the killer app you are designing, the bank routing and account numbers, or the plans for tomorrow's vehicle today.

Evaluate Impact

By this point you should have pretty much stepped through the attacks on one or more systems. Unfortunately, that means your job has just begun. You have identified key areas that are the systemic causes, whether that is a policy issue, a user issue, an application issue, or some other issue. Now, by taking those key areas, you know where you need to start.

By making effective changes in the areas where you were unrestricted in your actions, you can begin to build your defenses. You will obviously need a plan for securing these points. Hopefully, you did not skip ahead to read this chapter. If you did, go back and start at Chapter 1 to get an understanding of the type of security you can implement with Windows XP. There are unlimited ways to leverage key features, if you take the time. In reality, the time you spend now is a tiny fraction of what it could cost if you wait and fix things after they are broken.

TOOLS OF THE TRADE

All of the tools we discussed in this chapter are available free to aid you in performing a pen test. The following paragraphs offer a quick rundown of these tools. This is by no means an all-inclusive list, as an Internet search will reveal. However, most of the available tools perform similar functions. Those discussed below will give you the minimum you will need to perform a similar assessment, and you can add your favorites as you want. Many of these tools are native commands or are available through the Windows NT or Windows 2000 Resource Kits.

Net.exe　　We have to thank Microsoft for providing one of the most versatile multiprotocol tools available. While this command is native to all systems, it takes an advanced user to know all the intricacies available. When all else fails, this utility is the basic fallback and provides the tools to do the job. The syntax is available by typing **net** at a command prompt.

Fscan.exe　　Fscan is one of the only port scanners you need for internal work. While lacking in the more advanced techniques, such as FIN or ACK scanning, Fscan is a tremendously versatile, fast, and easy-to-use command line utility. The tool is designed to make it easy to tailor your scan times and delays to your environment, and is capable of traversing class B networks in minutes rather than the more typical hours. Syntax is available by typing **fscan**. The tool is available free from the Foundstone web site: http://www.foundstone.com.

PStools These tools are indispensable. Aside from the venerable Psexec command, which allows you to run any command remotely on a system with the appropriate privileges, Mark Russinovich has provided tools to perform remote service controls (allowing you to specify user credentials) and a remote tool to display users logged on locally. It includes nearly a dozen tools, to complement even the most complete toolkit. Syntax for any PStool component is available by typing the tool name. The tools are available from the Sysinternals web site: http://www.sysinternals.com.

DumpSec.exe Previously known as DumpAcl from Somarsoft, this tool is now provided as DumpSec by SystemTools.com for free and provides information on users, groups, shares, and corresponding ACLs. This tool can be run from the command line with arguments as defined in the help file. The tool is available from http://www.systemtools.com.

NC.exe Netcat, as it is known, is the Swiss Army Knife of hacker tools. This utility can be used to connect to or create a TCP or UDP socket. Full mastery of Netcat allows it to be used as a port scanner or to be set up in the background as a backdoor for a later visit. Newer incarnations incorporate encryption to protect your data as it traverses the wire and limit connections to those with the correct key. Syntax for NC.exe can be obtained by typing **nc -h**. The tool is available from the @stake web site: http://www.atstake.com/research/tools/.

Userdump.exe Created to remotely retrieve the account names from systems with Restrict Anonymous set to 1, this tool allows you to use a known account name to obtain the system SID transparently and then provide all the users on the system based on the number of queries you run. The syntax can be obtained by typing the command name. The tool is available from Tim Mullen on the security focus web site: http://online.securityfocus.com/tools/1931.

Nltest.exe A component of the Windows NT 4.0/2000 Resource Kit, Nltest provides the ability to obtain and test domain trust issues. This utility can come in very handy when trying to identify a domain controller on a network. Syntax for Nltest can be obtained by typing the command name.

SQLdict.exe A robust Microsoft SQL scanner, this GUI-based utility is easy to use, only requiring the input of a password list and username. The tool then attempts to authenticate against Microsoft SQL servers. The tool is available from Arne Vidstrom's web site at http://ntsecurity.nu.

Whisker.pl A versatile vulnerability scanner for web servers, this utility is command line–based and requires a Perl interpreter. Updated features include support for SSL, and the open source community is actively updating the signatures. The tool is available from RFP at http://www.wiretrip.net.

Pwdump3e.exe Pwdump3e is a critical tool for any security professional or administrator. On a Windows system, this tool allows you to extract the LanMan and NT password hashes. This tool is a variation on Pwdump/Pwdump2; you can run it remotely and utilize encryption to protect the hashes as they come across the network. The tool is available at http://www.polivec.com/pwdump3.html.

LSAdump2.exe This is a great utility that takes advantage of the secrets stored in the LSA. This tool requires you to have debug privileges and must be run locally. The syntax of the command is **lsadump2**. If you don't have debug privileges, you will need to assign them through the User Rights interface described in Chapter 1, or with the Resource Kit utility NTrights.exe. The tool is available from Todd Sabin at http://razor.bindview.com.

CHECKLIST: PENETRATION TESTING

Attempting to penetrate your own network defenses is a great way to identify security weaknesses that need to be addressed. The initial steps of reconnaissance and interrogation will give you a much better picture of what exactly is running on your own network. Following this phase with the steps described in the "Attack and Overcome" section will give you precise insight into just where security defenses break down on your network.

- [ ] First identify the scope. Determine the ranges of all the hosts within your environment. Determine the boundaries that should not be crossed, such as adjacent networks or partner systems.

- [ ] Then perform reconnaissance. Perform port scans and host queries to determine what servers and services are available.

- [ ] Next, interrogate the targets. Using the appropriate tools, initiate connections to the services and determine what information is available.

- [ ] Break the barriers. Using a mix of exploit tools, poor design, and poor user actions, obtain some level of host access on the domain. Then, once you have become a user, the next level is privileged user. This can be accomplished by leveraging vulnerable services.

- [ ] Now achieve local access. Access on a host as a system- or administrative-level user provides the opportunity to look for host secrets or user secrets that can be used to gain access on other systems. After becoming an administrative-level user on a local host, gain access on a domain controller or other sensitive server.

- [ ] Finally, evaluate the impact. Evaluate all the results of your actions and how they apply to the enterprise as a whole. Your experience has either provided you a roadmap for better security or allowed you to gain a stronger sense of confidence in the efforts you've made to secure the enterprise.

CHAPTER 15

Incident Response

If you work in an organization with more than two employees and have some sort of connection to a public network, you have probably performed some sort of incident response, perhaps without realizing it. Most organizations lack a formal plan detailing what to do when something bad happens. Ad hoc approaches may work for a short time, but sooner or later you may find yourself in the position of a program manager, responsible for investigating the loss of several millions of dollars in product. At that point you will wish you had a formal incident response plan in place. During the course of incident response (IR) program development, an organization needs to understand how to respond to each platform used by the company.

In this chapter, we will take a look at how the Windows XP operating system fits into your incident response plan. Most of the steps remain the same as when responding to a Windows 2000 system. We will also provide a quick summary of the incident response process. The perfect companion to this chapter is the book by Kevin Mandia and Chris Prosise, *Incident Response: Investigating Computer Crime* (Osborne, 2001).

THE INCIDENT RESPONSE PROCESS

What is an *incident*? This definition is one of the first things that we at Foundstone establish when working with a company to build an incident response program. In the broadest definition, an incident may be a computer intrusion, a denial of service attack, theft of intellectual property, or any network activity that is unauthorized or unlawful. Often, it comes down to any event that violates a company policy or common law. You do have solid information security policies in place, right?

We have developed a process for handling incidents based on our experiences in government and commercial work. The process diagram, shown in Figure 15-1, helps

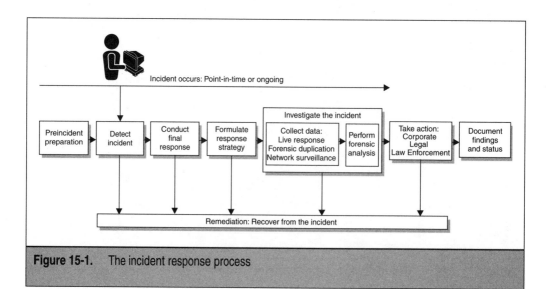

Figure 15-1.   The incident response process

us communicate the steps that we typically take toward management as well as technical staff. In this chapter we will investigate how the Windows XP operating system affects the way you and your team prepare for and respond to attacks on your infrastructure. In this regard, we will cover the following four important phases of a typical incident response plan:

- Preincident response preparation
- Conduct initial response
- Collect data
- Perform forensic analysis

PREINCIDENT RESPONSE PREPARATION

This section outlines some of the tasks specific to Windows XP that will help you position your group to respond quickly, effectively, and in an organized fashion. The goal is to prevent, minimize, and recoup potential losses to the greatest degree possible. Here is a short list of tasks that we suggest to organizations looking to form an IR program:

- *Verify that acceptable use policies are in place and have the approval of your legal department.* Be sure your employees understand that the use of the network implies consent to monitoring by the organization. This will allow you to perform network monitoring and forensic analysis.
- *Implement "baseline" installations of approved operating systems.* This is a part of configuration management that will help you detect and respond to problems before they become overwhelming. Baseline installations are where you implement security policies, host-based intrusion detection, and centralized logging.
- *Harden the operating systems on workstations and servers.* Practice defense in depth. Nearly all organizations we have performed external penetration tests against had what we call a "soft, chewy center." In other words, a firewall may be present, but it can be a single point of failure, allowing one security incident to affect all aspects of the organization's business.
- *Install and maintain host- and network-based intrusion detection systems.* Some security companies find these systems indispensable, others consider them a waste of time. Both views can be correct. If you don't have a set of knowledgeable eyes on the IDS consoles, it may be a waste of time. Properly configured and monitored, intrusion detection can be a powerful tool in detecting attacks in their early stages.
- *Create checklists and toolkits to ensure that the process is performed in a standard, consistent manner.* One of the key principles of IR and forensics is consistency.

- *Acquire tools and training for your staff that allow them to perform forensic duplication and examination.* Use only the tools that have been tested for their suitability for forensic analysis. The National Institute of Standards and Technology is currently working on a series of performance metrics for verifying forensics tools, and is a good reference for developing software and testing methods on your own.

- *Create initial response toolkits for each operating system used in your organization.* Be sure the team of "first responders" is knowledgeable about each OS and fully understands the entire IR process.

INITIAL RESPONSE ON WINDOWS XP

Initial response is a stage of preliminary information gathering designed to determine whether unlawful, unauthorized, or unacceptable activity has occurred. As investigators, we need to gather as much information as possible, especially if the information is in danger of being lost or destroyed. The information present in the computer system's memory will dictate the degree of examination you will perform while the computer remains on. Quite often, you will develop investigative leads based on the state of the network and the list of running processes. The steps outlined in this section are designed to ensure the integrity of the most volatile data on a computer system. It is critical to adhere to sound forensic principles and alter the state of the system as little as possible, if at all.

The following list is a summary of the manner in which computer systems store and process data. We have ordered the storage locations from most to least volatile. If power were to be disconnected from the system, you would lose the contents of the first four storage locations. The last two items, not surprisingly, were developed to solve this problem. During an initial response, we need to transfer the information contained in the first four locations to something more permanent.

- Registers, cache contents
- Memory contents
- State of network connections
- State of running processes
- Contents of storage media
- Contents of removable and backup media

In our experience, you will need to safely store the contents of the third and fourth types of data before you power off the system. When attempting to obtain data from the first two locations, you run the risk of modifying the system or taking it down entirely.

CAUTION   Avoid a live review, if possible. Recovering live data during the initial response should be attempted only when there is evidence of an ongoing network-based crime. This information is not always relevant to the investigation, and avoiding this type of collection is preferred.

You need to plan your approach to obtain all the information necessary to help your investigation without affecting potential evidence. You will be issuing commands with administrator rights on the system, so you will need to be particularly careful. Rule number one for incident response is *never alter or destroy evidence.* The best way to ensure your actions have no unintended consequences is to take the time to prepare a complete response toolkit.

Building a Trusted Toolkit

We often rely on standard system administration tools for gathering evidence during the initial response phase. We advise against using tools that use a graphical interface; instead stick to command line utilities that perform exactly the functionality that you expect. Most tools with a graphical user interface perform functions that are not immediately known to the user. All the tools we will present in this chapter are command line utilities. We suggest that you test any tool that you intend to use to become intimately familiar with its operation.

You need to ensure that your toolkit functions exactly as intended and will not alter the victim system. Your response disk should be completely self-contained, relying entirely on the software you place on the disk, not on the victim operating system. Unfortunately, in the Windows XP environment, you cannot avoid using some system libraries. The best you can do is set the execution search path to point solely to the media containing your response kit. We will provide a sample script in the next section. Table 15-1 lists the binaries that we include in our toolkit and the source for each one.

A large percentage of our tools are straight out of a standard installation of Windows XP or Windows 2000. When you assemble the toolkit, pull these from a fresh (or trusted) installation. The remaining utilities should be downloaded directly from the companies listed in the table. Use the md5sum command to generate a cryptographic checksum of each binary. You will want to record these MD5 hash values to verify the binaries against the original sources.

We have selected tools for their compatibility across as many Windows platforms as possible. If Windows XP or 2000 is the only operating system in use at your organization, each has a few new commands built in that can take the place of the ones we have listed. Windows XP and 2000 have a subsystem called the Windows Management Interface. This subsystem, through the use of the Wmic.exe application, gives an administrator access to much of the system information that we collect with

Command	Source
cmd	Built-in system command
date	Built-in system command
time	Built-in system command
netstat	Built-in system command
arp	Built-in system command
ifconfig	Built-in system command
at	Built-in system command
nbtstat	Built-in system command
dir	Built-in system command
auditpol	Microsoft Windows 2000 Resource Kit
ntlast	http://www.foundstone.com
fport	http://www.foundstone.com
pslist	http://www.sysinternals.com
psinfo	http://www.sysinternals.com
psfile	http://www.sysinternals.com
psloggedon	http://www.sysinternals.com
psloglist	http://www.sysinternals.com
md5sum	http://www.etree.org/md5com.html

Table 15-1. System Utilities in the Windows XP Initial Response Toolkit

Resource Kit or third-party tools. Two other executables, Openfiles.exe and Qprocess.exe, are very helpful in determining which processes are utilizing resources and network sockets. These applications can replace the fport command used in the next section. Remember to keep the scripts short, retrieve only what you will lose with a shutdown, and add each binary to your trusted toolkit.

Building the IR Scripts

Before you review a live system, create a step-by-step plan and stick to it. We cannot overstress the importance of documentation, because you will be executing commands and changing the environment on the victim machine. Document every step that you take in a spreadsheet or checklist. When you get to the later stages, where you are analyzing the file system, some of the information you discover may be a result of your actions during your initial response.

The following is a DOS batch file that we use to collect volatile data and system information from a Windows OS before we shut it down for forensic duplication. We try to keep this script as short as possible, and grab only what we need in order to protect volatile data and plan our next steps. This script is written to be portable to different versions of Windows, with one exception. The netstat command in Windows XP now includes a switch, -o, that will display the process ID of the application using the resource. Notice that our binaries in the script have been renamed to include a "t_" prefix. We renamed the files in our trusted toolkit to overcome any strange environment settings that may lead our scripts to the system binaries.

```
@echo off
echo Basic IR Script for Windows XP/2000
## Record actual time in agent notes to
## calculate clock drift deltas.
echo -- Start Timestamp --
echo. | t_date
echo. | t_time
echo -- Network Information --
t_netstat -ano
t_netstat -rn
t_arp -a
t_ifconfig /all
echo -- Open Network Ports --
t_fport
echo -- Process List --
t_pslist
t_psinfo
t_psfile
echo -- Scheduled Jobs --
t_at
echo -- Open SMB Connections --
t_nbtstat -c
echo -- Who is logged on
t_psloggedon
echo -- Last Accessed Timestamps - C Drive --
dir /t:a /o:d /s c:\
echo -- Last Modified Timestamps - C Drive --
dir /t:w /o:d /s c:\
echo -- Creation Timestamps - C Drive --
dir /t:c /o:d /s c:\
echo -- Audit Policies --
t_auditpol
echo -- Recent Logins --
t_ntlast
## Note that these last 3 items are optional
## because they can be run after the system
## has been duplicated.
```

```
echo -- Security Event Log --
t_psloglist -s -x security
echo -- Application Event Log --
t_psloglist -s -x application
echo -- System Event Log --
t_psloglist -s -x system
echo -- End Timestamp --
echo. | t_date
echo. | t_time
### The end.
```

You will want to place the script, the trusted binaries, and their libraries on removable media. Assuming your CD-ROM drive is E:\ on the victim system, start the trusted version of t_cmd.exe from the removable media by selecting Start → Run from the taskbar and type **e:\t_cmd.exe**. Type **echo $PATH** to view the file paths that the operating system will search when you issue a command. It will probably be a long string including the path C:\windows\system32. This needs to be limited to your trusted binaries and their libraries located on the removable media. If your CD-ROM disc were set up in the following manner, you would need to reset the PATH variable to point to e:\, e:\bin, e:\lib.

```
Contents of the E:\ drive:

t_cmd.exe
irscript.bat
/bin
      (trusted binaries)
/lib
      (trusted libraries)
```

To set the PATH variable, type the following command in your t_cmd.exe shell window:

```
set PATH=e:\,e:\bin,e:\lib
```

Running the Initial Response Procedure Safely

What do environmentalists and IR policy have in common? The following tenet: "Stay out of the wilderness if possible. If you must go in, leave no trace of your presence and change nothing." Our more environmentally conscious friends will probably give us a hard time for butchering their idea to fit this analogy, but the same principles clearly apply. Initial response is not something that one should do on a whim and without forethought. Additionally, you should make a reasonable effort to avoid leaving a trace of your actions. When collecting data from a system that you suspect has been compromised or used in the commission of a crime, be as creative as you want, but make sure that you practice this principle first and verify that everything was collected correctly.

We have used a few methods of collection in recent months. The first method is to save the data to the media on which the trusted toolkit is stored. This is obviously the safest route, since the information is written directly to media you own and is not transferred via a medium that can be monitored or altered. However, this method may not be feasible on large systems, where you end up retrieving a listing of the entire file system.

In the second collection method, we have used network sockets to transfer data from the compromised system to a laptop. Using Netcat or Cryptcat, the output from the IR script is sent over a TCP connection to our own laptop. Once the information has been transferred, we verify that the transfer was complete by calculating a cryptographic checksum with md5 or SHA1 for the data on both sides of the connection.

Finally, we have used network file shares to store the collected data when a massive amount of information was collected. When you go this route, ensure the file shares to which you are saving the data are secured by access lists and connection limits. Always assume the worst—that all passwords in the domain have been compromised and network monitoring is occurring. On your forensic workstation or laptop, set up a file share with sufficient disk space to hold the results of your initial response. When you define the file share, you will want to ensure that you are the only one who has access to the files, so apply strict connection filters (user lists, machine names, or IP addresses). When we perform initial response, we use Windows 2000, Windows XP, or UNIX on our forensic workstations, depending on the situation and the mood we are in that day. If you choose to send the results to a Windows system, set up a file share and remove all rights from it, including local and domain administrators' rights. Use a local account when you access the share, and make sure the password is changed before you begin. Lock the connection limit to one client (or the exact number of systems that you will run the IR script on concurrently). Figure 15-2 shows the settings recommended for securing a share during data collection.

If you choose to send the results to a UNIX system, you will need to open a file share using Samba. As with the Windows OS, lock the connections down to a specific user and allow connections only from the systems you are investigating. Here is an excerpt from a Samba configuration file that displays the proper method for creating a secure file share. This allows the systems you are investigating (victim1, victim2, victim3, and 192.168.8.8) to place files in the Unix directory /mnt/irstorage.

```
[irstorage]
    comment = IR storage
    path = /mnt/irstorage
    allow hosts = victim1, victim2, victim3, 192.168.8.8
    browseable = no
    printable = no
    public = no
    writable = yes
    create mode = 0700
```

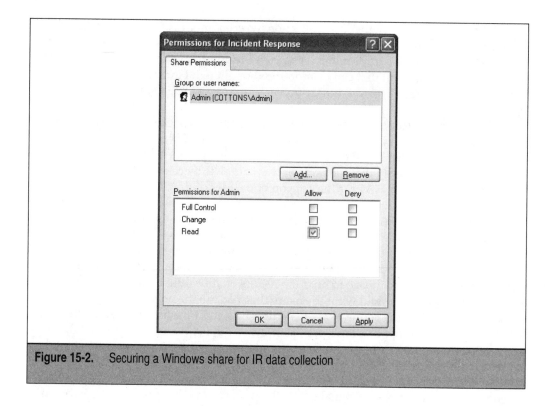

Figure 15-2. Securing a Windows share for IR data collection

Once the file share is set up and ready for use, connect to the share from each victim system, run the initial response scripts, and save the output to the remote share. This will keep you from storing data on the victim system, thereby altering the evidence as little as possible.

When all the data has been collected, store it in a secured location, and record the MD5 hash of the files in your notes. Before moving on to the next step of forensic duplication, review this information to determine whether additional live response steps are necessary.

Obtaining a Forensic Duplication

After you review the information you collected from your initial response, you need to decide whether to perform a forensic duplication of the victim system. The forensic duplication provides the bit-for-bit duplicate image that is required by the Federal Rules of Evidence, should your investigation ever reach the point where law enforcement becomes involved or the potential for civil litigation becomes high. We recommend that a forensic duplication be made in nearly every case, as it ensures the integrity of the evidence and provides a sound base on which to establish facts in the investigation. Your organization should have policies that define when and how your incident response teams acquire forensic duplications. Consider the following points when drafting the forensic duplication portion of your IR policy:

- Is there likely to be judicial action?
- Is it a high-profile incident?
- Is there a significant dollar loss due to a disruption of business?
- Is there a significant dollar loss due to extensive damage?
- Will you need to recover data to establish facts in the investigation?

This policy will probably depend on the type of incident as well as the type of systems involved. For example, you may choose to image the employee's workstations and obtain logical copies of mission-critical SQL servers that cannot be taken offline. If your organization utilizes mirrored RAID devices on its essential servers, you may be able to simply extract one drive from the RAID set and replace it with a new drive. Store the RAID drive you extracted as your best evidence.

TIP Be certain to check your hardware to be sure it is configured as a RAID mirror and that the single drive contains the complete file system. Keep in mind that the format of each RAID drive is slightly different than the typical layout of normal PC BIOS drives. These drives will probably have a small header added to the beginning, pushing the master partition table down a number of sectors. One of our clients, facing a very serious intrusion, was able to do this on practically every server at the facility. If we gave out awards, they would probably have won the one for best informal IR process. The collection of RAID drives saved an immense amount of time and manpower.

The most reliable tools used for forensic duplication are Safeback, EnCase, and the UNIX dd utility. Safeback, from NTI (http://www.forensics-intl.com), is the historical leader in this field and has been used in more criminal cases that any other software. EnCase, from Guidance Software (http://www.guidancesoftware.com), provides the capability to duplicate media as well as a means of examining the evidence without the need to restore the image. The Unix dd tool is preferred over the others by professional forensic examiners in government and commercial firms. It reliably images any type of media that the host operating system recognizes, and allows examiners to use any tool they wish to do the analysis.

Unfortunately, we don't have the space to talk about the process of forensic duplication. That subject could consume an entire chapter alone. It is essential that your team performs many trial runs and gains experience on whichever method suits your goals.

INVESTIGATING WINDOWS XP SYSTEMS

How do you establish facts that prove an allegation? Unearthing evidence from a mountain of files, slack space, and erased files takes time. Everyone seems to have his or her own method for searching a hard drive. Some people initially extract all documents and e-mail, some will skim the entire file system, and others prefer to follow checklists. The goals are to find the relevant information, document and track the metadata for each bit of important data, and finally determine where it came from. In some intrusion cases, the impact of the information on the organization may also need to be defined.

You can perform this examination in a variety of environments. We rotate among three tools, depending on the type of case that we are working on. A majority of the time, we will use Linux to view the file systems within a forensic duplication. By mounting the forensic image through a loopback driver in read-only mode, we are given the capability to use any number of UNIX utilities and Windows workstations to review the data. This is also the best way to allow multiple examiners to work on the same image concurrently. Two commercial products provide an excellent interface to perform analysis of FAT and NTFS file systems, Forensic Toolkit by AccessData and EnCase by Guidance Software. Both toolkits have their strengths and weaknesses. The best option is to try them out and work with whichever you are more comfortable with.

It is nearly impossible to provide a comprehensive flowchart for examining a forensic image—there are far too many variables. The following sections offer some ideas on where to start.

Identify Relevant Files

Occasionally, the files relevant to the investigation are obvious. You may need to find the Microsoft Excel spreadsheet that contains last quarter's financial information— from the last company the accountant worked for. Sometimes, it is more vague. You may need to find whether the chemist revealed the proprietary formula of your flagship product to the competition. In keeping with our "toolkit" approach, here are a few methods that we use to identify files relevant to an investigation.

String Searches

String searches work well when you have sample data available. Searches are fairly self-explanatory. Collect unique strings from documents, interviews, and your experience. Examples of good terms for a theft of intellectual property case would be document headers:

- "Proprietary"
- "Internal Use"
- Names of programmers
- Revision Control System headers
- URLs that should not be seen on your network

Strings describing unique functionality are another good possibility:

- "int poll_special_widget(int code, void *widget_structure)"
- "Volume Management Driver"

Filename Searches

One would think that the forensic analysis suites would include this simple function. Unfortunately, they all require you to select a directory tree (or the entire drive) and sort the immense list of files by filename. Forget searching for files that have *similar* names. As with most problems that occur during forensic analysis, the best solutions are going to come from your own ingenuity rather than a software company. If your forensic image was created with dd, you can perform searches using standard UNIX utilities. The following example shows all files on a drive that contain the string "pgp". This sample was created by mounting a forensic image of a hard drive under UNIX. After ensuring the drive was mounted with the read-only flag, it was searched with the find command.

```
[wedge:/Volumes/D]# find . -type f -name "*pgp*" -print
./cygwin/bin/pgpewrap
./cygwin/bin/pgpring.exe
./cygwin/usr/doc/mutt/samples/pgp2.rc
./cygwin/usr/doc/mutt/samples/pgp5.rc
./cygwin/usr/doc/mutt/samples/pgp6.rc
./Documents and Settings/Administrator/My Documents/Chris Weber.pgp
./Program Files/Netscape/Users/default/Cache/mvumpgpi.jpg
./storage/pgpvolume.pgd
./solaris/yassp/html_doc/pgp.html
```

MD5 Comparisons

It is a simple concept: determining relevance based on known hash values. If you have the AutoCAD specification file for a new picnic umbrella, and want to see if your lead umbrella developer has been a bit "entrepreneurial," calculate the MD5 hash value of the file and search for matches. The forensic processing suites do a good job of this, and will calculate hashes in a background process allowing the examiner to multitask. If your environment of choice is UNIX, the following line works well for gathering MD5 hashes of the file system:

```
[localhost:/] # find /Volumes/D/WINNT -type f -exec md5sum {} \;
```

This will give you output that looks like this:

```
d753eee17725526a67acddaa5d63ef68   system32//append.exe
6bf868c93d144a37f323c39c8c5dc4de   system32//arp.exe
0560fa9f135c0b2591c29abf13312122   system32//at.exe
dbfdc4865106039c5586101bebd86b54   system32//chcp.com
3d420efce68036721814af3e6c8fedec   system32//command.com
f6e368e10b600836dd349ff937b183a2   system32//edit.com
```

If you have the GNU version of find (most Linux distributions do), the following command line provides a more comprehensive file listing. It includes MAC (modify, access, create) time stamps, file size, ownership, and permissions, all in semicolon-delimited output. The GNU version of find is the only one that supports the printf command line option.

```
[localhost:/]# find / -type f -printf "%a;%t;%c;%s;" -exec md5sum {} \;
```

This command will give you a single-line summary of each file on the file system, perfect for searching and importing. The summary contains the following file metadata:

- Last accessed date
- Last modification date
- Last creation date
- File size
- MD5 hash
- Full path

```
Tue Sep  3 18:15:10 2002;Tue Dec  7 07:00:00 1999;Tue Dec  7 07:00:00
 1999;12498;d753eee17725526a67acddaa5d63ef68 D/WINNT/system32/append.exe
Tue Sep  3 18:15:10 2002;Tue Dec  7 07:00:00 1999;Tue Dec  7 07:00:00
 1999;19728;6bf868c93d144a37f323c39c8c5dc4de D/WINNT/system32/arp.exe
Tue Sep  3 18:15:10 2002;Tue Dec  7 07:00:00 1999;Tue Dec  7 07:00:00
 1999;23824;0560fa9f135c0b2591c29abf13312122 D/WINNT/system32/at.exe
Tue Sep  3 17:36:39 2002;Tue Dec  7 07:00:00 1999;Tue Dec  7 07:00:00
 1999;8464;dbfdc4865106039c5586101bebd86b54 D/WINNT/system32/chcp.com
Tue Sep  3 17:36:39 2002;Tue Dec  7 07:00:00 1999;Tue Dec  7 07:00:00
 1999;50620;3d420efce68036721814af3e6c8fedec D/WINNT/system32/command.com
Tue Sep  3 17:36:40 2002;Tue Dec  7 07:00:00 1999;Tue Dec  7 07:00:00
 1999;69886;f6e368e10b600836dd349ff937b183a2 D/WINNT/system32/edit.com
```

At this point, you can run searches on the output of this command to find duplicate files. When the files are large, and we intend to perform multiple searches and visualization, we import the data into Microsoft Excel. Sorting the data in an Excel worksheet can give the examiner a fairly good idea of the actions taken on the machine during certain periods of time.

File-by-File Review

Looking at filenames one by one is by far the best way to find anything on a hard drive. Unfortunately, it is unreasonably resource intensive and requires a good amount of Red Bull. Many cases will require this level of analysis, and any tools that can help you speed it up are invaluable. Known File Hashes is one way to whittle down the domain of your review. Both Forensic Toolkit and EnCase will flag files whose MD5 hash matches that of a vendor-provided file. The National Drug Intelligence Center (http://www.hashkeeper.org) has compiled a database of hashes for most operating systems and commercial products.

Temporary and Swap Files

Our favorite places to find data are in the temporary files and swap files used by applications and the operating system. Search through each user's Temporary Internet Files and Temp directories. Most applications will place cached copies of documents, presentations, and e-mails in these directories. When you are working with your computer and have a file open that has not been saved or is not tied to an actual file in your documents directory, there is a good chance that it is saved in a temporary file. The swap file or partition will contain pages, or blocks of memory, that have been removed from the active pages in RAM for one reason or another. This activity occurs when large files are opened, many applications are running, or the system has been in use for a while. You can use a file viewer such as QuickView Plus (http://www.inso.com) or the forensic toolkits to view the files in the temporary directories, but you will need to open the swap file with a hex editor.

Determine How Relevant Files Were Obtained

Say you have finally found the files that amount to the smoking gun. You have rounded up all the valid string search hits and recorded their locations on the file system. The next question is, "How did that information get on the computer?" Occasionally, it will be readily apparent: Microsoft Word documents that match the Word temporary files and program registration GUID, digital images with the creator ID of the digital camera sitting across the room. Other times, the clues may be found by searching through the user's e-mail or Internet browser history.

Examine E-mail Storage Files

A user's e-mail store can be fertile ground for obtaining evidence. To read the store files, you will typically need to view them in their native application. This involves copying the store file from the forensic image onto your forensic workstation and opening it in Netscape Messenger, Microsoft Outlook, or whatever application is appropriate.

Netscape Messenger stores the e-mail in a plain text file. These files are typically stored in /Program Files/Netscape/ Users/*account name*/Mail. Netscape stores two files for every mailbox. One is an index file with an .snm extension, and the other is a file named after the mail folder. For example, the Inbox mail folder would be composed of Inbox.snm and Inbox. The actual mail is stored in the second file (Inbox) in a format that can be read through Notepad. You can also import the mailbox into a new installation of Netscape Messenger.

Microsoft Outlook stores e-mail messages in a proprietary format that must be read through Outlook. You will find a user's mail store in the /Documents and Settings/ *user name*/Local Settings/Application Data/Microsoft/Outlook/ directory. Outlook names the files with a .pst extension. You may want to do a search across the entire file system for files that end in .pst, as the user can place archived mail in any location. In contrast to the Netscape Messenger application, Outlook stores everything in one large file. To view this file in its native format, copy the .pst file onto your forensic workstation, and open your local copy of Outlook. Use the File menu (File → Open → Personal Folders File) to browse to the suspect's .pst file and import it.

Examine Internet Browser History

Of equal importance to the e-mail storage files is the user's activity on the Web. All browsers will maintain logs and caches of the pages viewed by the user. The two browsers with the largest user base are Microsoft Internet Explorer (IE) and Netscape Navigator/ Mozilla. Both applications keep their histories and cache databases in private binary formats, making it impossible to parse through them with a text editor. A wonderful tool, the Internet History Viewer, has been written by Scott Ponder (e-mail saponder@ earthlink.net) to decode the browser cache files. This little application will decode files from both Microsoft and Netscape. Figure 15-3 shows the Internet History Viewer in action, decoding an index.dat file from IE.

Internet Explorer stores its web browser cache files in the /Documents and Settings/ *user name*/Local Settings/Temporary Internet Files/ directory. This directory contains all the files downloaded from various web sites. The index.dat file that maps cached files to their respective URLs, dates, and times is located in the /Documents and Settings/ *user name*/Application Data/Microsoft/Internet Explorer/UserData/ directory. The index.dat file is what you will need to load into the Internet History Viewer program.

Netscape and Mozilla store web browser history and cache files in one of two directories. The older versions store these files in /Program Files/Netscape/Users/*user name*/. Version 6 stores the information in the /Documents and Settings/Application Data/Netscape/ directory. The files you will need to open in the history viewer are named fat.db and netscape.hst.

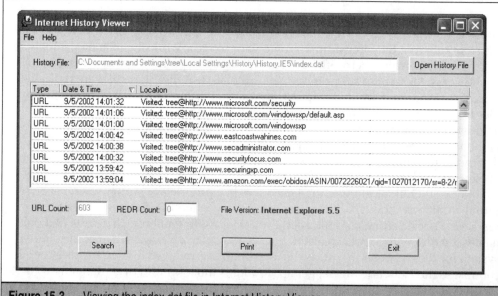

Figure 15-3. Viewing the index.dat file in Internet History Viewer

TOOLS OF THE TRADE

We have discussed a large number of tools we use for incident response. Here is a quick list of the tools we use for each phase.

Initial Response

- **cmd, date, time, netstat, arp, ifconfig, at, nbtstat, dir**   Built-in commands from Windows XP
- **Auditpol**   Microsoft Windows 2000 Resource Kit
- **NTlast, Fport**   http://www.foundstone.com
- **Pslist, Psinfo, Psfile, Psloggedon, Psloglist**   http://www.sysinternals.com
- **MD5sum**   www.etree.org/md5com.html

Forensic Duplication

- **NTI Safeback**   http://www.forensics-intl.com
- **EnCase**   http://www.guidancesoftware.com

Forensic Examination

- **Access Data's Forensic Toolkit**   http://www.access-data.com
- **EnCase**   http://www.guidancesoftware.com
- **NCIC File Hash Database**   http://www.hashkeeper.org
- **Quickview Plus**   http://www.inso.com
- **Internet History Viewer**   e-mail saponder@earthlink.net

CHECKLIST: INCIDENT RESPONSE

The following is a list of recommended examination steps to perform when investigating incidents:

- ☐ Acquire and restore the forensic duplication.
- ☐ Recover deleted files.
- ☐ Review unallocated and free space.
- ☐ Review slack space.
- ☐ Generate file lists containing MD5 hash values and file system metadata.
- ☐ Identify known system files (hash sets).
- ☐ Obtain and review the time and date stamps.
- ☐ Perform keyword searches.
- ☐ Perform file signature analysis.

The following is a short list of examination steps to perform during the review of a logical file system:

- ☐ Review all pertinent log files.
- ☐ Identify rogue processes.
- ☐ Search for unusual or hidden files.
- ☐ Check for unauthorized backdoors.
- ☐ Examine jobs run by the scheduler service.
- ☐ Determine the patch level.
- ☐ Analyze trust relationships.
- ☐ Review temporary files.
- ☐ Review swap files.
- ☐ Review graphic files.
- ☐ Reconstruct files in the recycle bin.
- ☐ Reconstruct printer spools.
- ☐ Extract and review all e-mail and attachments.
- ☐ Review Internet browser history.
- ☐ Review installed applications.

APPENDIX

Default and Recommended Security Settings

All of the security and service settings described in this appendix should be tested in a lab before they are deployed in a production environment. We have only made recommendations where the default setting should be changed.

These settings only apply to Windows XP Professional. Any recommended security setting that is preceded with an asterisk should be considered only for domains in which only Windows 2000 SP2 or higher and Windows XP/.NET computers will be communicating. Otherwise, these settings will prevent down-level client or server communications.

The recommended security and service settings do not represent the most secure, or strictest possible. Rather, they are designed to maintain Windows functionality while providing a much higher level of security than is provided by default.

Chapter 1 provides a complete reference to each of the security settings listed under the following "Account Policies" and "Local Policies" sections.

ACCOUNT POLICIES

This container provides settings for password and account lockout security. These settings are most effectively enforced at a domain or organizational unit level within Active Directory, where they provide one of the most basic means of networkwide security.

Password Policy Settings

Policy	Default	Recommended
Enforce password history	0 passwords remembered	10
Maximum password age	42 days	90
Minimum password age	0 days	1
Minimum password length	0 characters	7
Password must meet complexity requirements	Disabled	Enabled
Store password using reversible encryption for all users in the domain	Disabled	

Account Policy Settings

Policy	Default	Recommended
Account lockout duration	Not applicable	30 minutes
Account lockout threshold	0 invalid logon attempts	3
Reset account lockout counter after	Not applicable	30 minutes

LOCAL POLICIES

This most-important container has settings for audit policy, user rights, and other security options. Every build of Windows XP should be secured.

Audit Policy Settings

Policy	Default	Recommended
Audit account logon events	No auditing	Success, Failure
Audit account management	No auditing	Success, Failure
Audit directory service access	No auditing	
Audit logon events	No auditing	Success, Failure
Audit object access	No auditing	Failure
Audit policy change	No auditing	Success, Failure
Audit privilege use	No auditing	Failure
Audit process tracking	No auditing	
Audit system events	No auditing	Success, Failure

User Rights Assignment

Policy	Default	Recommended
Access this computer from the network	Everyone, Administrators, Users, Power Users, Backup Operators	Authenticated Users, Administrators
Act as part of the operating system		
Add workstations to domain		
Adjust memory quotas for a process	Local Service, Network Service, Administrators	
Allow logon through Terminal Services	Administrators, Remote Desktop Users	
Back up files and directories	Administrators, Backup Operators	
Bypass traverse checking	Everyone, Administrators, Users, Power Users, Backup Operators	Authenticated Users, Administrators
Change the system time	Administrators, Power Users	
Create a pagefile	Administrators	
Create a token object		
Create permanent shared objects		
Debug programs	Administrators	None
Deny access to this computer from the network	SUPPORT_388945a0, Guest	

Policy	Default	Recommended
Deny logon as a batch job		
Deny logon as a service		
Deny logon locally	SUPPORT_388945a0, Guest	
Deny logon through Terminal Services		
Enable computer and user accounts to be trusted for delegation		
Force shutdown from a remote system	Administrators	
Generate security audits	Local Service, Network Service	
Increase scheduling priority	Administrators	
Load and unload device drivers	Administrators	
Lock pages in memory		
Log on as a batch job	Support_388945a0	None
Log on as a service	Network Service	
Log on locally	Guest, Administrators, Users, Power Users, Backup Operators	Authenticated Users, Administrators
Manage auditing and security log	Administrators	
Modify firmware environment values	Administrators	
Perform volume maintenance tasks	Administrators	
Profile single process	Administrators, Power Users	Administrators
Profile system performance	Administrators	
Remove computer from docking station	Administrators, Users, Power Users	Authenticated Users, Administrators
Replace a process level token	Local Service, Network Service	
Restore files and directories	Administrators, Backup Operators	
Shut down the system	Administrators, Users, Power Users, Backup Operators	Authenticated Users, Administrators
Synchronize directory service data		
Take ownership of files or other objects	Administrators	

Security Options

Policy	Default	Recommended
Accounts: Administrator account status	Enabled	
Accounts: Guest account status	Disabled	
Accounts: Limit local account use of blank passwords to console logon only	Enabled	
Accounts: Rename administrator account	Administrator	
Accounts: Rename guest account	Guest	
Audit: Audit the access of global system objects	Disabled	

Policy	Default	Recommended
Audit: Audit the use of Backup and Restore privilege	Disabled	Enabled
Audit: Shut down system immediately if unable to log security audits	Disabled	
Devices: Allow undock without having to log on	Enabled	
Devices: Allowed to format and eject removable media	Administrators	
Devices: Prevent users from installing printer drivers	Disabled	
Devices: Restrict CD-ROM access to locally logged-on user only	Disabled	
Devices: Restrict floppy access to locally logged-on user only	Disabled	
Devices: Unsigned driver installation behavior	Warn but allow installation	
Domain controller: Allow server operators to schedule tasks	Not defined	
Domain controller: LDAP server signing requirements	Not defined	
Domain controller: Refuse machine account password changes	Not defined	
Domain member: Digitally encrypt or sign secure channel data (always)	Disabled	*Enabled
Domain member: Digitally encrypt secure channel data (when possible)	Enabled	
Domain member: Digitally sign secure channel data (when possible)	Enabled	
Domain member: Disable machine account password changes	Disabled	
Domain member: Maximum machine account password age	30 days	
Domain member: Require strong (Windows 2000 or later) session key	Disabled	*Enabled
Interactive logon: Do not display last user name	Disabled	Enabled
Interactive logon: Do not require CTRL+ALT+DEL	Not defined	Disabled
Interactive logon: Message text for users attempting to log on		Usage of this system is for authorized users only. All individuals using this computer are subject to having their activities monitored and recorded. By using this system you consent to the aforesaid monitoring. Be advised that if this monitoring reveals possible evidence of criminal activity, the evidence may be provided to law enforcement officials.
Interactive logon: Message title for users attempting to log on		Company Legal Notice

Policy	Default	Recommended
Interactive logon: Number of previous logons to cache (in case domain controller is not available)	10 logons	1
Interactive logon: Prompt user to change password before expiration	14 days	
Interactive logon: Require Domain Controller authentication to unlock workstation	Disabled	Enabled
Interactive logon: Smart card removal behavior	No action	Lock Workstation
Microsoft network client: Digitally sign communications (always)	Disabled	*Enabled
Microsoft network client: Digitally sign communications (if server agrees)	Enabled	
Microsoft network client: Send unencrypted password to third-party SMB servers	Disabled	
Microsoft network server: Amount of idle time required before suspending session	15 minutes	
Microsoft network server: Digitally sign communications (always)	Disabled	*Enabled
Microsoft network server: Digitally sign communications (if client agrees)	Disabled	Enabled
Microsoft network server: Disconnect clients when logon hours expire	Enabled	
Network access: Allow anonymous SID/Name translation	Disabled	
Network access: Do not allow anonymous enumeration of SAM accounts	Enabled	
Network access: Do not allow anonymous enumeration of SAM accounts and shares	Disabled	Enabled
Network access: Do not allow storage of credentials or .NET Passports for network authentication	Disabled	
Network access: Let Everyone permissions apply to anonymous users	Disabled	
Network access: Named pipes that can be accessed anonymously	COMNAP COMNODE SQL\QUERY SPOOLSS LLSRPC EPMAPPER LOCATOR TrkWks TrkSvr	Note: Refer to Chapter 1

Policy	Default	Recommended
Network access: Remotely accessible registry paths	System\CurrentControlSet\ Control\ProductOptions System\CurrentControlSet\ Control\Print\Printers System\CurrentControlSet\ Control\Server Applications System\CurrentControlSet\ Services\EventlogSoftware\ Microsoft\ OLAP Server Software\ Microsoft\Windows NT\ CurrentVersion System\ CurrentControlSet\Control\ ContentIndex System\CurrentControlSet\ Control\Terminal Server System\CurrentControlSet\ Control\Terminal Server\ UserConfig System\CurrentControlSet\ Control\Terminal Server\ DefaultUserConfiguration	Note: Refer to Chapter 1
Network access: Shares that can be accessed anonymously	COMCFG DFS$	Note: Refer to Chapter 1
Network access: Sharing and security model for local accounts	Guest only; local users authenticate as Guest	
Network security: Do not store LAN Manager hash value on next password change	Disabled	Enabled
Network security: Force logoff when logon hours expire	Disabled	Enabled
Network security: LAN Manager authentication level	Send LM & NTLM responses	Send LM & NTLM; use NTLMv2 session security if negotiated. *Send NTLMv2 response only; refuse LM
Network security: LDAP client signing requirements	Negotiate signing	
Network security: Minimum session security for NTLM SSP based (including secure RPC) clients	No minimum	*Integrity *Confidentiality *NTLMv2 *128-bit encryption
Network security: Minimum session security for NTLM SSP based (including secure RPC) servers	No minimum	*Integrity *Confidentiality *NTLMv2 *128-bit encryption
Recovery console: Allow automatic administrative logon	Disabled	

Policy	Default	Recommended
Recovery console: Allow floppy copy and access to all drives and all folders	Disabled	
Shutdown: Allow system to be shut down without having to log on	Enabled	Disabled
Shutdown: Clear virtual memory pagefile	Disabled	Enabled
System cryptography: Use FIPS compliant algorithms for encryption, hashing, and signing	Disabled	Enabled
System objects: Default owner for objects created by members of the Administrators group	Object creator	Administrators group
System objects: Require case insensitivity for non-Windows subsystems	Enabled	
System objects: Strengthen default permissions of internal system objects (e.g. Symbolic Links)	Enabled	

SERVICES SETTINGS

The following table is an alphabetical listing of all services installed on a default build of Windows XP. (OEM builds may install additional services.) The table lists the process responsible for launching the service, dependencies for each service, the default startup setting, and the recommended startup setting.

Service Name	Process	Dependencies	Default Setting	Recommended Setting
Alerter	Services.exe	Workstation	Manual	Disabled
Application Layer Gateway Service	Alg.exe	None	Manual	Manual
Application Management	Svchost.exe	None	Manual	Manual
Automatic Updates	Svchost.exe	None	Automatic	Disabled
Background Intelligent Transfer Service	Svchost.exe	Remote Procedure Call (RPC), Workstation	Manual	Disabled
ClipBook	Clipsrv.exe	Network DDE	Manual	Disabled
COM+ Event System	Svchost.exe	Remote Procedure Call (RPC)	Manual	Manual
COM+ System Application	Dllhost.exe	Remote Procedure Call (RPC)	Manual	Manual
Computer Browser	Svchost.exe	Server Workstation	Automatic	Automatic
Cryptographic Services	Svchost.exe	Remote Procedure Call (RPC)	Automatic	Automatic

Service Name	Process	Dependencies	Default Setting	Recommended Setting
DHCP Client	Svchost.exe	AFD Networking Support Environment NetBios over TCP/IP TCP/IP Protocol Driver	Automatic	Automatic
Distributed Link Tracking Client	Svchost.exe	Remote Procedure Call (RPC)	Automatic	Disabled
Distributed Transaction Coordinator	Msdtc.exe	Remote Procedure Call (RPC) Security Accounts Manager	Manual	Disabled
DNS Client	Svchost.exe	TCP/IP Protocol Driver	Automatic	Automatic
Error Reporting Service	Svchost.exe	Remote Procedure Call (RPC)	Automatic	Disabled
Event Log	Services.exe	None	Automatic	Automatic
Fast User Switching Compatibility	Svchost.exe	Terminal Services	Manual	Disabled
Fax	Fxssvc.exe	Plug and Play Print Spooler Remote Procedure Call (RPC) Telephony	Not installed	Disabled
Help and Support	Svchost.exe	Remote Procedure Call (RPC)	Automatic	Disabled
Human Interface Device Access	Svchost.exe	Remote Procedure Call (RPC)	Disabled	Disabled
IMAPI CD-Burning COM Service	Imapi.exe	None	Manual	Disabled
Indexing Service	Cisvc.exe	Remote Procedure Call (RPC)	Manual	Disabled
Internet Connection Firewall (ICF) /Internet Connection Sharing (ICS)	Svchost.exe	Application Layer Gateway Service Network Connections Network Location Awareness (NLA) Remote Access Connection Manager	Automatic	Automatic
IPSec Services	Lsass.exe	IPSec Driver Remote Procedure Call (RPC) TCP/IP Protocol Driver	Automatic	Manual
Logical Disk Manager	Svchost.exe	Plug and Play Remote Procedure Call (RPC)	Automatic	Manual
Logical Disk Manager Administrative Service	DMAdmin.exe	Logical Disk Manager Plug and Play Remote Procedure Call (RPC)	Manual	Manual

Service Name	Process	Dependencies	Default Setting	Recommended Setting
Messenger	Services.exe	NetBIOS Interface Plug and Play Remote Procedure Call (RPC) Workstation	Automatic	Disabled
Microsoft Software Shadow Copy Provider	Dllhost.exe	Remote Procedure Call (RPC)	Manual	Manual
Net Logon	Lsass.exe	Workstation	Automatic	Manual
NetMeeting Remote Desktop Sharing	MNMsrvc.exe	None	Manual	Disabled
Network Connections	Svchost.exe	Remote Procedure Call (RPC)	Manual	Automatic
Network DDE	Netdde.exe	Network DDE DSDM	Manual	Disabled
Network DDE DSDM	Netdde.exe	None	Manual	Disabled
Network Location Awareness (NLA)	Svchost.exe	AFD Networking Support Environment TCP/IP Protocol Driver	Manual	Automatic
NTLM Security Support Provider	Lsass.exe	None	Manual	Disabled
Performance Logs and Alerts	Smlogsvc.exe	None	Manual	Disabled
Plug and Play	Services.exe	None	Automatic	Automatic
Portable Media Serial Number	Svchost.exe	None	Automatic	Disabled
Print Spooler	Spoolsv.exe	Remote Procedure Call (RPC)	Automatic	Automatic
Protected Storage	Lsass.exe	Remote Procedure Call (RPC)	Automatic	Automatic
QoS RSVP	RSVP.exe	AFD Networking Support Environment Remote Procedure Call (RPC) TCP/IP Protocol Driver	Manual	Disabled
Remote Access Auto Connection Manager	Svchost.exe	Remote Access Connection Manager Telephony	Manual	Manual
Remote Access Connection Manager	Svchost.exe	Telephony	Manual	Automatic
Remote Desktop Help Session Manager	Sessmgr.exe	Remote Procedure Call (RPC)	Manual	Disabled
Remote Procedure Call (RPC)	Svchost.exe	None (but a lot depends on it)	Automatic	Automatic
Remote Procedure Call (RPC) Locator	Locator.exe	Workstation	Manual	Manual
Remote Registry	Svchost.exe	Remote Procedure Call (RPC)	Automatic	Disabled
Removable Storage	Svchost.exe	Remote Procedure Call (RPC)	Manual	Disabled

Service Name	Process	Dependencies	Default Setting	Recommended Setting
Routing and Remote Access	Svchost.exe	NetBIOSGroup Remote Procedure Call (RPC)	Disabled	Disabled
Secondary Logon	Svchost.exe	None	Automatic	Automatic
Security Accounts Manager	Lsass.exe	Remote Procedure Call (RPC)	Automatic	Automatic
Server	Svchost.exe	None	Automatic	Automatic
Shell Hardware Detection	Svchost.exe	Remote Procedure Call (RPC)	Automatic	Disabled
Smart Card	SCardSvr.exe	Plug and Play	Manual	Manual
Smart Card Helper	SCardSvr.exe	None	Manual	Manual
SSDP Discovery Service	Svchost.exe	None	Manual	Disabled
System Event Notification	Svchost.exe	COM+ Event System	Automatic	Automatic
System Restore Service	Svchost.exe	Remote Procedure Call (RPC)	Automatic	Disabled
Task Scheduler	Svchost.exe	Remote Procedure Call (RPC)	Automatic	Disabled
TCP/IP NetBIOS Helper Service	Svchost.exe	AFD Networking Support Environment NetBios over TCP/IP	Automatic	Automatic
Telephony	Svchost.exe	Plug and Play Remote Procedure Call (RPC)	Manual	Automatic
Telnet	Tlntsvr.exe	NTLM Security Support Provider Remote Procedure Call (RPC) TCP/IP Protocol Driver	Manual	Disabled
Terminal Services	Svchost.exe	Remote Procedure Call (RPC)	Manual	Disabled
Themes	Svchost.exe	None	Automatic	Disabled
Uninterruptible Power Supply	UPS.exe	None	Manual	Disabled
Universal Plug and Play Device Host	Svchost.exe	SSDP Discovery Service	Manual	Disabled
Upload Manager	Svchost.exe	Remote Procedure Call (RPC)	Automatic	Disabled
Volume Shadow Copy	Vssvc.exe	Remote Procedure Call (RPC)	Manual	Manual
WebClient	Svchost.exe	WebDav Client Redirector	Automatic	Disabled
Windows Audio	Svchost.exe	Plug and Play Remote Procedure Call (RPC)	Automatic	Manual
Windows Image Acquisition (WIA)	Svchost.exe	Remote Procedure Call (RPC)	Manual	Disabled
Windows Installer	Msiexec.exe	Remote Procedure Call (RPC)	Manual	Manual

Service Name	Process	Dependencies	Default Setting	Recommended Setting
Windows Management Instrumentation	Svchost.exe	Event Log Remote Procedure Call (RPC)	Automatic	Automatic
Windows Management Instrumentation Driver Extension	Svchost.exe	None	Manual	Manual
Windows Time	Svchost.exe	None	Automatic	Automatic
Wireless Zero Configuration	Svchost.exe	NDIS Usermode I/O Protocol Remote Procedure Call (RPC)	Automatic	Disabled
WMI Performance Adapter	WMIapsrv.exe	Remote Procedure Call (RPC)	Manual	Disabled
Workstation	Svchost.exe	None (but plenty depend on it)	Automatic	Automatic

Index

❖ E

F

❖ O

Q

R

X

 Z

INTERNATIONAL CONTACT INFORMATION

AUSTRALIA
McGraw-Hill Book Company Australia Pty. Ltd.
TEL +61-2-9900-1800
FAX +61-2-9878-8881
http://www.mcgraw-hill.com.au
books-it_sydney@mcgraw-hill.com

CANADA
McGraw-Hill Ryerson Ltd.
TEL +905-430-5000
FAX +905-430-5020
http://www.mcgraw-hill.ca

GREECE, MIDDLE EAST, & AFRICA
(Excluding South Africa)
McGraw-Hill Hellas
TEL +30-1-656-0990-3-4
FAX +30-1-654-5525

MEXICO (Also serving Latin America)
McGraw-Hill Interamericana Editores S.A. de C.V.
TEL +525-117-1583
FAX +525-117-1589
http://www.mcgraw-hill.com.mx
fernando_castellanos@mcgraw-hill.com

SINGAPORE (Serving Asia)
McGraw-Hill Book Company
TEL +65-863-1580
FAX +65-862-3354
http://www.mcgraw-hill.com.sg
mghasia@mcgraw-hill.com

SOUTH AFRICA
McGraw-Hill South Africa
TEL +27-11-622-7512
FAX +27-11-622-9045
robyn_swanepoel@mcgraw-hill.com

SPAIN
McGraw-Hill/Interamericana de España, S.A.U.
TEL +34-91-180-3000
FAX +34-91-372-8513
http://www.mcgraw-hill.es
professional@mcgraw-hill.es

UNITED KINGDOM, NORTHERN,
EASTERN, & CENTRAL EUROPE
McGraw-Hill Education Europe
TEL +44-1-628-502500
FAX +44-1-628-770224
http://www.mcgraw-hill.co.uk
computing_neurope@mcgraw-hill.com

ALL OTHER INQUIRIES Contact:
Osborne/McGraw-Hill
TEL +1-510-549-6600
FAX +1-510-883-7600
http://www.osborne.com
omg_international@mcgraw-hill.com

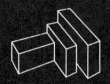